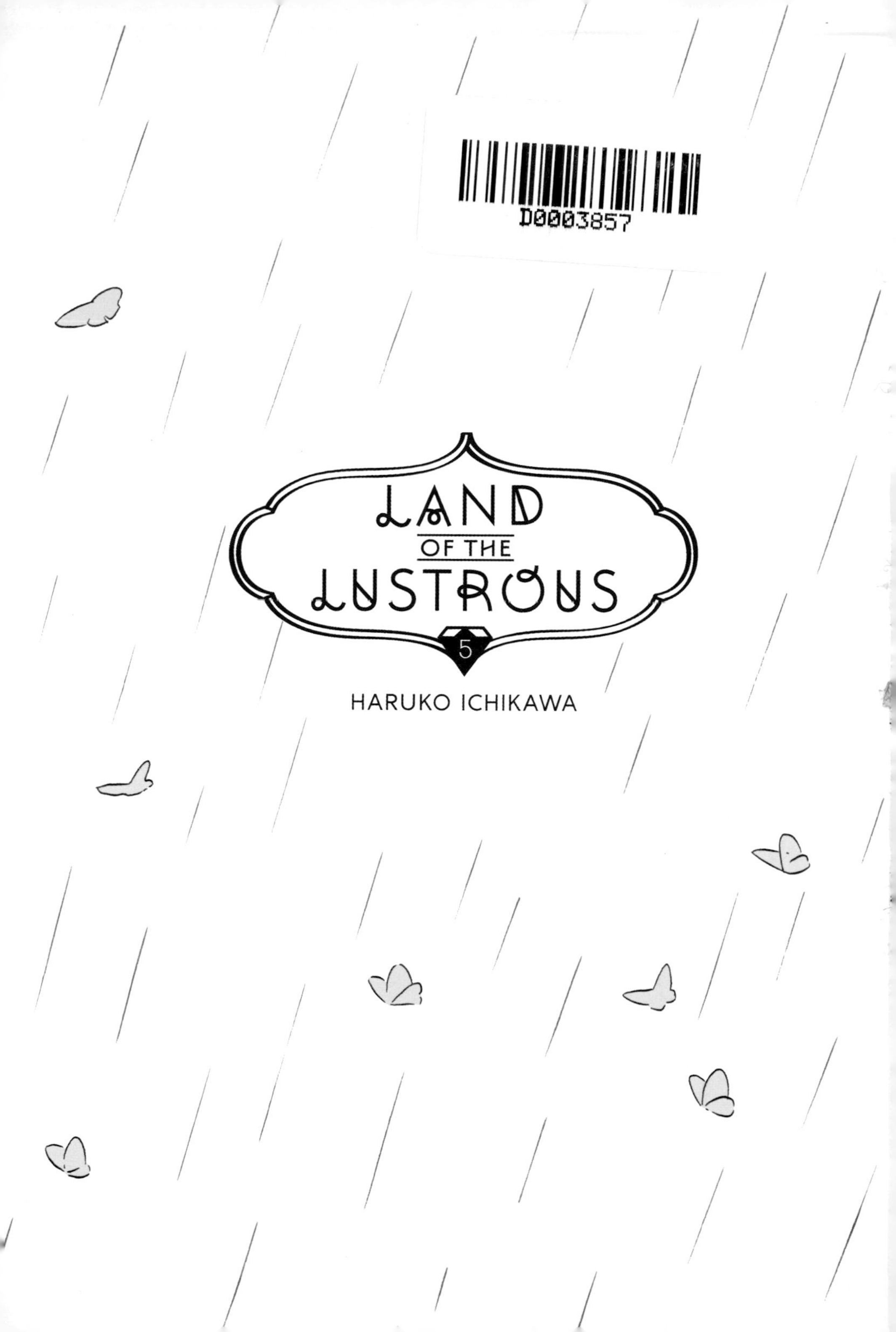

LAND OF THE LUSTROUS

5

HARUKO ICHIKAWA

CHARACTER INTRODUCTIONS

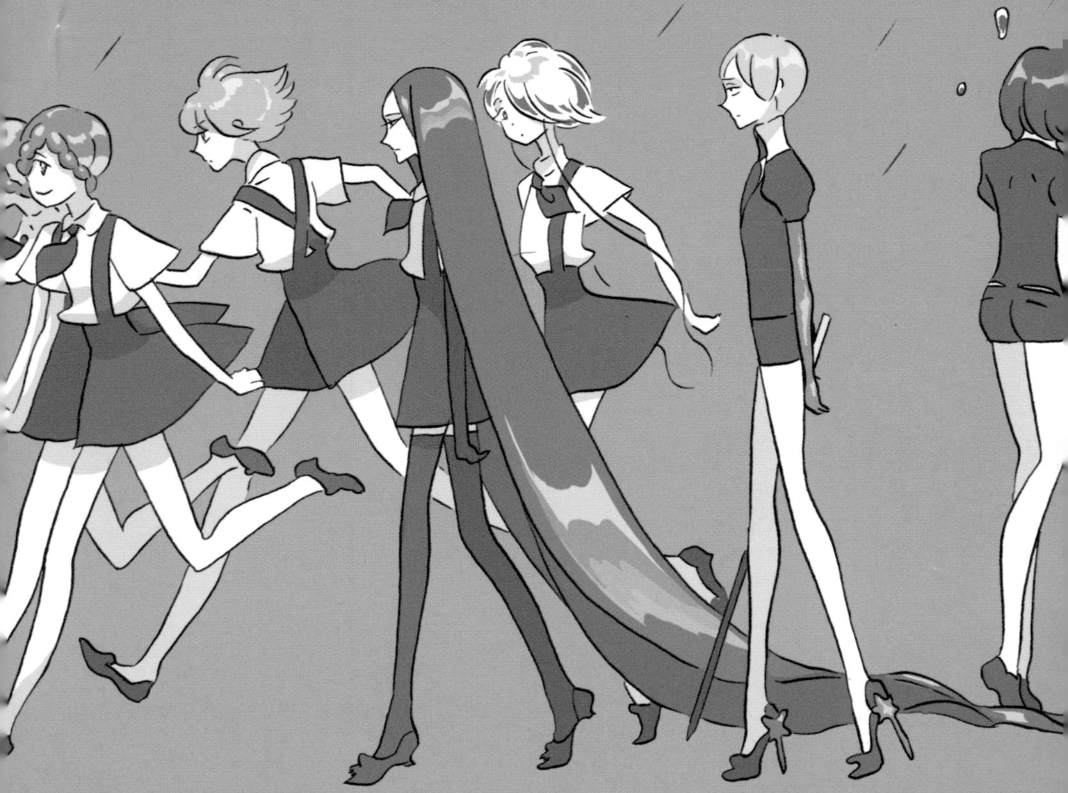

Amethyst
HARDNESS: 7
Apparently they switch places sometimes, but no one notices.

Zircon
HARDNESS: 7.5
So hard-working and diligent that others occasionally fear for the gem's well-being.

Bort
HARDNESS: 10
A battle geek. Recently discovered to have a taste for correcting others' battle styles.

Ghost Quartz
HARDNESS: 7
A quiet gem who does many inexplicable things. Has a body made of more than one crystal.

Phosphophyllite
HARDNESS: 3.5
The hero of our story. Has apparently been experiencing trippy hallucinations lately. Seriously damaged.

Cinnabar
HARDNESS: 2
Being clever sometimes makes it impossible to take action.

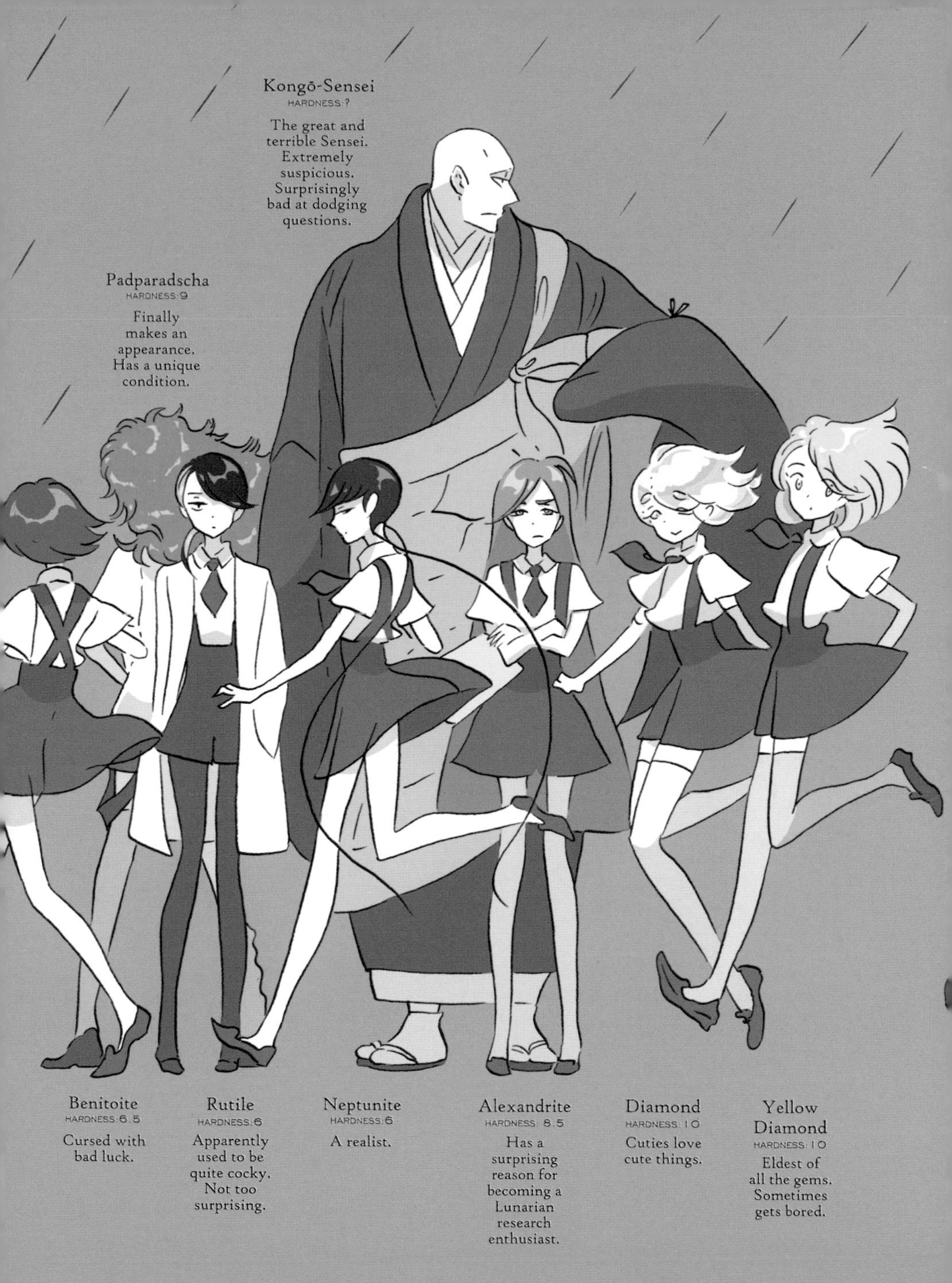

Kongō-Sensei
HARDNESS:?
The great and terrible Sensei. Extremely suspicious. Surprisingly bad at dodging questions.
Padparadscha
HARDNESS:9
Finally makes an appearance. Has a unique condition.
Benitoite
HARDNESS:6.5
Cursed with bad luck.
Rutile
HARDNESS:6
Apparently used to be quite cocky. Not too surprising.
Neptunite
HARDNESS:6
A realist.
Alexandrite
HARDNESS: 8.5
Has a surprising reason for becoming a Lunarian research enthusiast.
Diamond
HARDNESS: 10
Cuties love cute things.
Yellow Diamond
HARDNESS: 10
Eldest of all the gems. Sometimes gets bored.

CONTENTS

CHAPTER 29:

Padparadscha

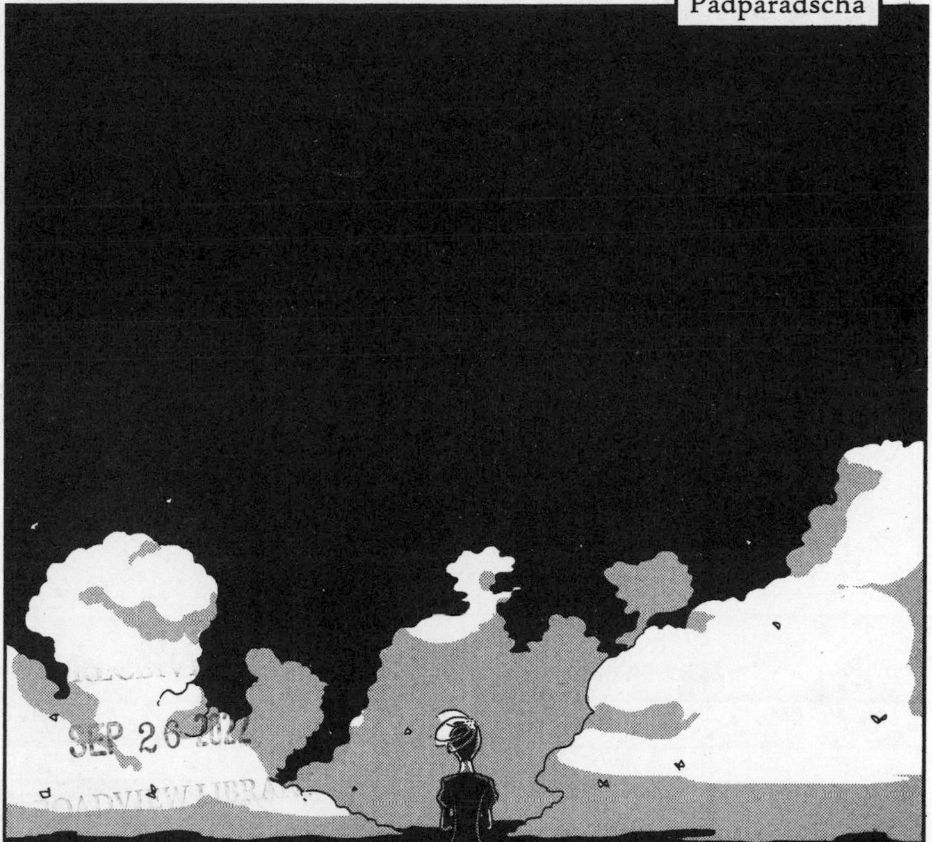

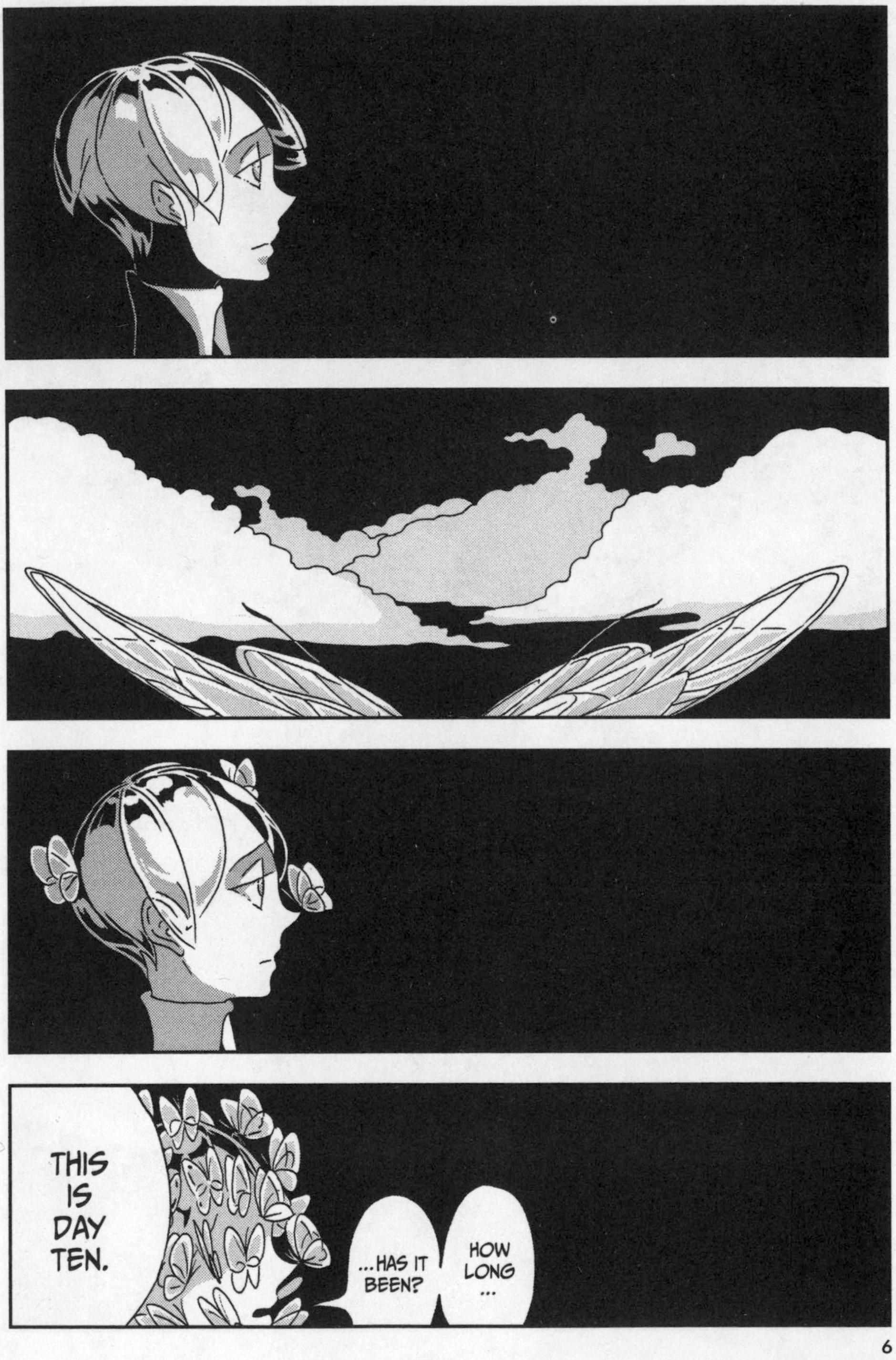
HOW LONG ...
...HAS IT BEEN?
THIS IS DAY TEN.

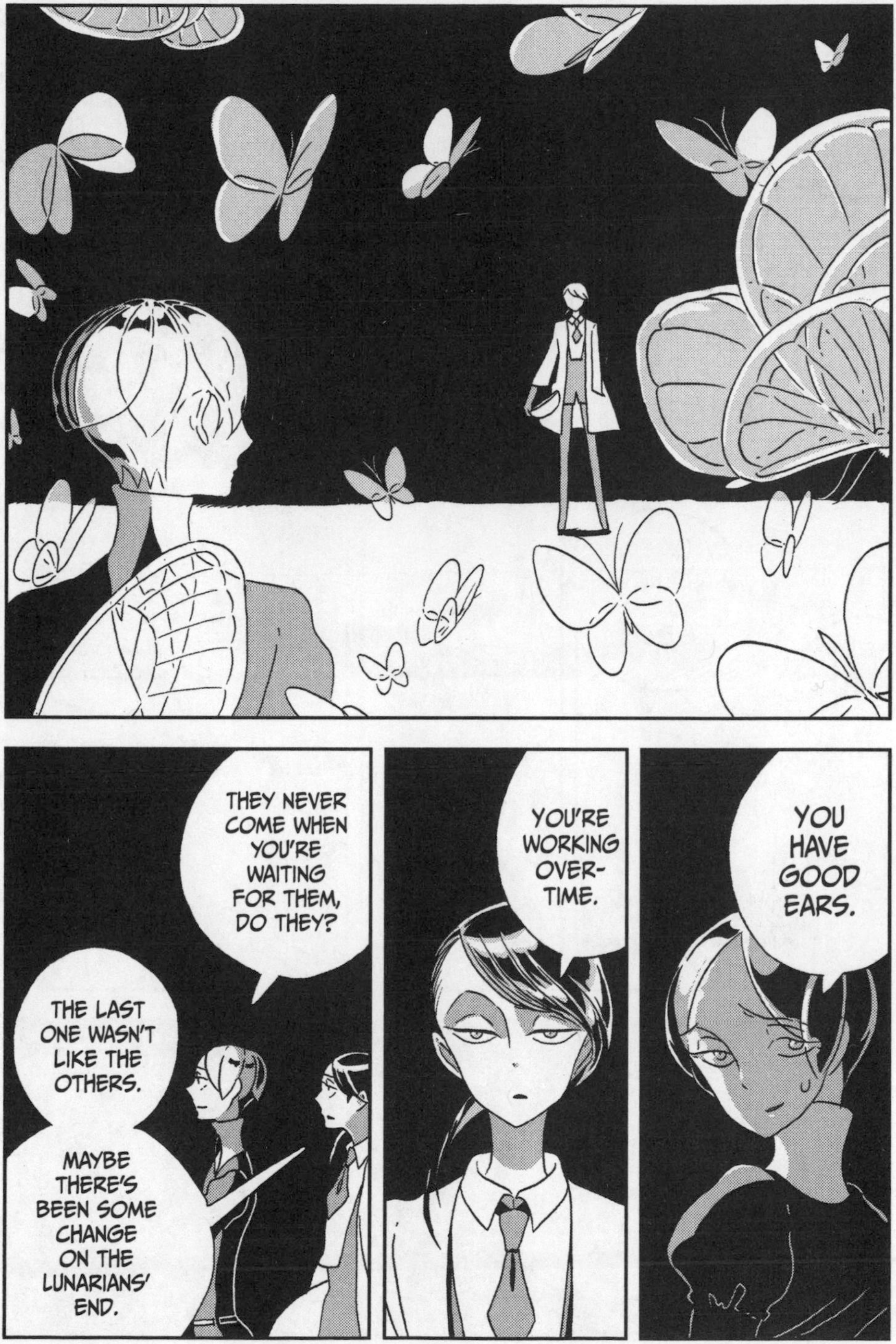
YOU HAVE GOOD EARS.
YOU'RE WORKING OVER-TIME.
THEY NEVER COME WHEN YOU'RE WAITING FOR THEM, DO THEY?
THE LAST ONE WASN'T LIKE THE OTHERS.
MAYBE THERE'S BEEN SOME CHANGE ON THE LUNARIANS' END.

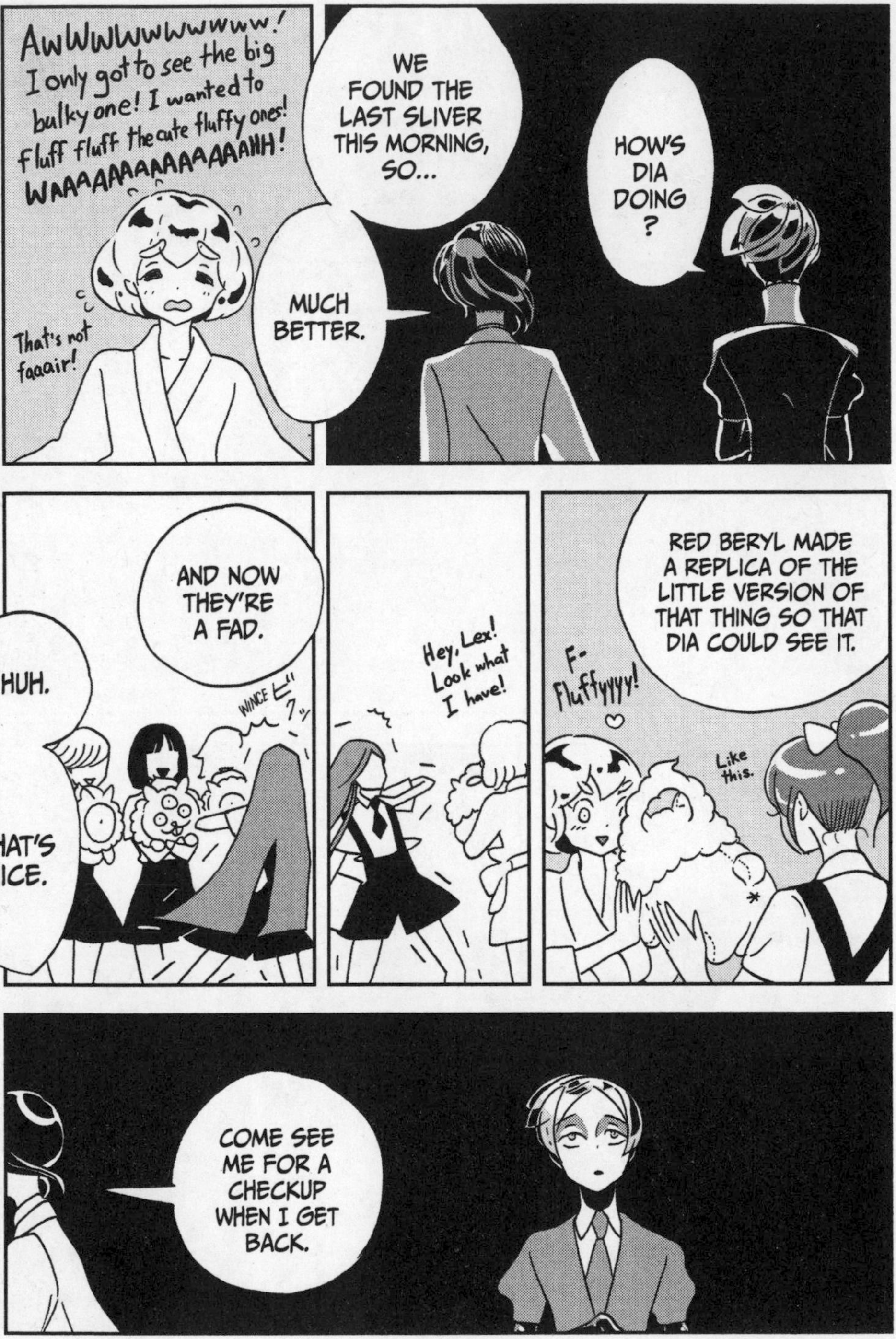
HOW'S DIA DOING?
WE FOUND THE LAST SLIVER THIS MORNING, SO...
MUCH BETTER.
AwWWWWWWWWW! I only got to see the big bulky one! I wanted to fluff fluff the cute fluffy ones! WAAAAAAAAAAAAAHH!
That's not faaair!
RED BERYL MADE A REPLICA OF THE LITTLE VERSION OF THAT THING SO THAT DIA COULD SEE IT.
F-Fluffyyyy!
Like this.
Hey, Lex! Look what I have!
AND NOW THEY'RE A FAD.
WINCE
HUH.
THAT'S NICE.
COME SEE ME FOR A CHECKUP WHEN I GET BACK.

ARE YOU GOING SOME-WHERE?
THE SHORE OF NASCENCY.
OH.
TO FIND PARTS FOR PADPARADSCHA.
HM?

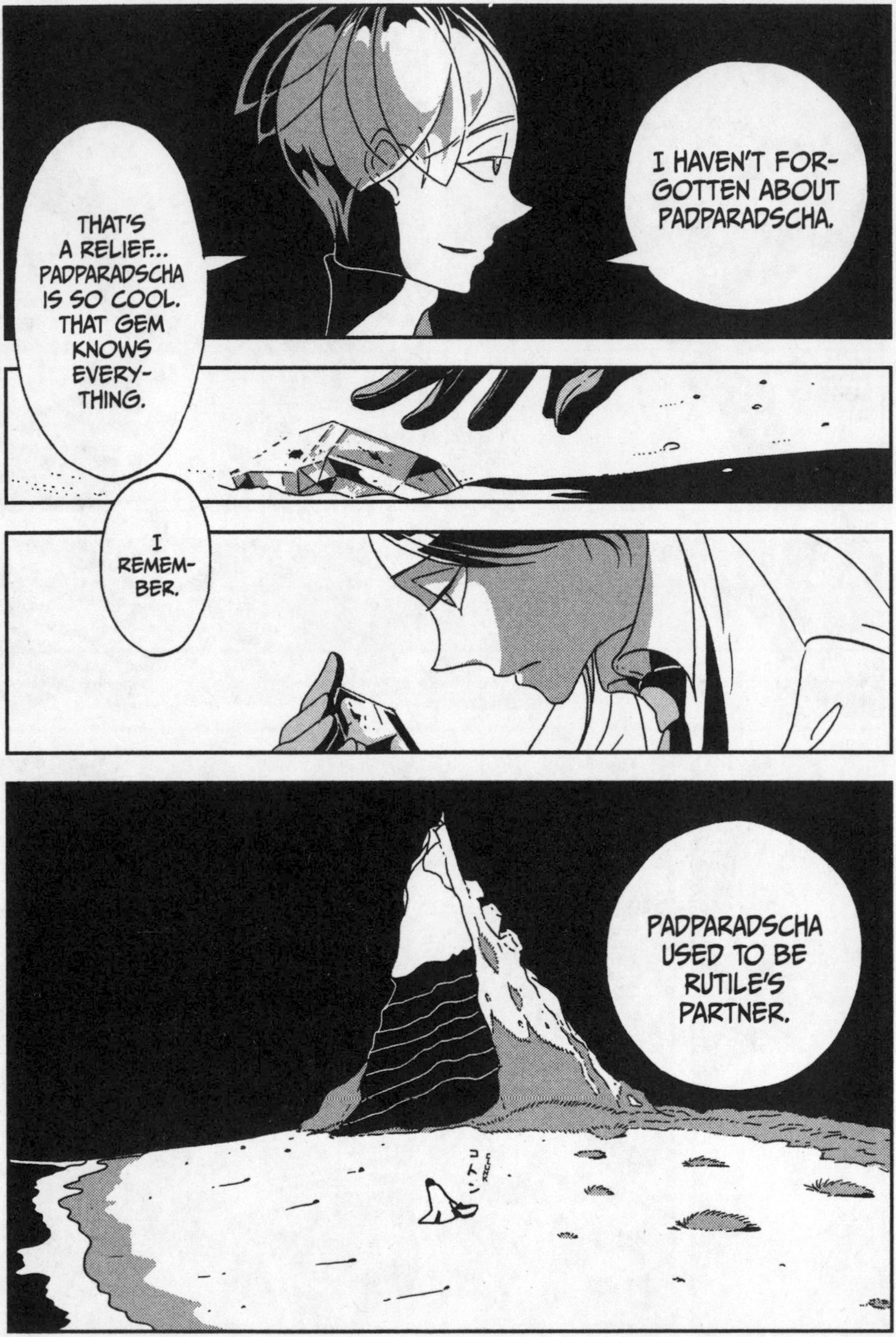
I HAVEN'T FOR-GOTTEN ABOUT PADPARADSCHA.
THAT'S A RELIEF... PADPARADSCHA IS SO COOL. THAT GEM KNOWS EVERY-THING.
I REMEM-BER.
PADPARADSCHA USED TO BE RUTILE'S PARTNER.

AND...
PA-KING
カッ TAK
カッ TAK
カッ TAK
カッ TAK
カッ TAK
カッ TAK
ZH

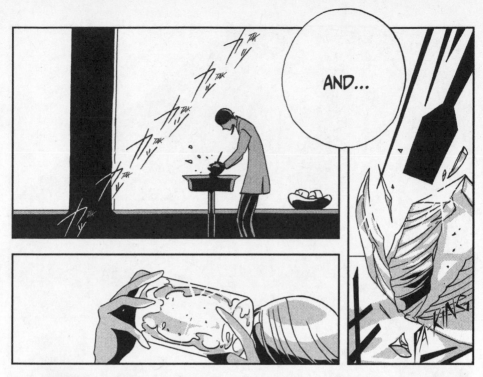

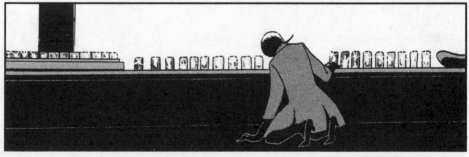

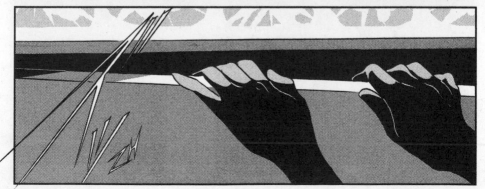

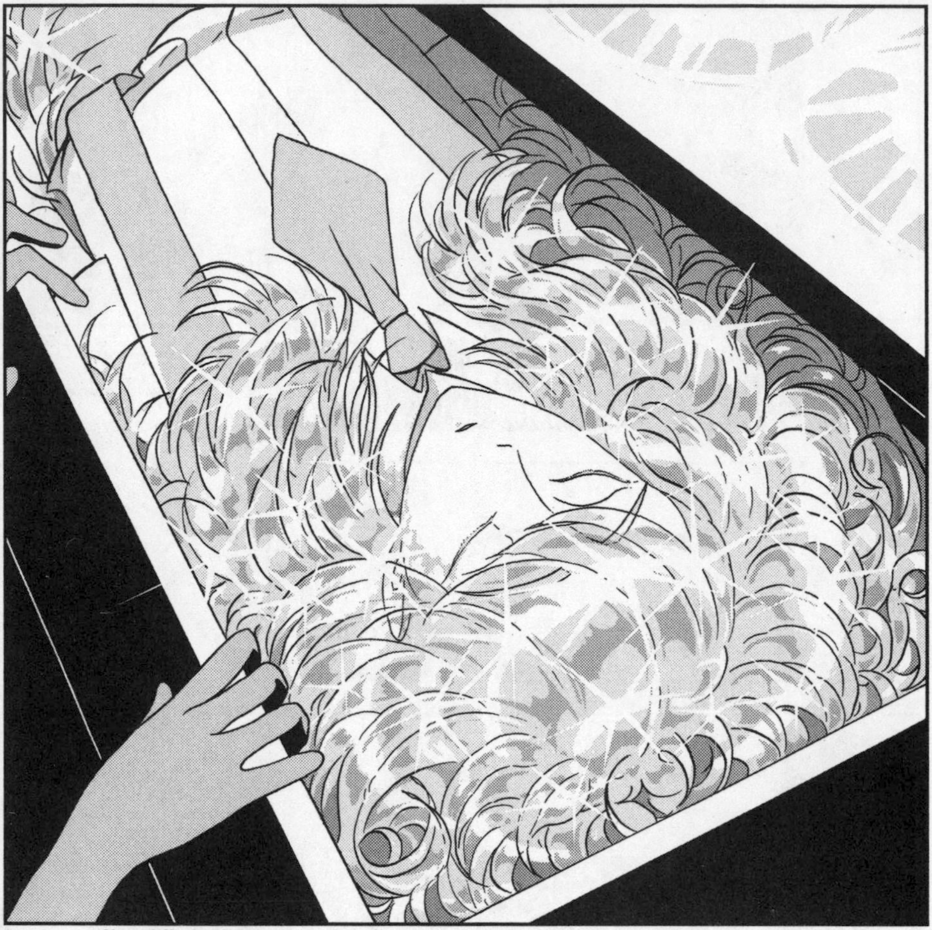

*A measure of how difficult it is to break a gem.

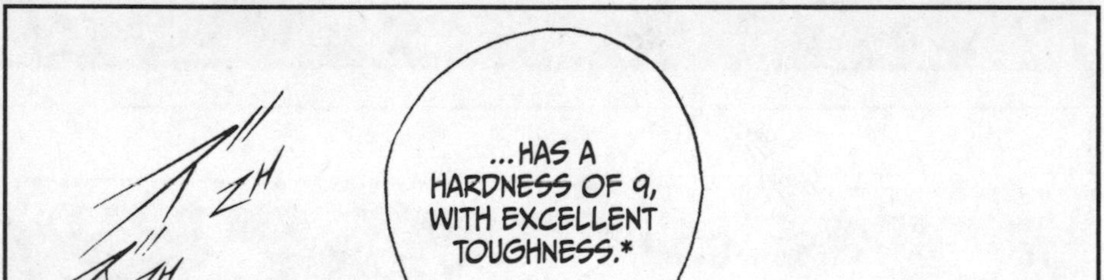
...HAS A HARDNESS OF 9, WITH EXCELLENT TOUGHNESS.*
ZH
ZH

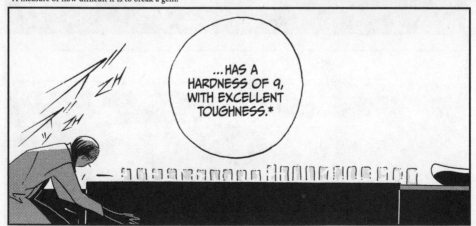

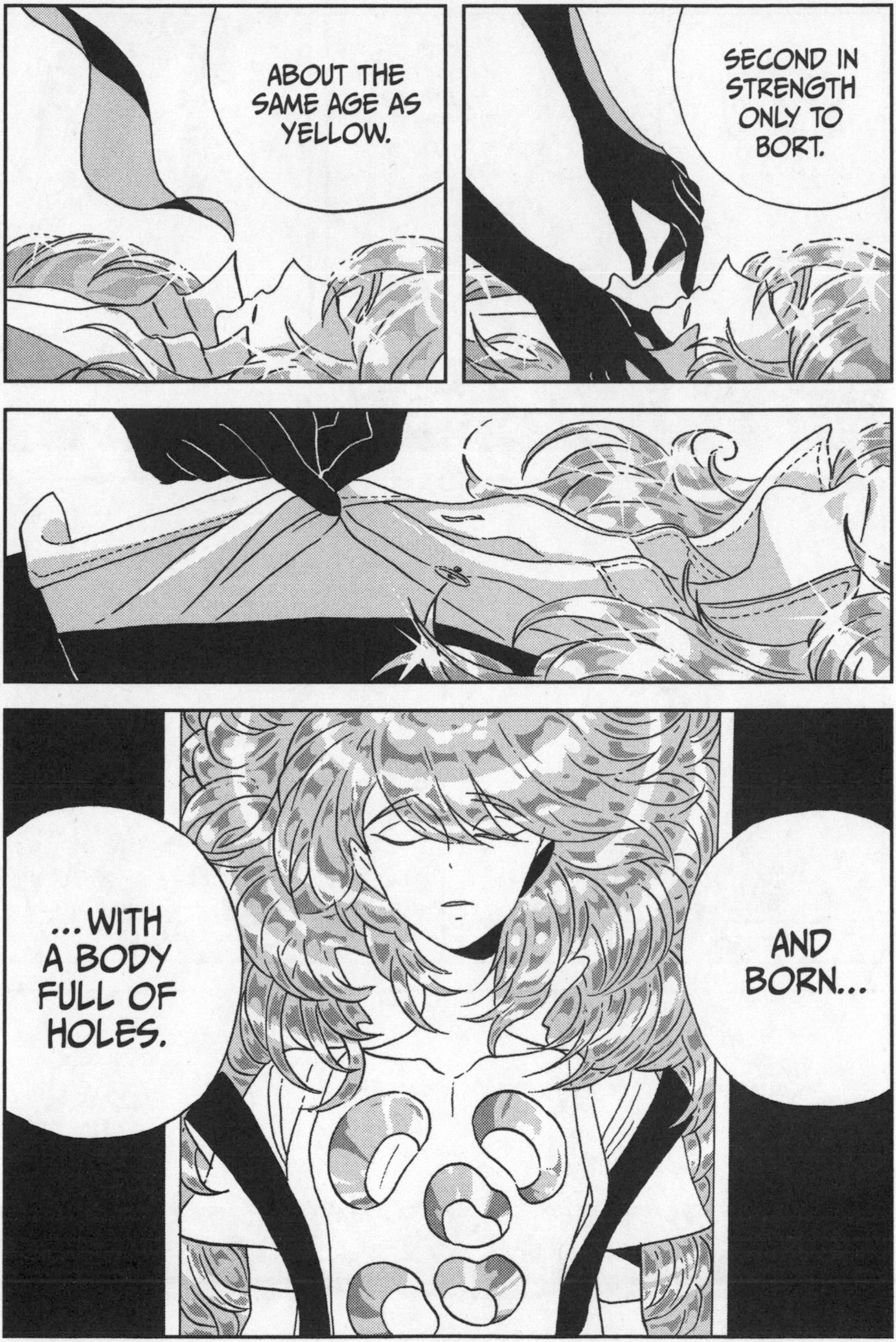
SECOND IN STRENGTH ONLY TO BORT.
ABOUT THE SAME AGE AS YELLOW.
AND BORN...
...WITH A BODY FULL OF HOLES.

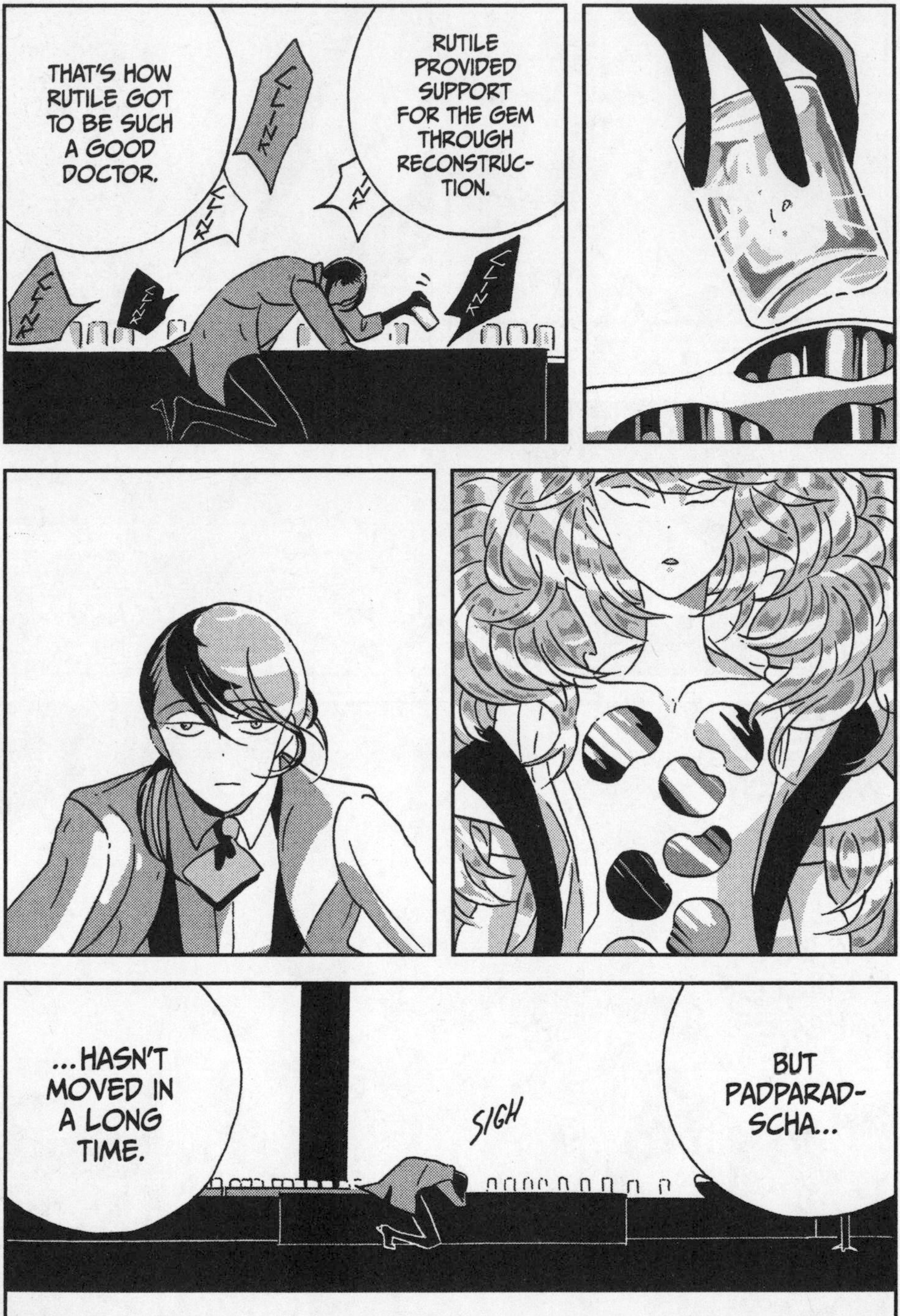
CLINK
RUTILE PROVIDED SUPPORT FOR THE GEM THROUGH RECONSTRUCTION.
CLINK
CLINK
CLINK
THAT'S HOW RUTILE GOT TO BE SUCH A GOOD DOCTOR.
CLINK
CLINK
BUT PADPARADSCHA...
SIGH
...HASN'T MOVED IN A LONG TIME.

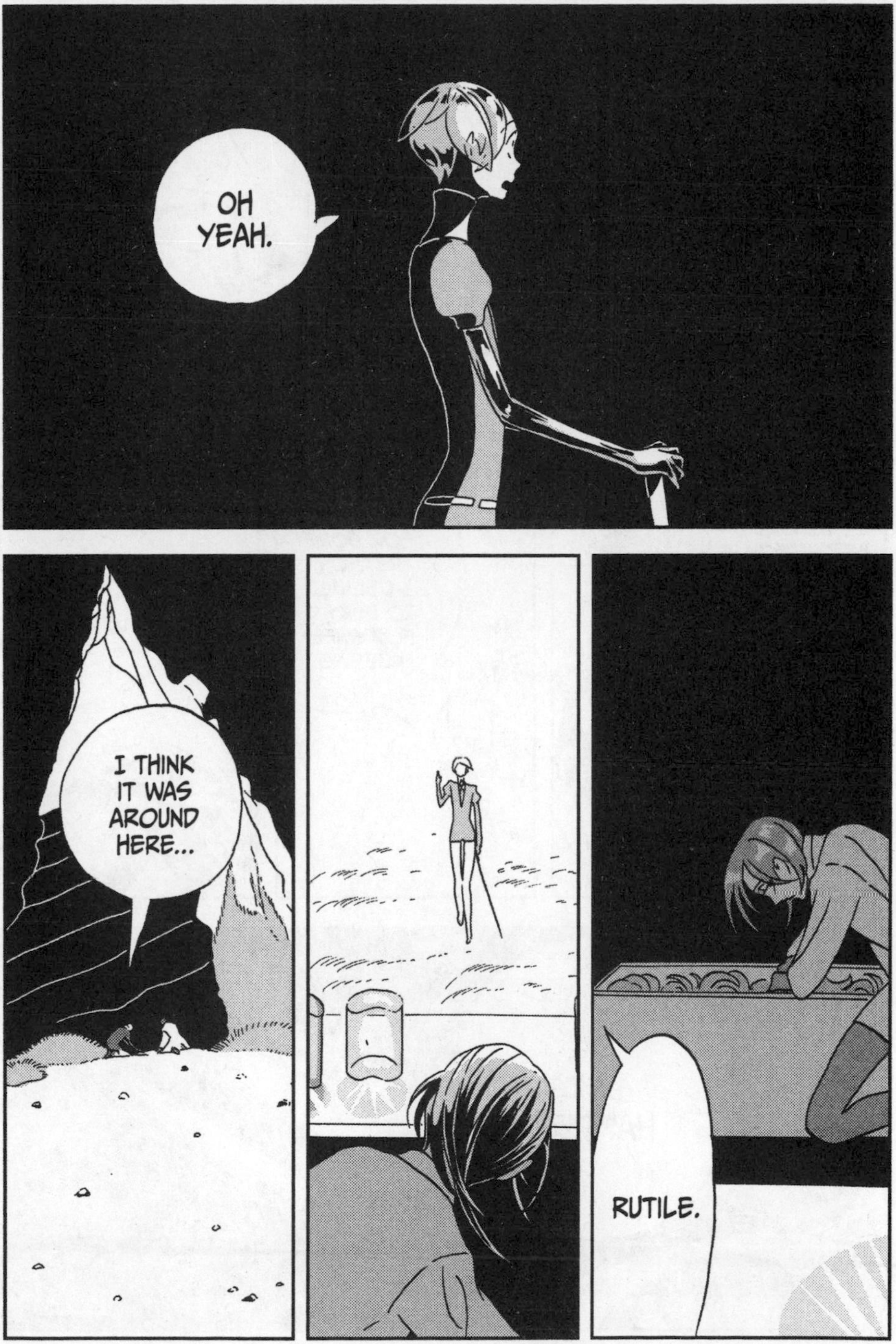
OH YEAH.
RUTILE.
I THINK IT WAS AROUND HERE...

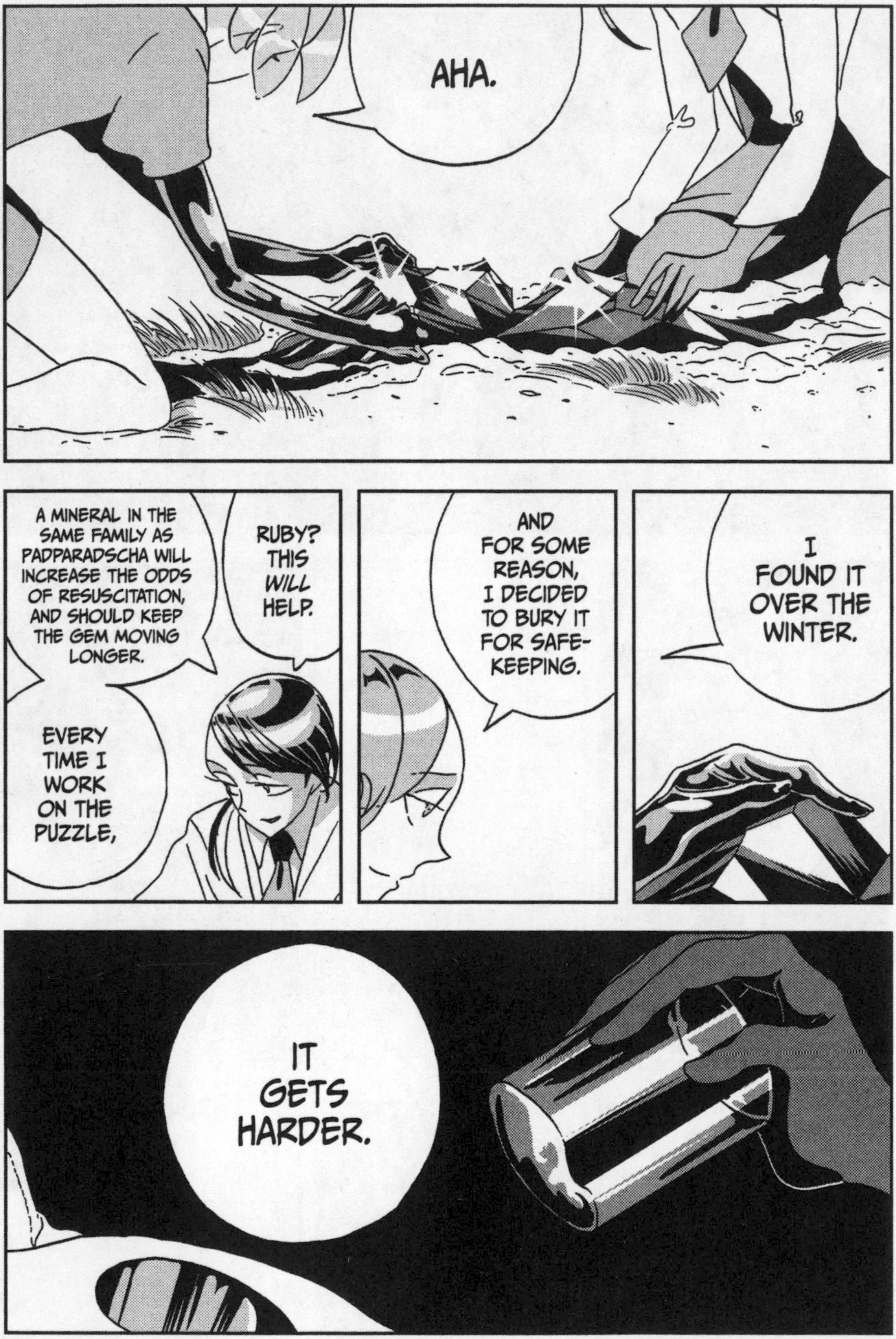
AHA.
I FOUND IT OVER THE WINTER.
AND FOR SOME REASON, I DECIDED TO BURY IT FOR SAFE-KEEPING.
RUBY? THIS *WILL* HELP.
A MINERAL IN THE SAME FAMILY AS PADPARADSCHA WILL INCREASE THE ODDS OF RESUSCITATION, AND SHOULD KEEP THE GEM MOVING LONGER.
EVERY TIME I WORK ON THE PUZZLE,
IT GETS HARDER.

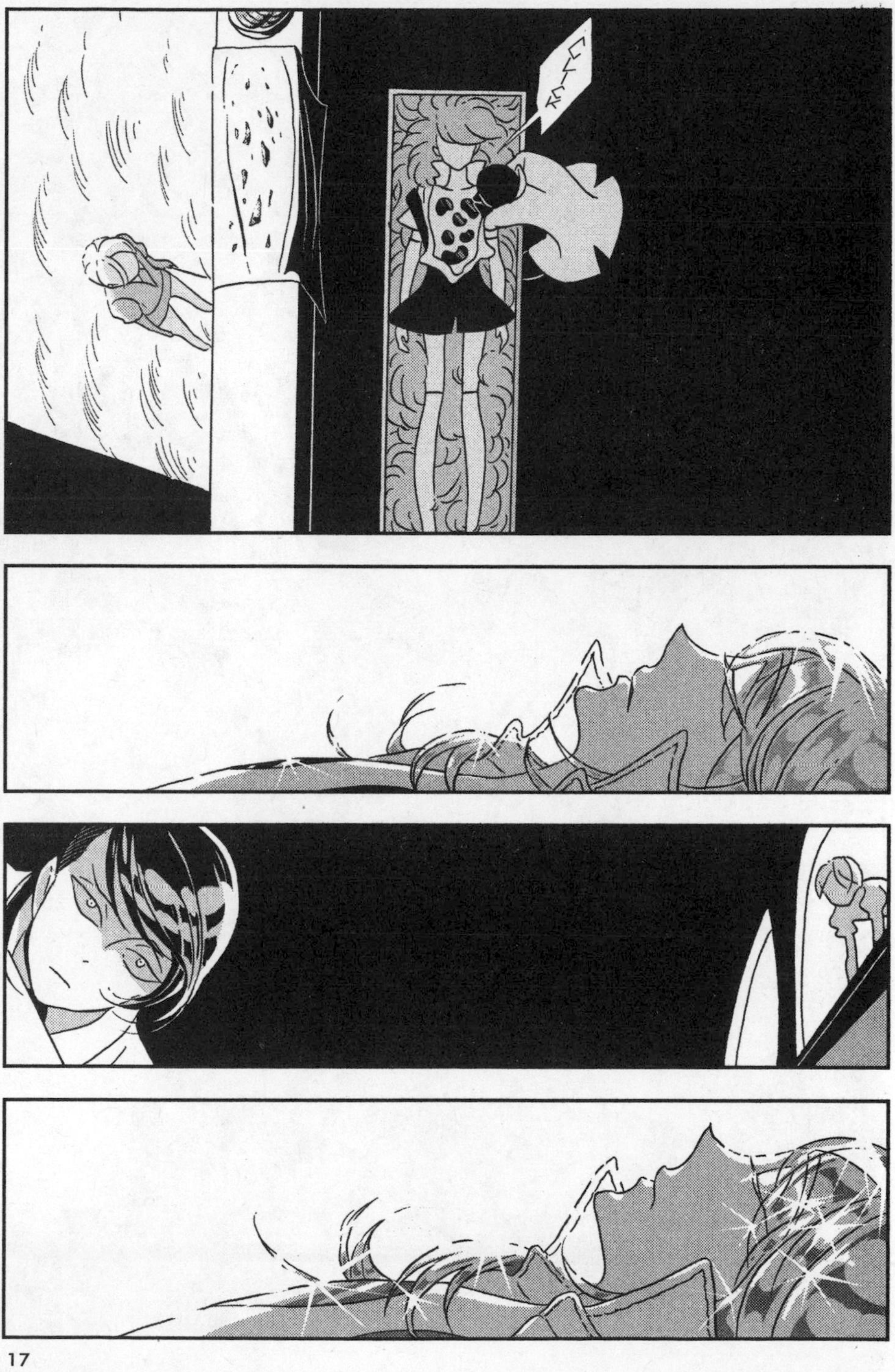
CLICK

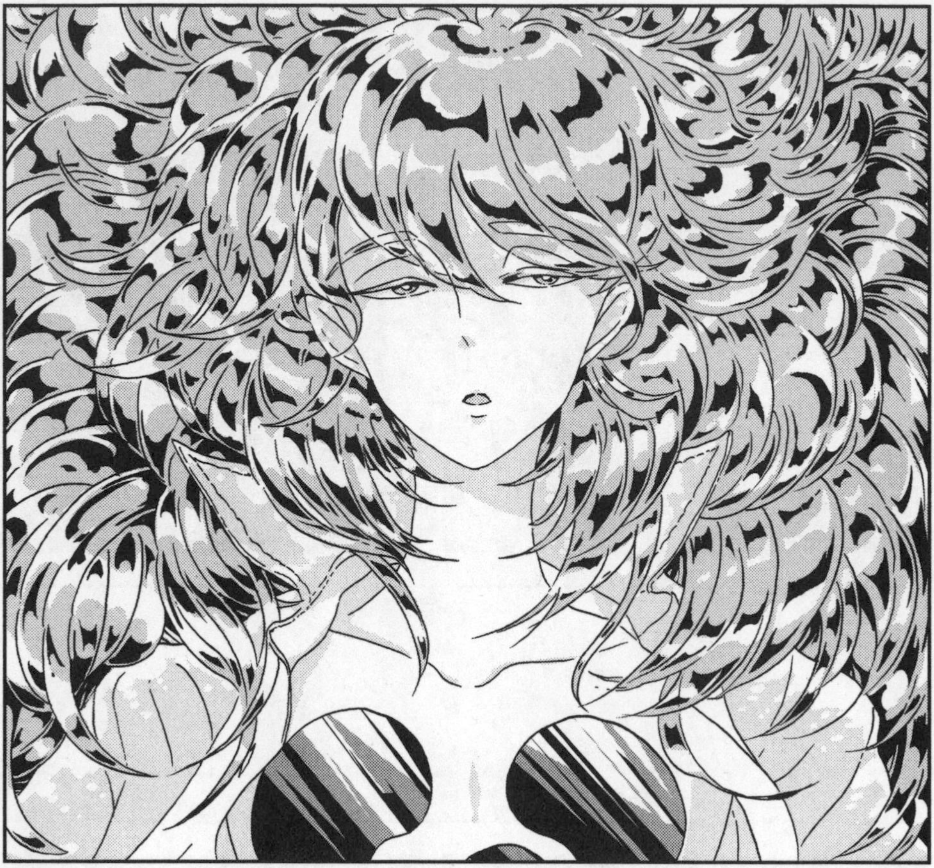

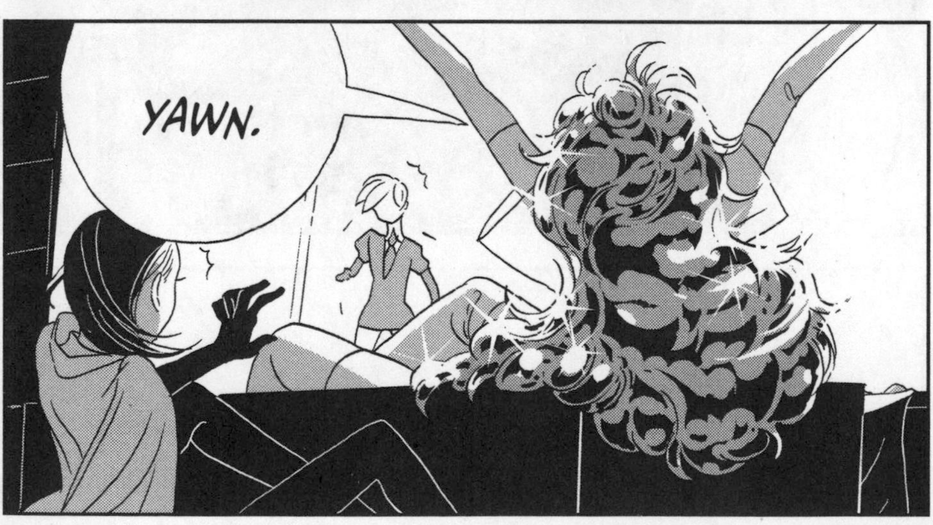
YAWN.

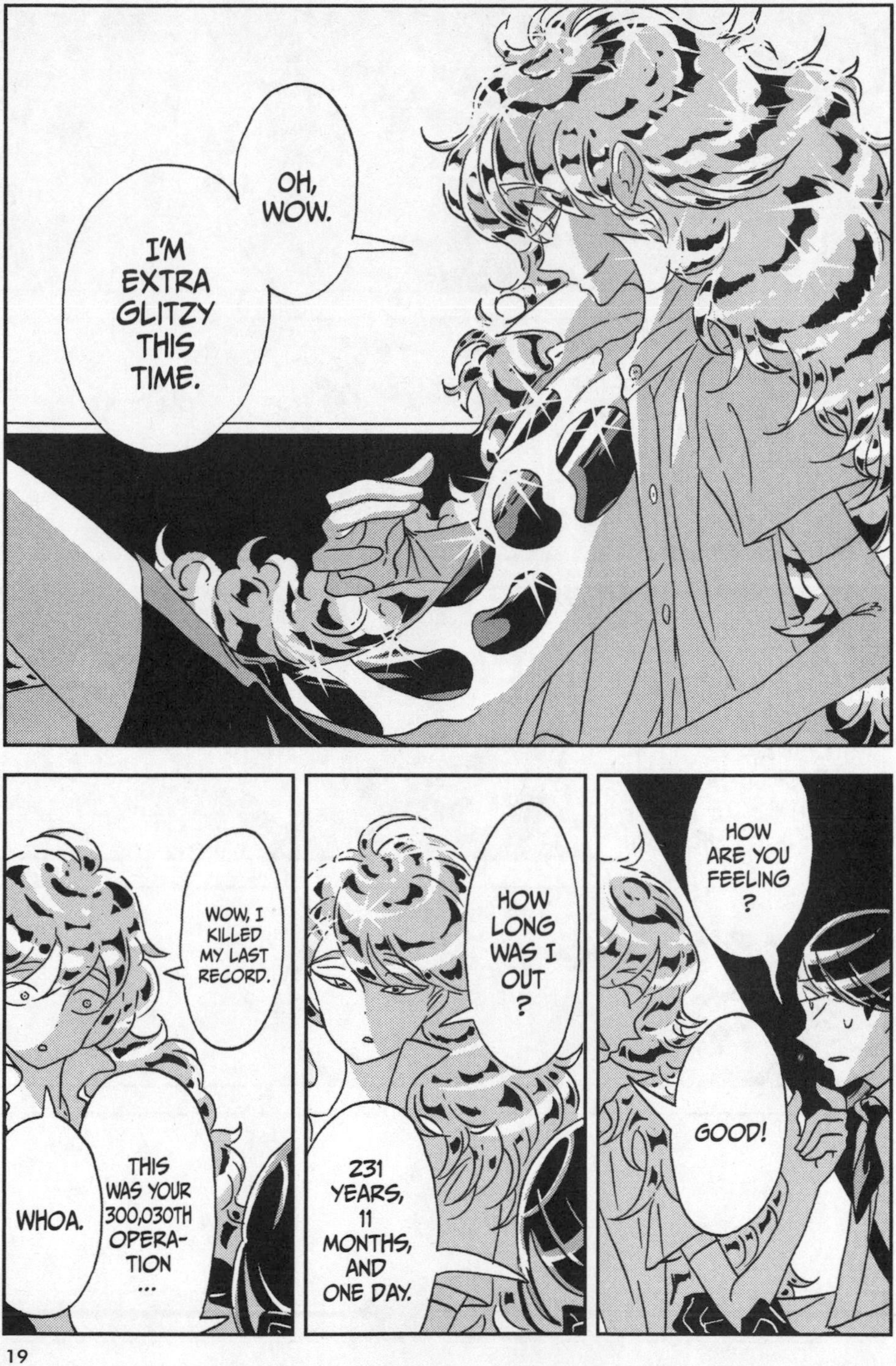
OH, WOW.
I'M EXTRA GLITZY THIS TIME.
HOW ARE YOU FEELING?
GOOD!
HOW LONG WAS I OUT?
231 YEARS, 11 MONTHS, AND ONE DAY.
WOW, I KILLED MY LAST RECORD.
THIS WAS YOUR 300,030TH OPERATION...
WHOA.

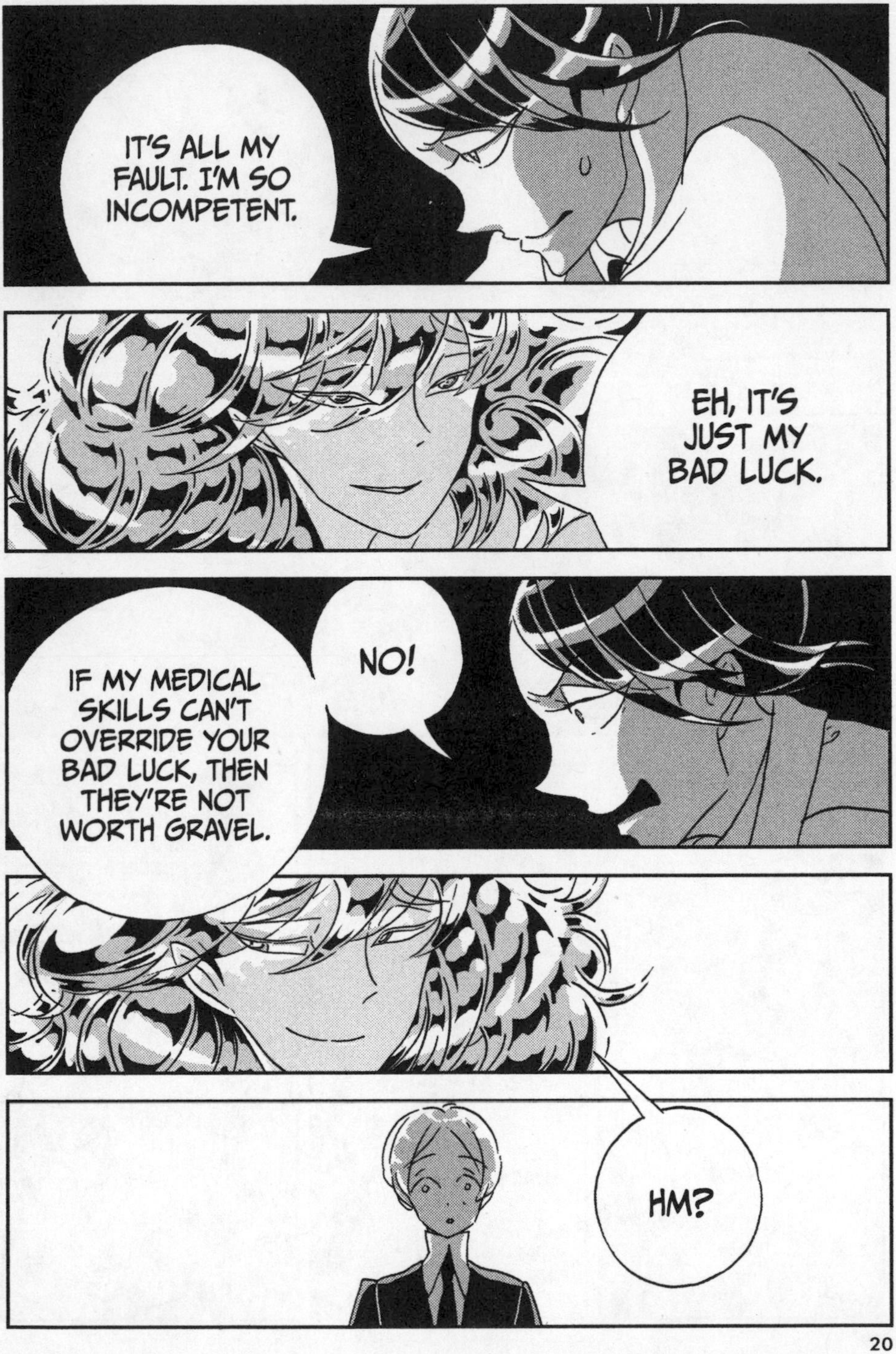
IT'S ALL MY FAULT. I'M SO INCOMPETENT.
EH, IT'S JUST MY BAD LUCK.
NO!
IF MY MEDICAL SKILLS CAN'T OVERRIDE YOUR BAD LUCK, THEN THEY'RE NOT WORTH GRAVEL.
HM?

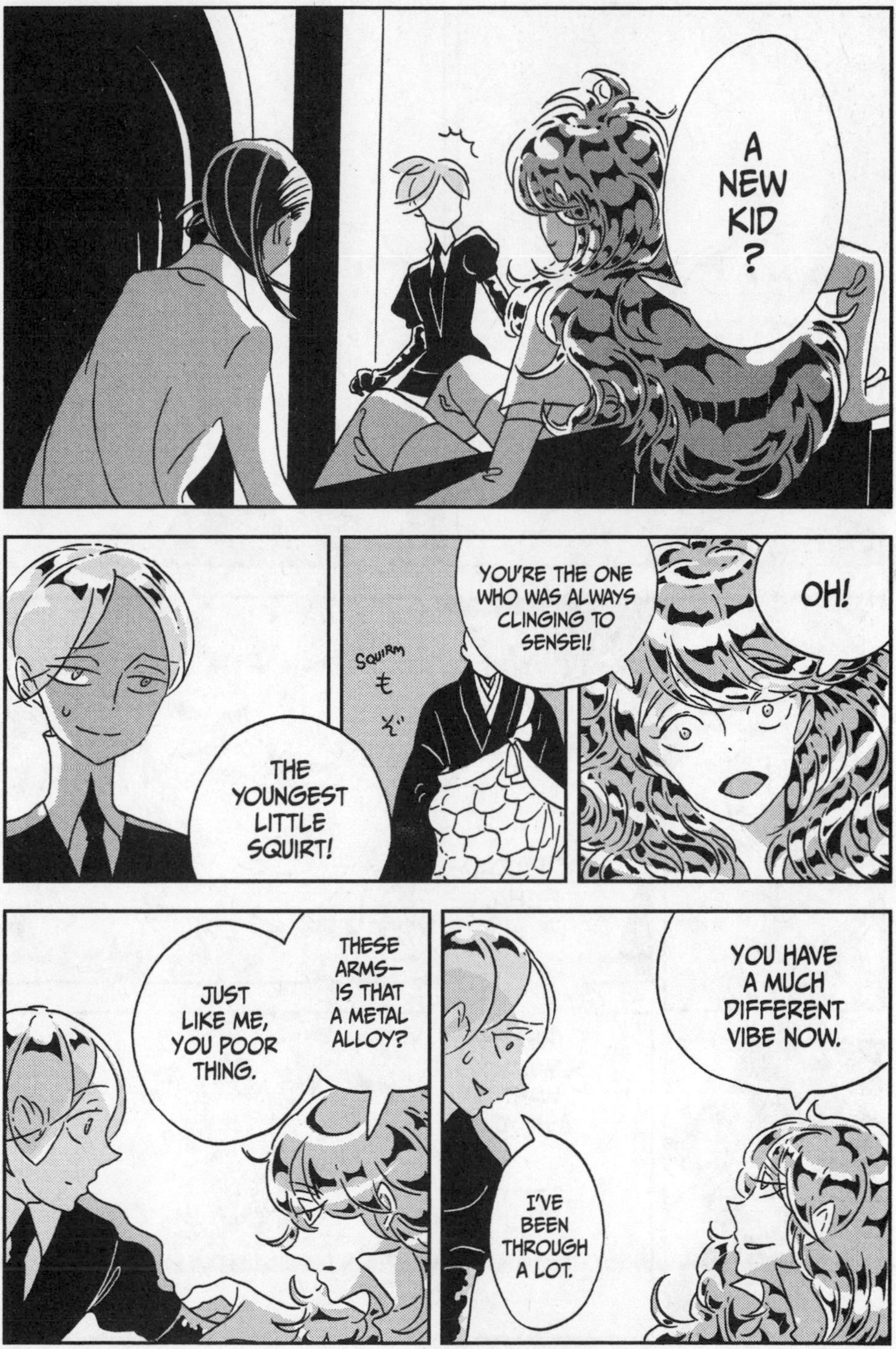
A NEW KID?
OH!
YOU'RE THE ONE WHO WAS ALWAYS CLINGING TO SENSEI!
SQUIRM
もぞ
THE YOUNGEST LITTLE SQUIRT!
YOU HAVE A MUCH DIFFERENT VIBE NOW.
I'VE BEEN THROUGH A LOT.
THESE ARMS— IS THAT A METAL ALLOY?
JUST LIKE ME, YOU POOR THING.

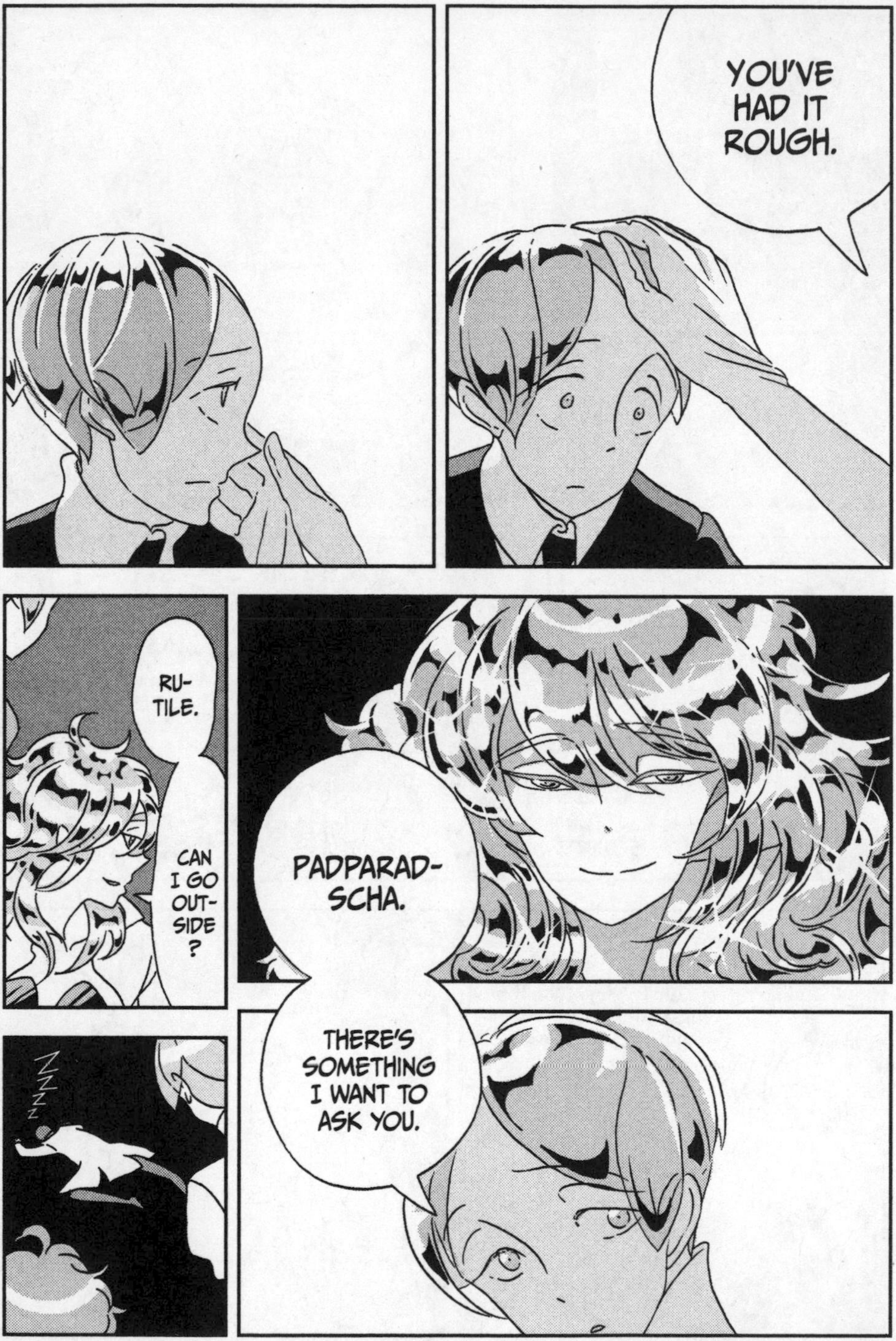
YOU'VE HAD IT ROUGH.
PADPARAD-SCHA.
RU-TILE.
CAN I GO OUT-SIDE?
THERE'S SOMETHING I WANT TO ASK YOU.
ZZZZ

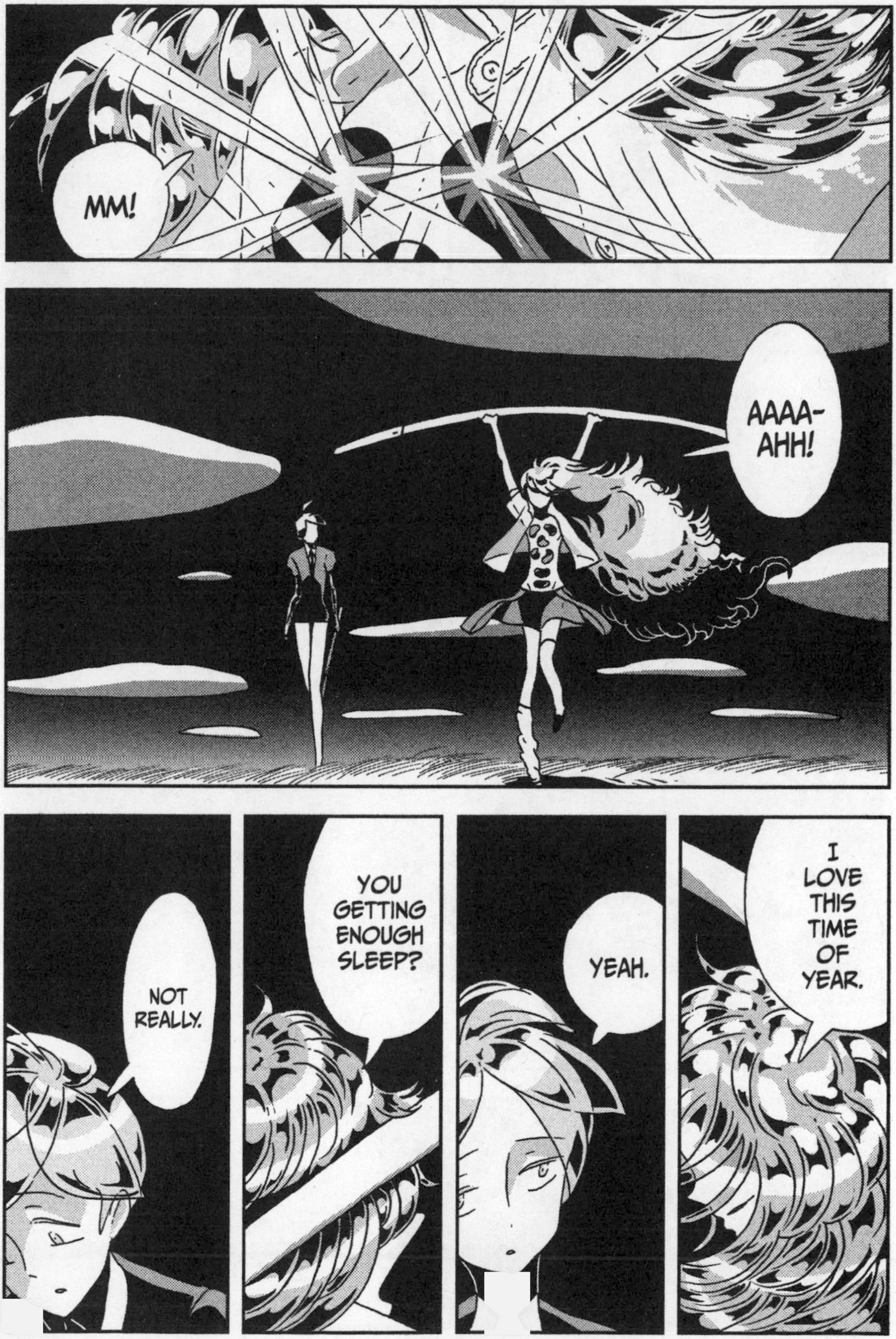
MM!
AAAA-AHH!
I LOVE THIS TIME OF YEAR.
YEAH.
YOU GETTING ENOUGH SLEEP?
NOT REALLY.

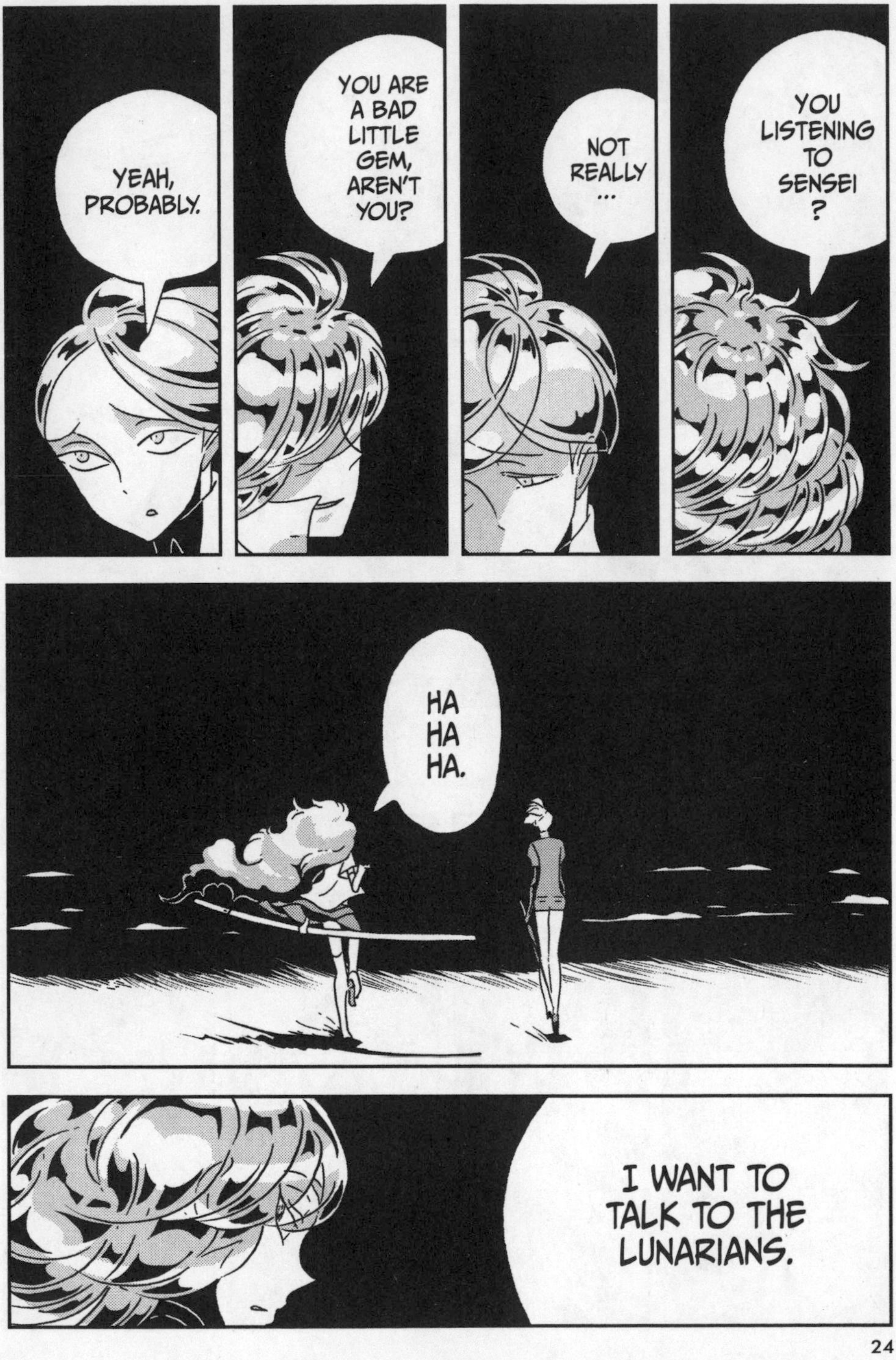
YOU LISTENING TO SENSEI ?
NOT REALLY ...
YOU ARE A BAD LITTLE GEM, AREN'T YOU?
YEAH, PROBABLY.
HA HA HA.
I WANT TO TALK TO THE LUNARIANS.

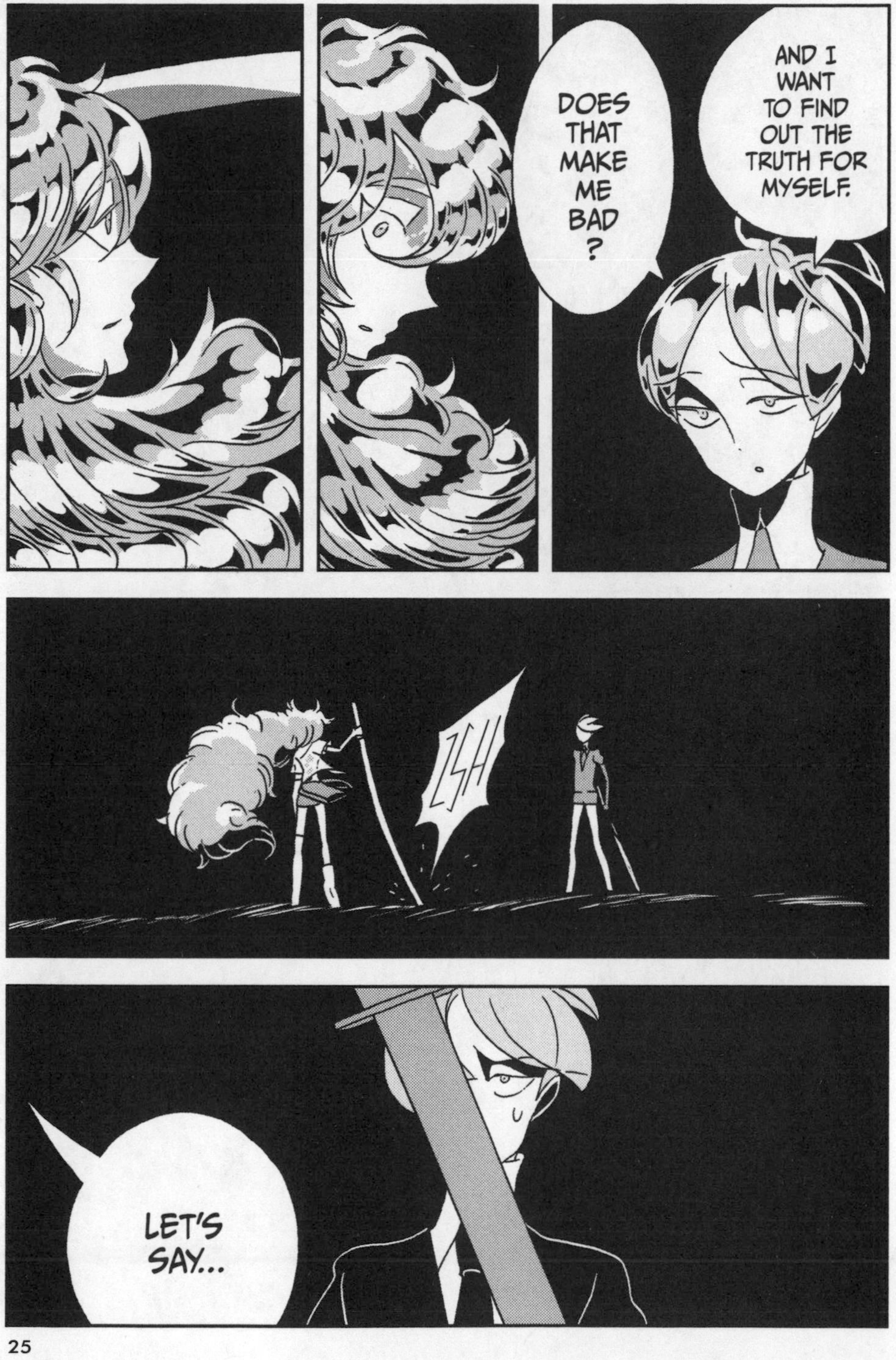
AND I WANT TO FIND OUT THE TRUTH FOR MYSELF.
DOES THAT MAKE ME BAD?
ZSH
LET'S SAY...

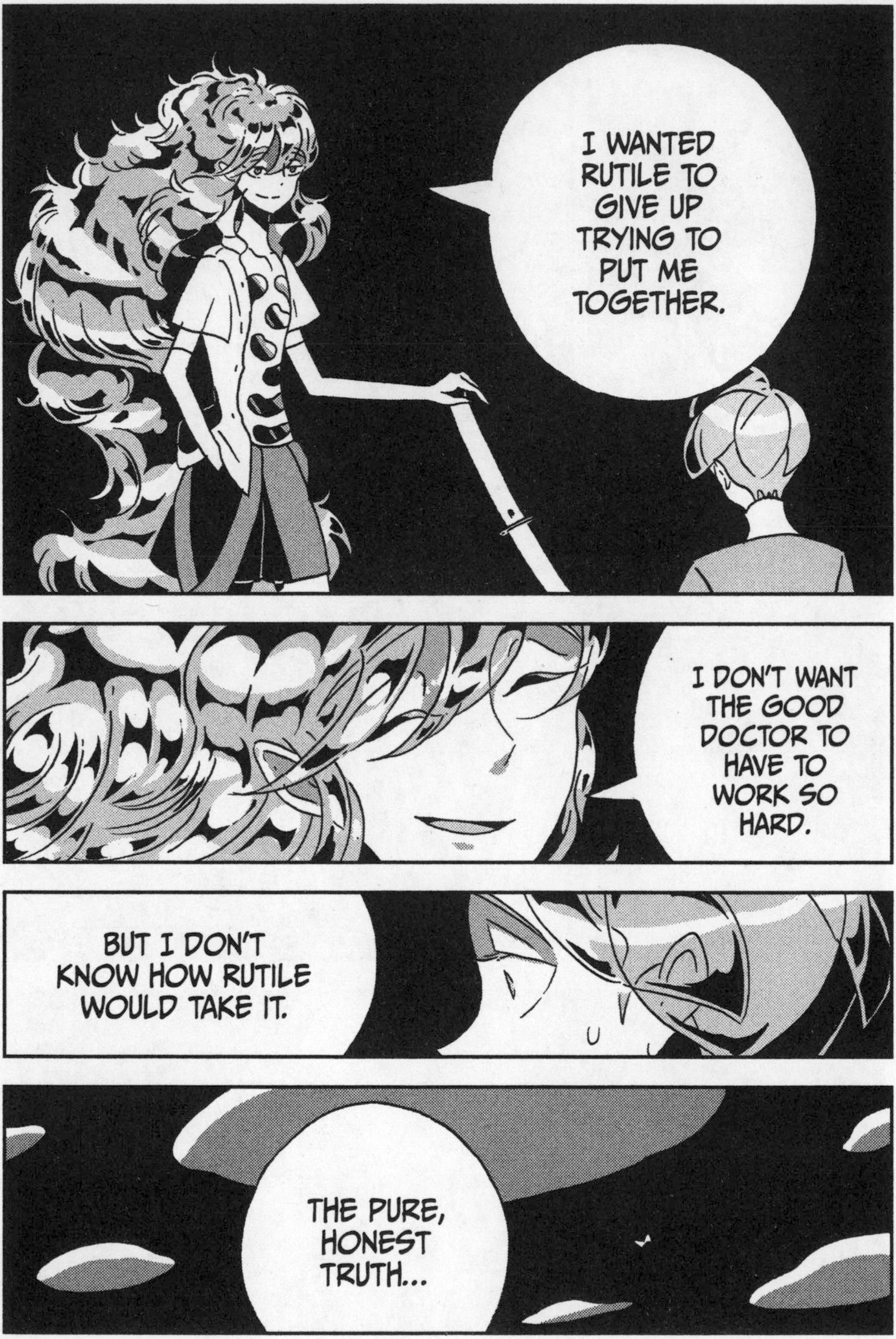
I WANTED RUTILE TO GIVE UP TRYING TO PUT ME TOGETHER.
I DON'T WANT THE GOOD DOCTOR TO HAVE TO WORK SO HARD.
BUT I DON'T KNOW HOW RUTILE WOULD TAKE IT.
THE PURE, HONEST TRUTH...

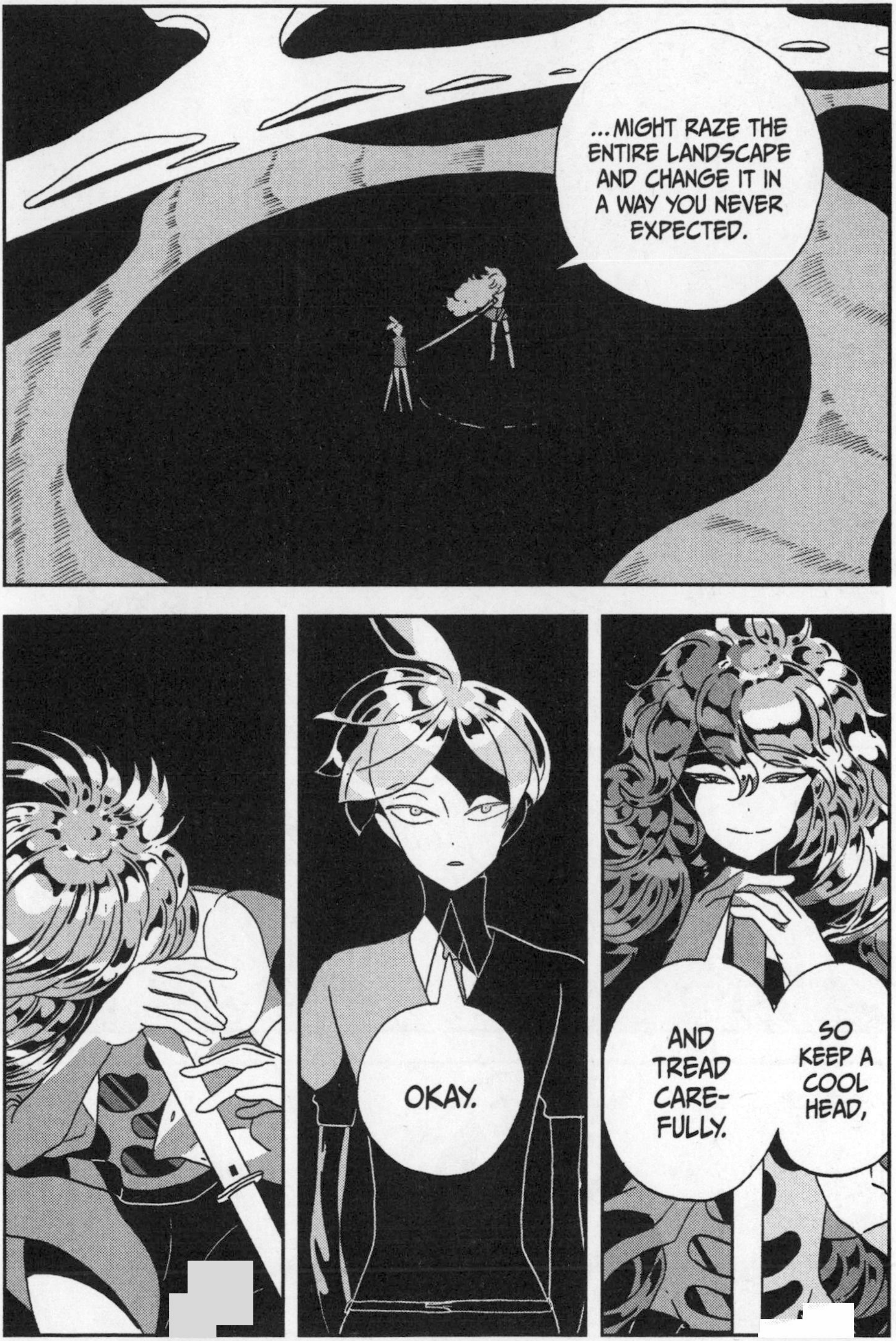
...MIGHT RAZE THE ENTIRE LANDSCAPE AND CHANGE IT IN A WAY YOU NEVER EXPECTED.
SO KEEP A COOL HEAD,
AND TREAD CARE-FULLY.
OKAY.

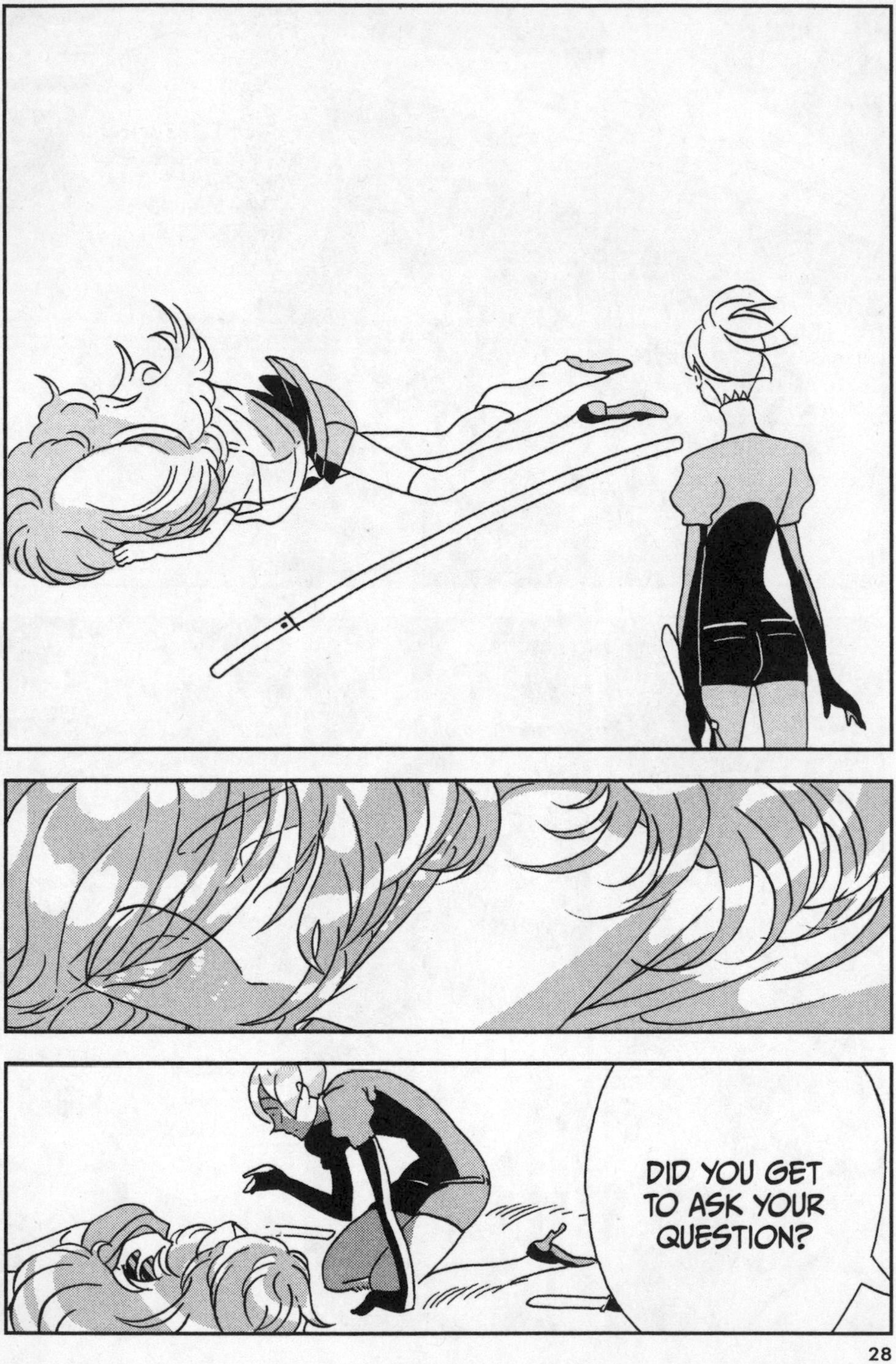
DID YOU GET TO ASK YOUR QUESTION?

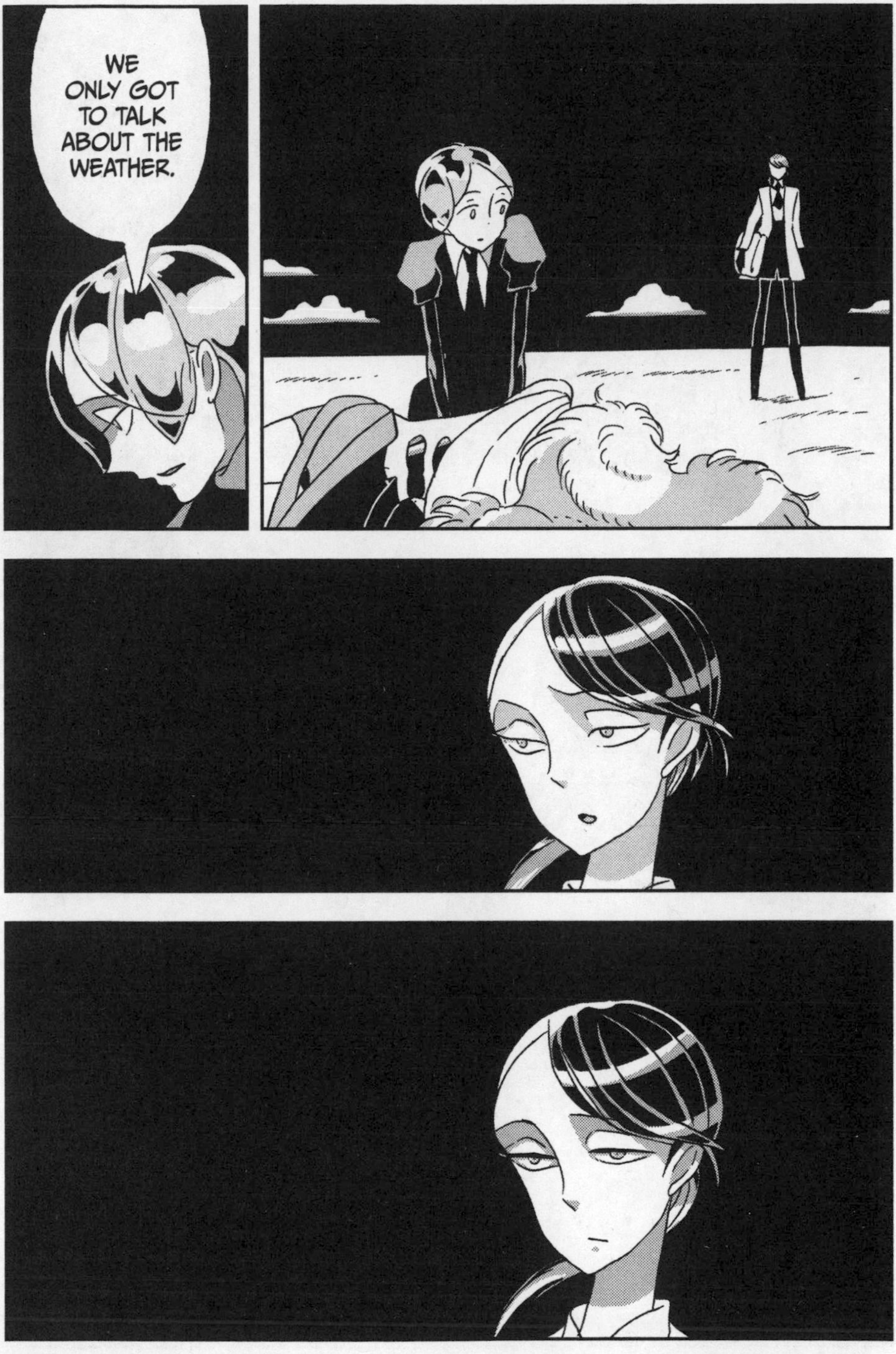
WE ONLY GOT TO TALK ABOUT THE WEATHER.

CHAPTER 29: Padparadscha END

CHAPTER 30:

Empty Black Spot

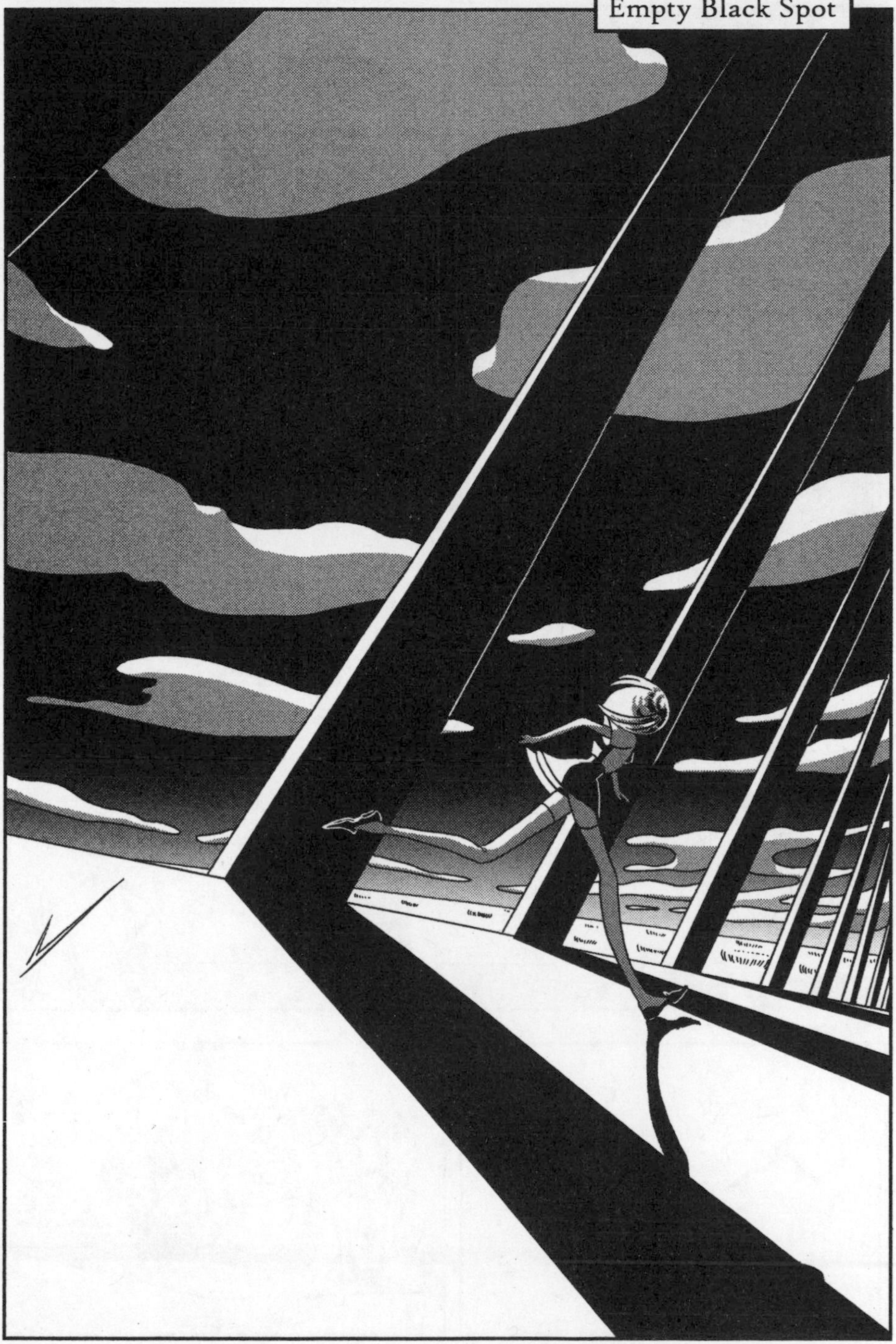

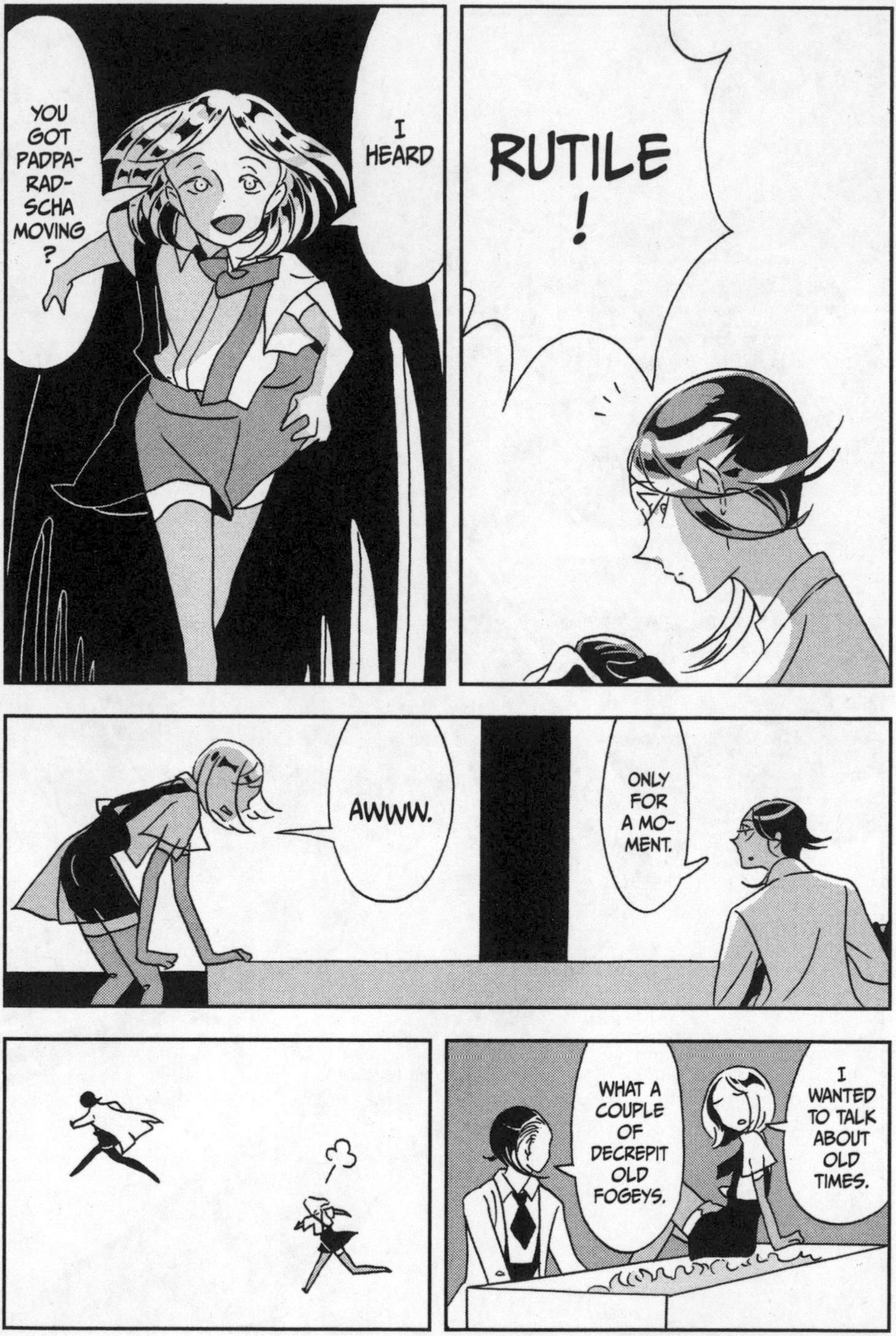
RUTILE!
I HEARD
YOU GOT PADPARADSCHA MOVING?
ONLY FOR A MOMENT.
AWWW.
I WANTED TO TALK ABOUT OLD TIMES.
WHAT A COUPLE OF DECREPIT OLD FOGEYS.

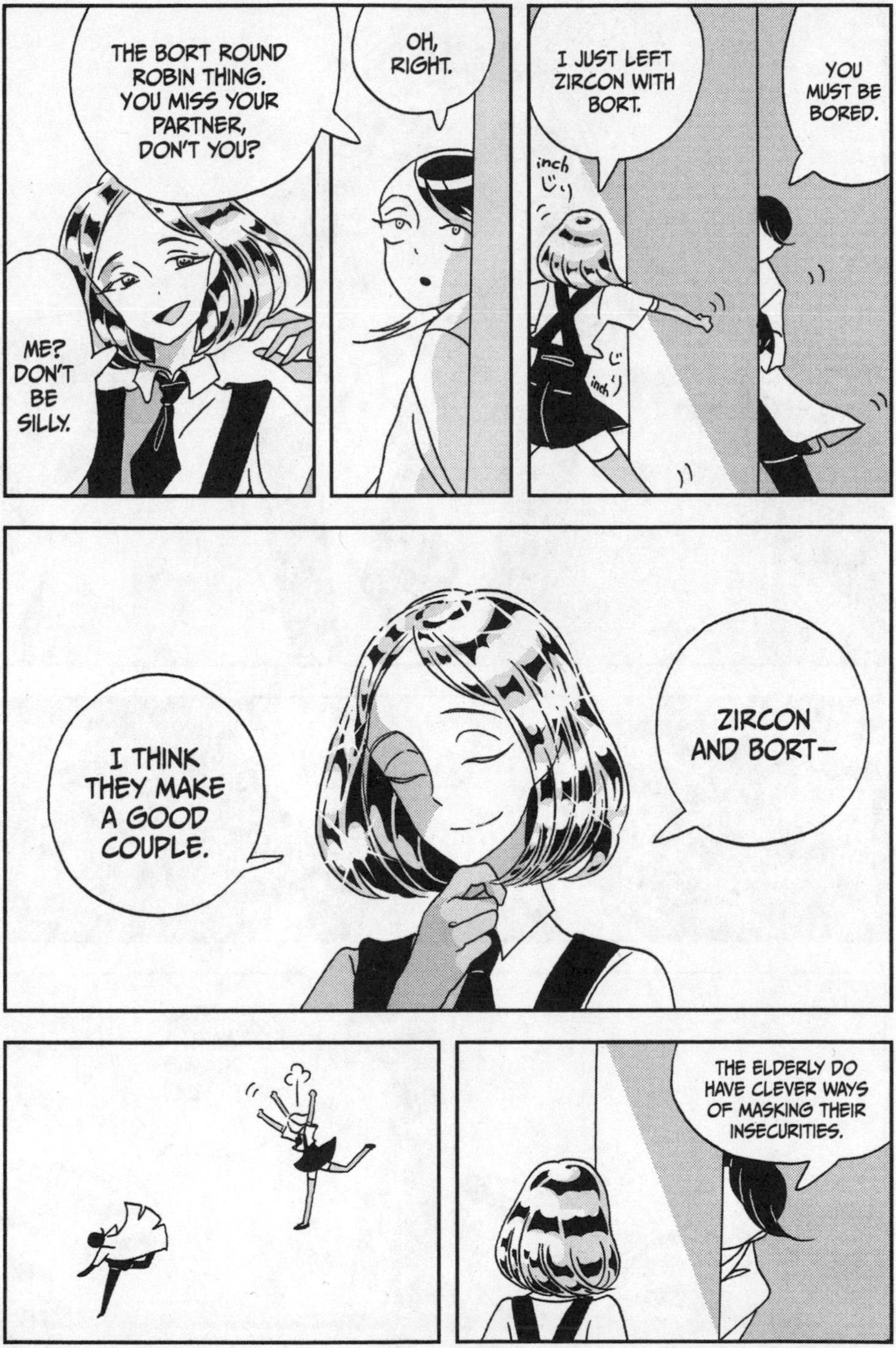

YOU MUST BE BORED.
I JUST LEFT ZIRCON WITH BORT.
inch じり
じり inch
OH, RIGHT.
THE BORT ROUND ROBIN THING. YOU MISS YOUR PARTNER, DON'T YOU?
ME? DON'T BE SILLY.
ZIRCON AND BORT—
I THINK THEY MAKE A GOOD COUPLE.
THE ELDERLY DO HAVE CLEVER WAYS OF MASKING THEIR INSECURITIES.

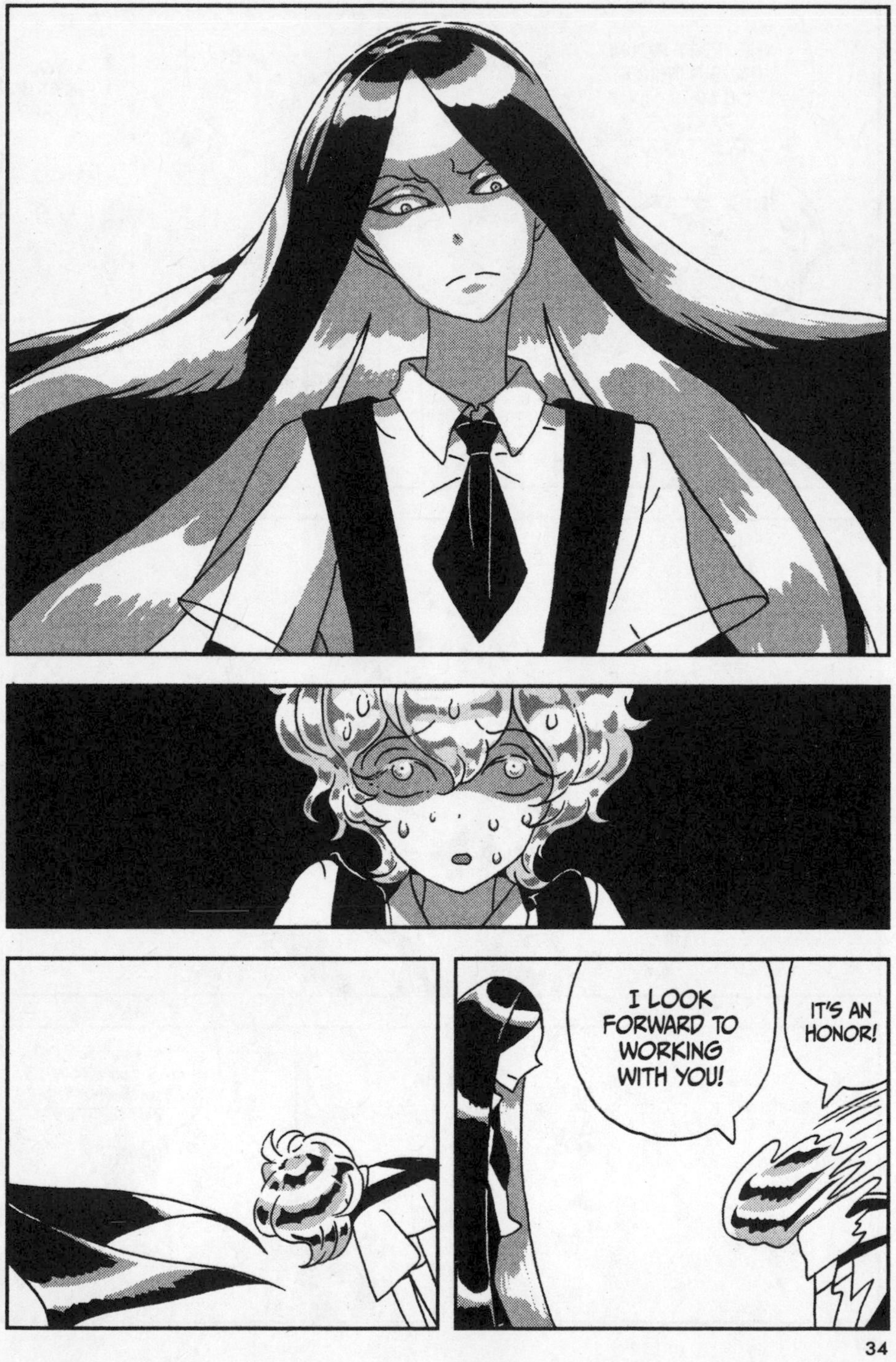
IT'S AN HONOR!
I LOOK FORWARD TO WORKING WITH YOU!

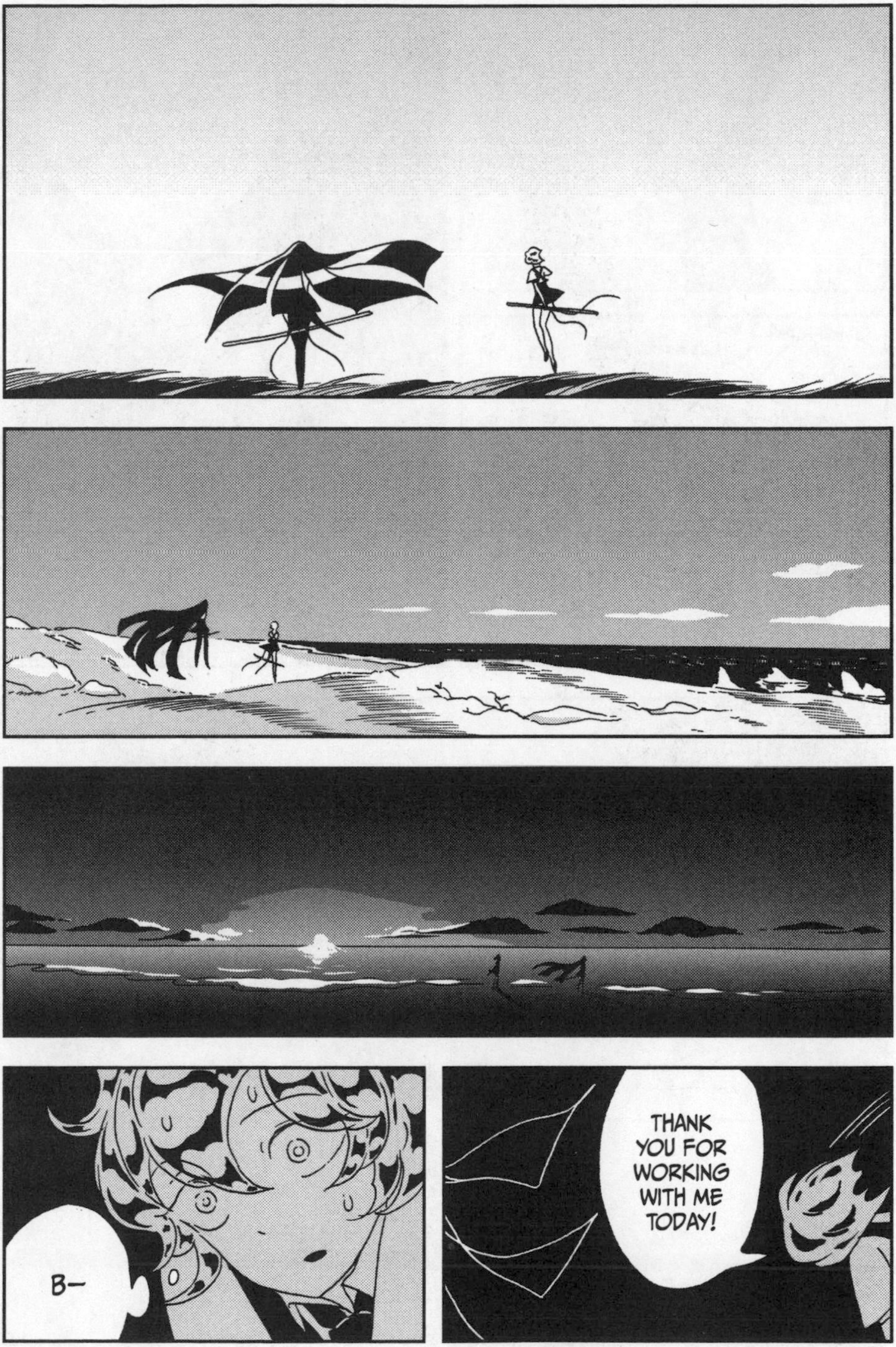
THANK YOU FOR WORKING WITH ME TODAY!
B—

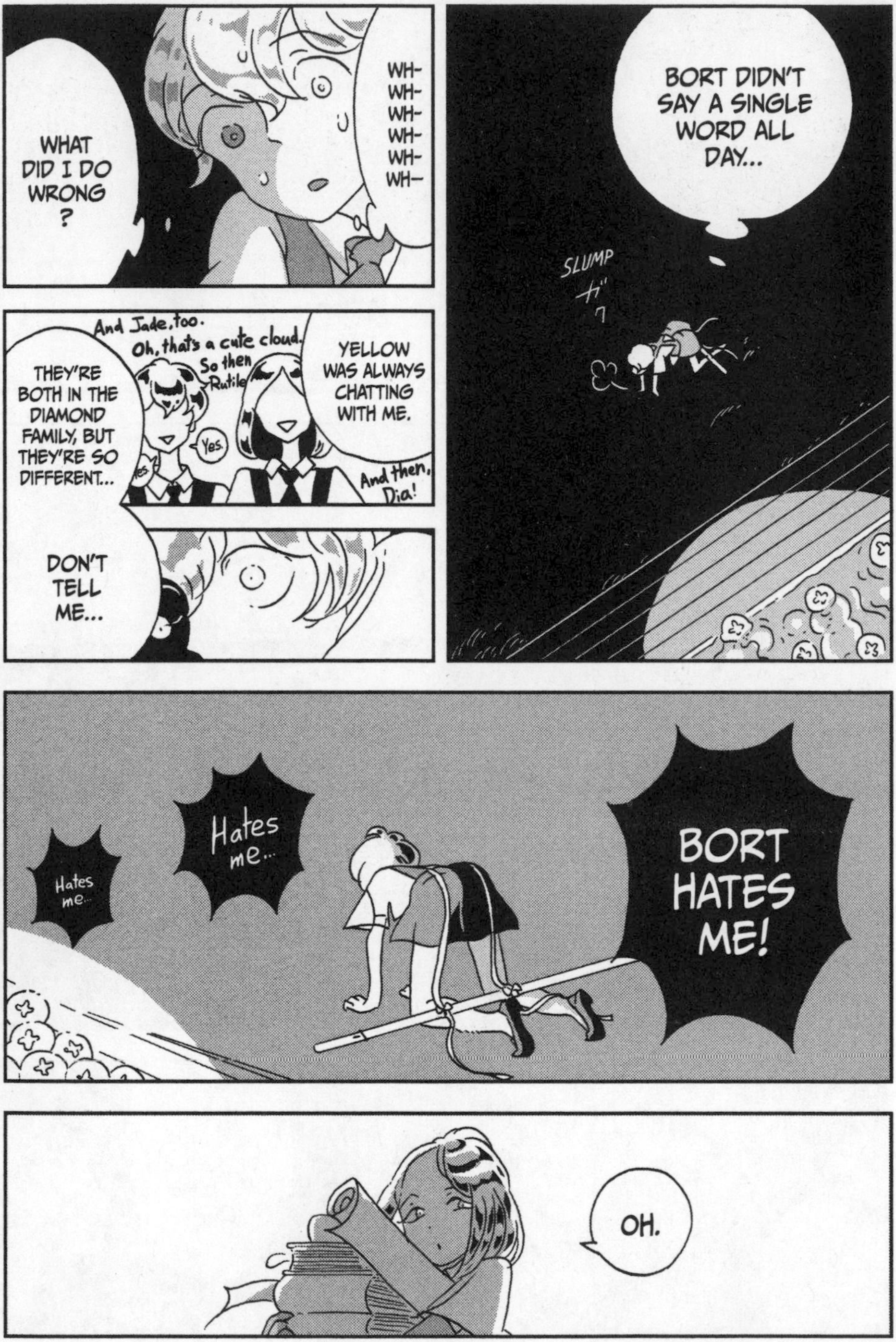
BORT DIDN'T SAY A SINGLE WORD ALL DAY...
SLUMP
WH- WH- WH- WH- WH- WH-
WHAT DID I DO WRONG ?
YELLOW WAS ALWAYS CHATTING WITH ME.
And Jade, too.
Oh, that's a cute cloud.
So then Rutile
And then, Dia!
Yes.
THEY'RE BOTH IN THE DIAMOND FAMILY, BUT THEY'RE SO DIFFERENT...
DON'T TELL ME...
BORT HATES ME!
Hates me...
Hates me...
OH.

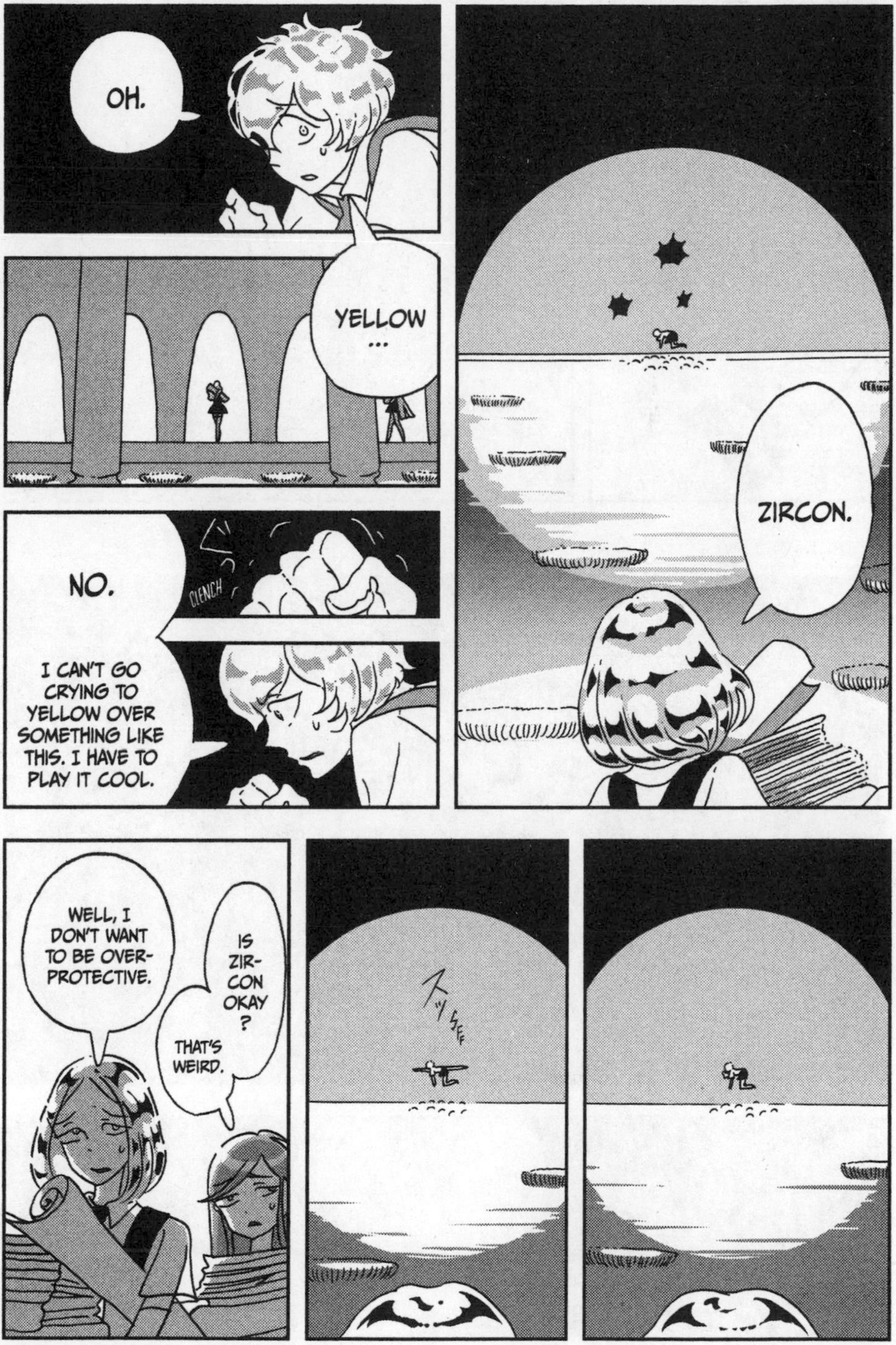
ZIRCON.
OH.
YELLOW ...
NO.
CLENCH
I CAN'T GO CRYING TO YELLOW OVER SOMETHING LIKE THIS. I HAVE TO PLAY IT COOL.
スッ SEE
IS ZIR-CON OKAY?
THAT'S WEIRD.
WELL, I DON'T WANT TO BE OVER-PROTECTIVE.

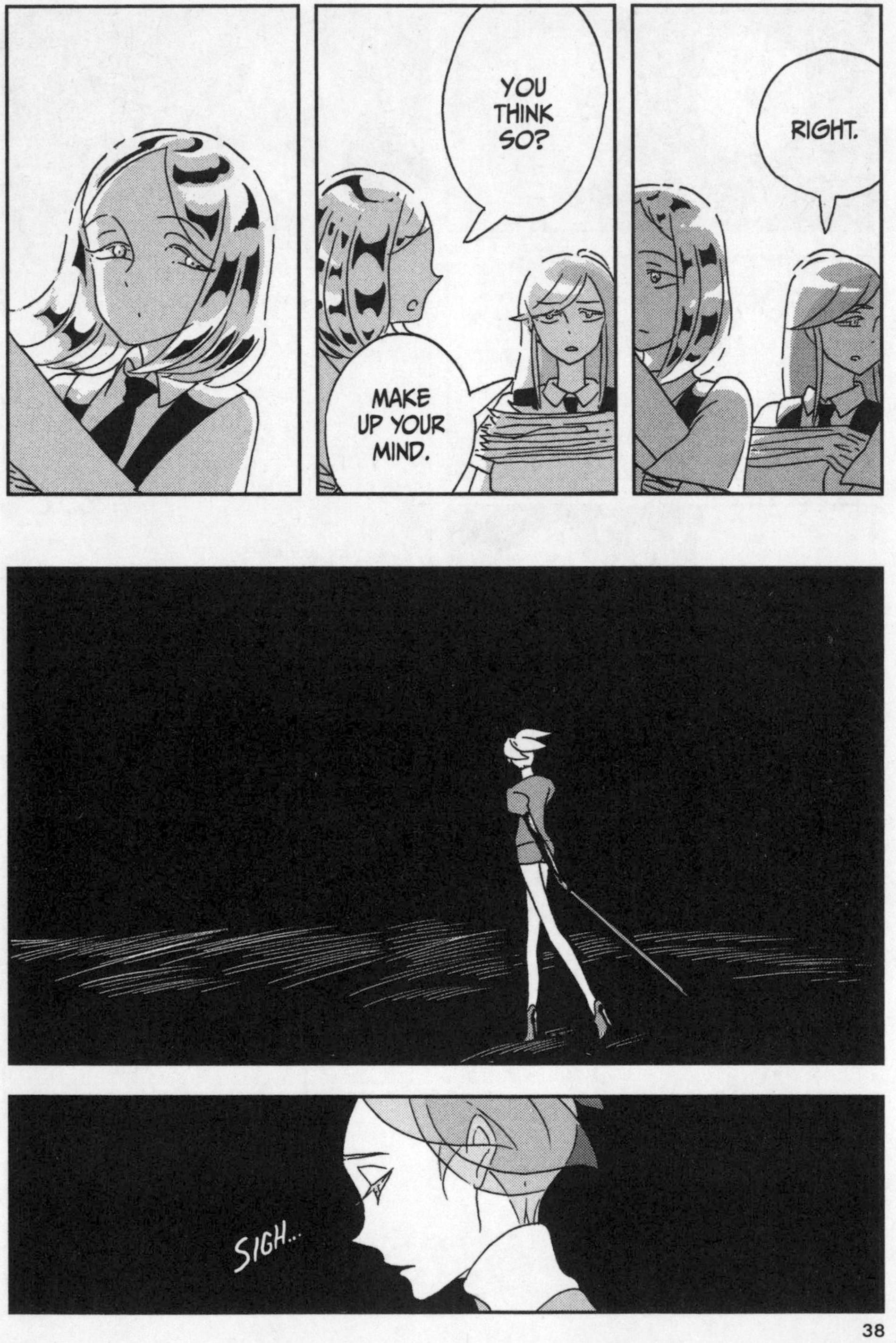
RIGHT.
YOU THINK SO?
MAKE UP YOUR MIND.
SIGH...

ANOTHER DAY...
...ANOTHER FAILURE.
DWAH!
YOU WERE HERE?
YES, I WAS.
PLEASE HELP ME!
HUH?
NO, YOU'RE SCARING ME!
PLEASE HELP ANYWAY!
ZSHH
BORT WON'T TALK TO YOU?

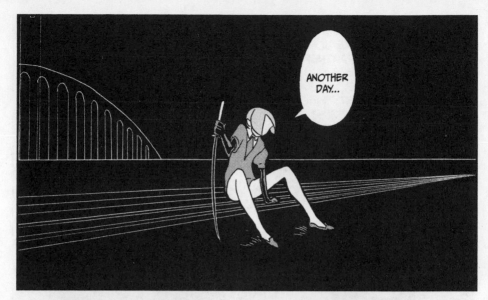

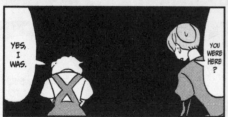

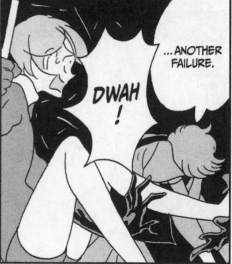

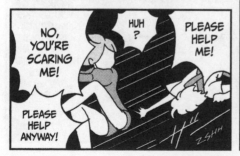

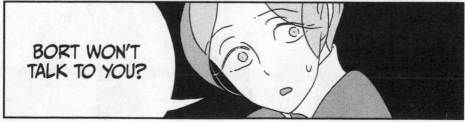

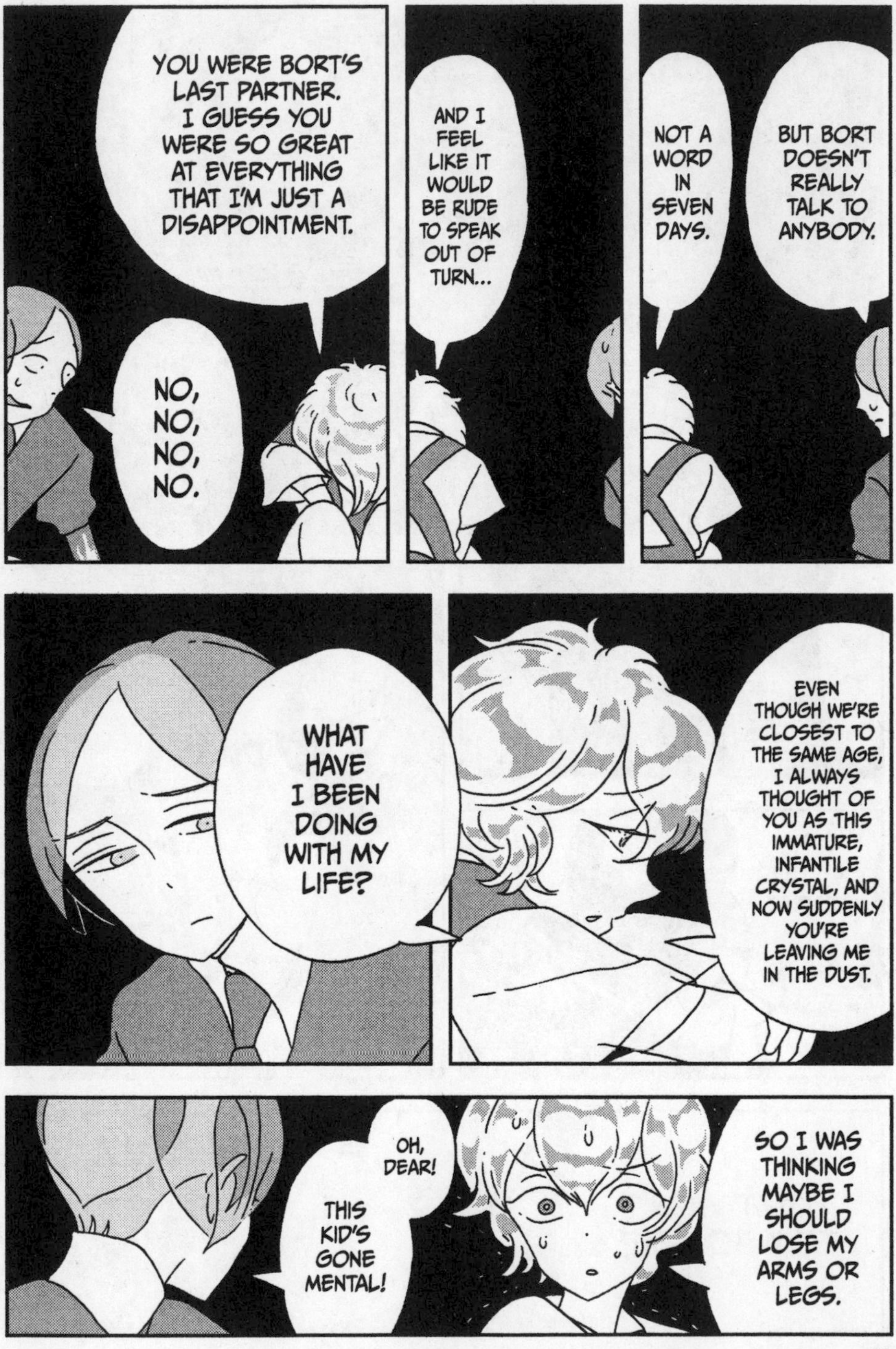
BUT BORT DOESN'T REALLY TALK TO ANYBODY.
NOT A WORD IN SEVEN DAYS.
AND I FEEL LIKE IT WOULD BE RUDE TO SPEAK OUT OF TURN...
YOU WERE BORT'S LAST PARTNER. I GUESS YOU WERE SO GREAT AT EVERYTHING THAT I'M JUST A DISAPPOINTMENT.
NO, NO, NO, NO.
EVEN THOUGH WE'RE CLOSEST TO THE SAME AGE, I ALWAYS THOUGHT OF YOU AS THIS IMMATURE, INFANTILE CRYSTAL, AND NOW SUDDENLY YOU'RE LEAVING ME IN THE DUST.
WHAT HAVE I BEEN DOING WITH MY LIFE?
SO I WAS THINKING MAYBE I SHOULD LOSE MY ARMS OR LEGS.
OH, DEAR!
THIS KID'S GONE MENTAL!

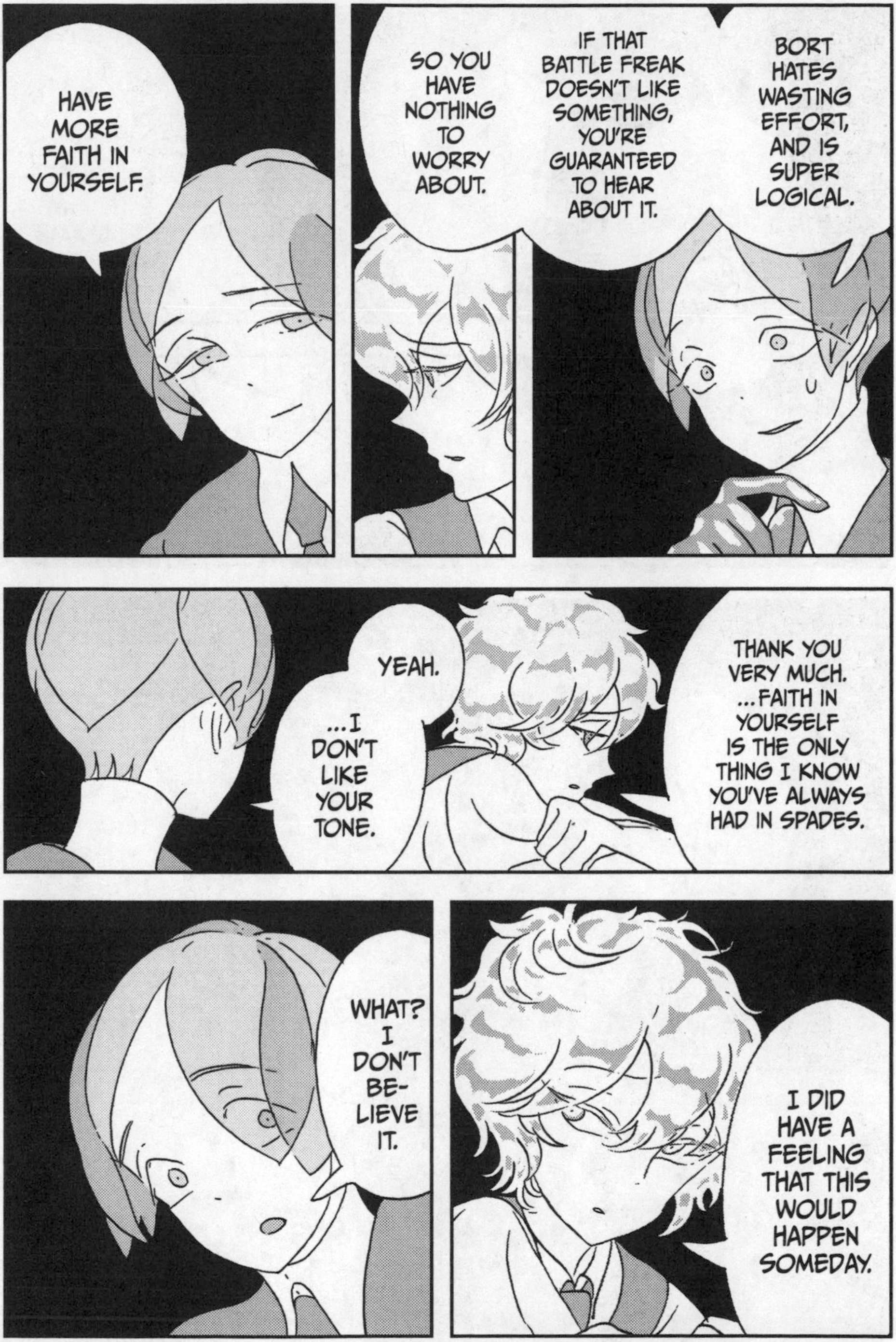
BORT HATES WASTING EFFORT, AND IS SUPER LOGICAL.
IF THAT BATTLE FREAK DOESN'T LIKE SOMETHING, YOU'RE GUARANTEED TO HEAR ABOUT IT.
SO YOU HAVE NOTHING TO WORRY ABOUT.
HAVE MORE FAITH IN YOURSELF.
THANK YOU VERY MUCH. ...FAITH IN YOURSELF IS THE ONLY THING I KNOW YOU'VE ALWAYS HAD IN SPADES.
YEAH.
...I DON'T LIKE YOUR TONE.
I DID HAVE A FEELING THAT THIS WOULD HAPPEN SOMEDAY.
WHAT? I DON'T BE- LIEVE IT.

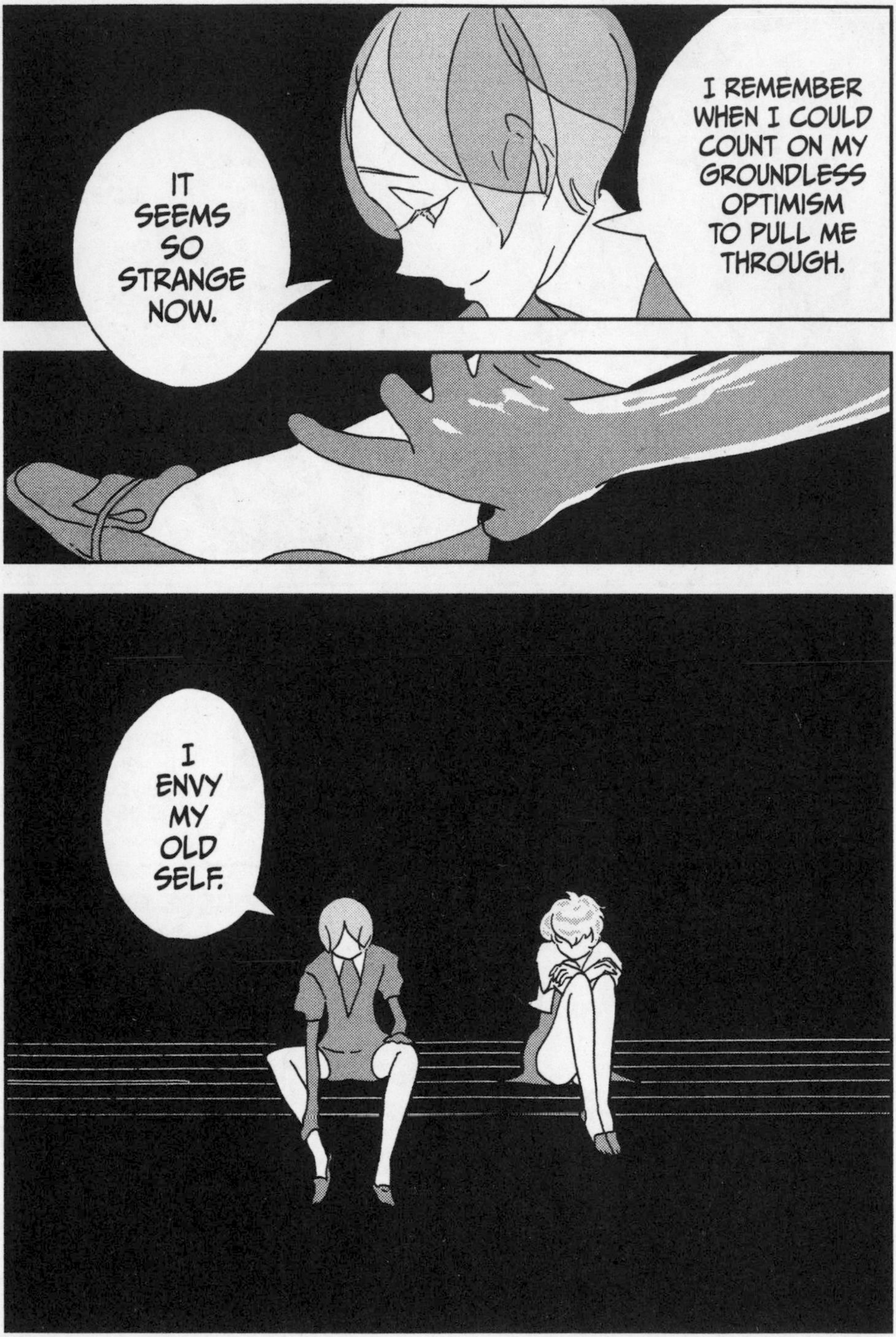
I REMEMBER WHEN I COULD COUNT ON MY GROUNDLESS OPTIMISM TO PULL ME THROUGH.
IT SEEMS SO STRANGE NOW.
I ENVY MY OLD SELF.

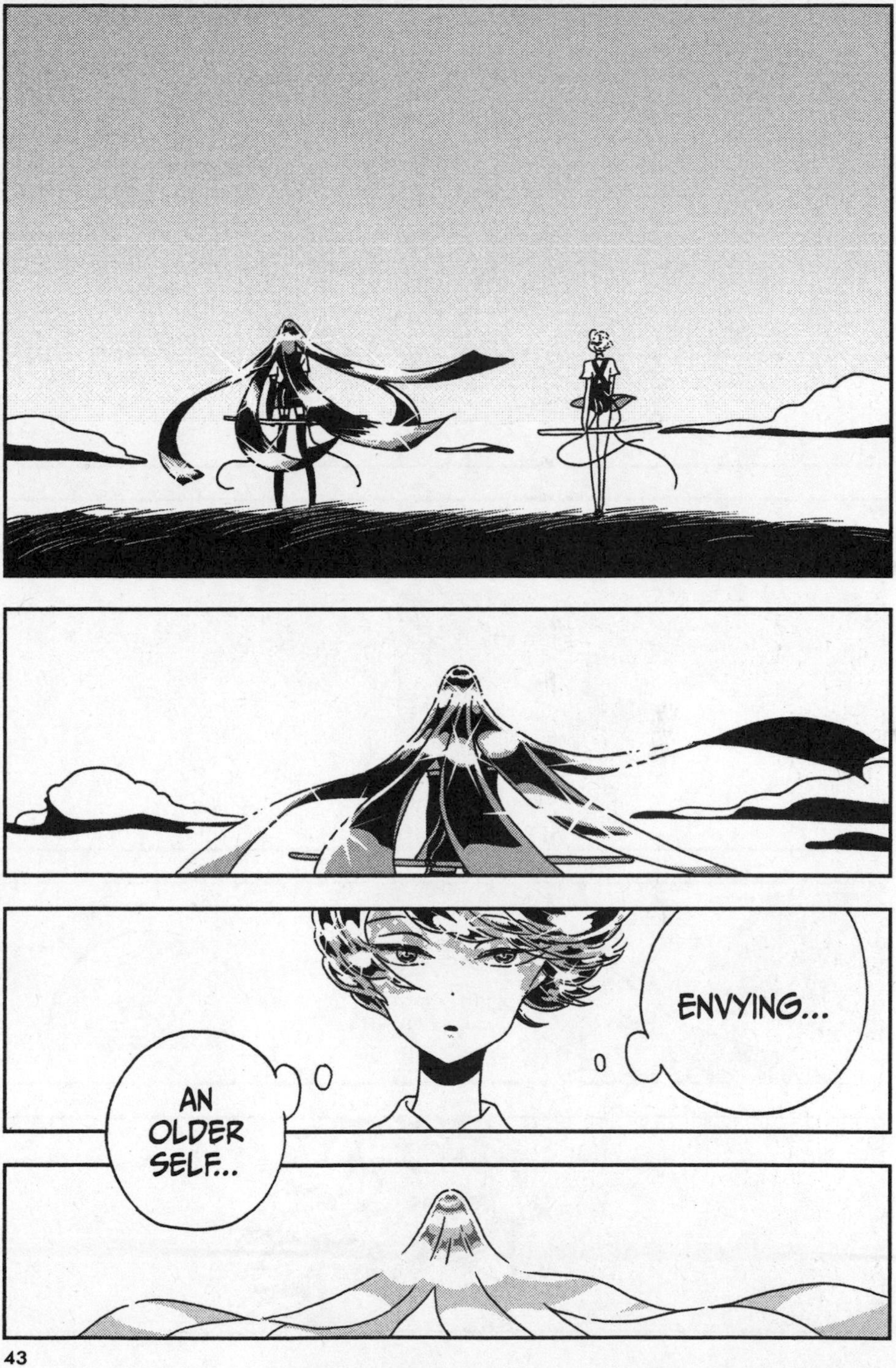
ENVYING...
AN OLDER SELF...

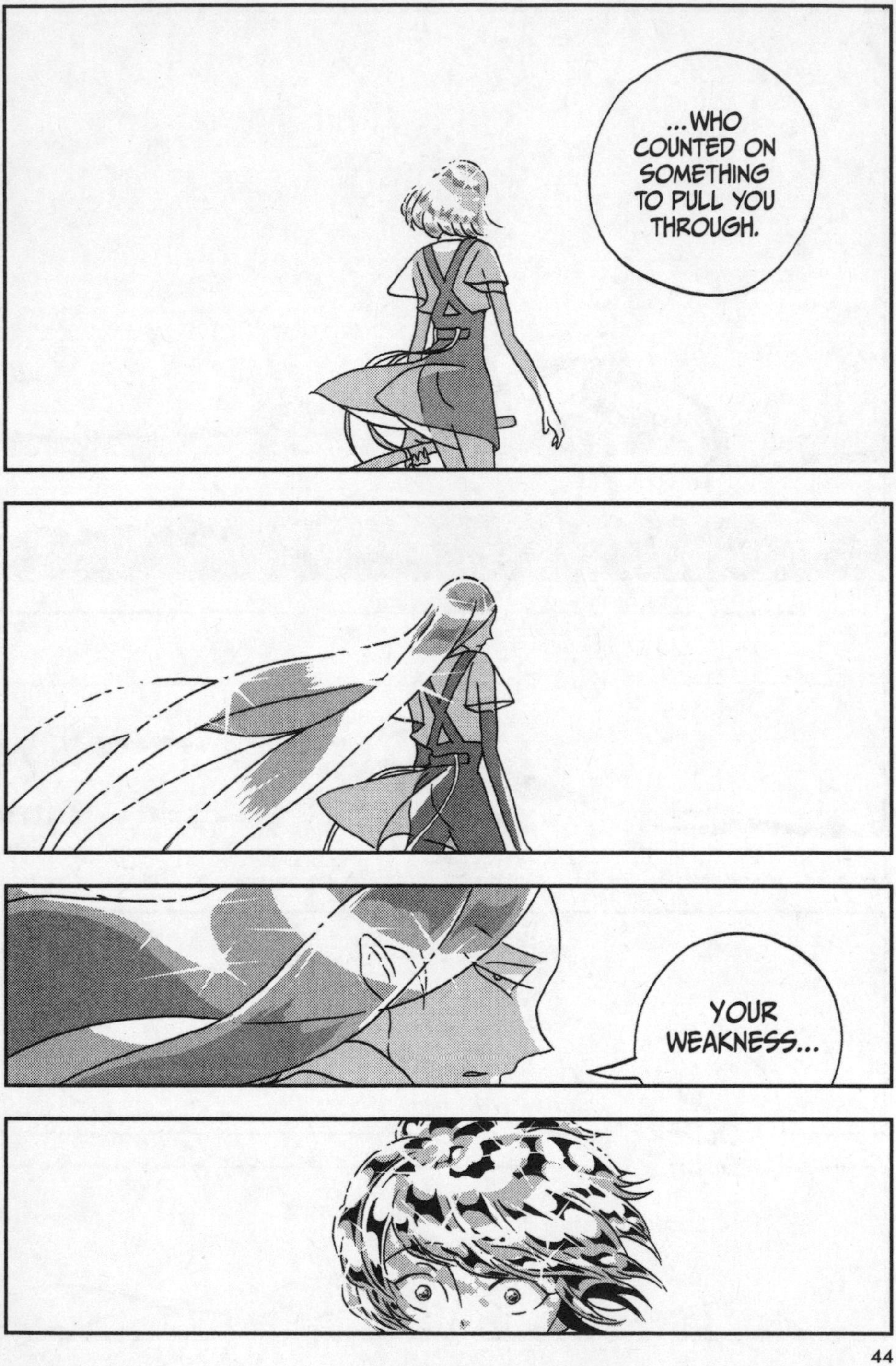
...WHO COUNTED ON SOMETHING TO PULL YOU THROUGH.
YOUR WEAKNESS...

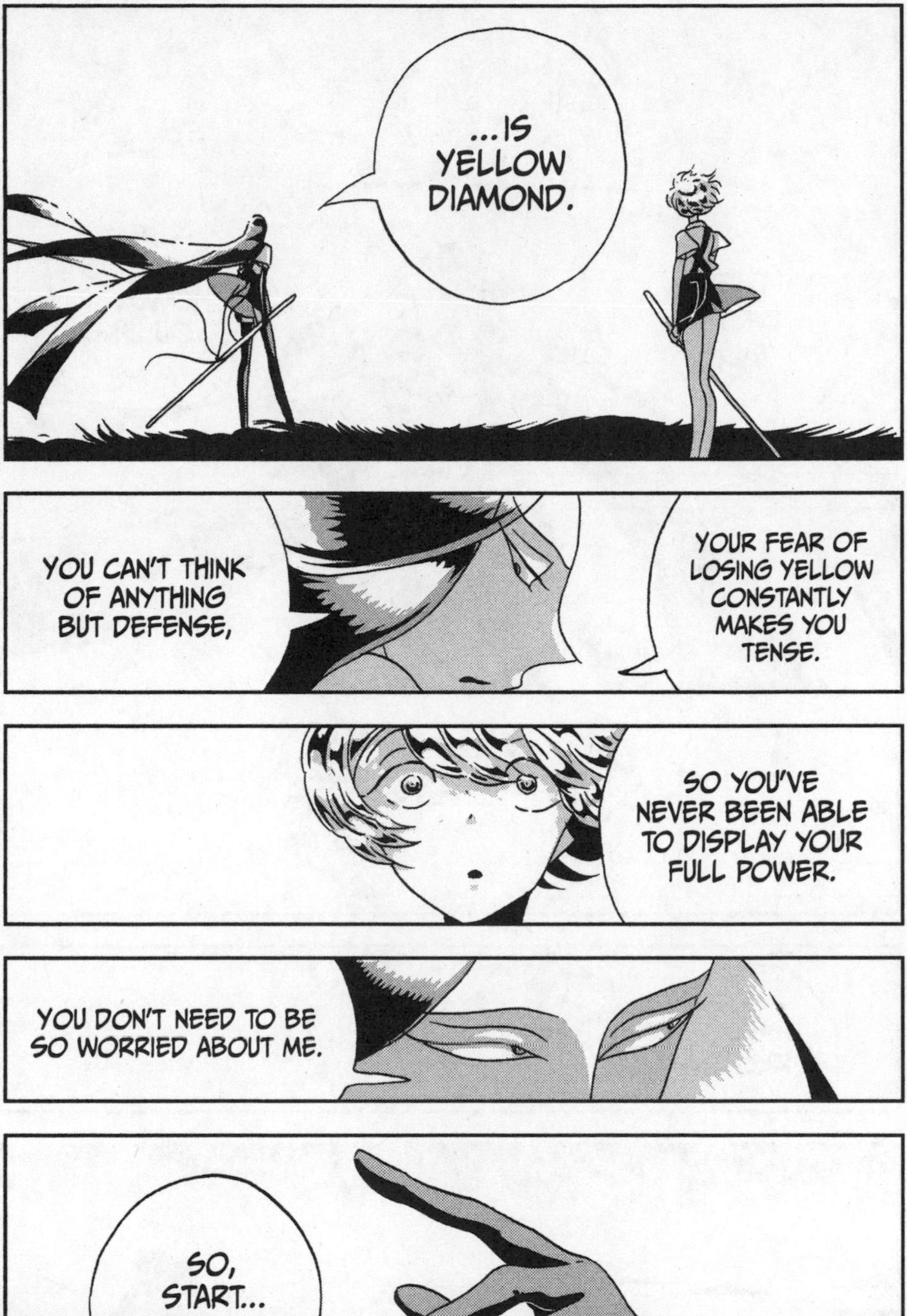
...IS YELLOW DIAMOND.
YOUR FEAR OF LOSING YELLOW CONSTANTLY MAKES YOU TENSE.
YOU CAN'T THINK OF ANYTHING BUT DEFENSE,
SO YOU'VE NEVER BEEN ABLE TO DISPLAY YOUR FULL POWER.
YOU DON'T NEED TO BE SO WORRIED ABOUT ME.
SO, START...

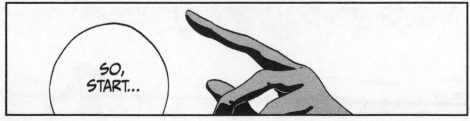

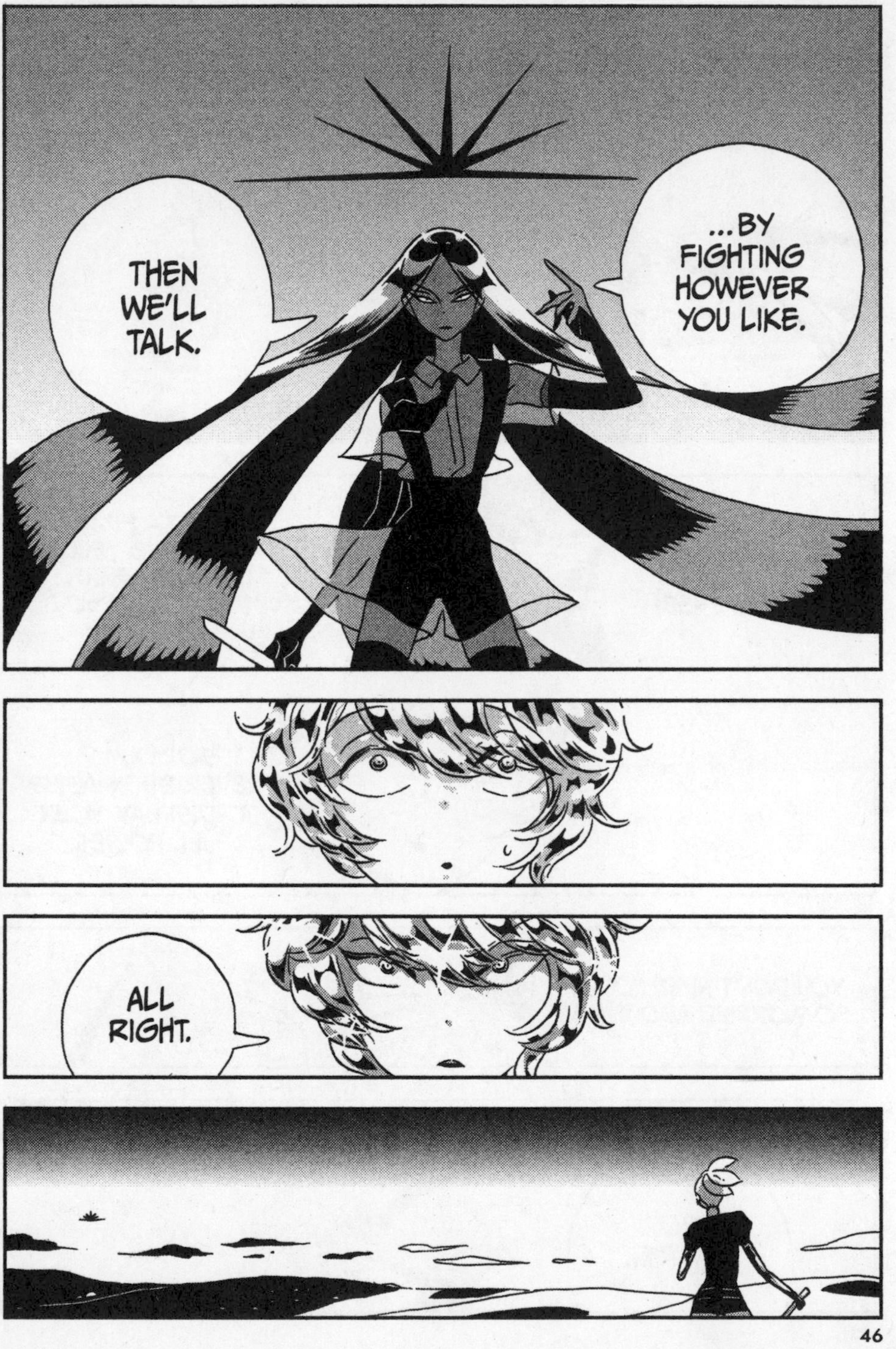
...BY FIGHTING HOWEVER YOU LIKE.
THEN WE'LL TALK.
ALL RIGHT.

THEY'RE
HERE!

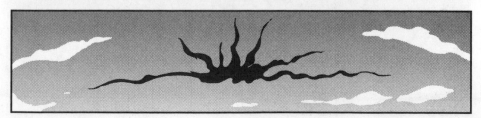

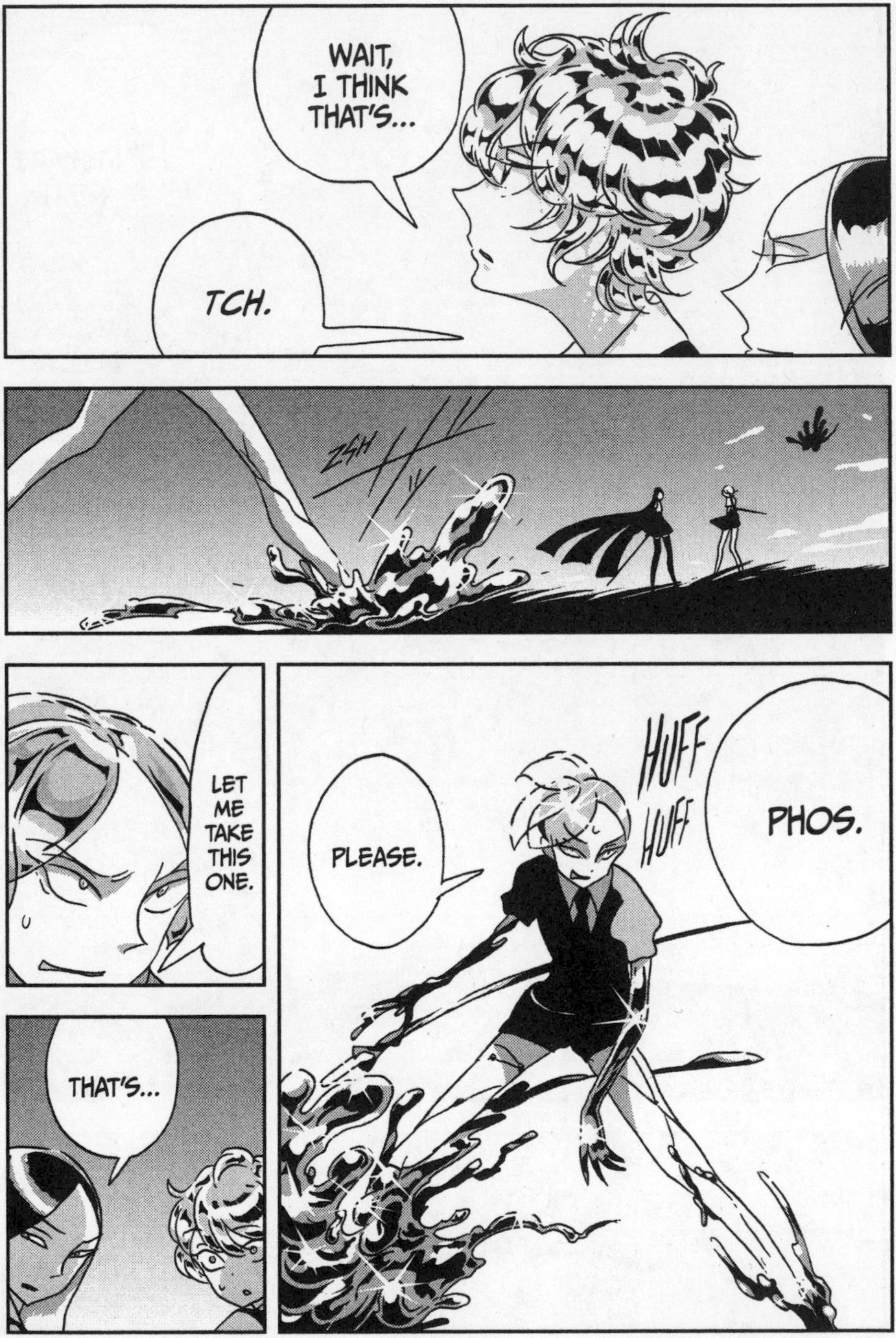
WAIT, I THINK THAT'S...
TCH.
ZSH
PHOS.
HUFF HUFF
PLEASE.
LET ME TAKE THIS ONE.
THAT'S...

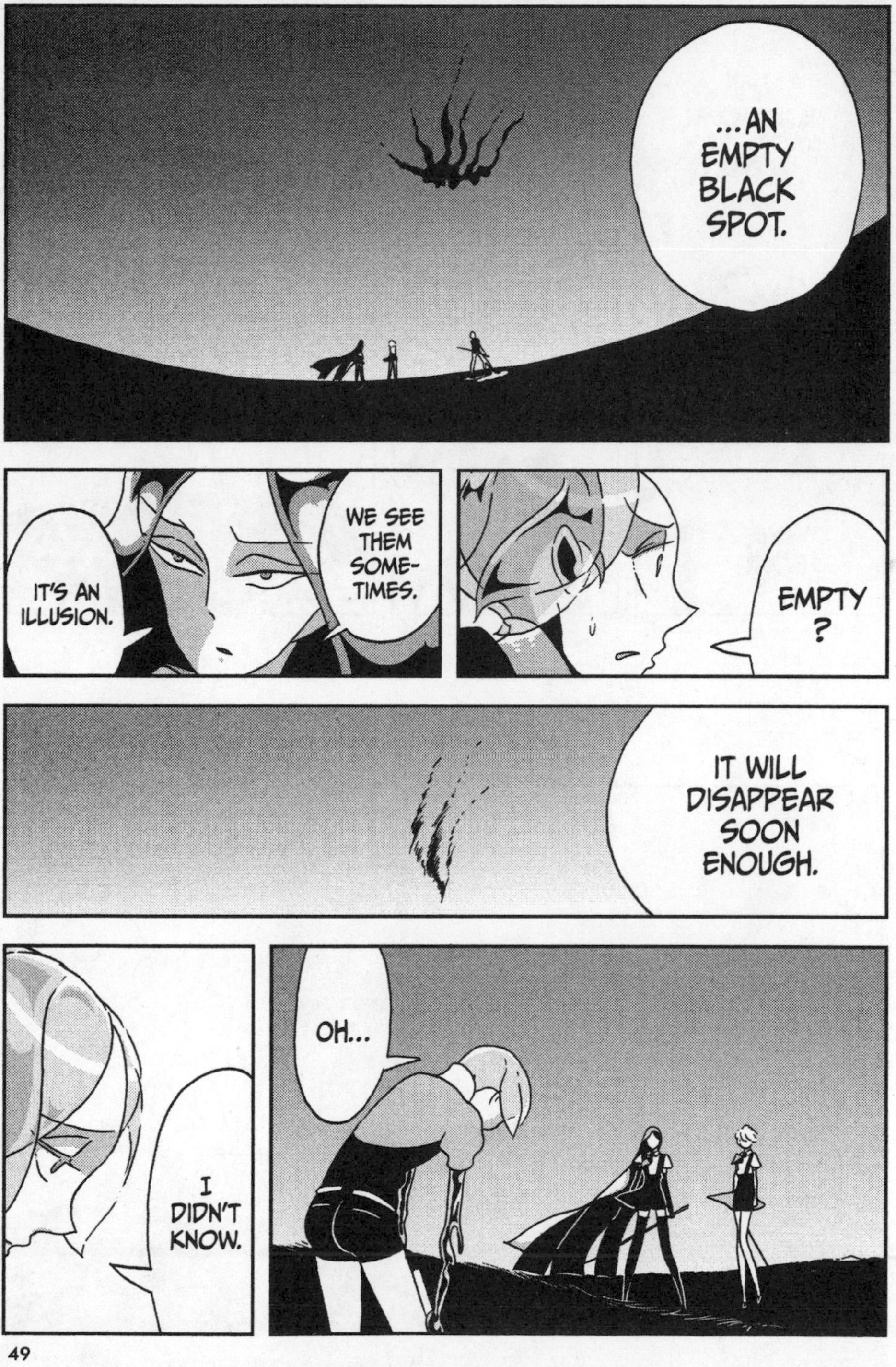
...AN EMPTY BLACK SPOT.
EMPTY?
WE SEE THEM SOMETIMES.
IT'S AN ILLUSION.
IT WILL DISAPPEAR SOON ENOUGH.
OH...
I DIDN'T KNOW.

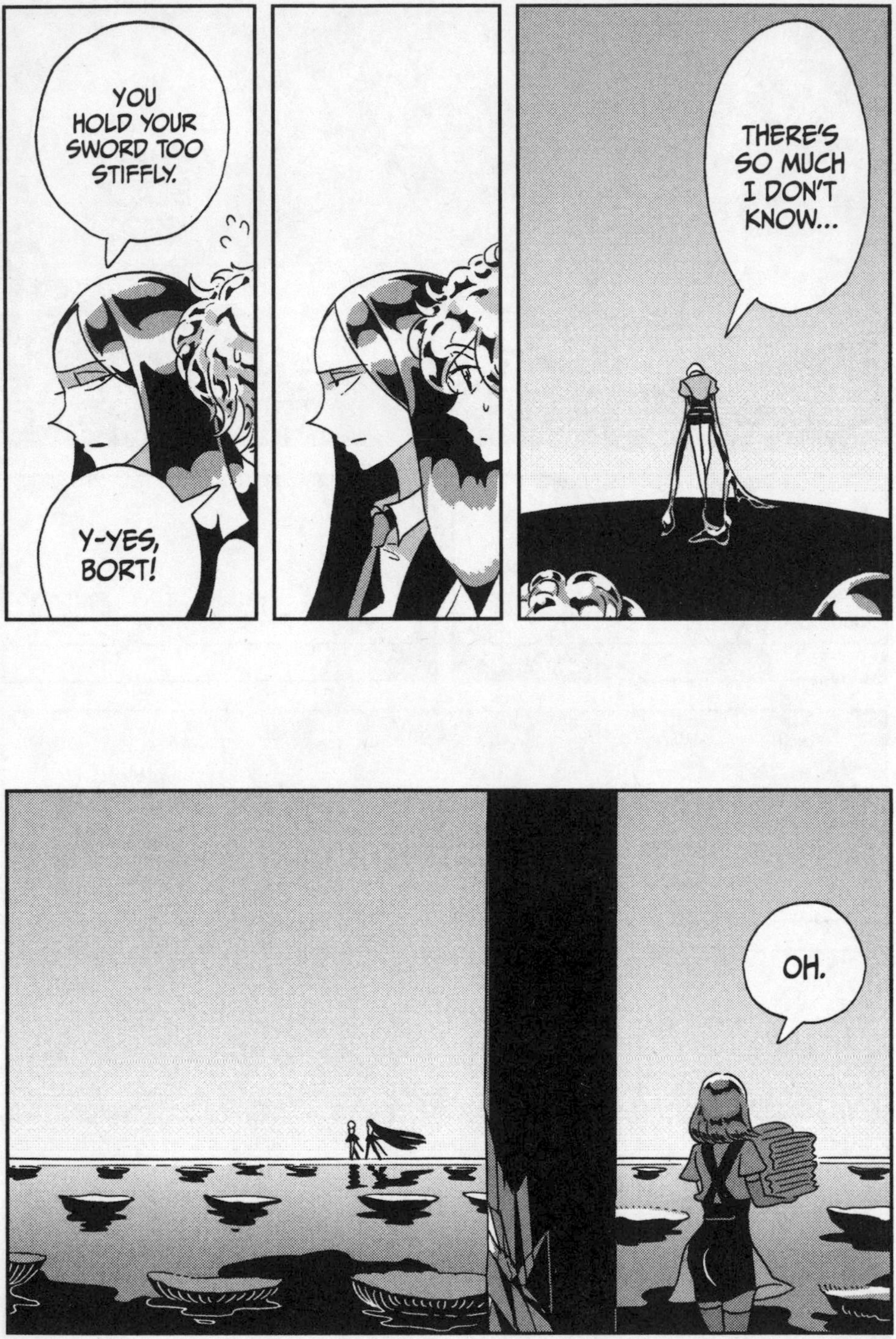
THERE'S SO MUCH I DON'T KNOW...
YOU HOLD YOUR SWORD TOO STIFFLY.
Y-YES, BORT!
OH.

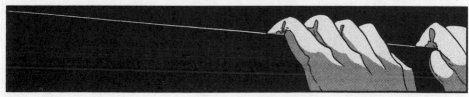

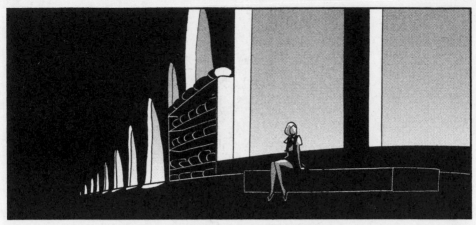

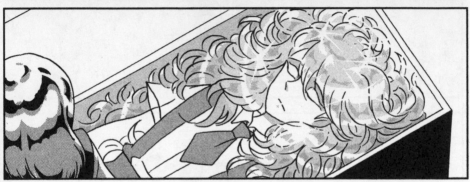

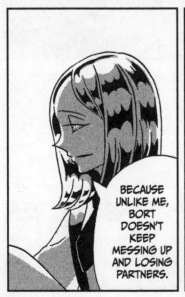

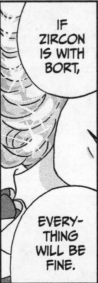

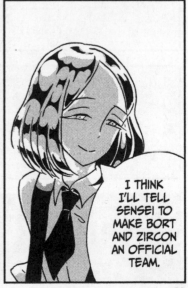

I THINK I'LL TELL SENSEI TO MAKE BORT AND ZIRCON AN OFFICIAL TEAM.
IF ZIRCON IS WITH BORT,
EVERY-THING WILL BE FINE.
BECAUSE UNLIKE ME, BORT DOESN'T KEEP MESSING UP AND LOSING PARTNERS.

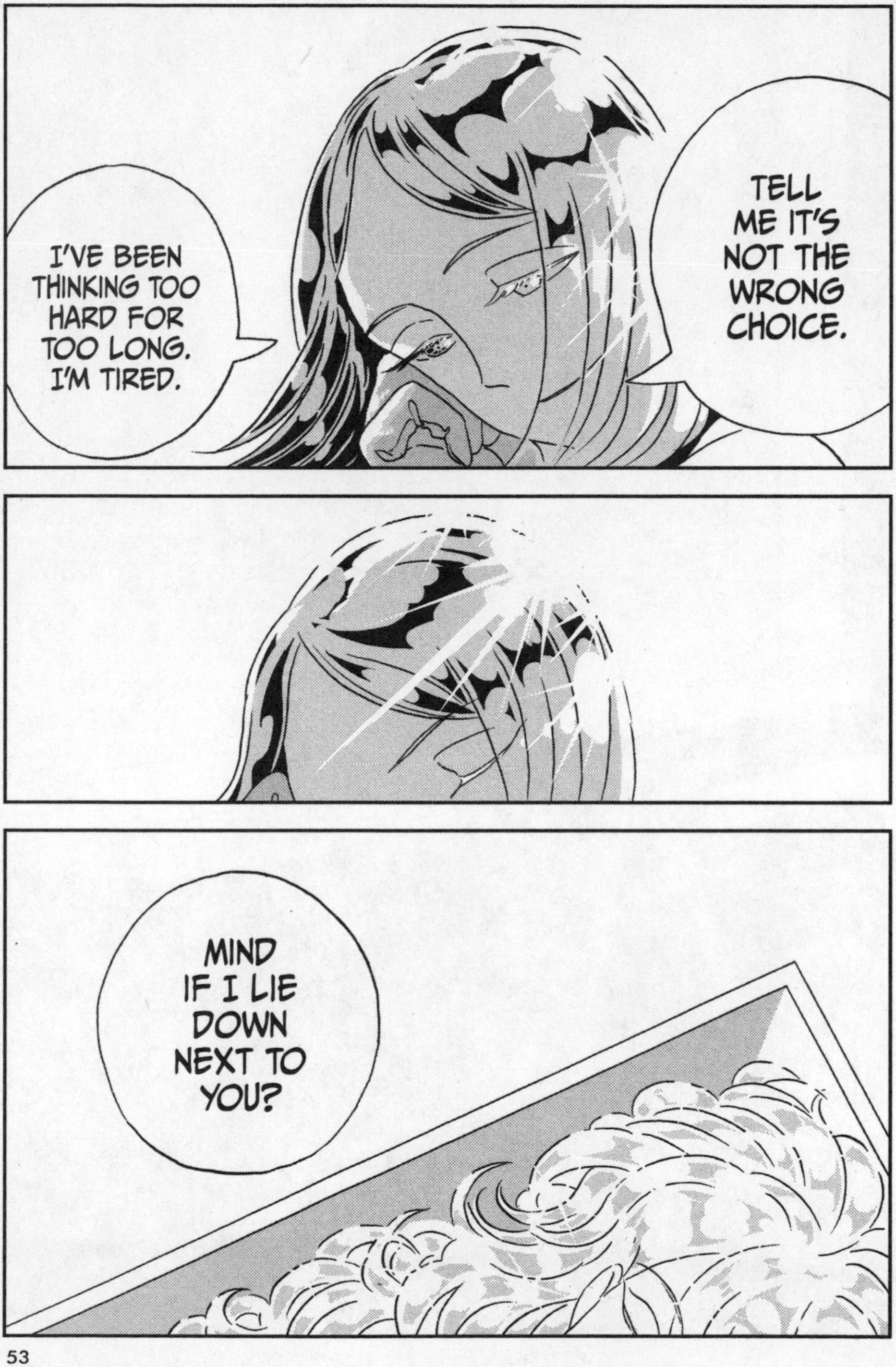
TELL ME IT'S NOT THE WRONG CHOICE.
I'VE BEEN THINKING TOO HARD FOR TOO LONG. I'M TIRED.
MIND IF I LIE DOWN NEXT TO YOU?

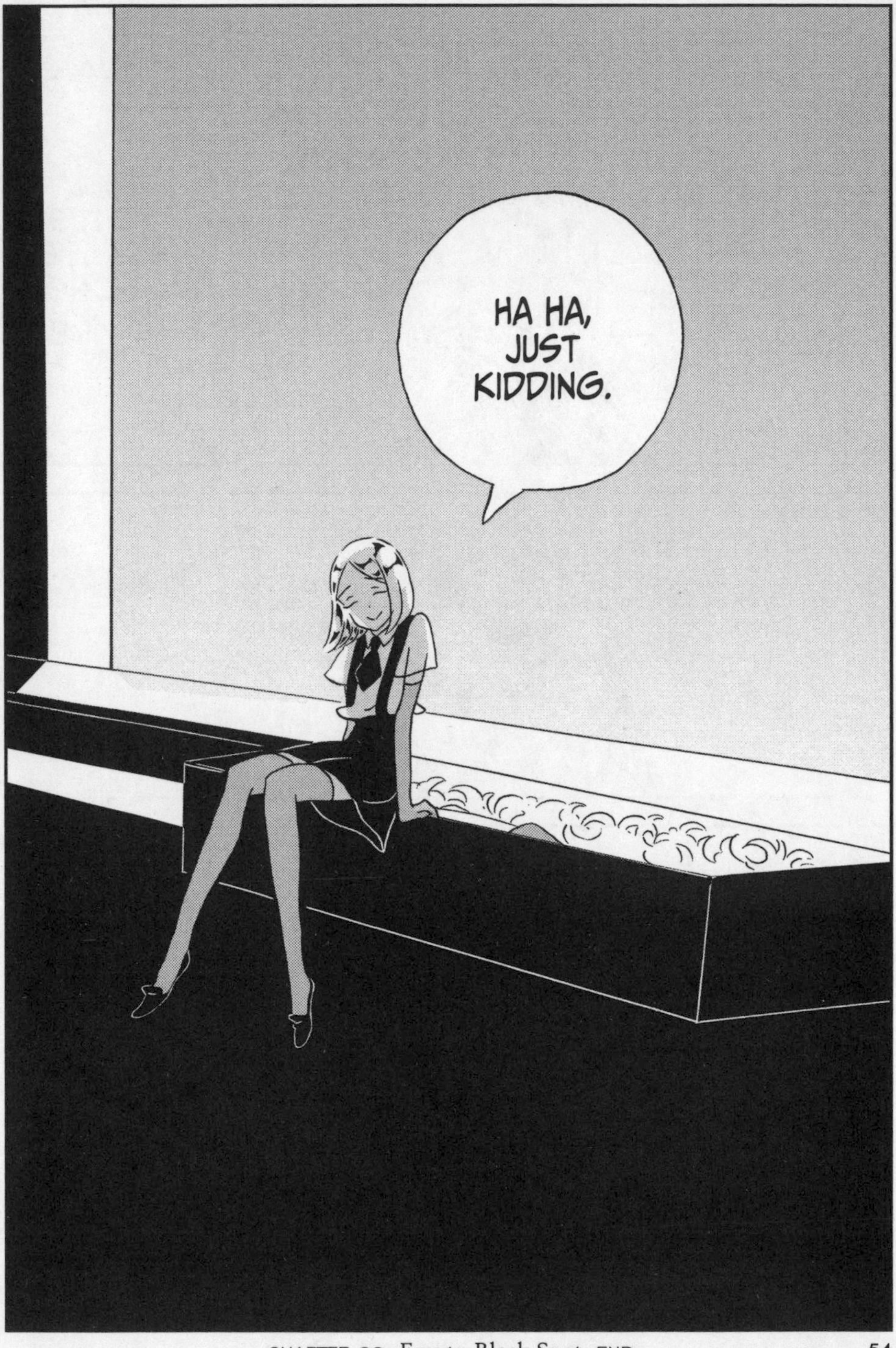
HA HA, JUST KIDDING.

CHAPTER 31:

Fresh

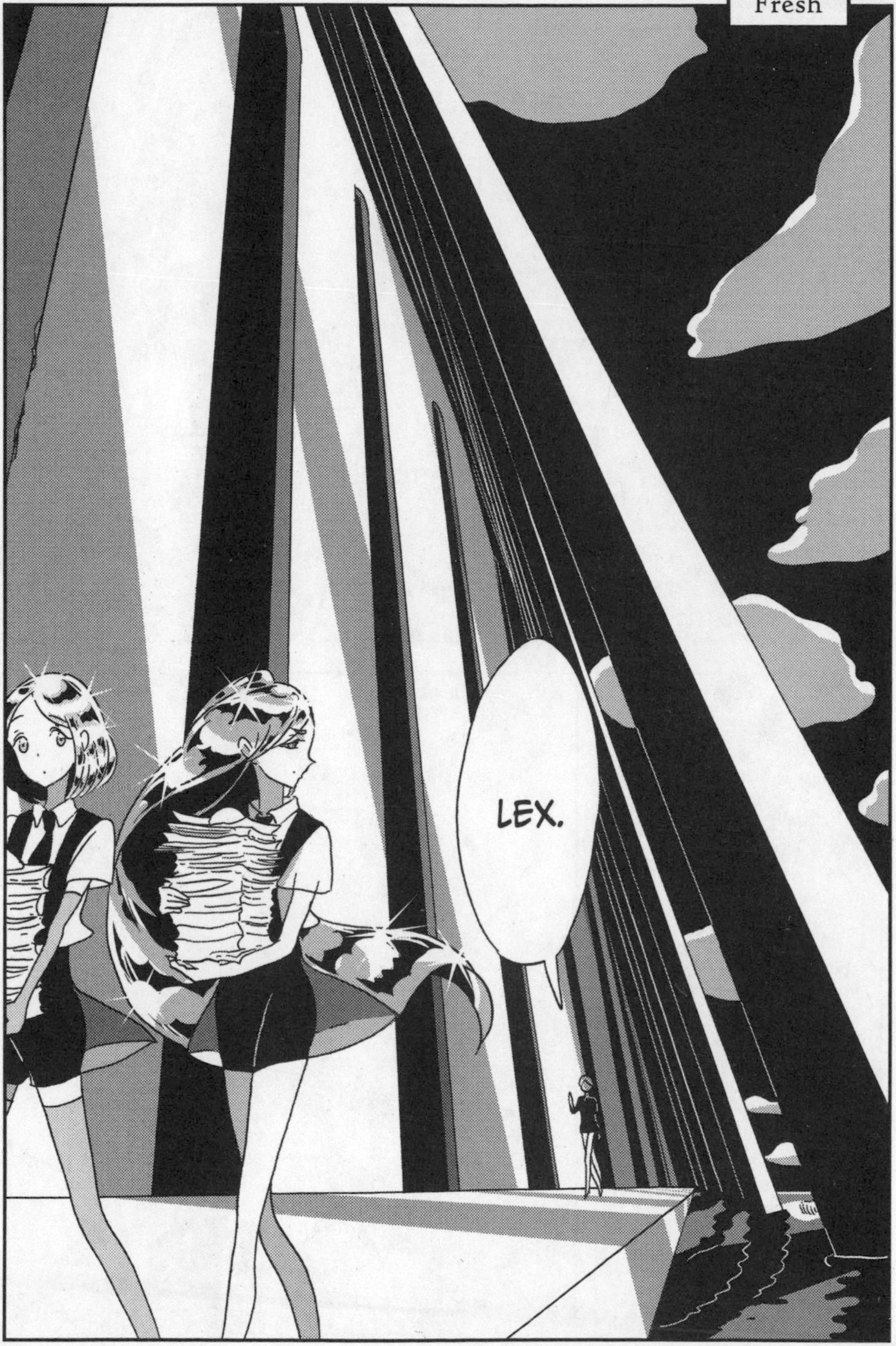
LEX.

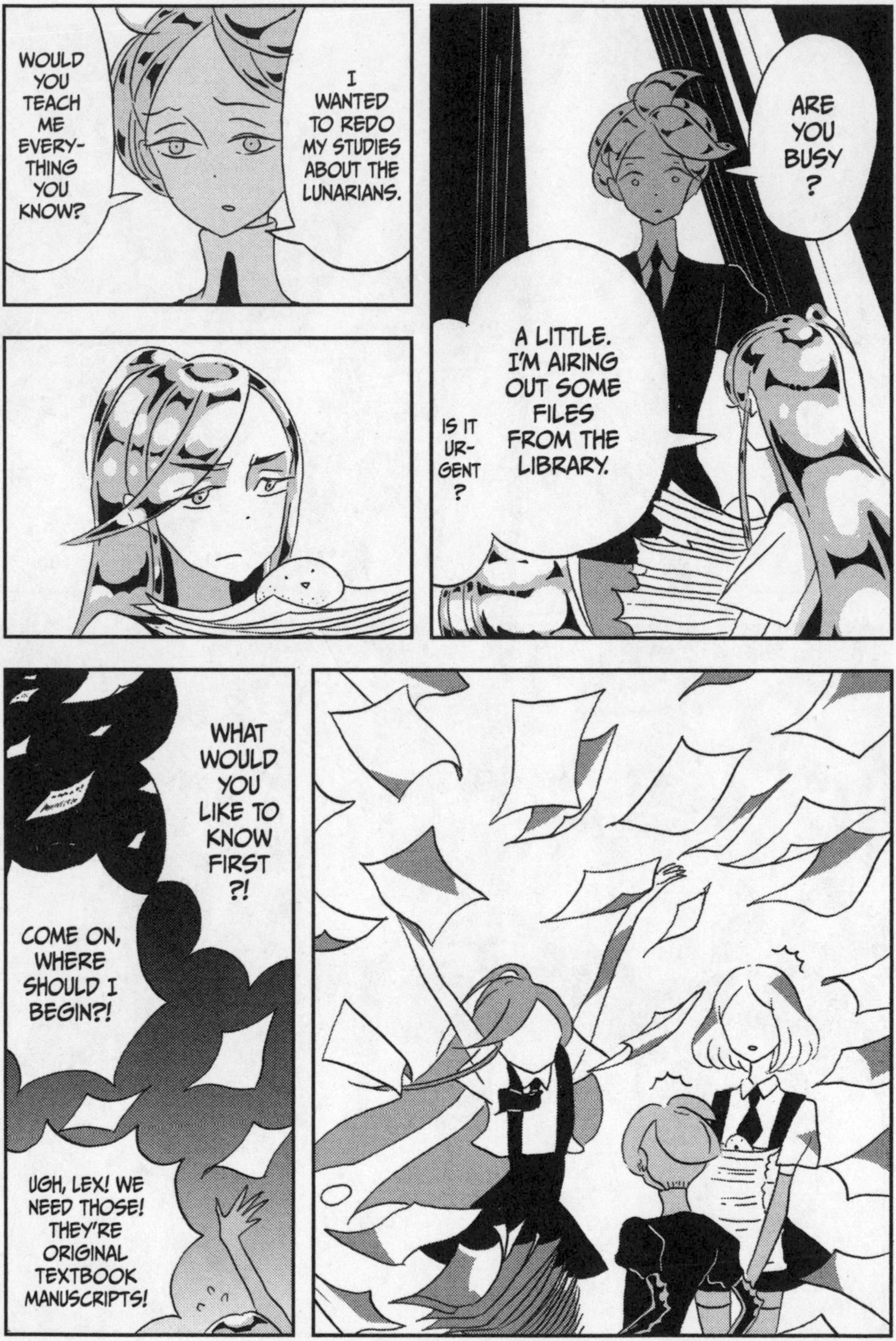
ARE YOU BUSY?
A LITTLE. I'M AIRING OUT SOME FILES FROM THE LIBRARY.
IS IT URGENT?
I WANTED TO REDO MY STUDIES ABOUT THE LUNARIANS.
WOULD YOU TEACH ME EVERYTHING YOU KNOW?
WHAT WOULD YOU LIKE TO KNOW FIRST?!
COME ON, WHERE SHOULD I BEGIN?!
UGH, LEX! WE NEED THOSE! THEY'RE ORIGINAL TEXTBOOK MANUSCRIPTS!

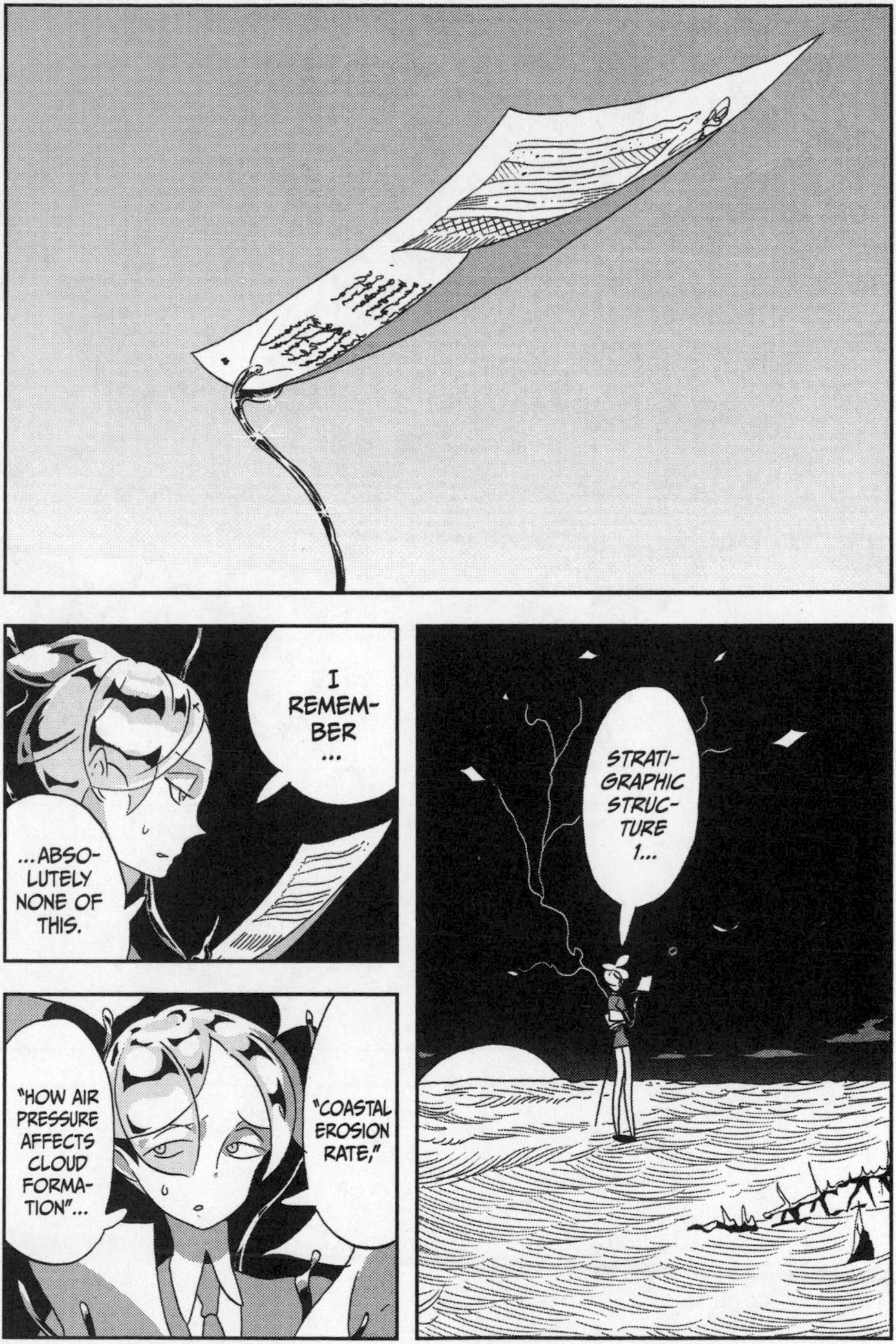
STRATI-GRAPHIC STRUC-TURE 1...
I REMEM-BER ...
...ABSO-LUTELY NONE OF THIS.
"COASTAL EROSION RATE,"
"HOW AIR PRESSURE AFFECTS CLOUD FORMA-TION"...

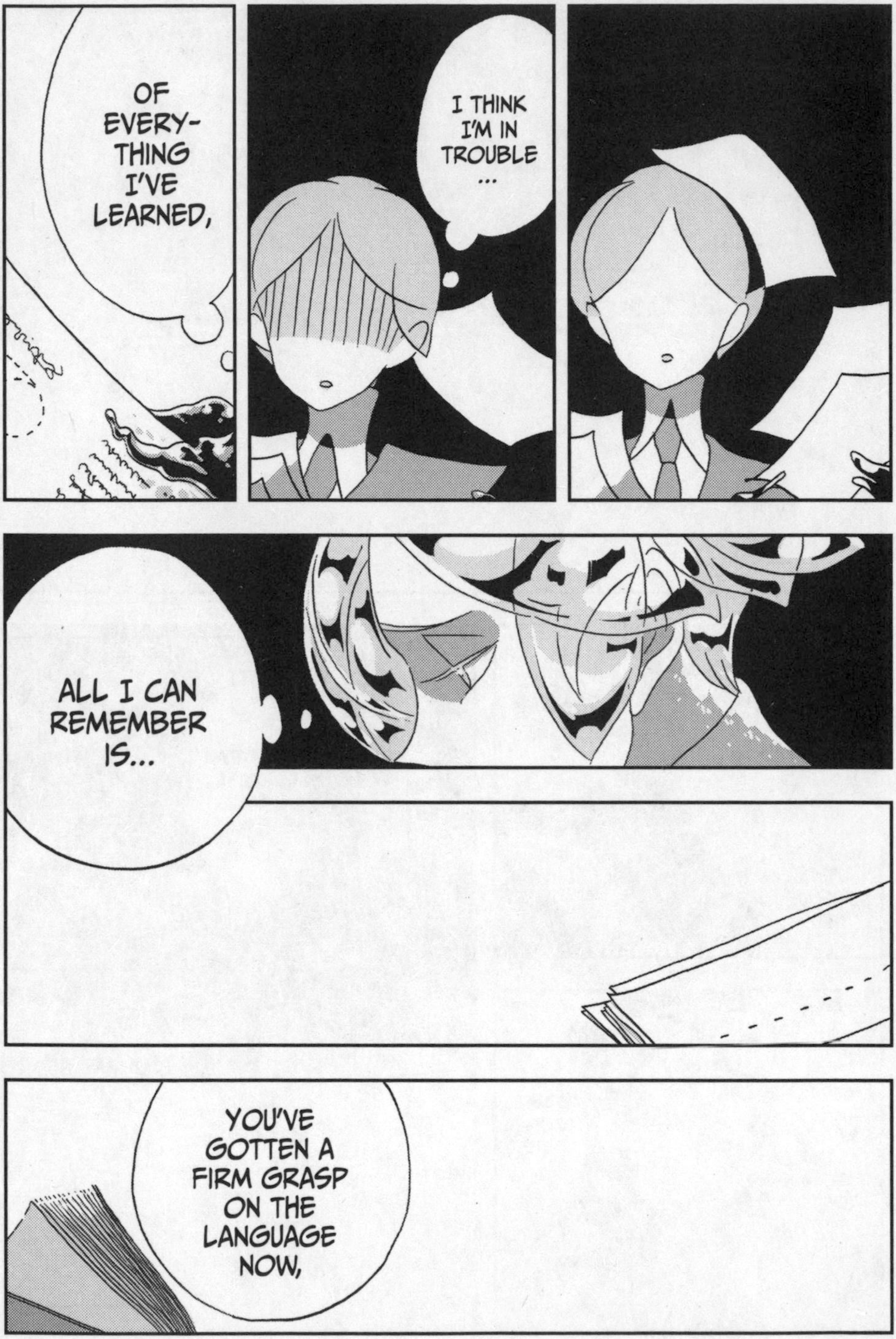
I THINK I'M IN TROUBLE ...
OF EVERY-THING I'VE LEARNED,
ALL I CAN REMEMBER IS...
YOU'VE GOTTEN A FIRM GRASP ON THE LANGUAGE NOW,

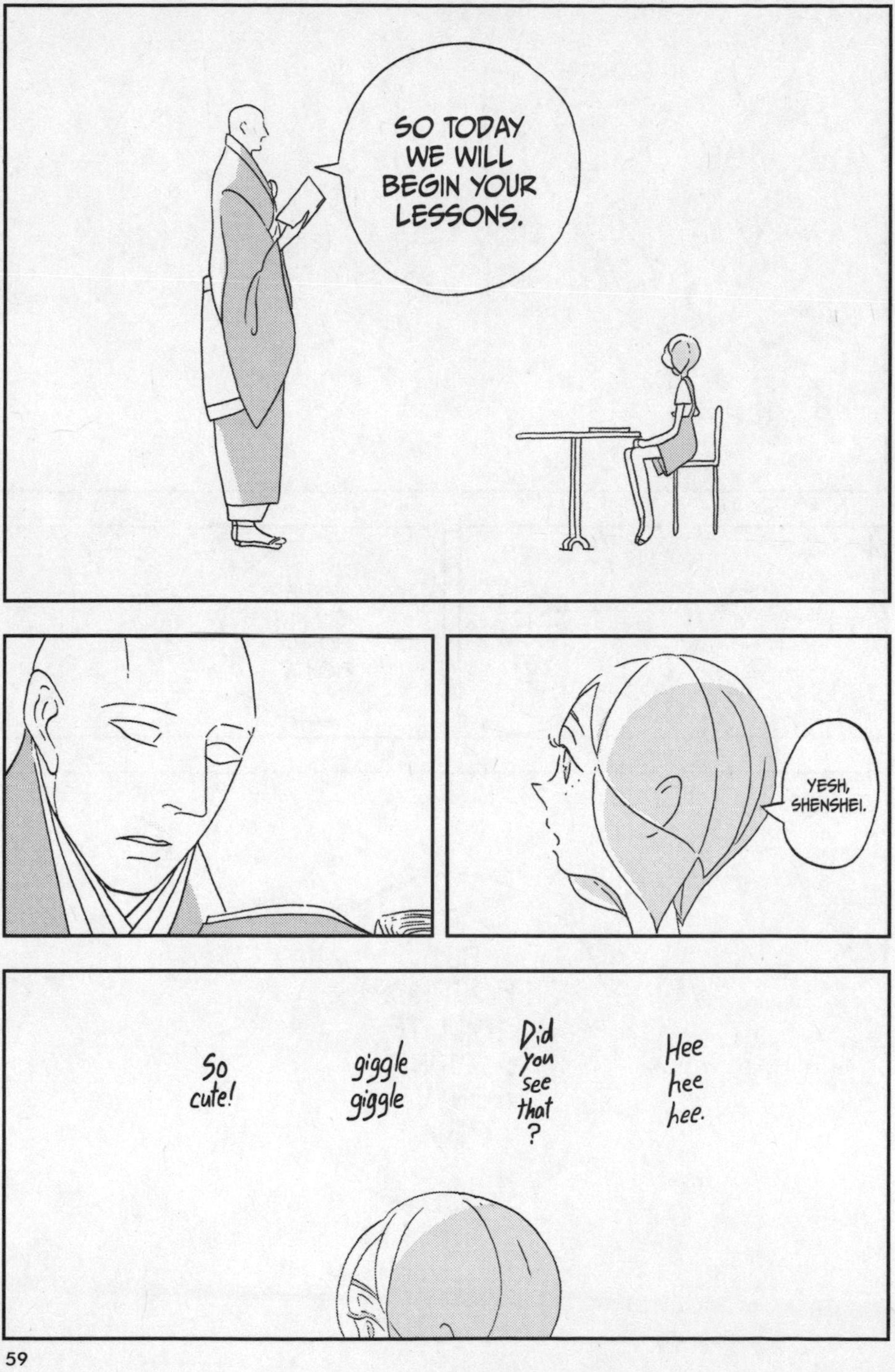
SO TODAY WE WILL BEGIN YOUR LESSONS.
YESH, SHENSHEI.
Hee hee hee.
Did you see that?
giggle giggle
So cute!

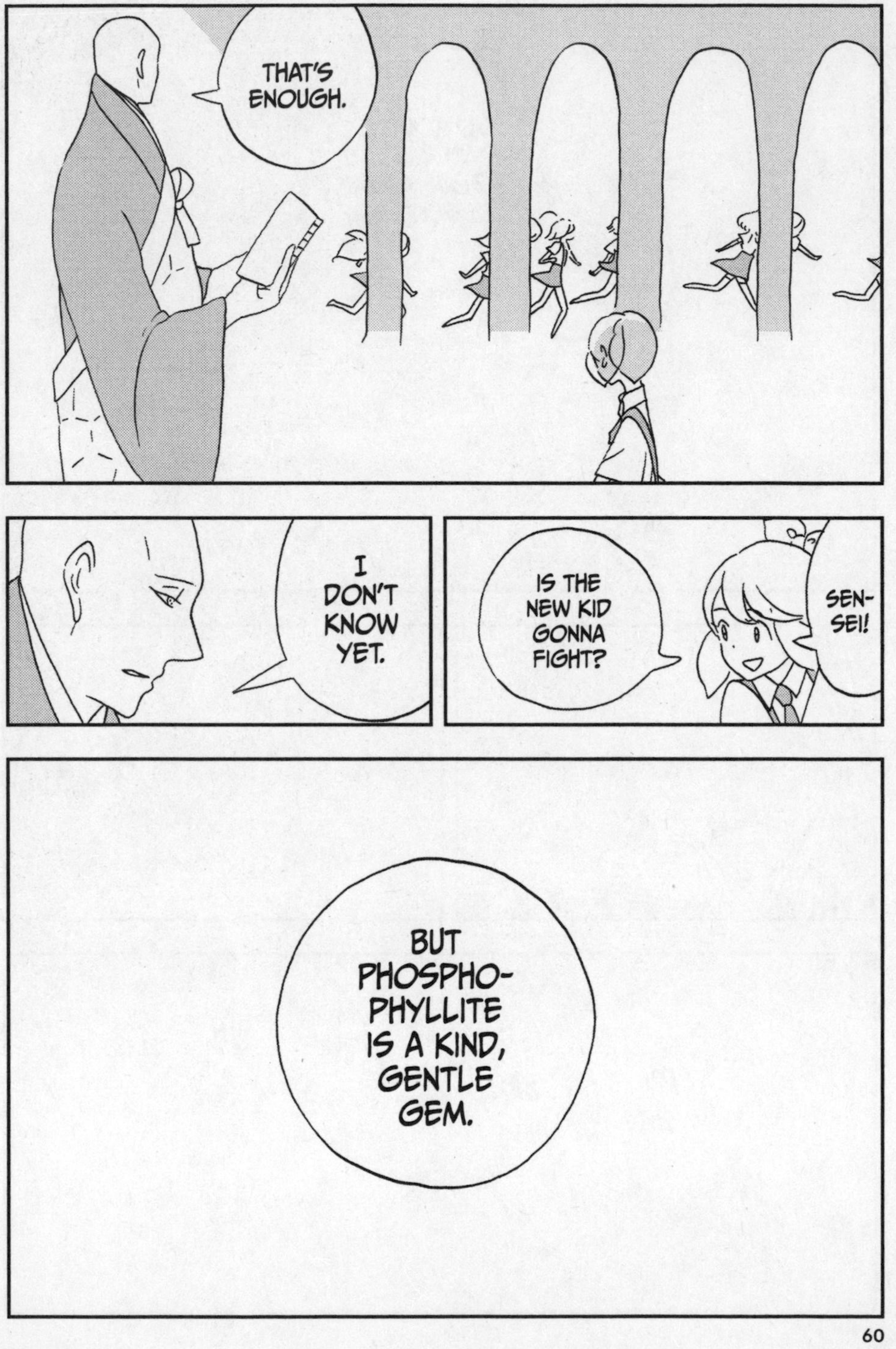
THAT'S ENOUGH.
SENSEI!
IS THE NEW KID GONNA FIGHT?
I DON'T KNOW YET.
BUT PHOSPHOPHYLLITE IS A KIND, GENTLE GEM.

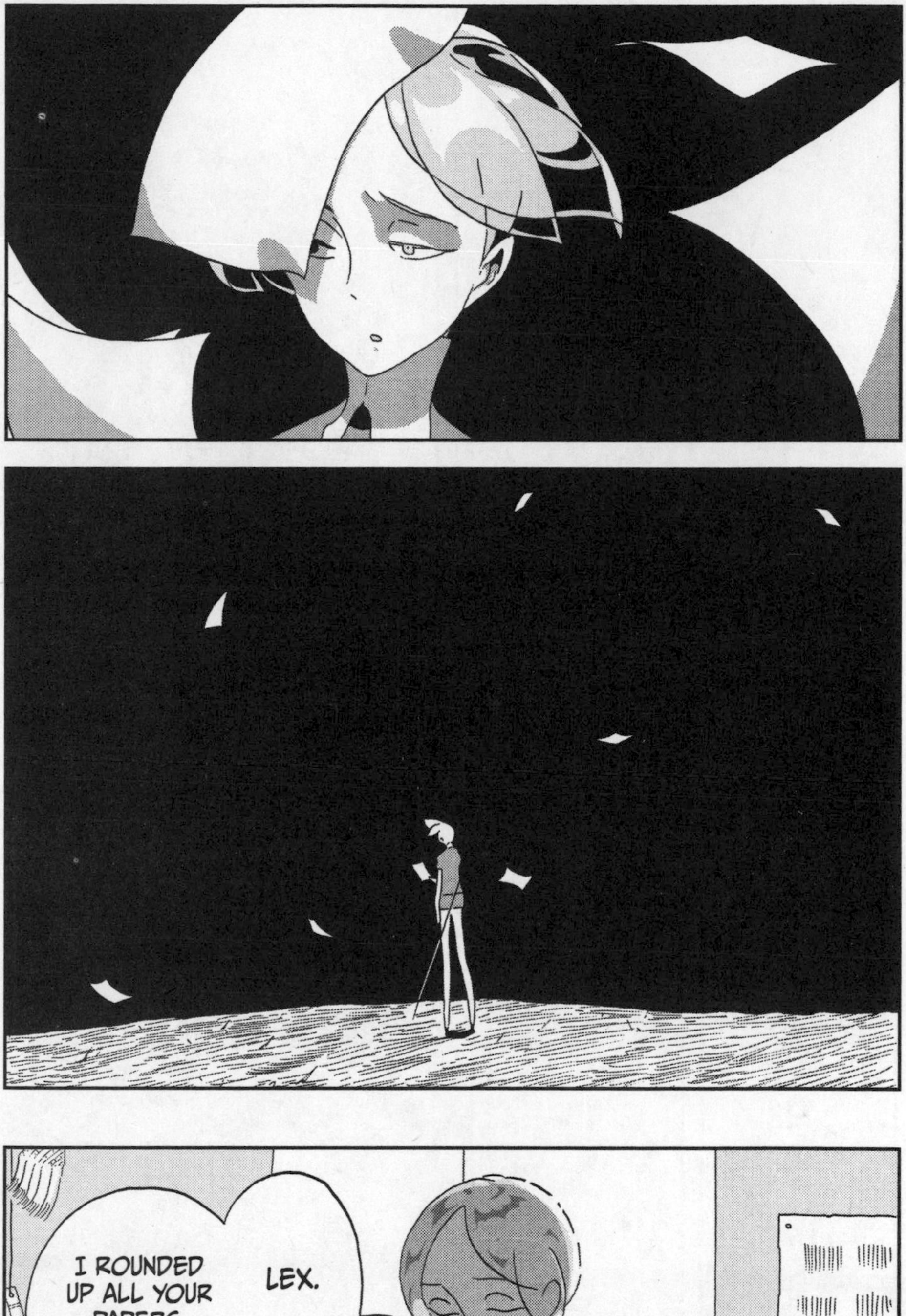
LEX.
I ROUNDED UP ALL YOUR PAPERS.

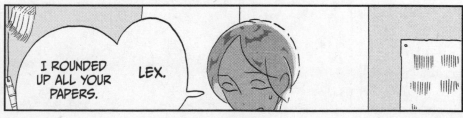

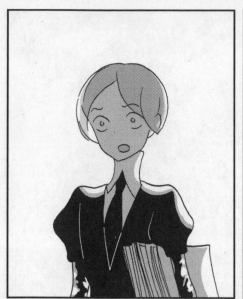

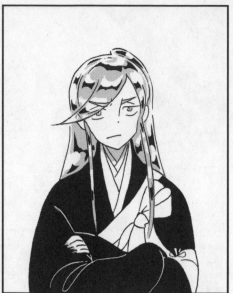

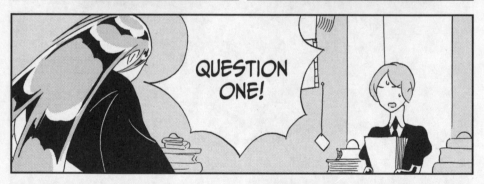

QUESTION ONE!
TELL ME THE TYPE OF LUNARIAN THAT APPEARED ON THE SECOND DAY OF THE FIFTH MONTH, 109 YEARS AGO.
WITH ITS OFFICIAL NAME.
HOW SHOULD I KNOW?
A QUIZ GAME?
I THOUGHT IT WOULD BE MORE FUN THIS WAY.
I JUST WANT TO LEARN.
THEN TAKE THESE.
DA-DUN

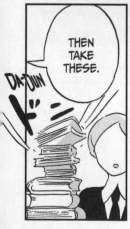

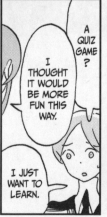

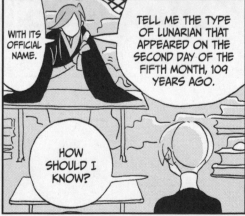

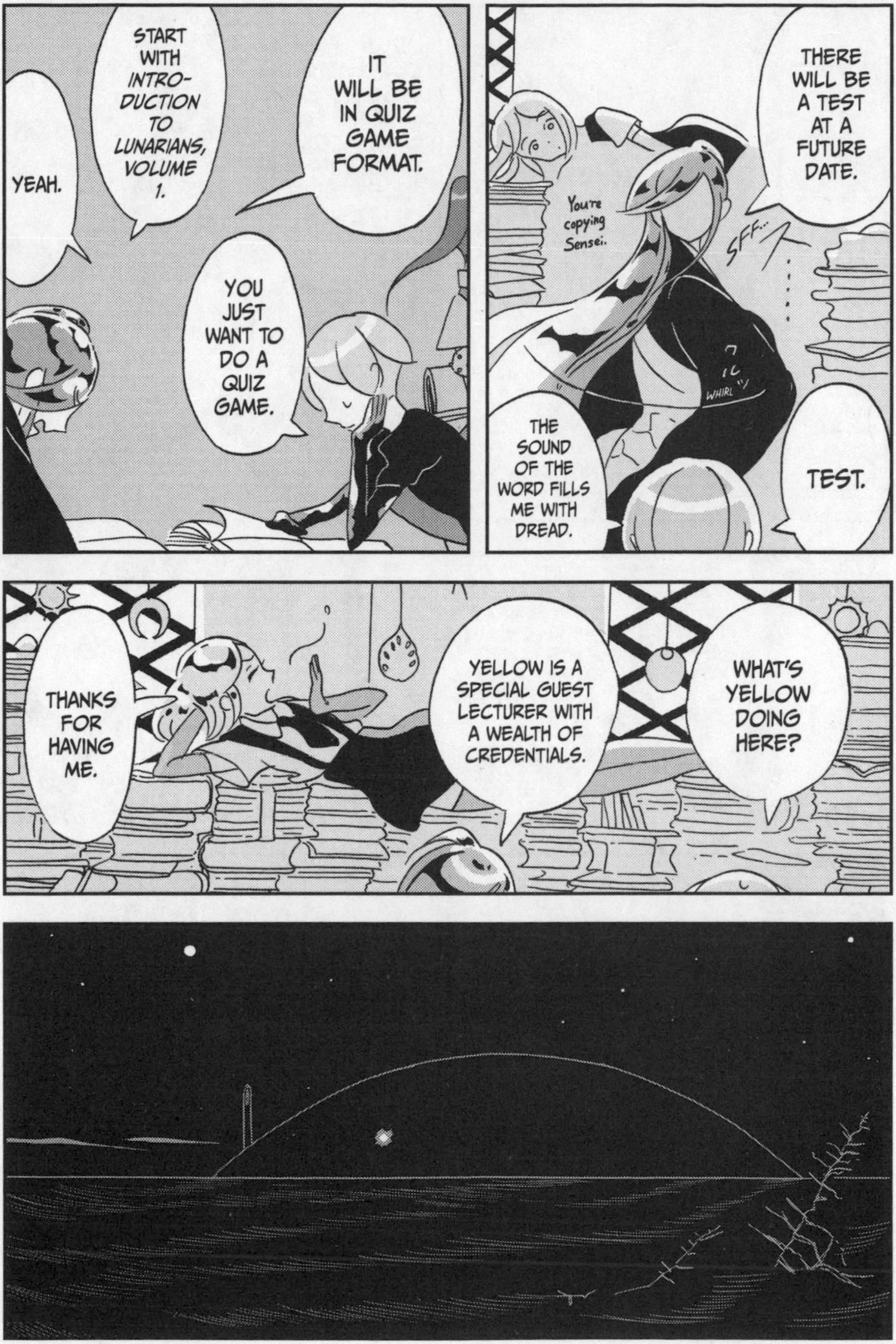
THERE WILL BE A TEST AT A FUTURE DATE.
SFF...
You're copying Sensei.
WHIRL
TEST.
THE SOUND OF THE WORD FILLS ME WITH DREAD.
IT WILL BE IN QUIZ GAME FORMAT.
START WITH INTRO-DUCTION TO LUNARIANS, VOLUME 1.
YEAH.
YOU JUST WANT TO DO A QUIZ GAME.
WHAT'S YELLOW DOING HERE?
YELLOW IS A SPECIAL GUEST LECTURER WITH A WEALTH OF CREDENTIALS.
THANKS FOR HAVING ME.

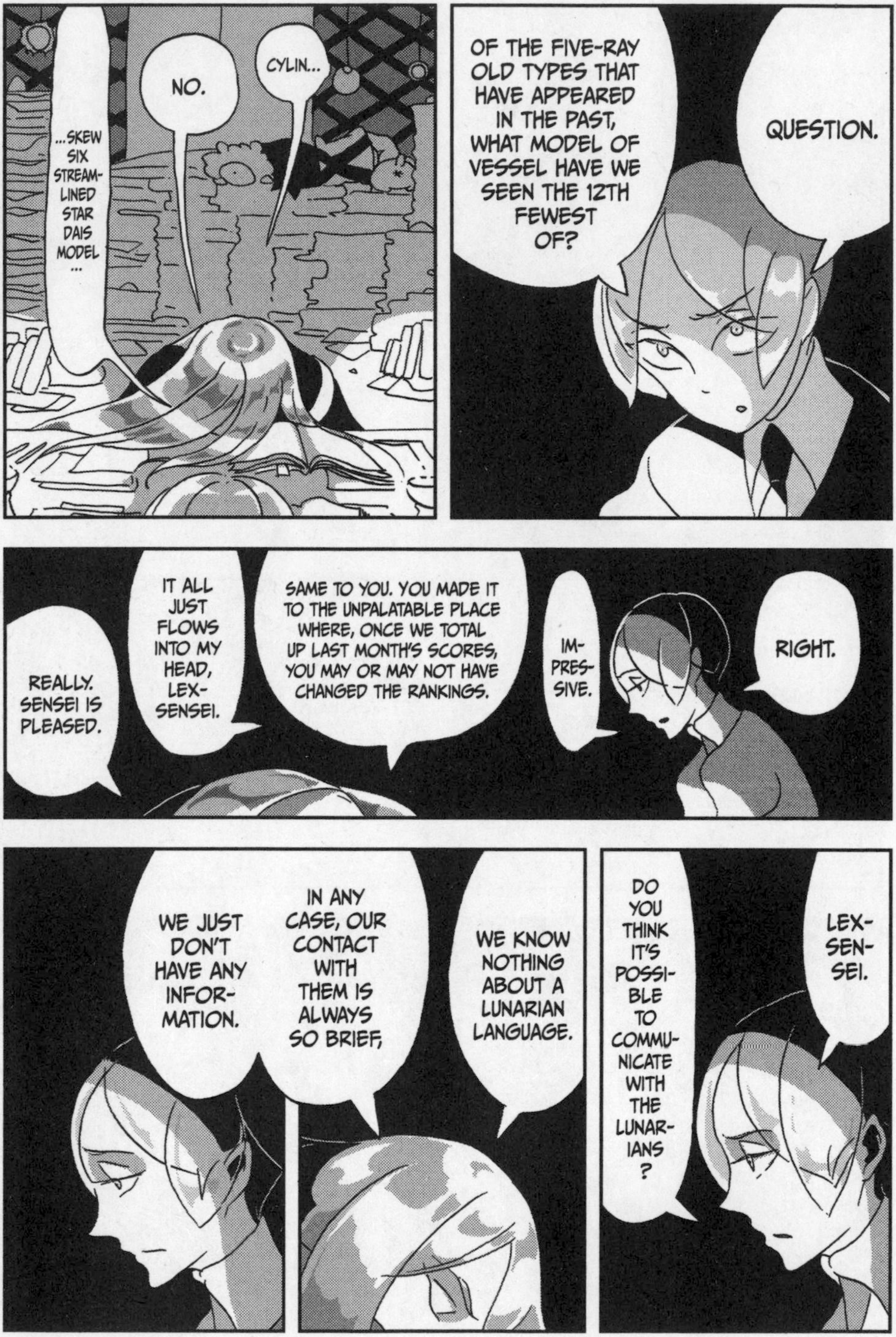
QUESTION.
OF THE FIVE-RAY OLD TYPES THAT HAVE APPEARED IN THE PAST, WHAT MODEL OF VESSEL HAVE WE SEEN THE 12TH FEWEST OF?
CYLIN...
NO.
...SKEW SIX STREAM-LINED STAR DAIS MODEL ...
RIGHT.
IM-PRES-SIVE.
SAME TO YOU. YOU MADE IT TO THE UNPALATABLE PLACE WHERE, ONCE WE TOTAL UP LAST MONTH'S SCORES, YOU MAY OR MAY NOT HAVE CHANGED THE RANKINGS.
IT ALL JUST FLOWS INTO MY HEAD, LEX-SENSEI.
REALLY. SENSEI IS PLEASED.
LEX-SEN-SEI.
DO YOU THINK IT'S POSSI-BLE TO COMMU-NICATE WITH THE LUNAR-IANS ?
WE KNOW NOTHING ABOUT A LUNARIAN LANGUAGE.
IN ANY CASE, OUR CONTACT WITH THEM IS ALWAYS SO BRIEF,
WE JUST DON'T HAVE ANY INFOR-MATION.

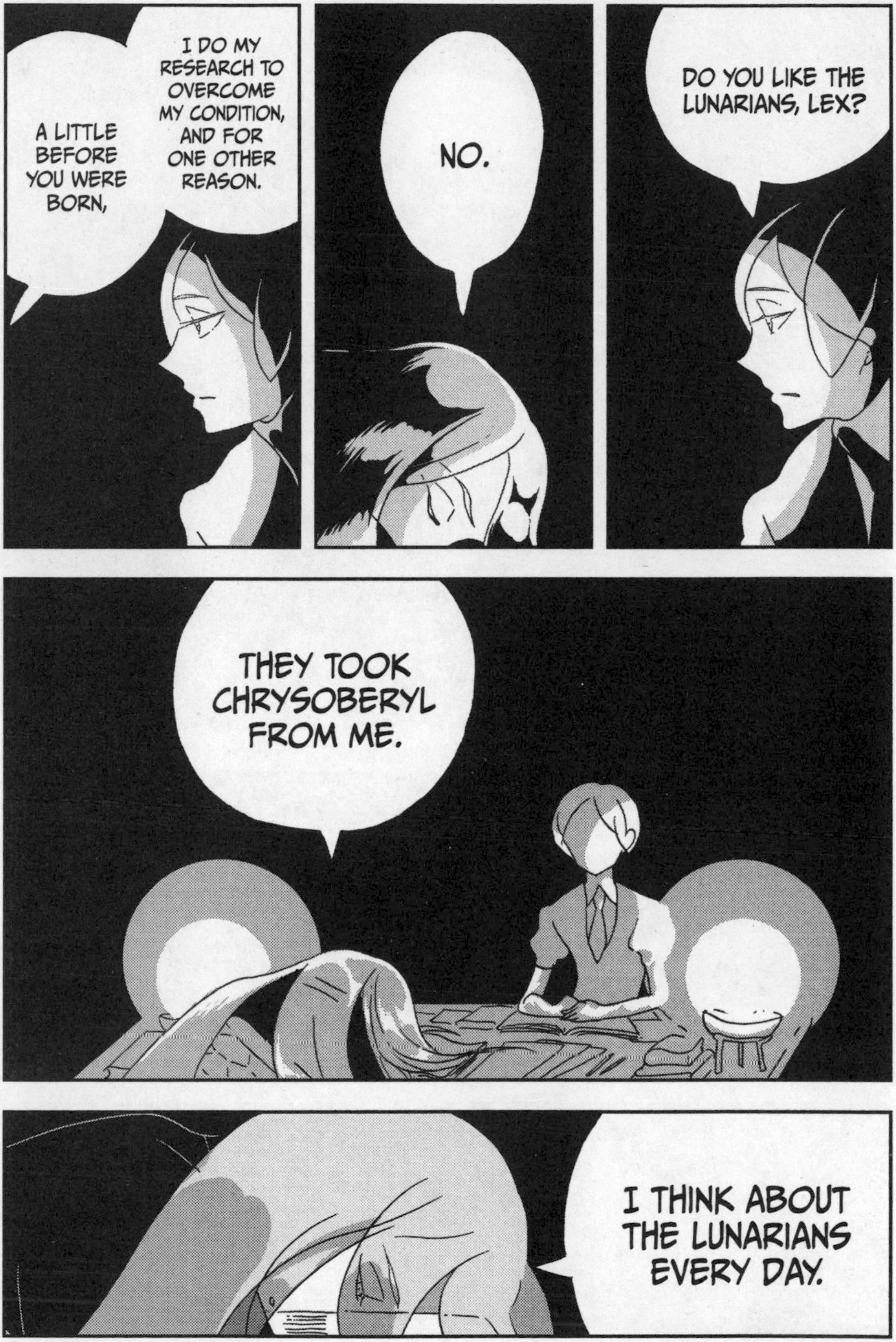
DO YOU LIKE THE LUNARIANS, LEX?
NO.
I DO MY RESEARCH TO OVERCOME MY CONDITION, AND FOR ONE OTHER REASON.
A LITTLE BEFORE YOU WERE BORN,
THEY TOOK CHRYSOBERYL FROM ME.
I THINK ABOUT THE LUNARIANS EVERY DAY.

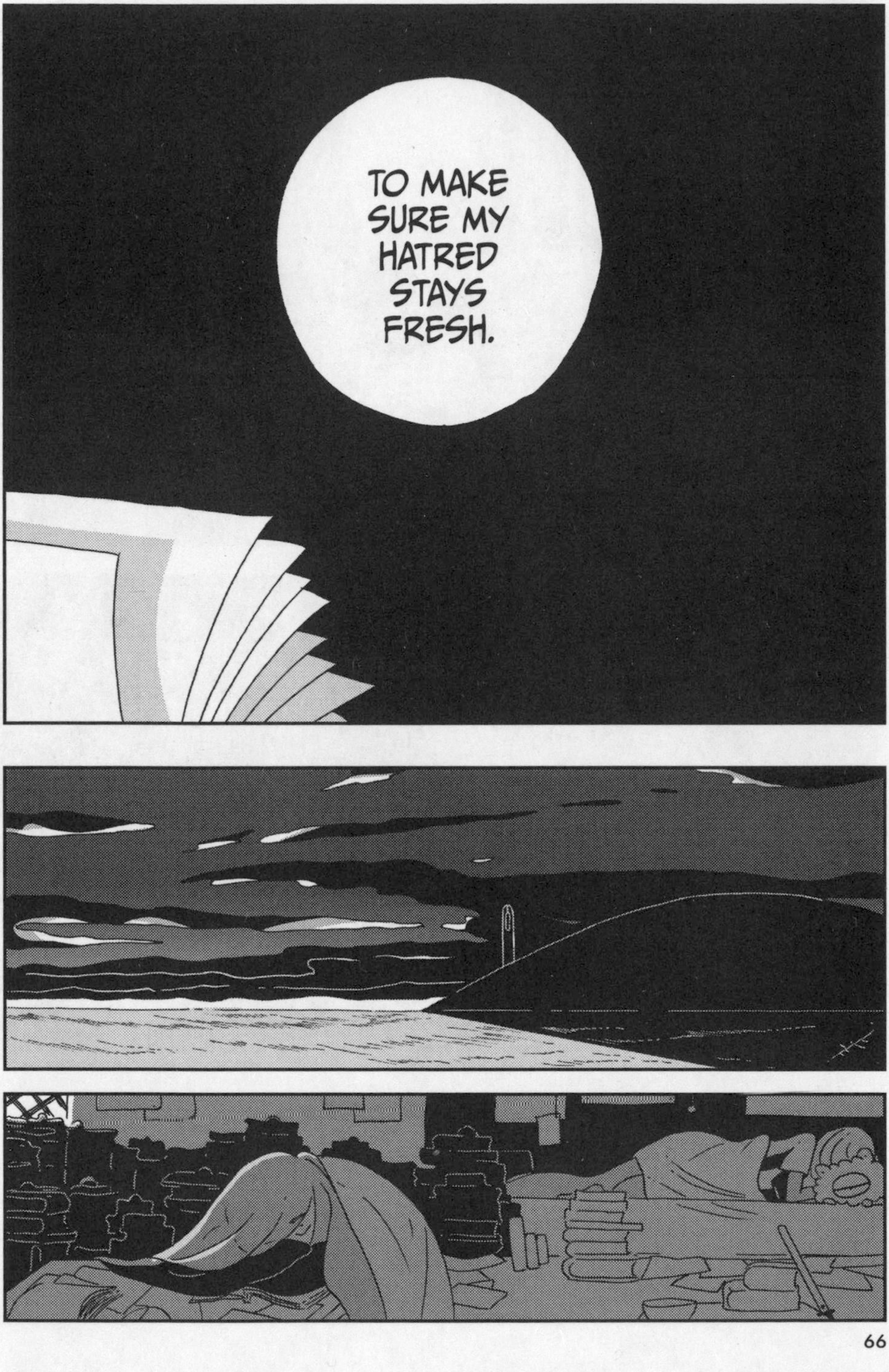
TO MAKE SURE MY HATRED STAYS FRESH.

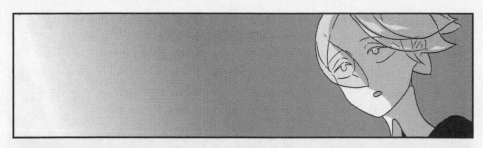

HM...

FRESH, EH?

OLD TYPE.

A THREE-RAY MODEL.

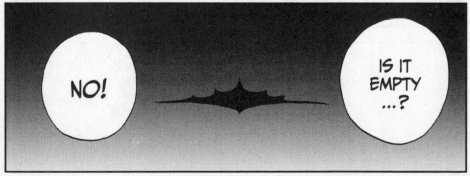

NO!

IS IT EMPTY ...?

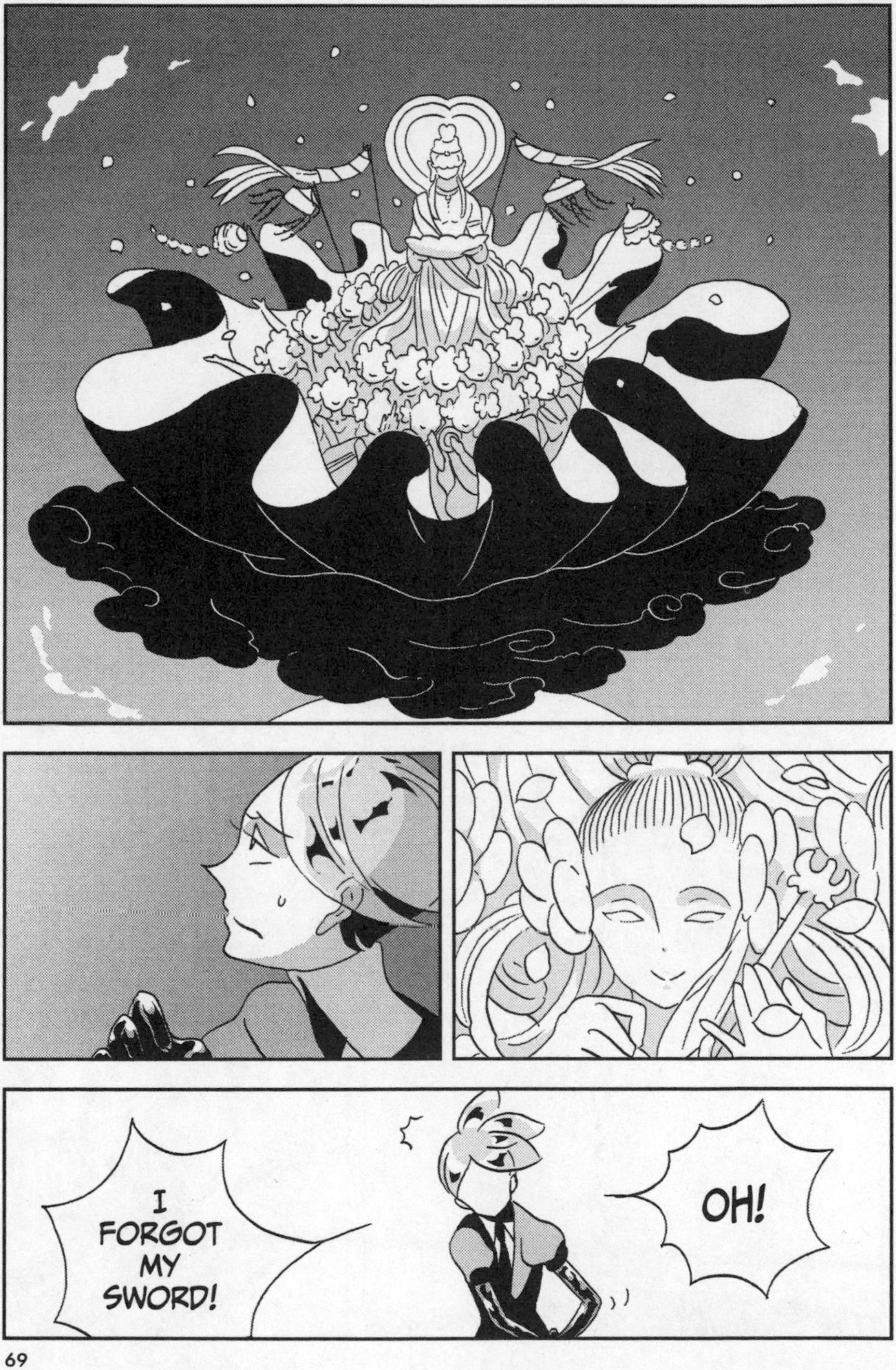
OH!
I FORGOT MY SWORD!

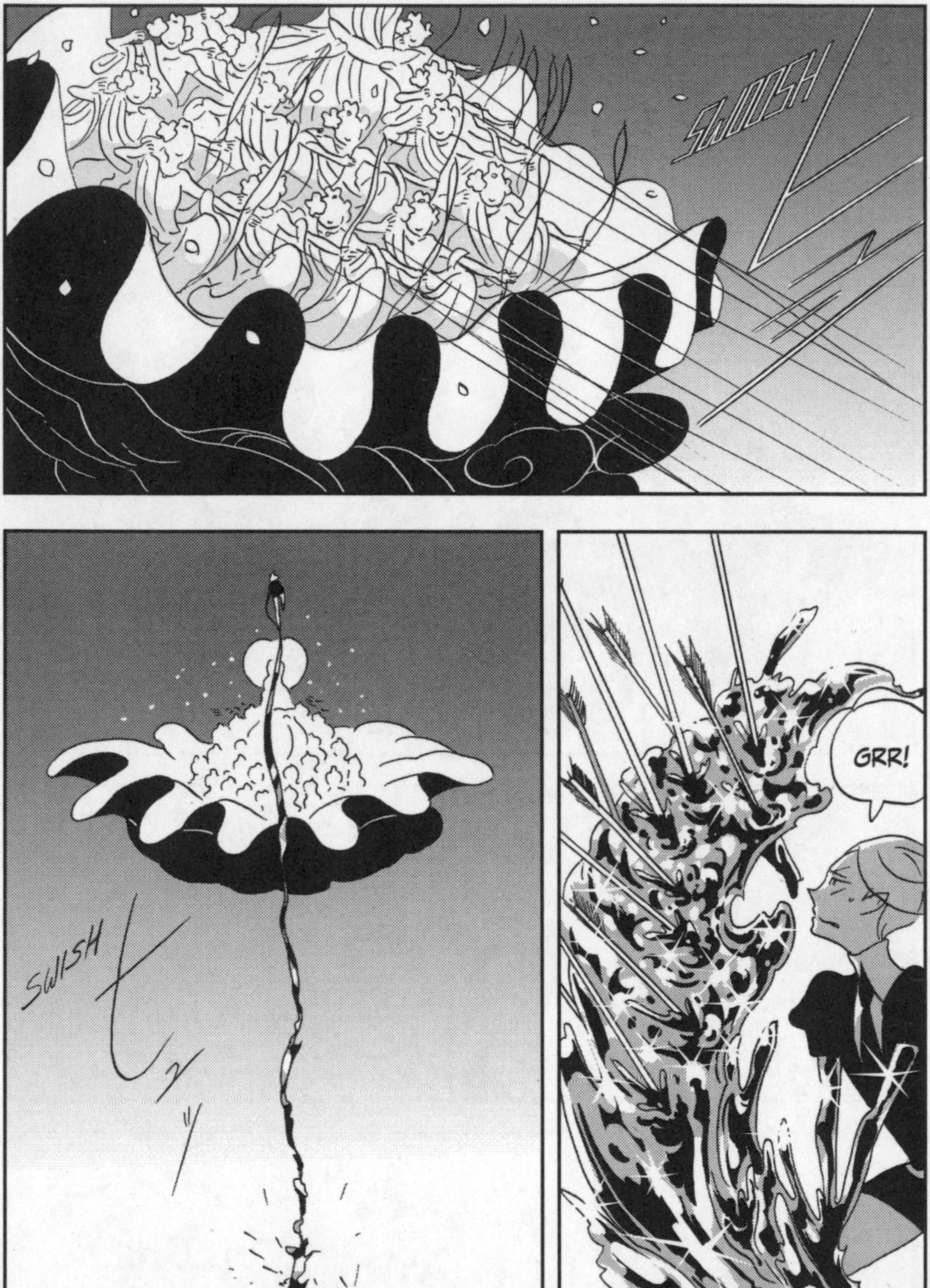
SWOOSH
GRR!
SWISH

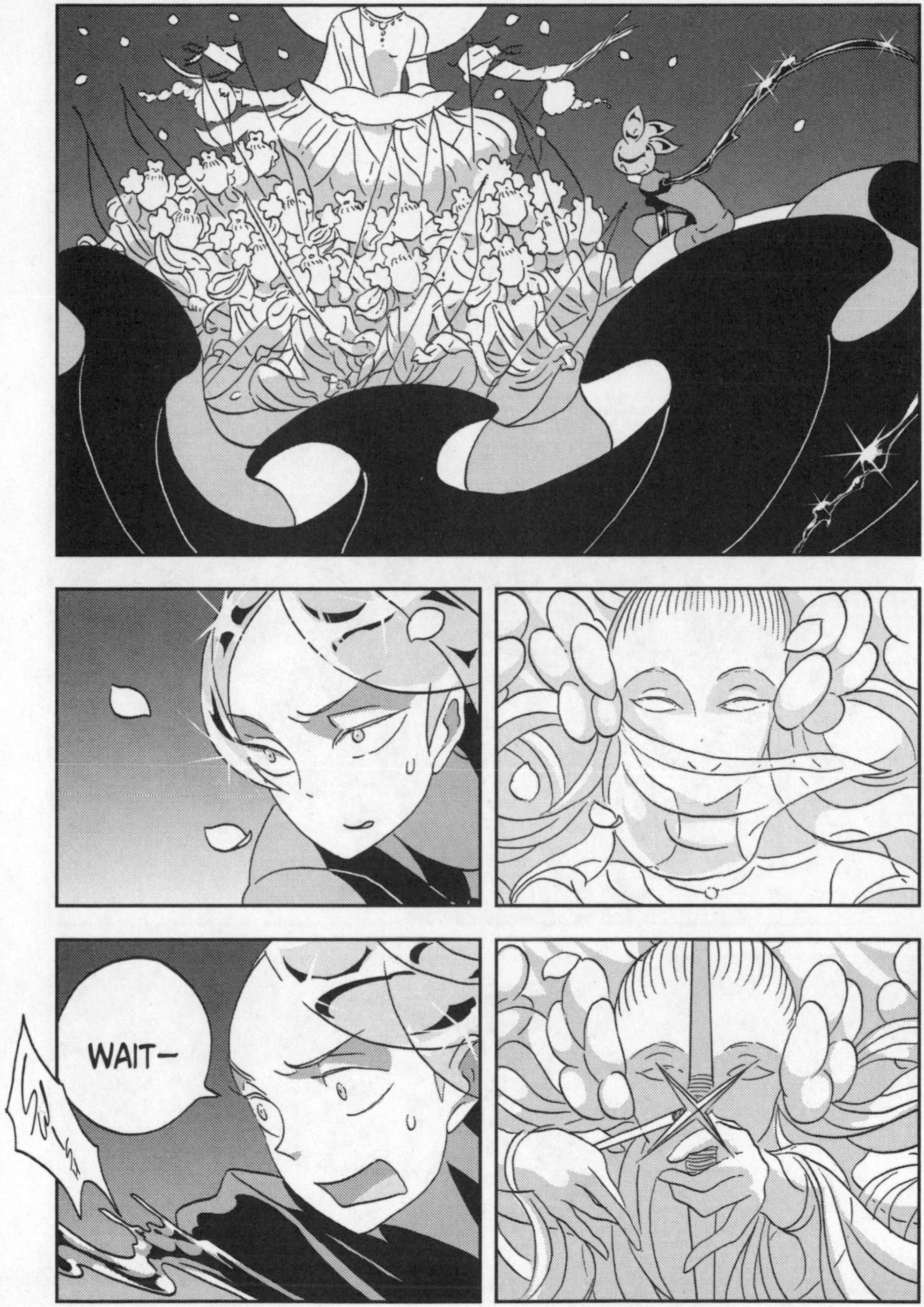
WAIT–

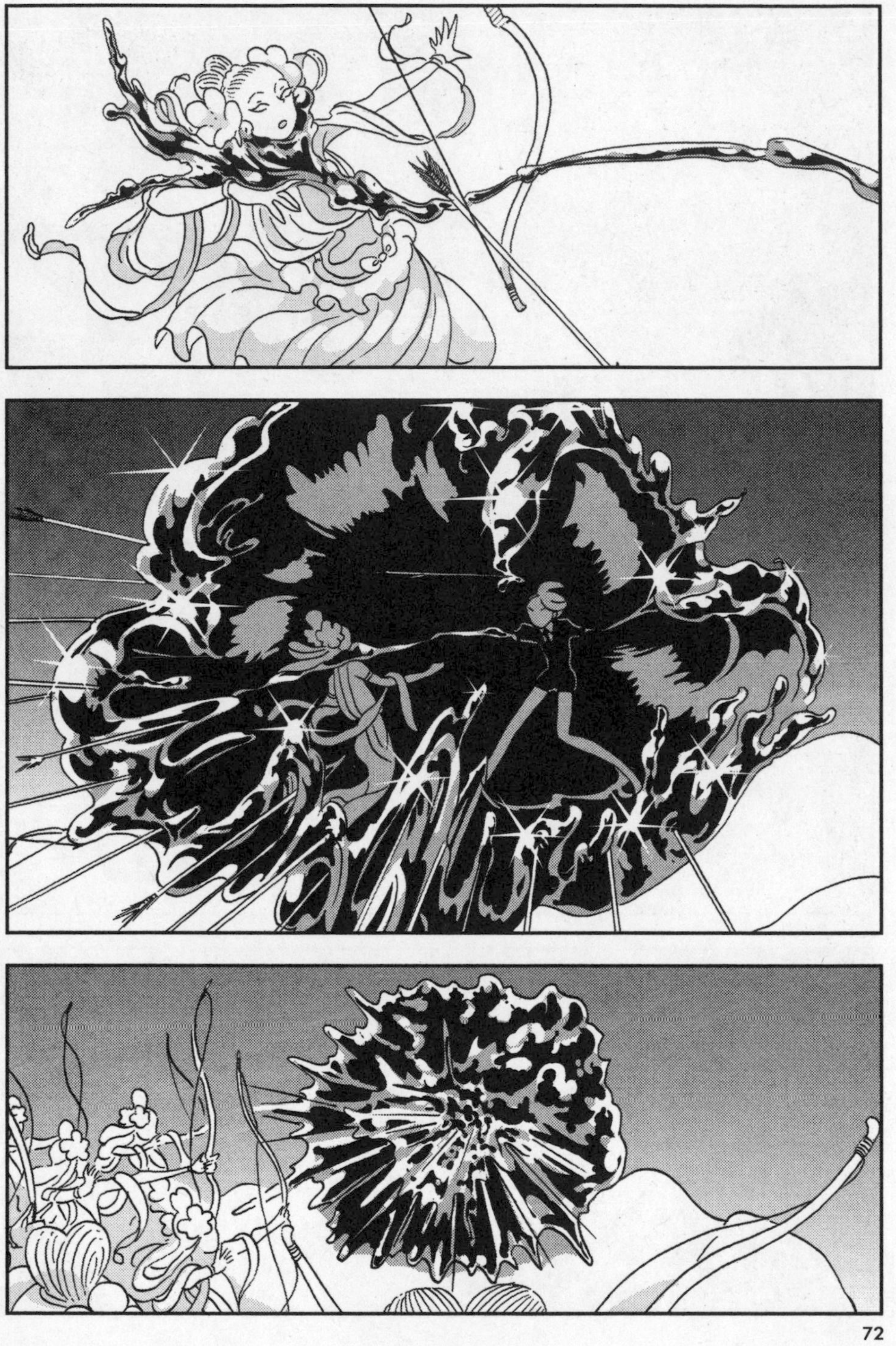

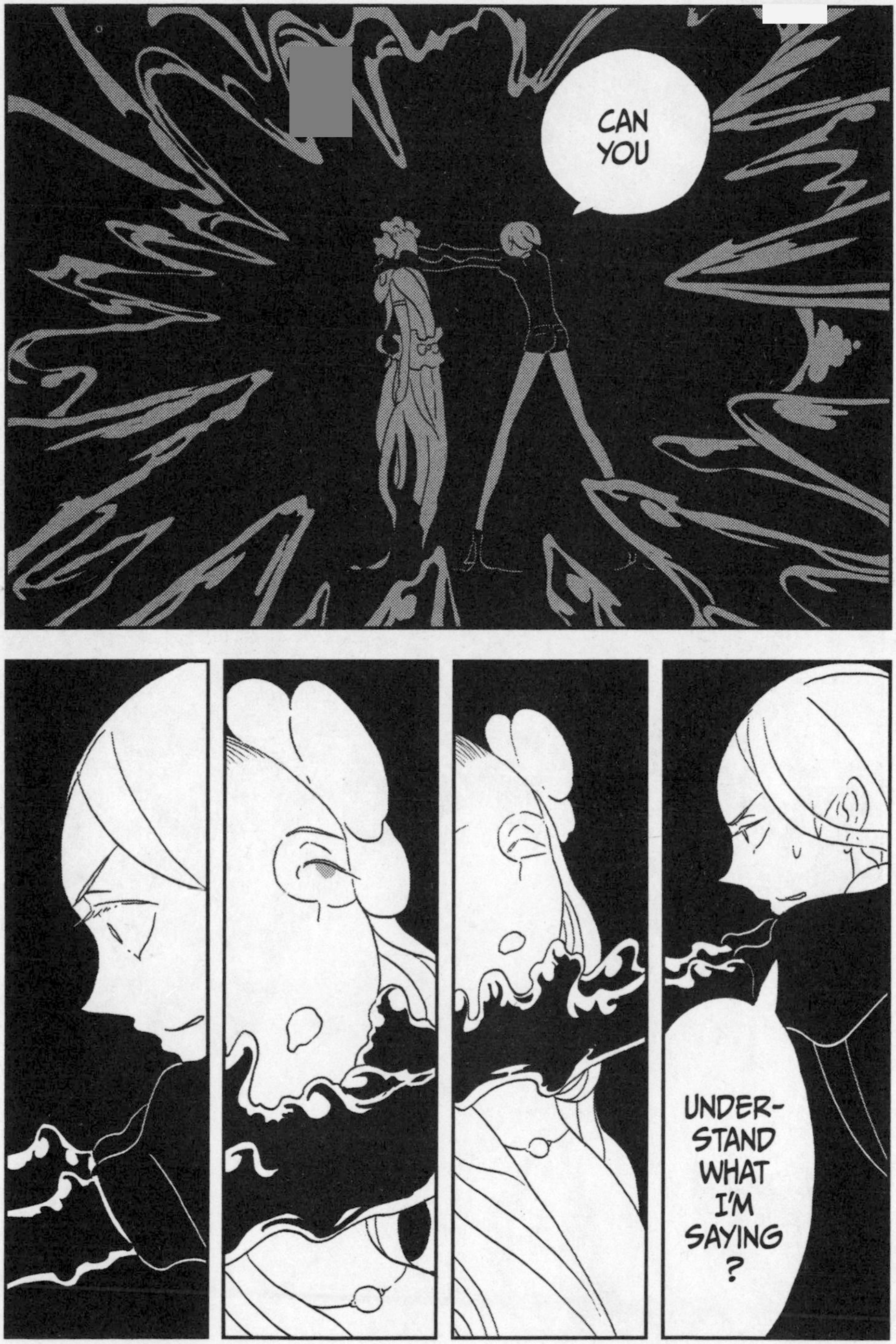
CAN YOU
UNDER-STAND WHAT I'M SAYING ?

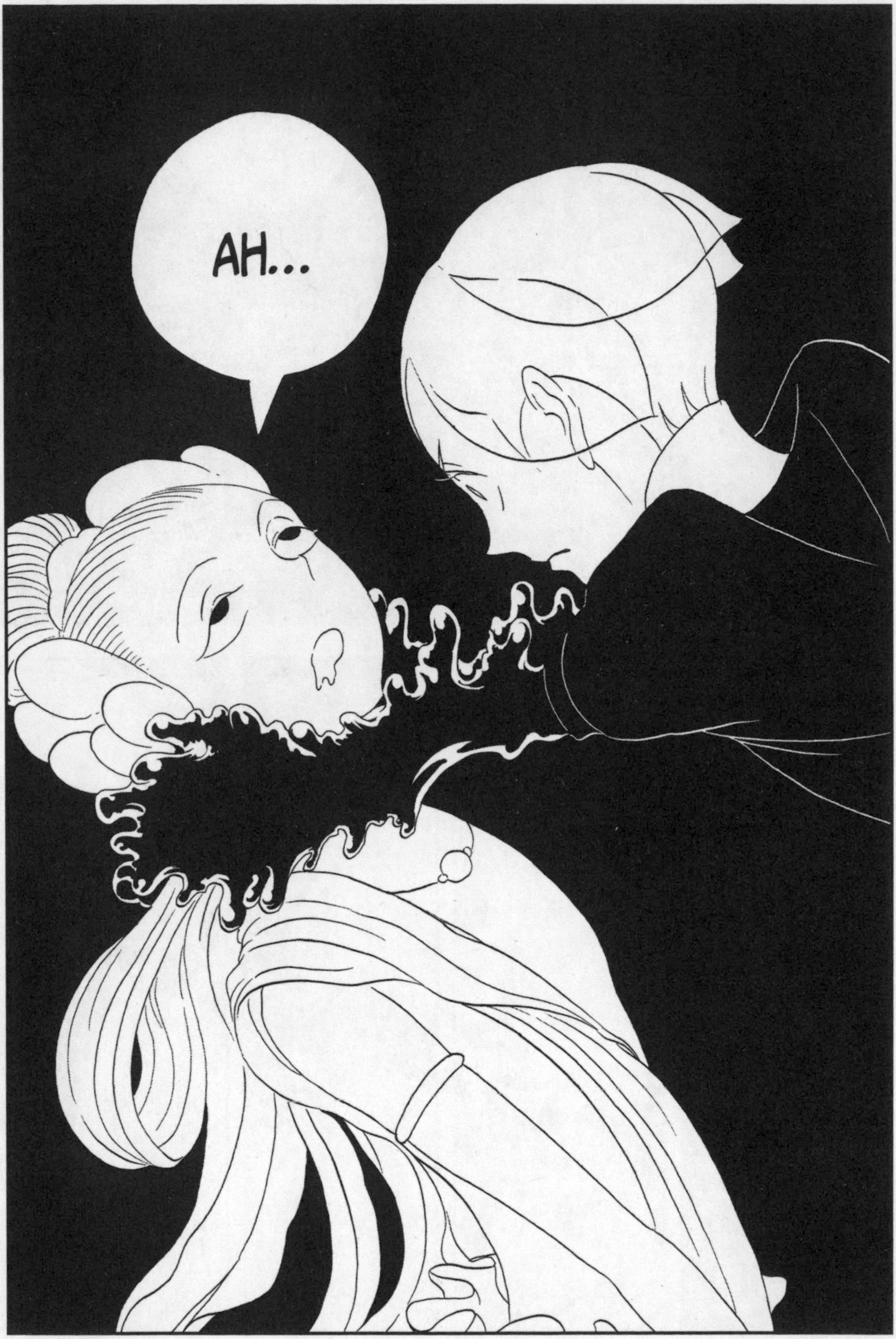
AH...

CHAPTER 32:

Angst

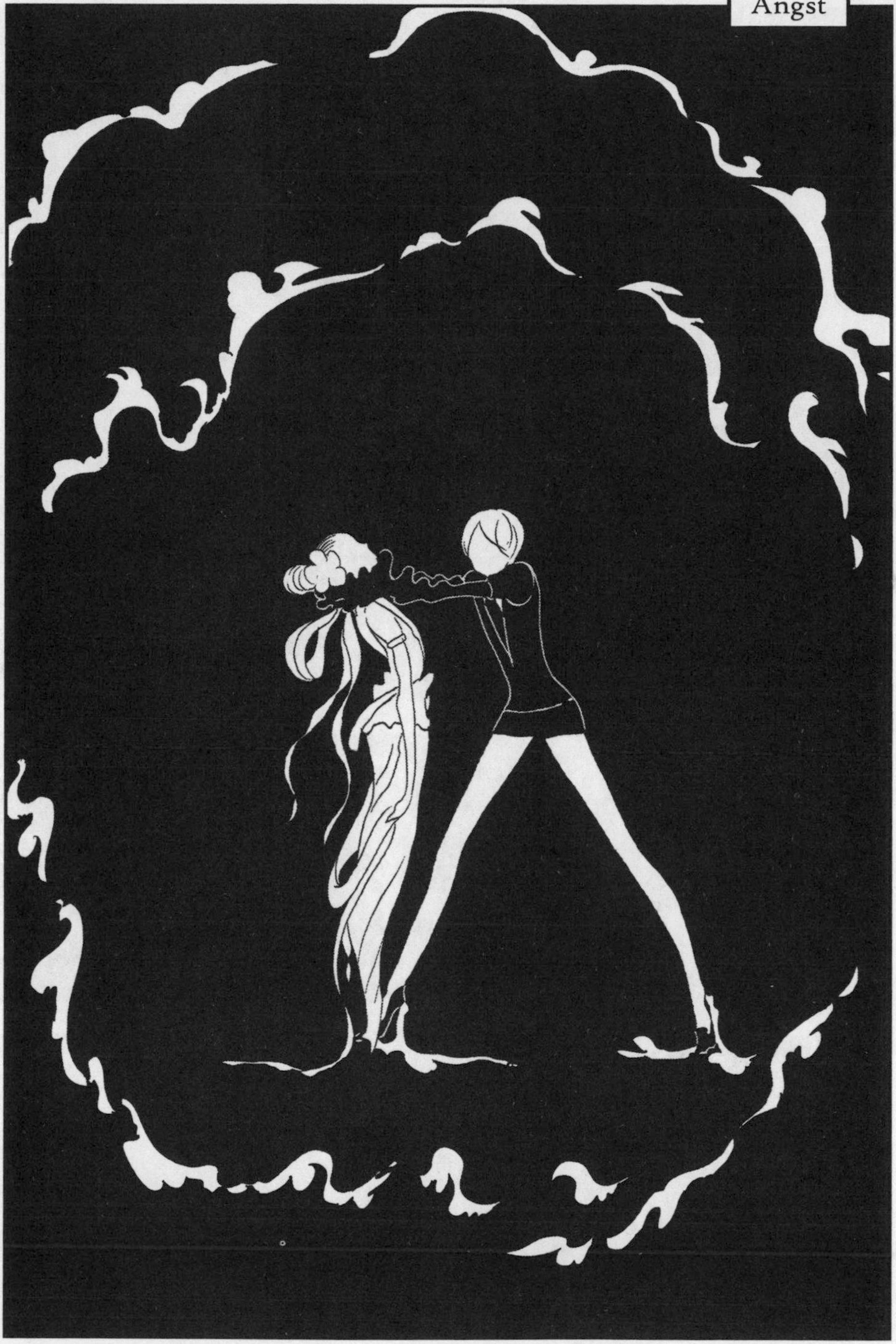

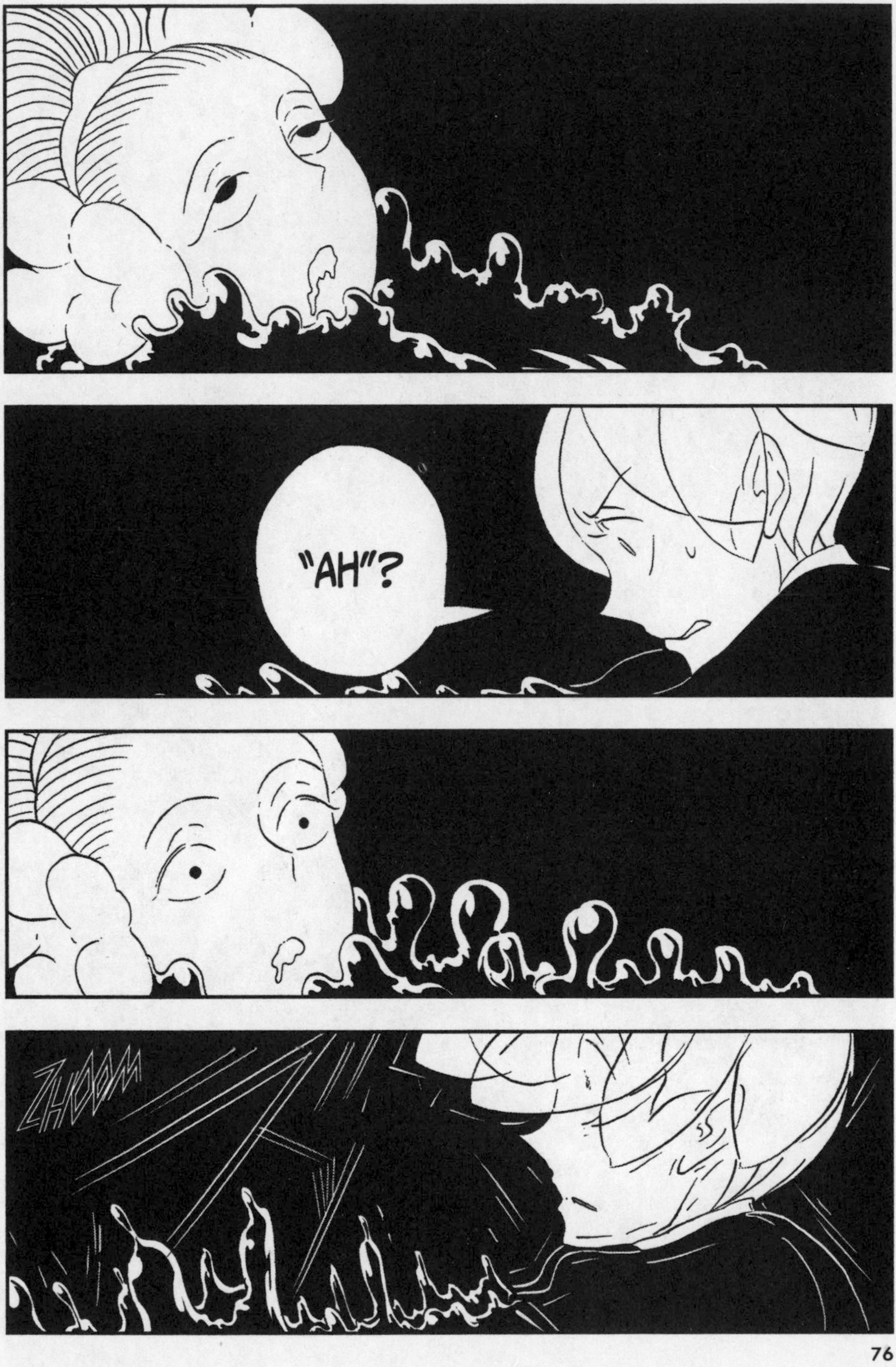
"AH"?
ZHOOM

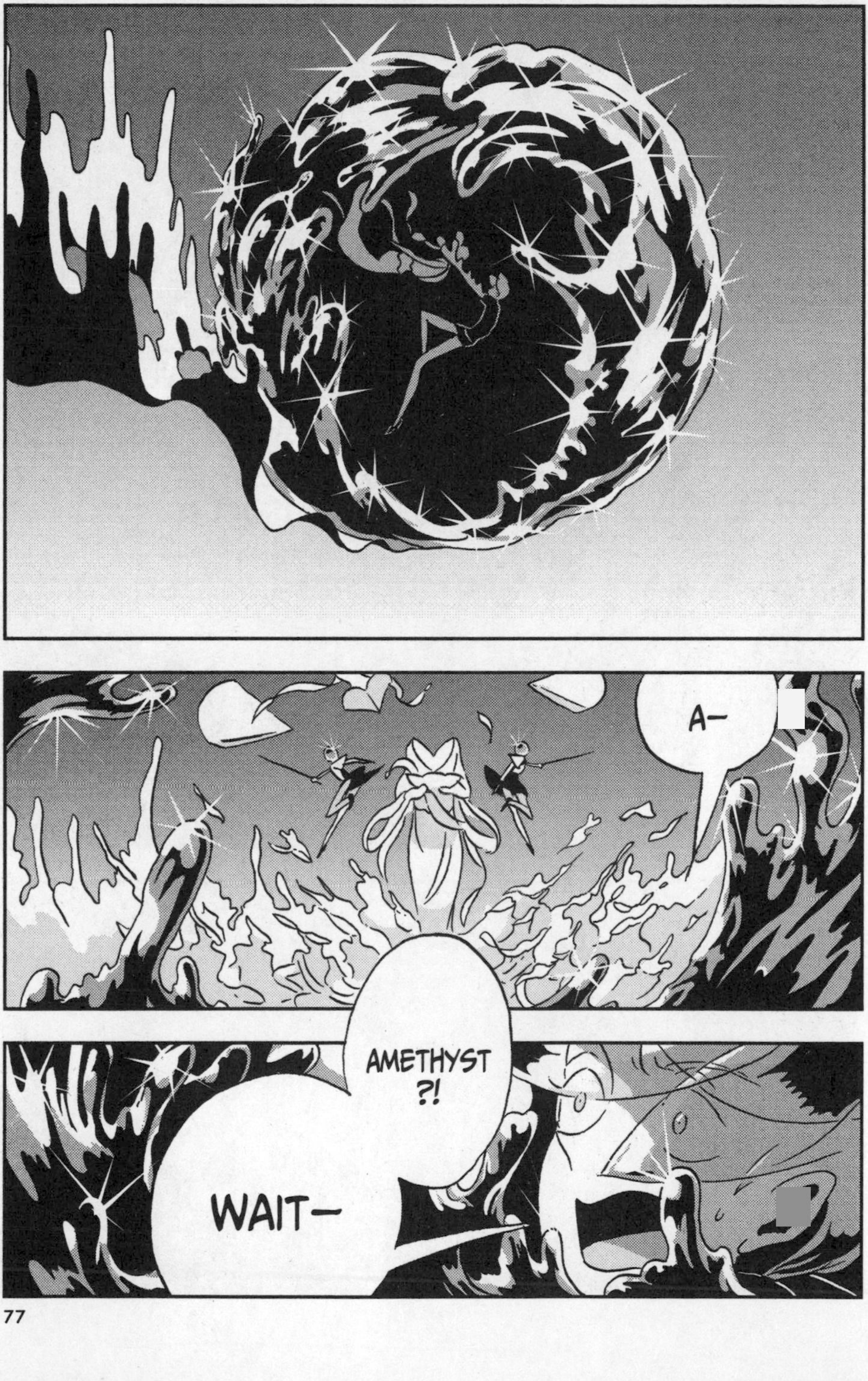
A-
AMETHYST ?!
WAIT-

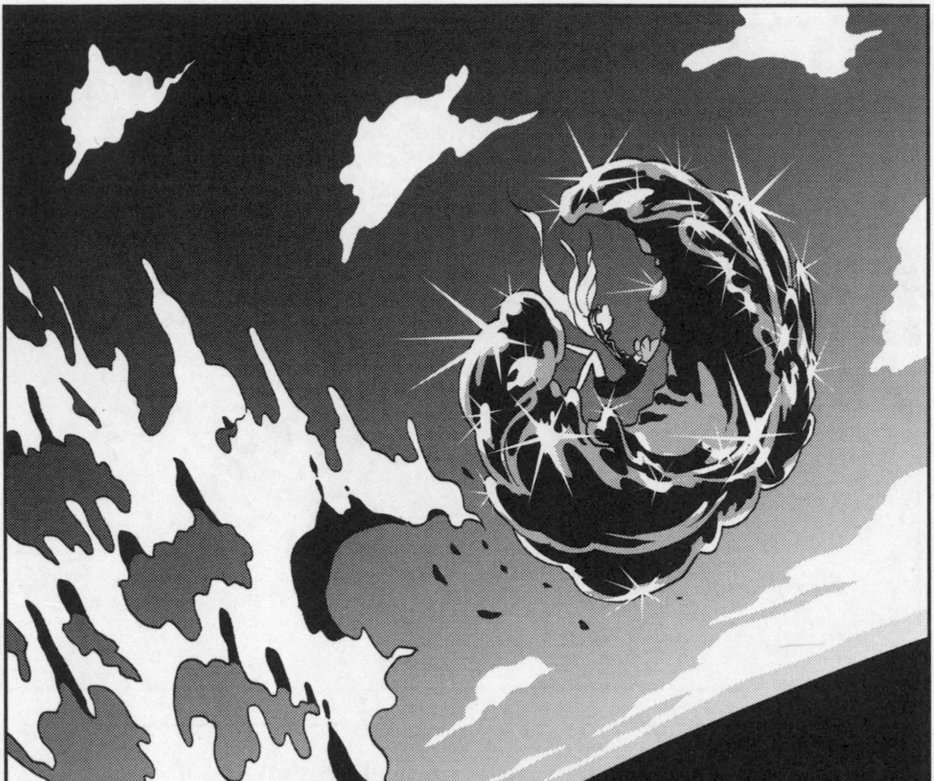

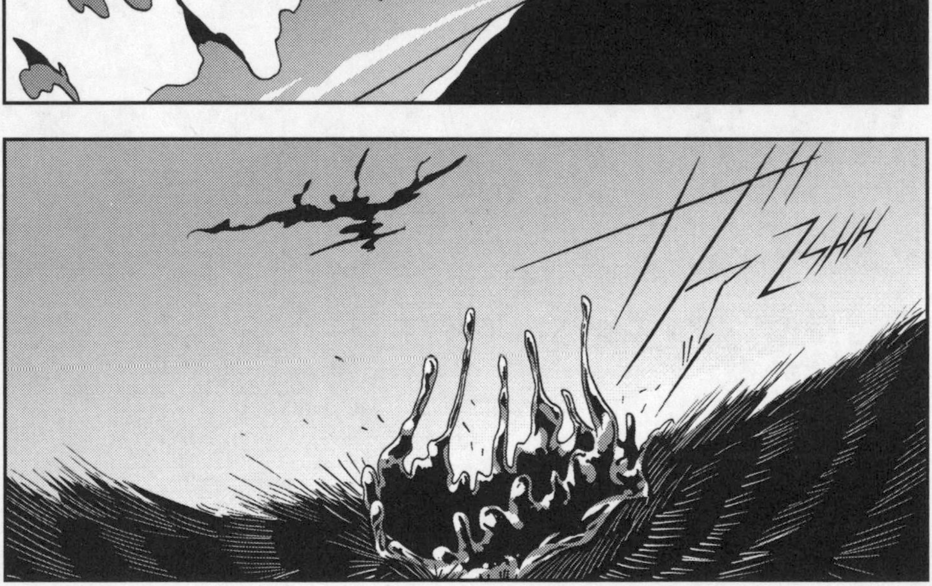
ZSHH

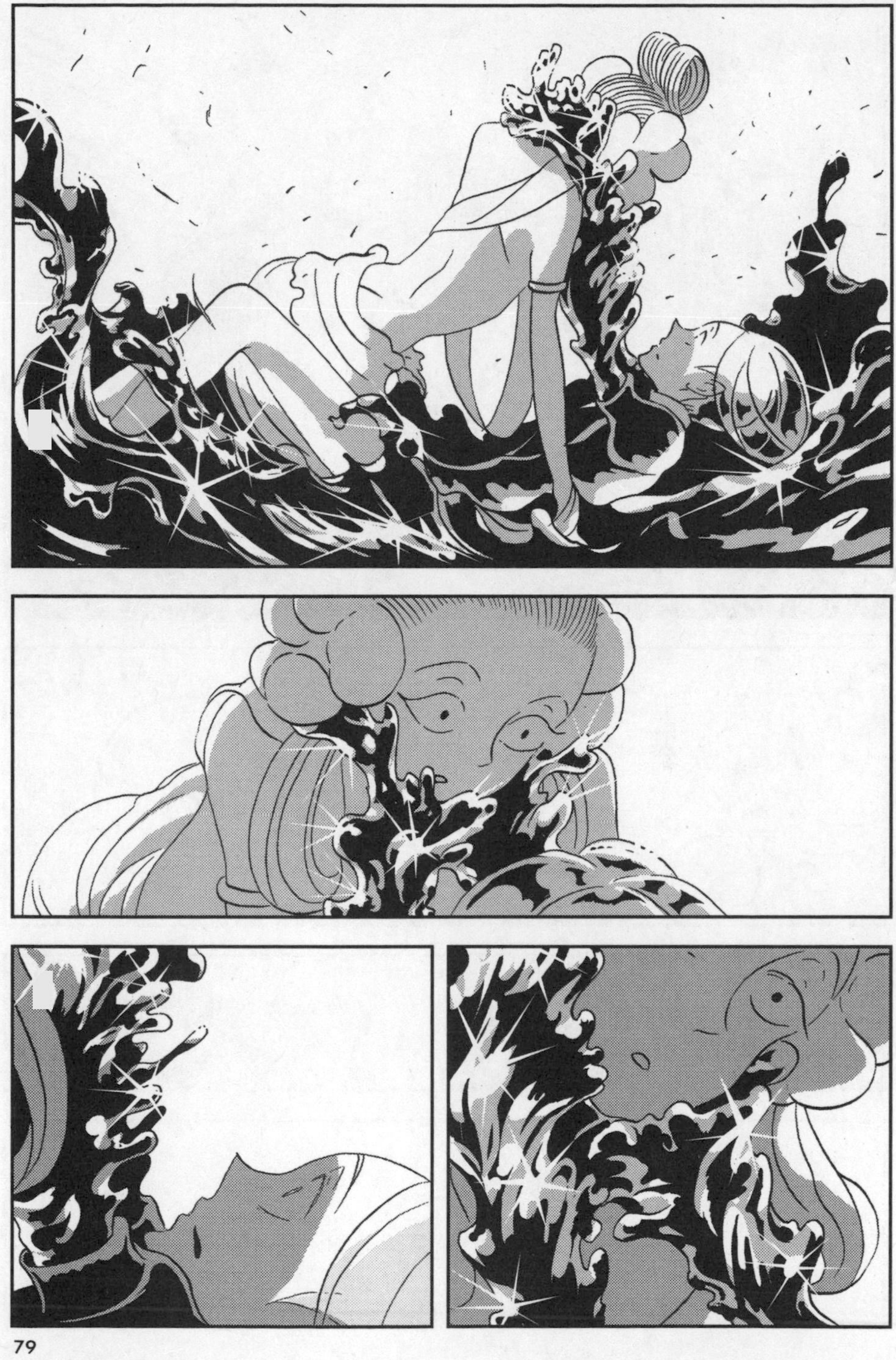

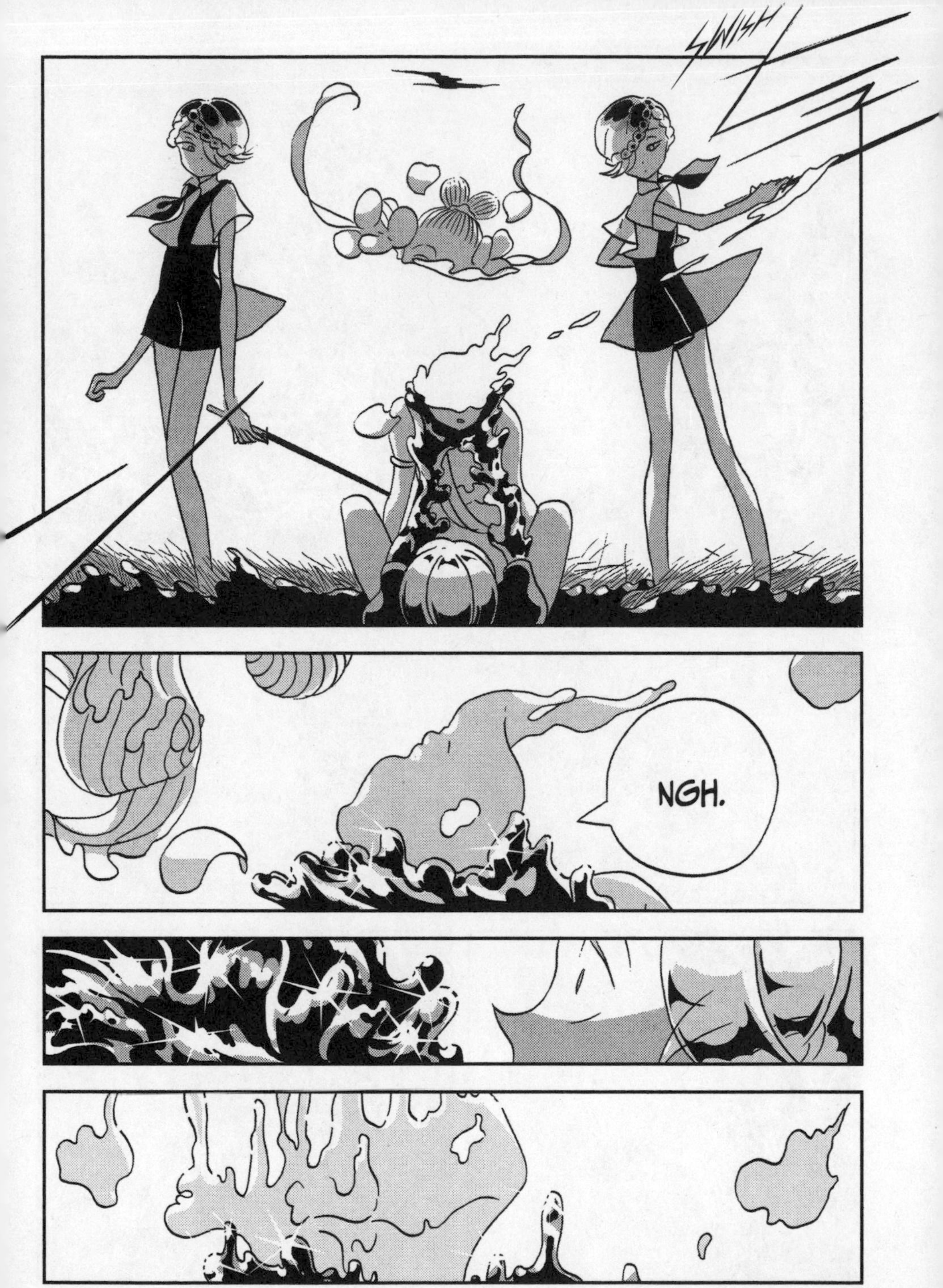
SWISH
NGH.

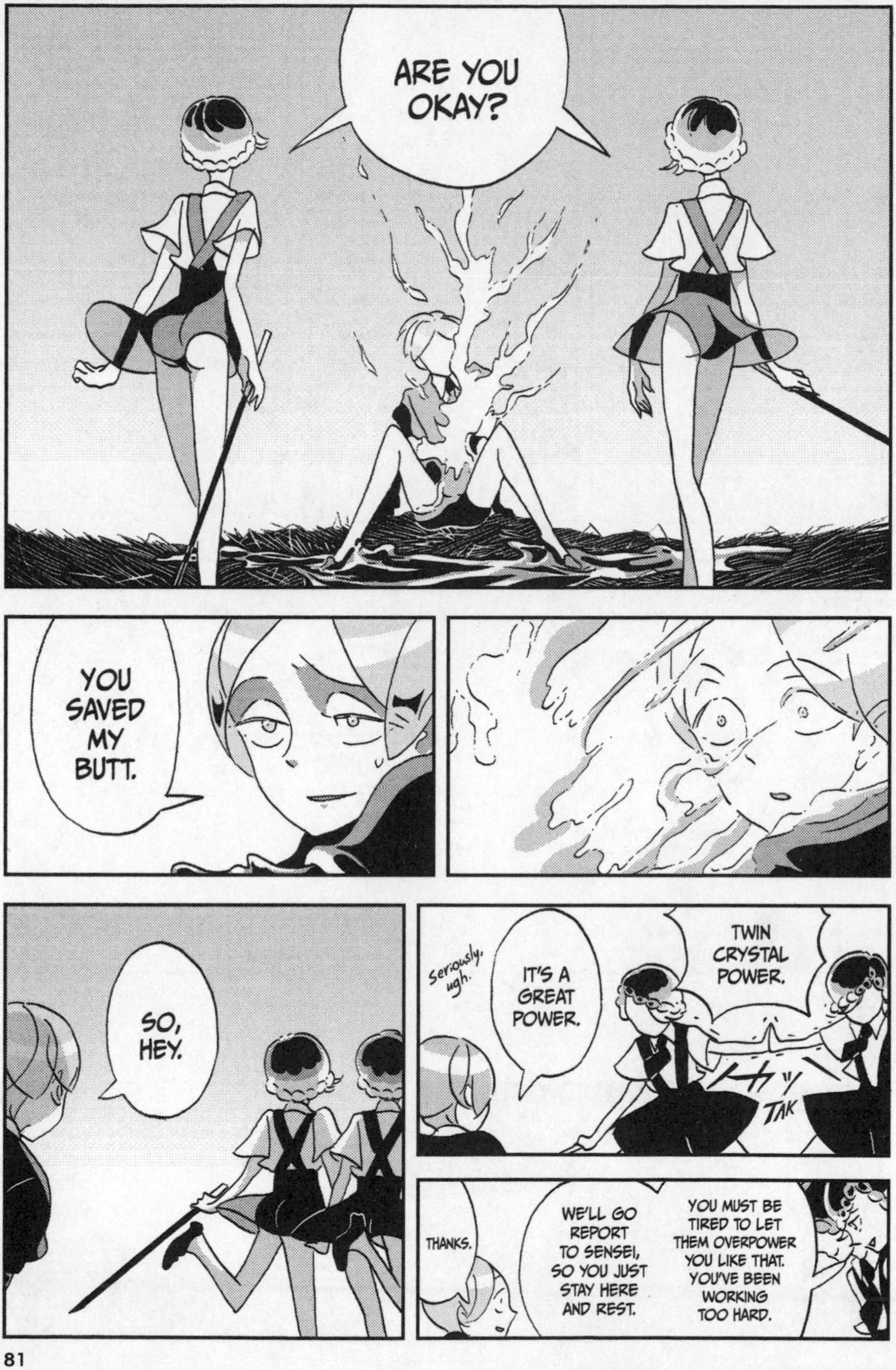
ARE YOU OKAY?
YOU SAVED MY BUTT.
TWIN CRYSTAL POWER.
IT'S A GREAT POWER.
Seriously, ugh.
TAK
YOU MUST BE TIRED TO LET THEM OVERPOWER YOU LIKE THAT. YOU'VE BEEN WORKING TOO HARD.
WE'LL GO REPORT TO SENSEI, SO YOU JUST STAY HERE AND REST.
THANKS.
SO, HEY.

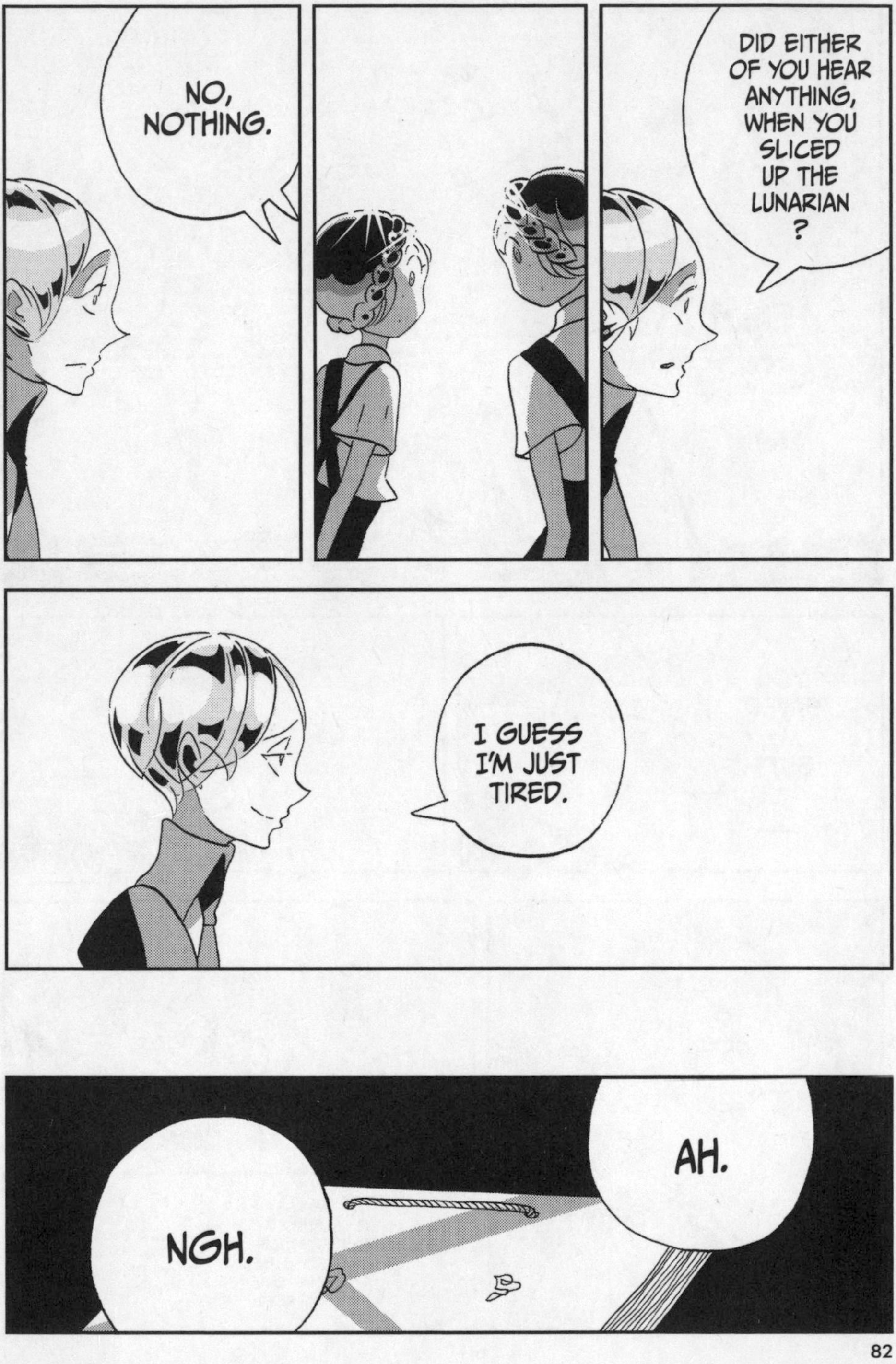
DID EITHER OF YOU HEAR ANYTHING, WHEN YOU SLICED UP THE LUNARIAN ?
NO, NOTHING.
I GUESS I'M JUST TIRED.
AH.
NGH.

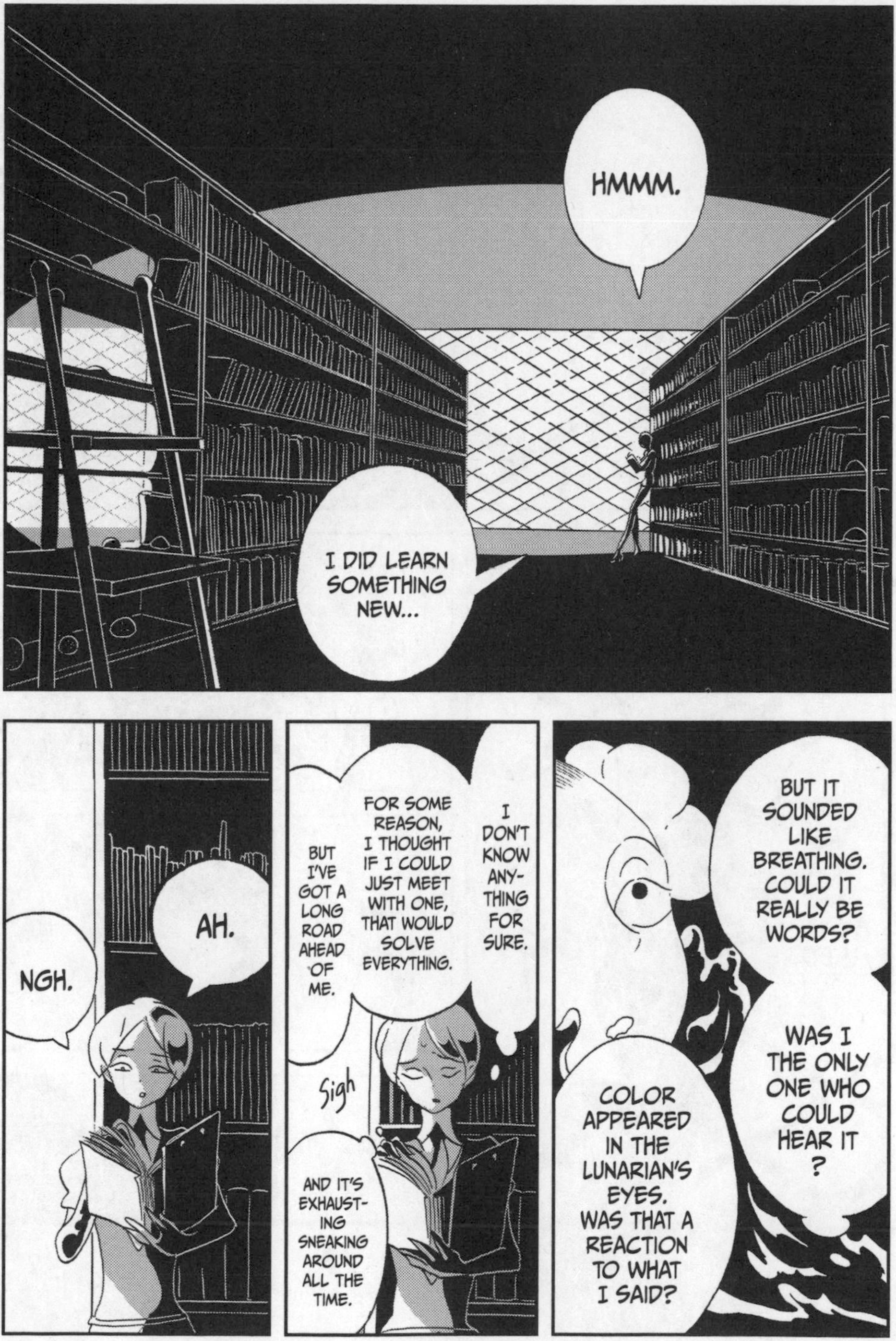
HMMM.
I DID LEARN SOMETHING NEW...
BUT IT SOUNDED LIKE BREATHING. COULD IT REALLY BE WORDS?
WAS I THE ONLY ONE WHO COULD HEAR IT ?
COLOR APPEARED IN THE LUNARIAN'S EYES. WAS THAT A REACTION TO WHAT I SAID?
I DON'T KNOW ANY-THING FOR SURE.
FOR SOME REASON, I THOUGHT IF I COULD JUST MEET WITH ONE, THAT WOULD SOLVE EVERYTHING.
BUT I'VE GOT A LONG ROAD AHEAD OF ME.
Sigh
AND IT'S EXHAUST-ING SNEAKING AROUND ALL THE TIME.
AH.
NGH.

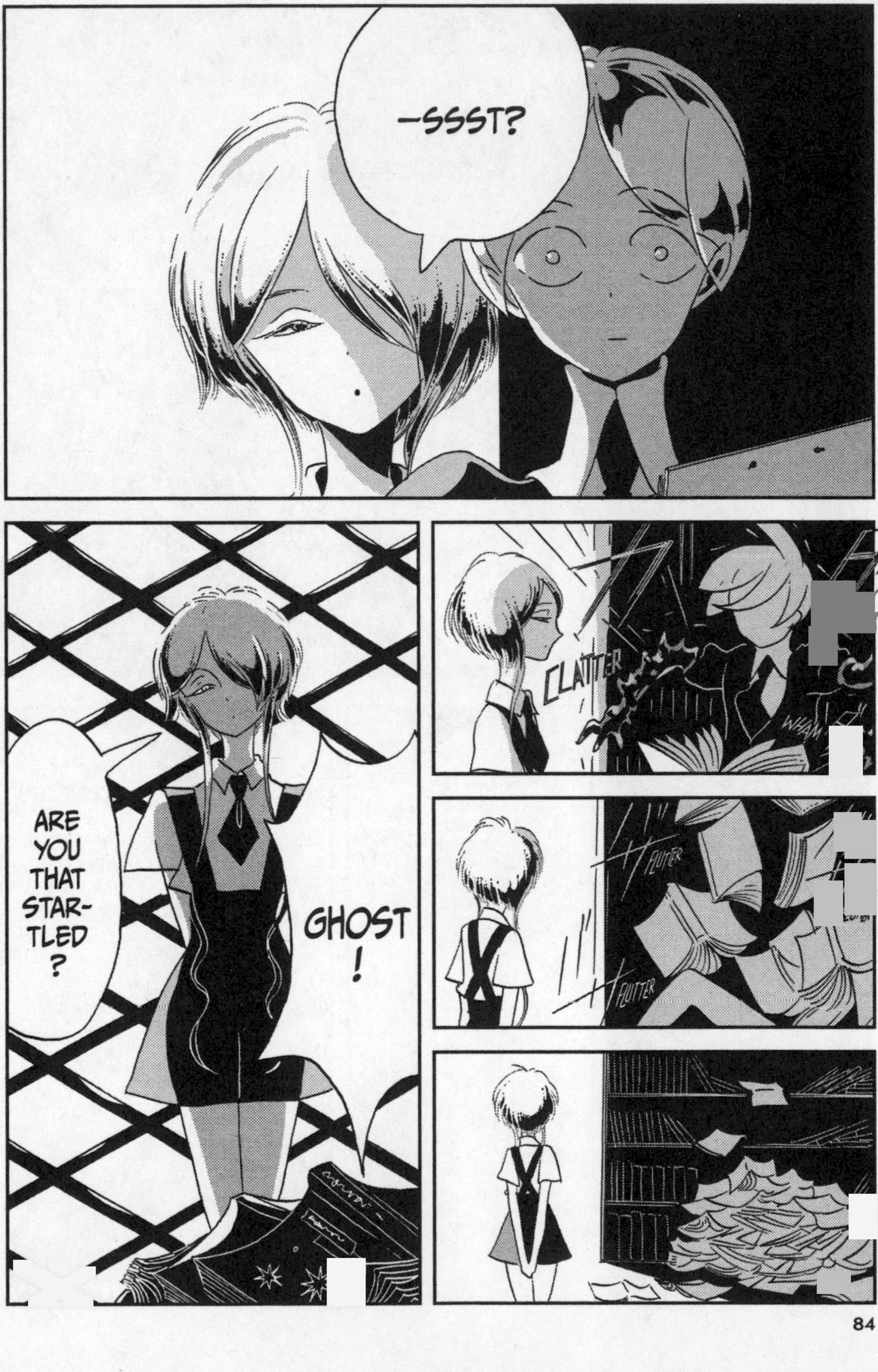
—SSST?
CLATTER
WHAM
FLUTTER
FLUTTER
GHOST!
ARE YOU THAT STARTLED?

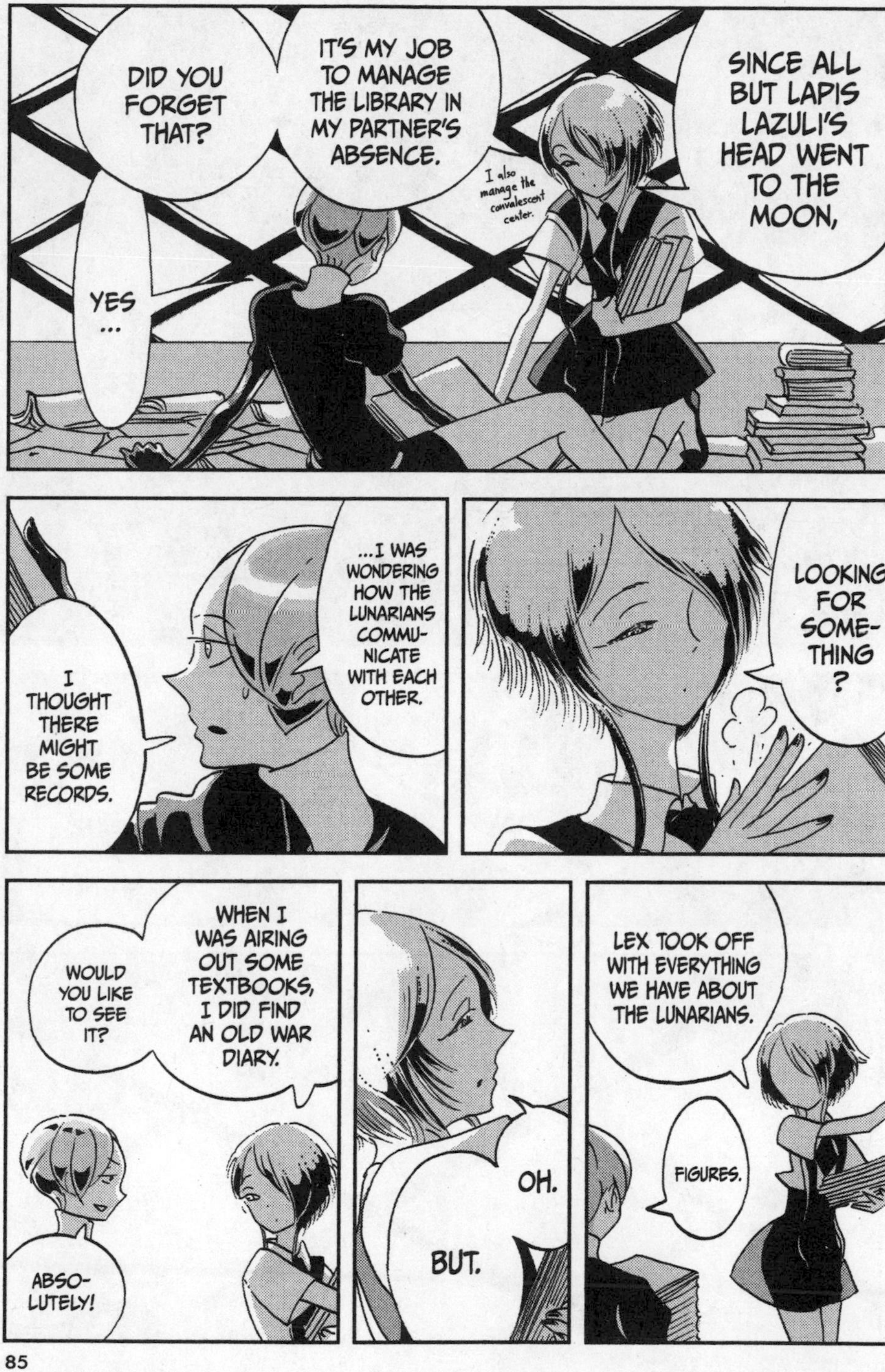
SINCE ALL BUT LAPIS LAZULI'S HEAD WENT TO THE MOON,
I also manage the convalescent center.
IT'S MY JOB TO MANAGE THE LIBRARY IN MY PARTNER'S ABSENCE.
DID YOU FORGET THAT?
YES ...
LOOKING FOR SOME-THING ?
...I WAS WONDERING HOW THE LUNARIANS COMMU-NICATE WITH EACH OTHER.
I THOUGHT THERE MIGHT BE SOME RECORDS.
LEX TOOK OFF WITH EVERYTHING WE HAVE ABOUT THE LUNARIANS.
FIGURES.
OH.
BUT.
WHEN I WAS AIRING OUT SOME TEXTBOOKS, I DID FIND AN OLD WAR DIARY.
WOULD YOU LIKE TO SEE IT?
ABSO-LUTELY!

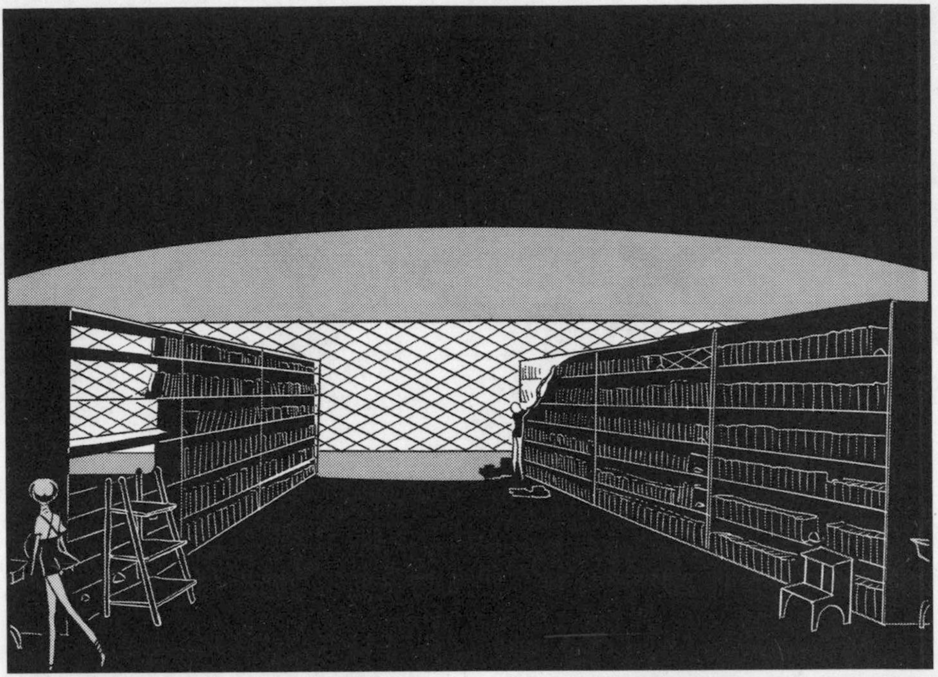

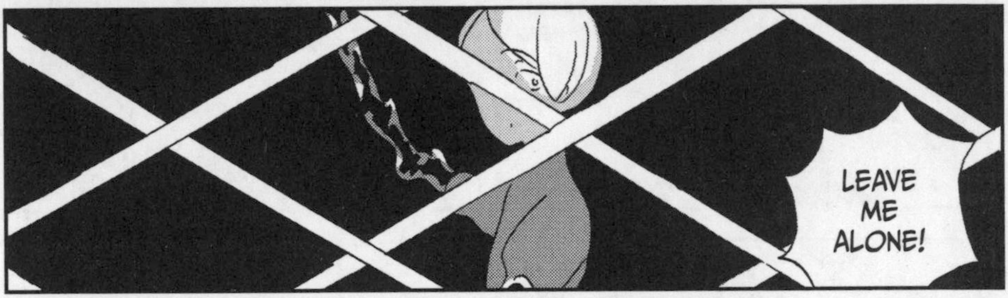
LEAVE ME ALONE!

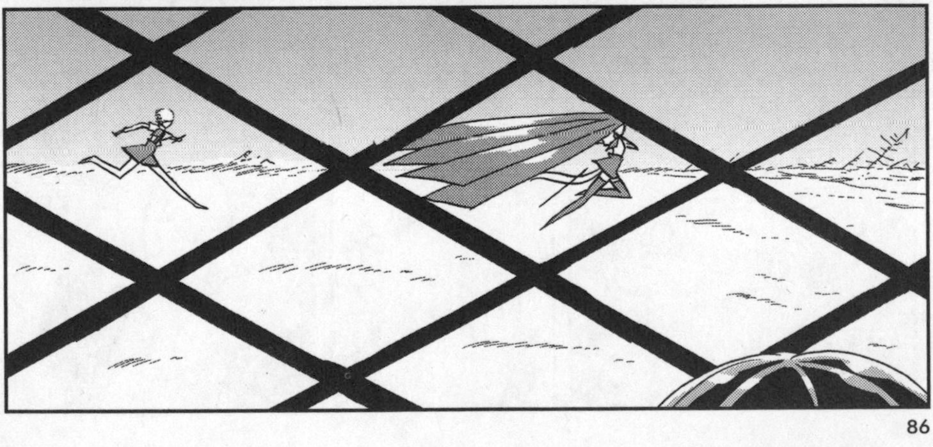

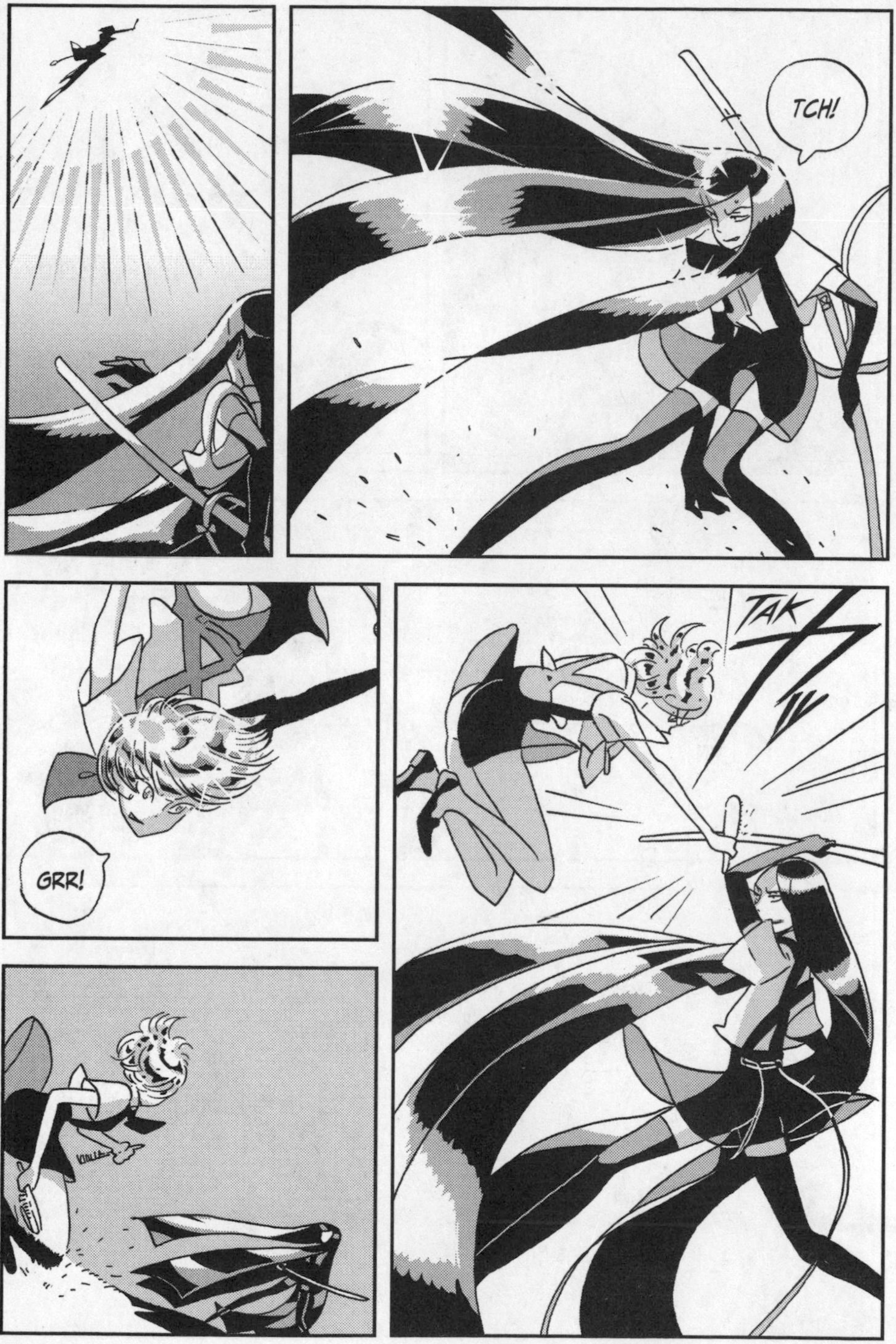
TCH!
TAK
GRR!

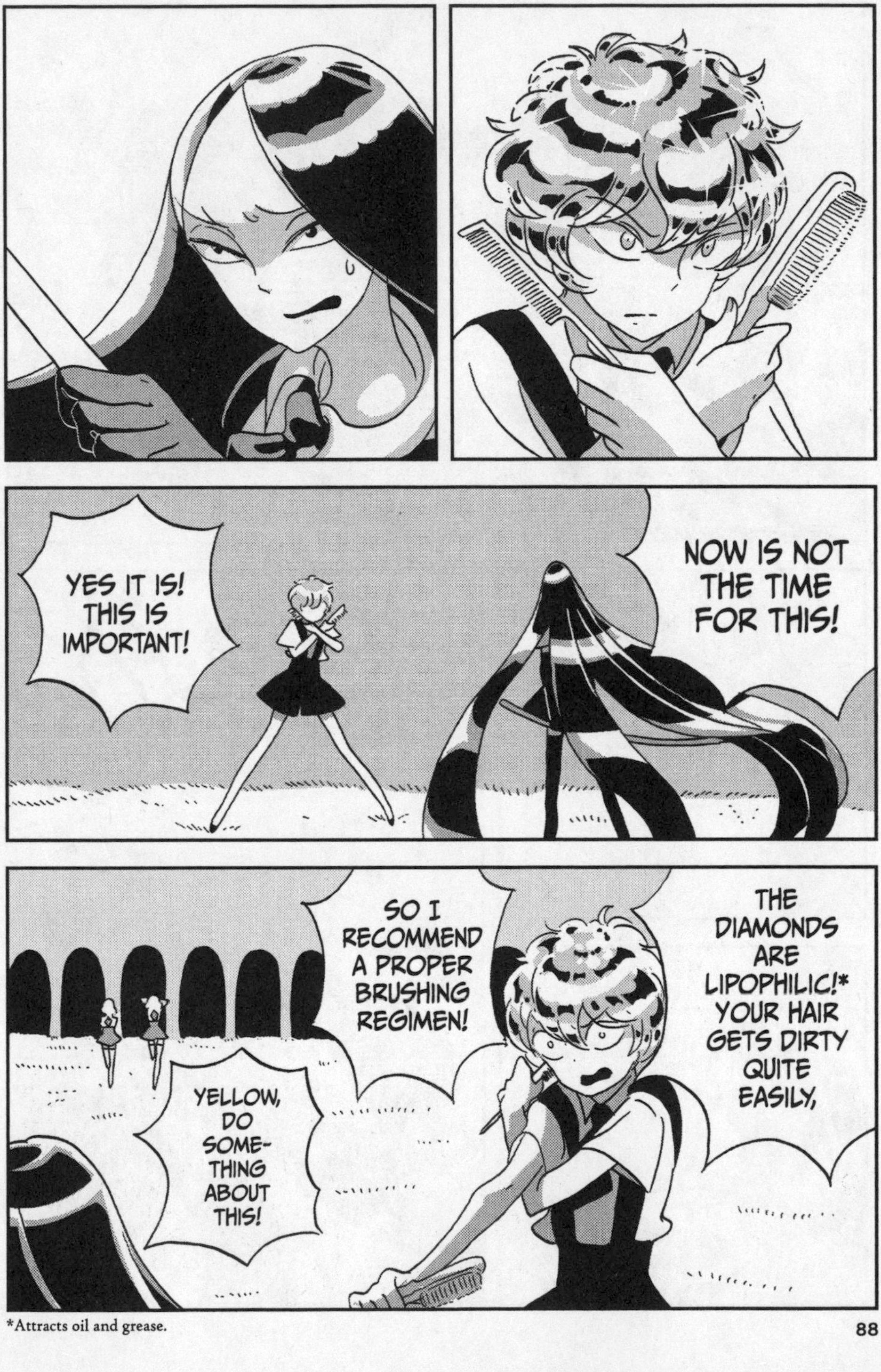
NOW IS NOT THE TIME FOR THIS!
YES IT IS! THIS IS IMPORTANT!
THE DIAMONDS ARE LIPOPHILIC!* YOUR HAIR GETS DIRTY QUITE EASILY,
SO I RECOMMEND A PROPER BRUSHING REGIMEN!
YELLOW, DO SOMETHING ABOUT THIS!

*Attracts oil and grease.

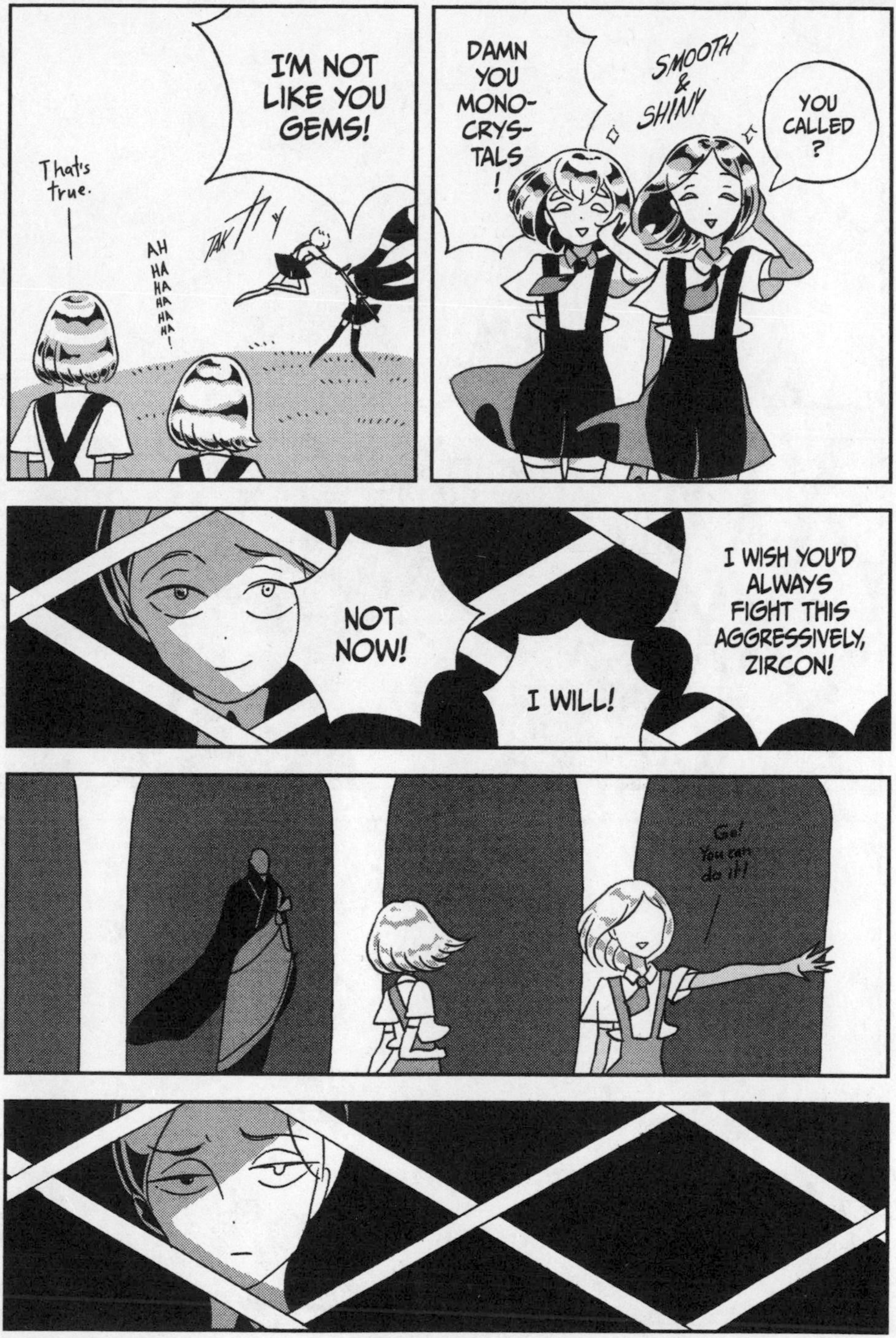

YOU CALLED?
SMOOTH & SHINY
DAMN YOU MONO-CRYSTALS!
I'M NOT LIKE YOU GEMS!
TAK
AH HA HA HA HA HA!
That's true.
I WISH YOU'D ALWAYS FIGHT THIS AGGRESSIVELY, ZIRCON!
I WILL!
NOT NOW!
Go! You can do it!

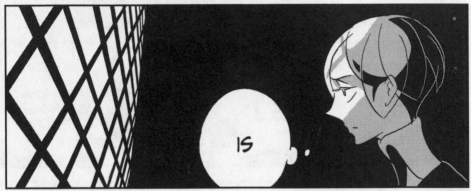

IS

WHAT I'M SEEING NOW

THE REAL SENSEI?

OR...

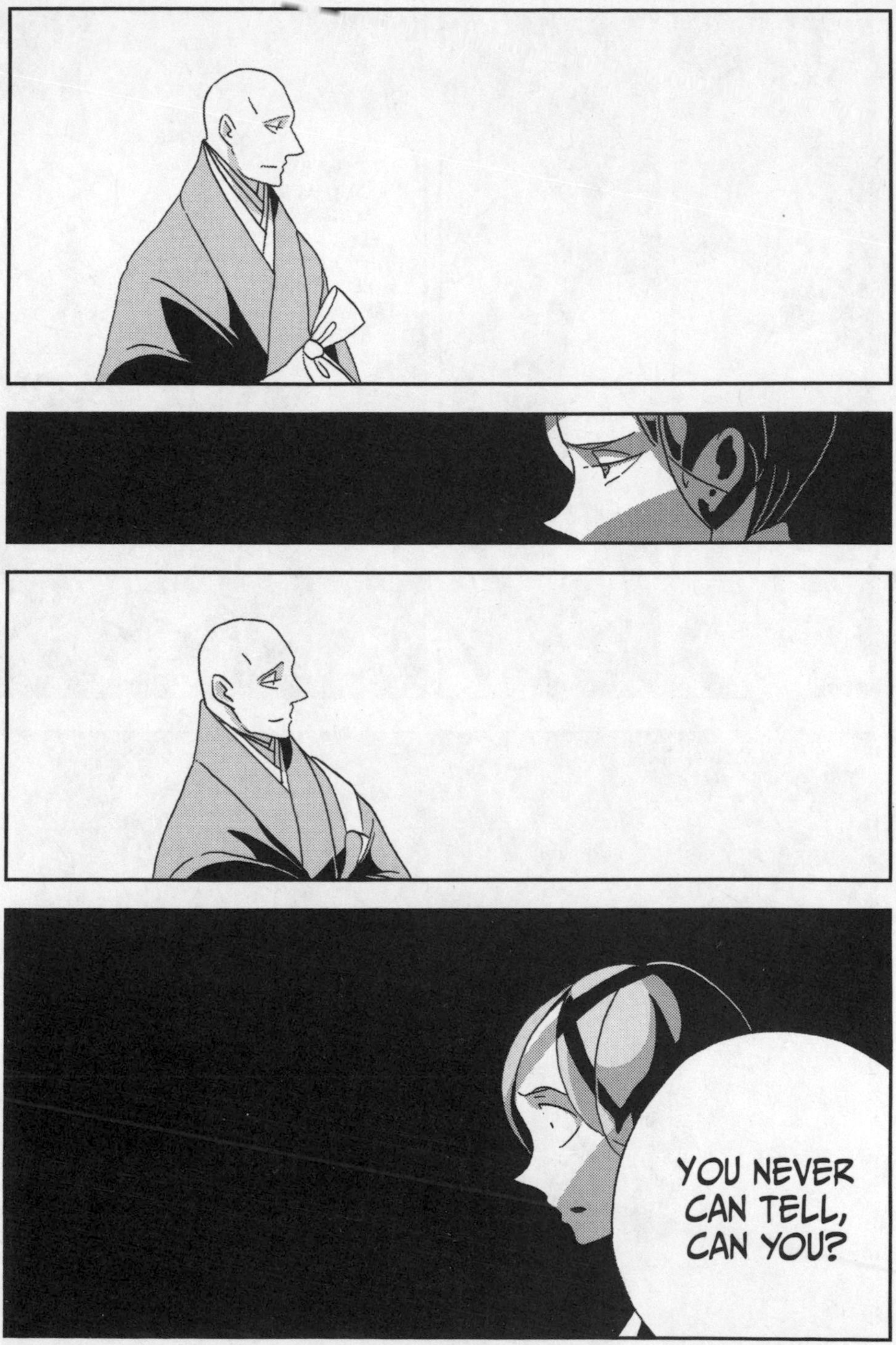
YOU NEVER CAN TELL, CAN YOU?

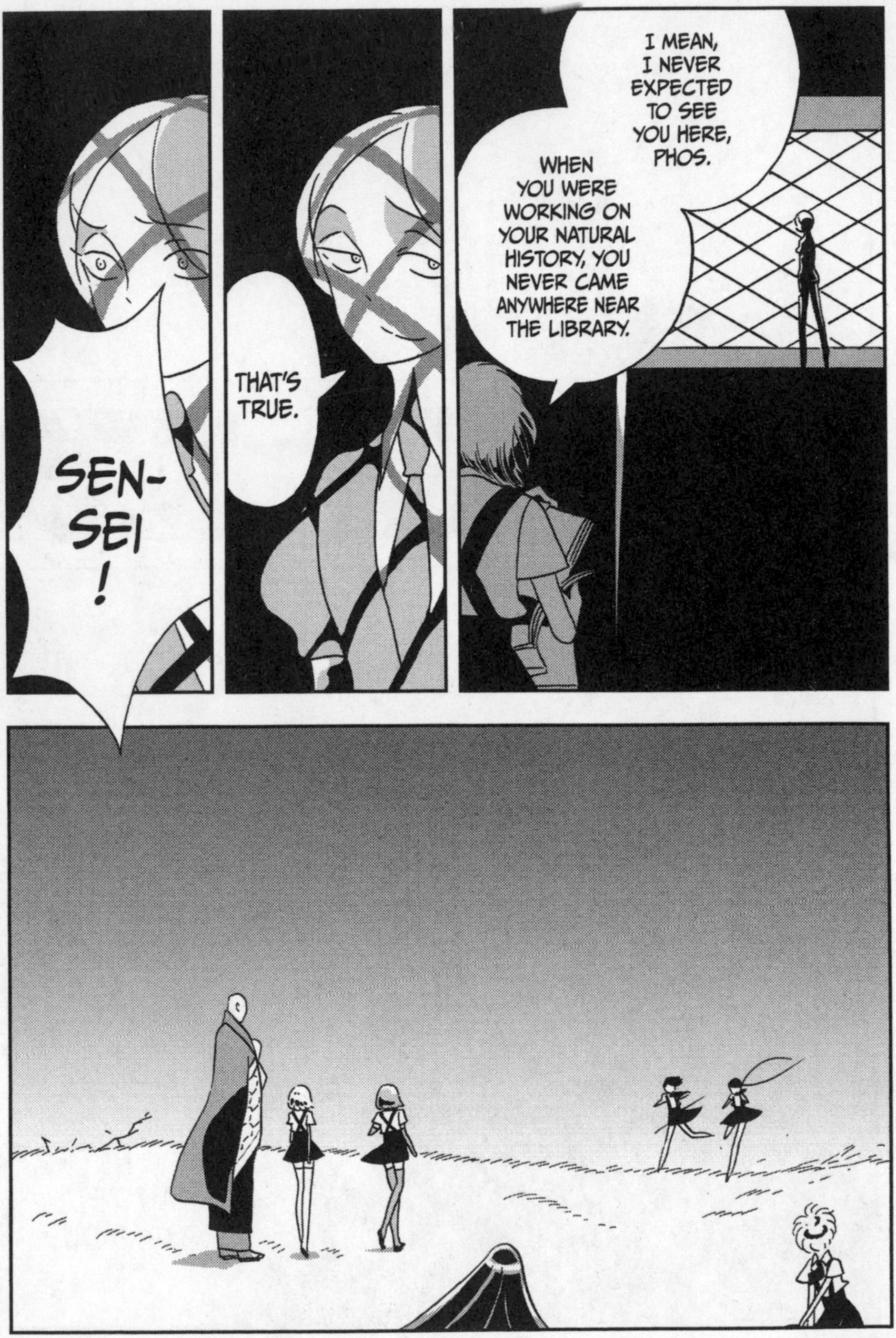
I MEAN, I NEVER EXPECTED TO SEE YOU HERE, PHOS.
WHEN YOU WERE WORKING ON YOUR NATURAL HISTORY, YOU NEVER CAME ANYWHERE NEAR THE LIBRARY.
THAT'S TRUE.
SEN-SEI!

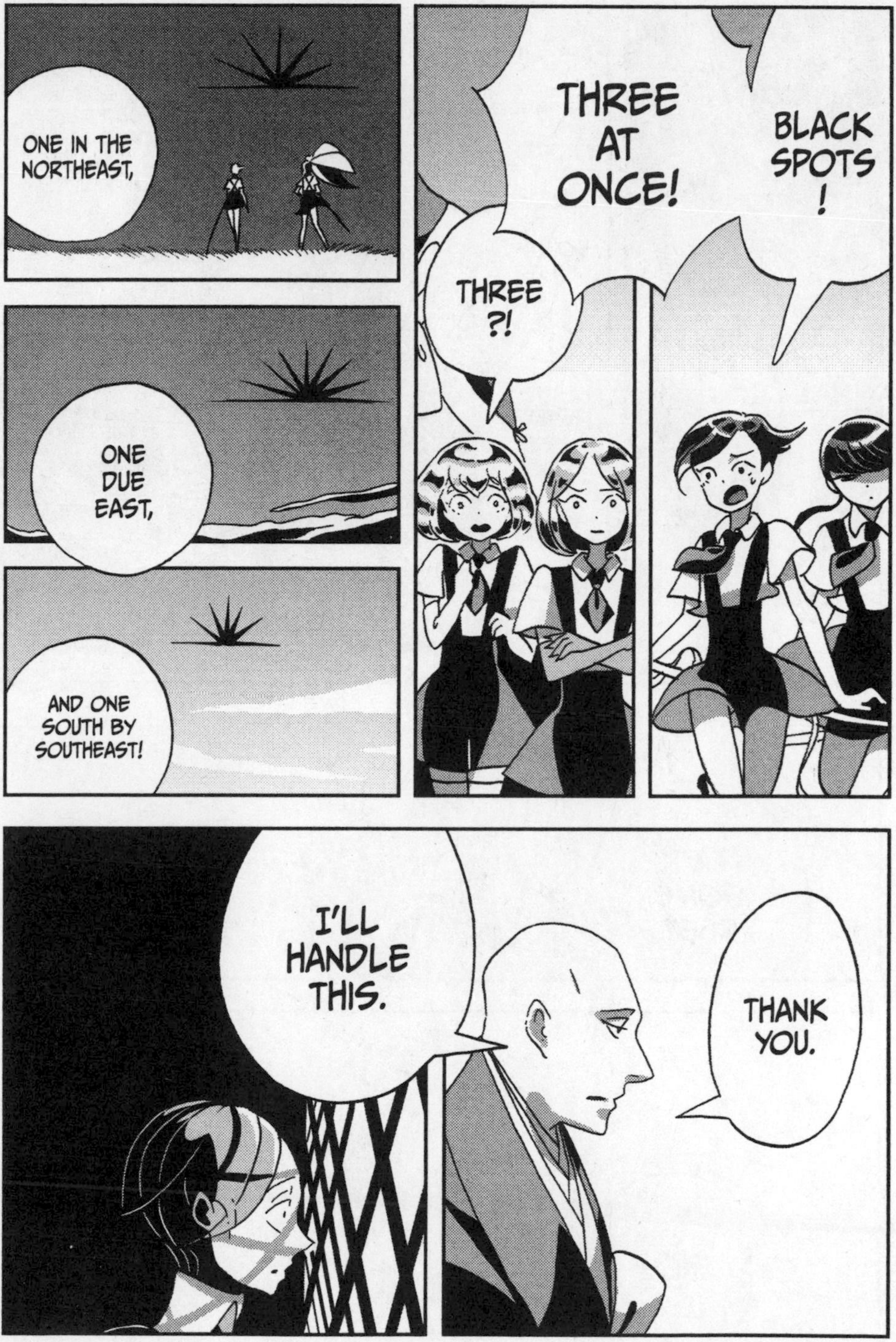
BLACK SPOTS!
THREE AT ONCE!
THREE?!
ONE IN THE NORTHEAST,
ONE DUE EAST,
AND ONE SOUTH BY SOUTHEAST!
THANK YOU.
I'LL HANDLE THIS.

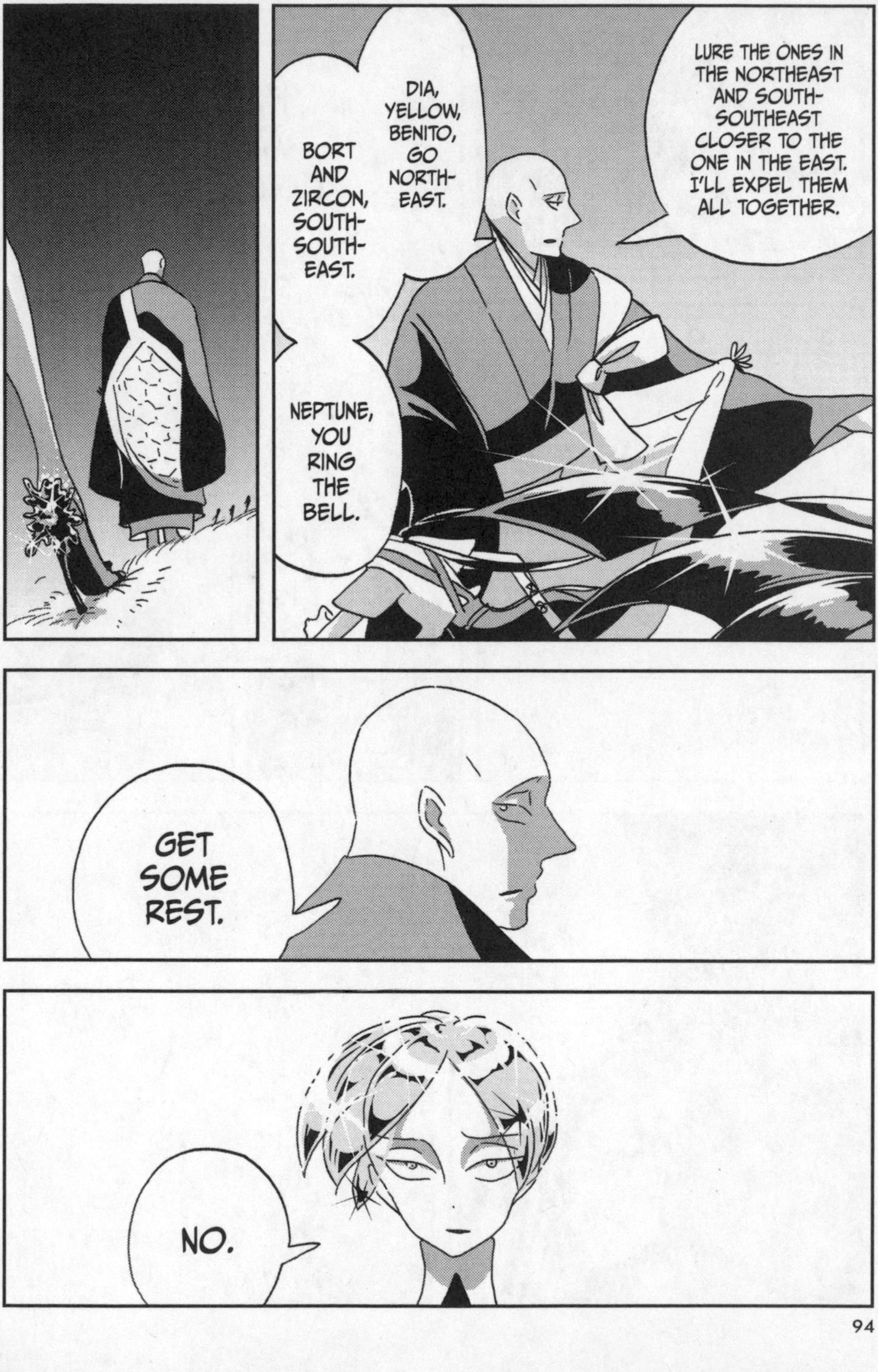

LURE THE ONES IN THE NORTHEAST AND SOUTH-SOUTHEAST CLOSER TO THE ONE IN THE EAST. I'LL EXPEL THEM ALL TOGETHER.
DIA, YELLOW, BENITO, GO NORTH-EAST.
BORT AND ZIRCON, SOUTH-SOUTH-EAST.
NEPTUNE, YOU RING THE BELL.
GET SOME REST.
NO.

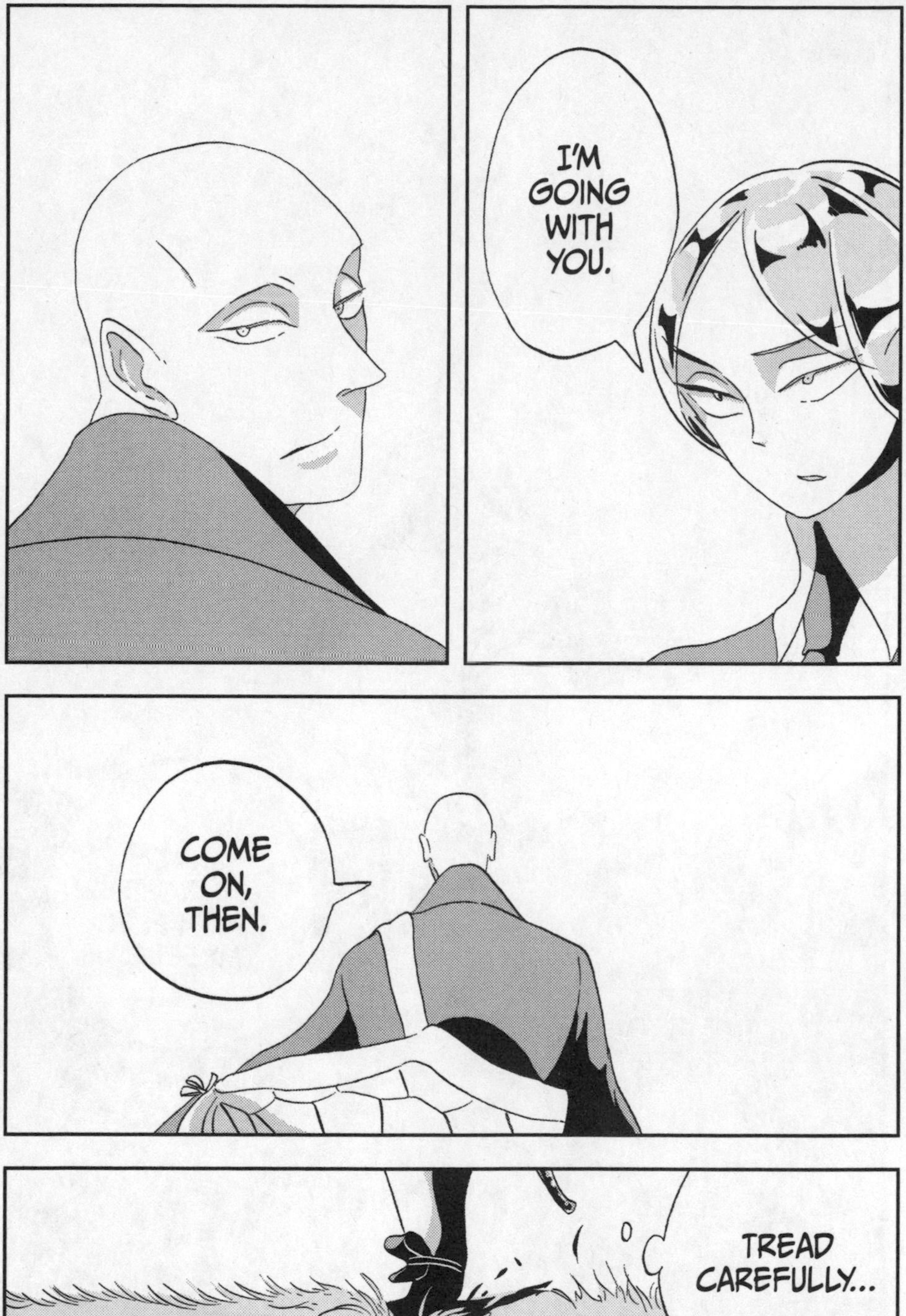
I'M GOING WITH YOU.
COME ON, THEN.
TREAD CAREFULLY...

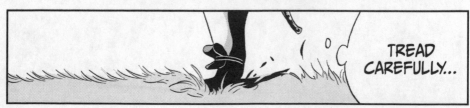

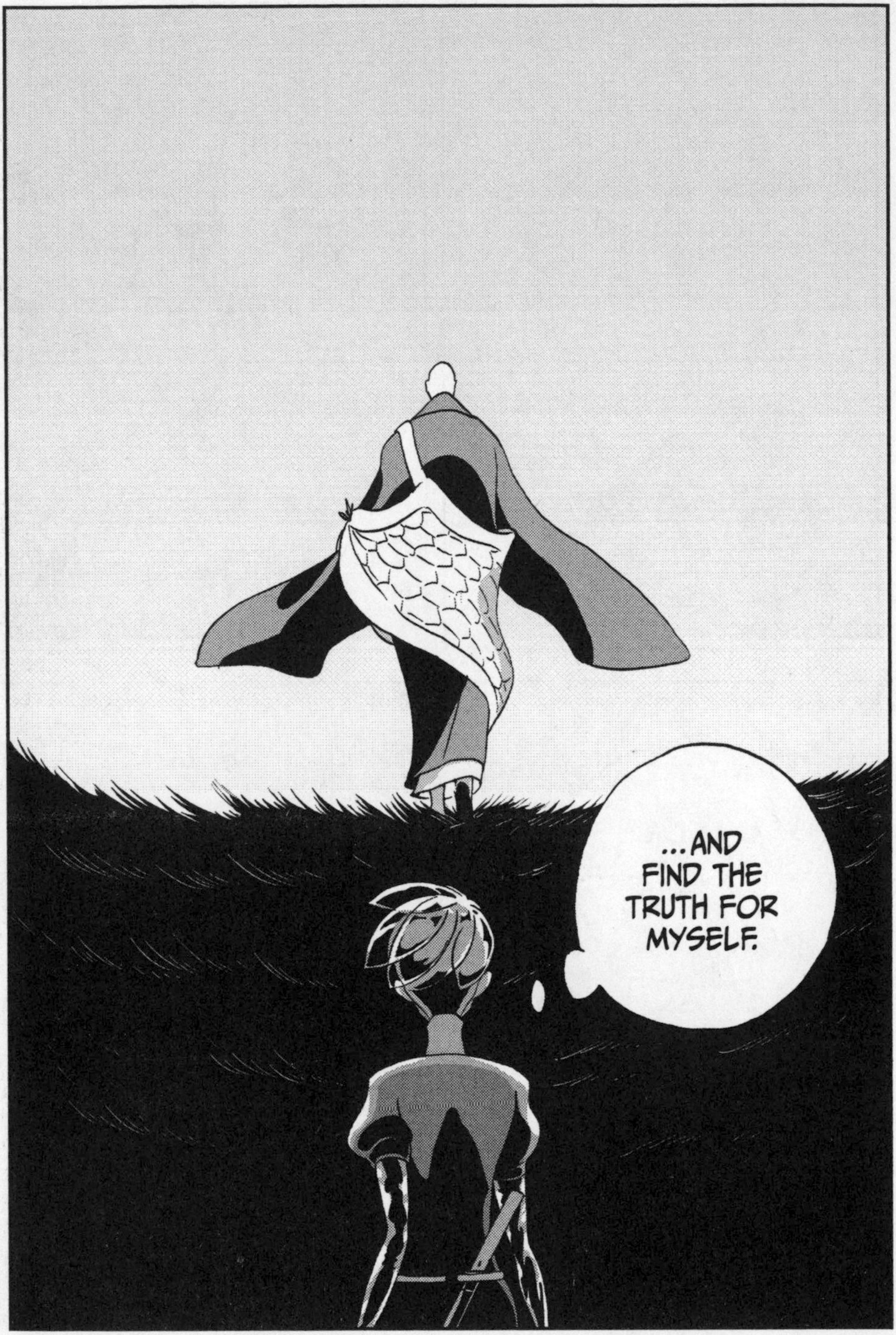
...AND FIND THE TRUTH FOR MYSELF.

CHAPTER 32: Angst END

CHAPTER 33:

Distance

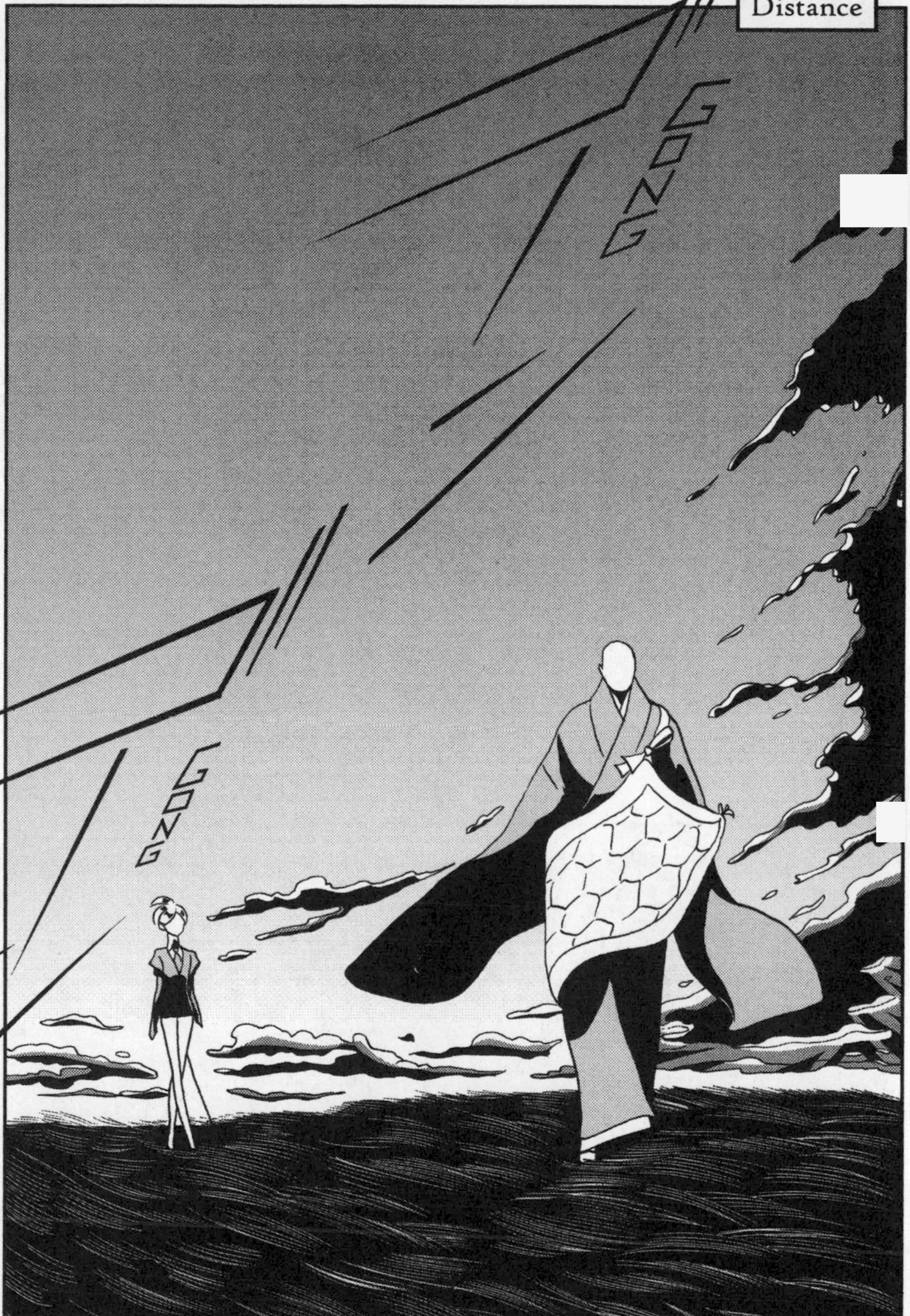
GONG
GONG

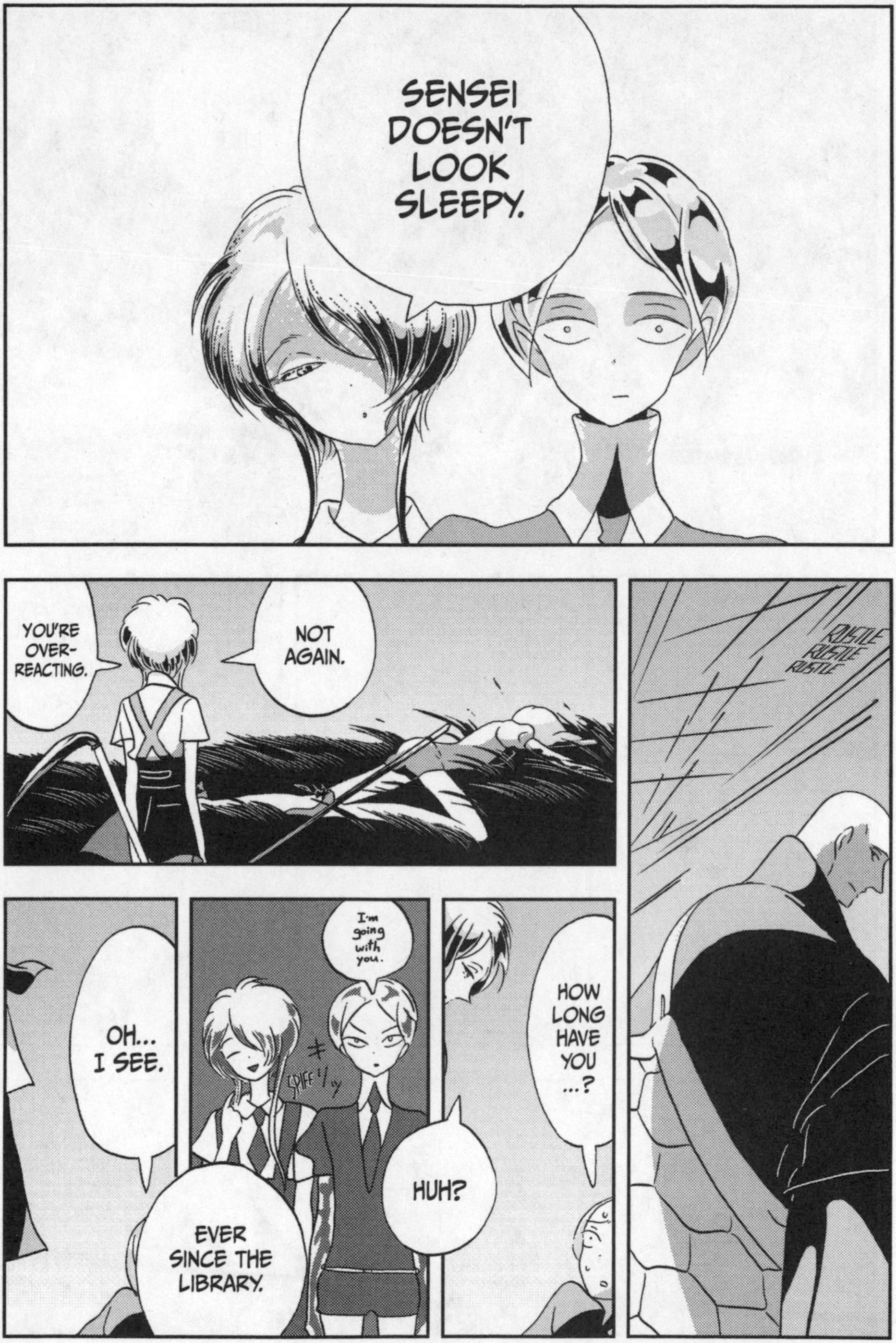
SENSEI DOESN'T LOOK SLEEPY.
RUSTLE RUSTLE RUSTLE
NOT AGAIN.
YOU'RE OVER-REACTING.
HOW LONG HAVE YOU ...?
I'm going with you.
SPIFF
HUH?
OH... I SEE.
EVER SINCE THE LIBRARY.

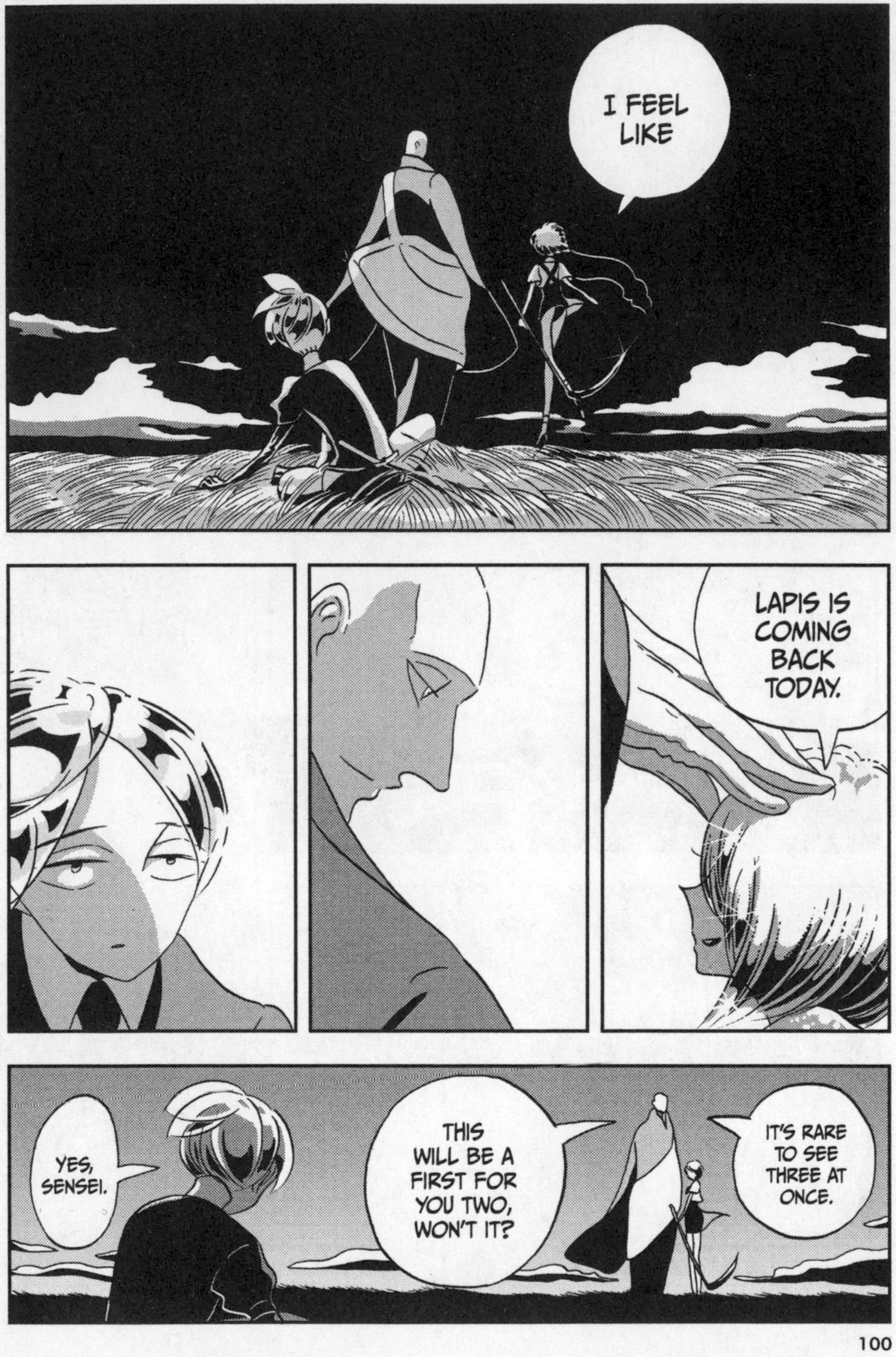
I FEEL LIKE
LAPIS IS COMING BACK TODAY.
IT'S RARE TO SEE THREE AT ONCE.
THIS WILL BE A FIRST FOR YOU TWO, WON'T IT?
YES, SENSEI.

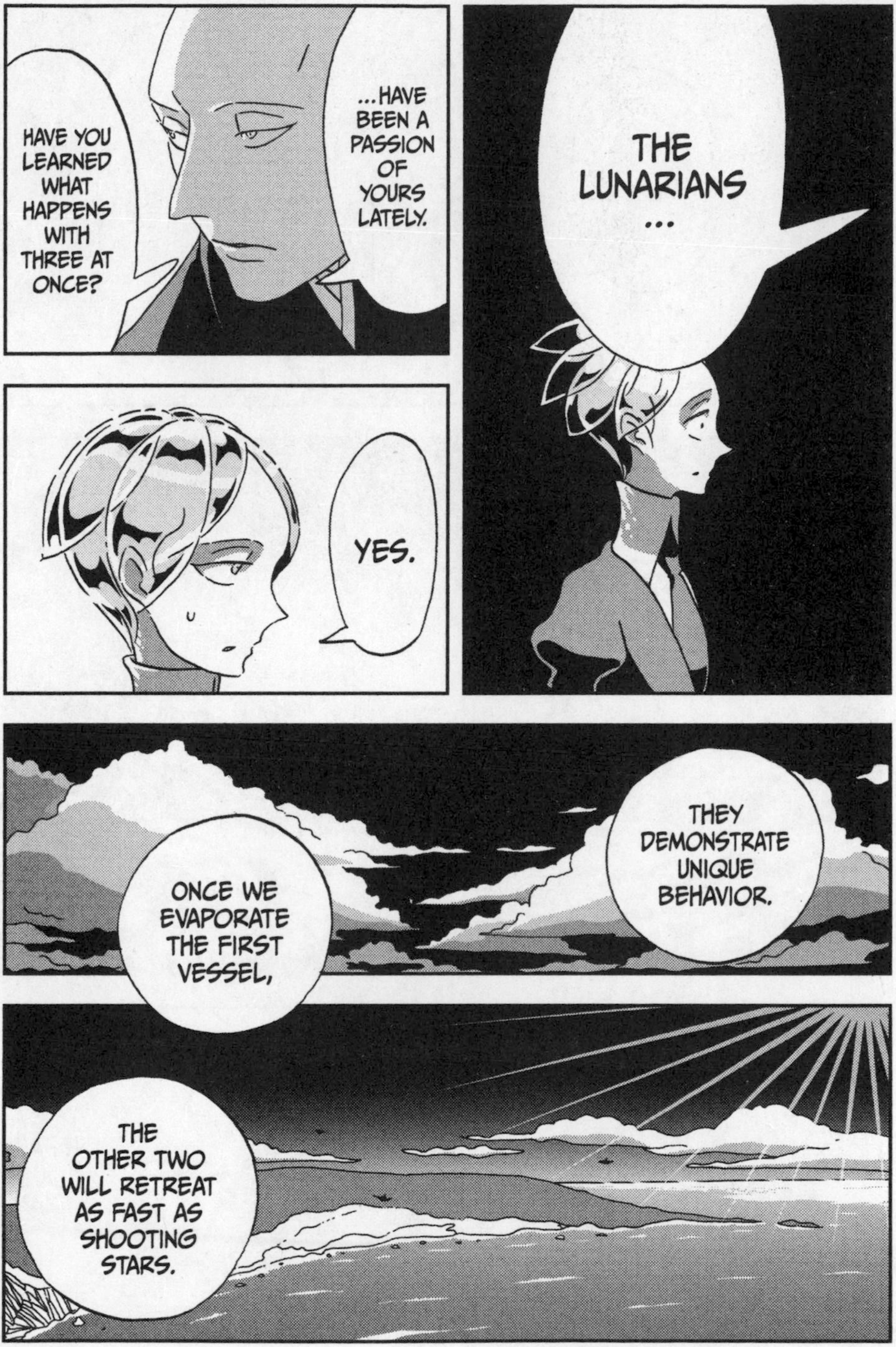
THE LUNARIANS ...
...HAVE BEEN A PASSION OF YOURS LATELY.
HAVE YOU LEARNED WHAT HAPPENS WITH THREE AT ONCE?
YES.
THEY DEMONSTRATE UNIQUE BEHAVIOR.
ONCE WE EVAPORATE THE FIRST VESSEL,
THE OTHER TWO WILL RETREAT AS FAST AS SHOOTING STARS.

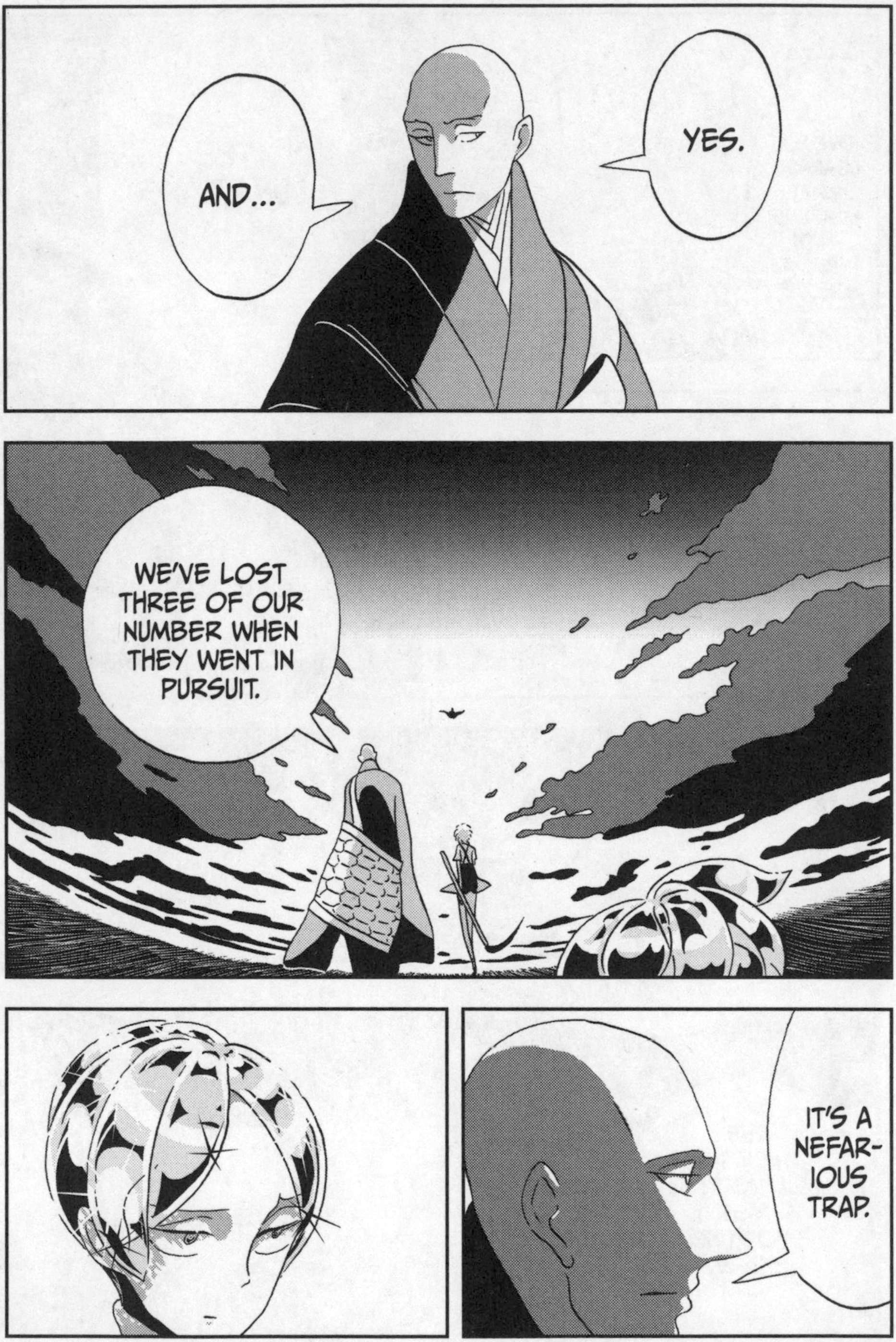
YES.
AND...
WE'VE LOST THREE OF OUR NUMBER WHEN THEY WENT IN PURSUIT.
IT'S A NEFARIOUS TRAP.

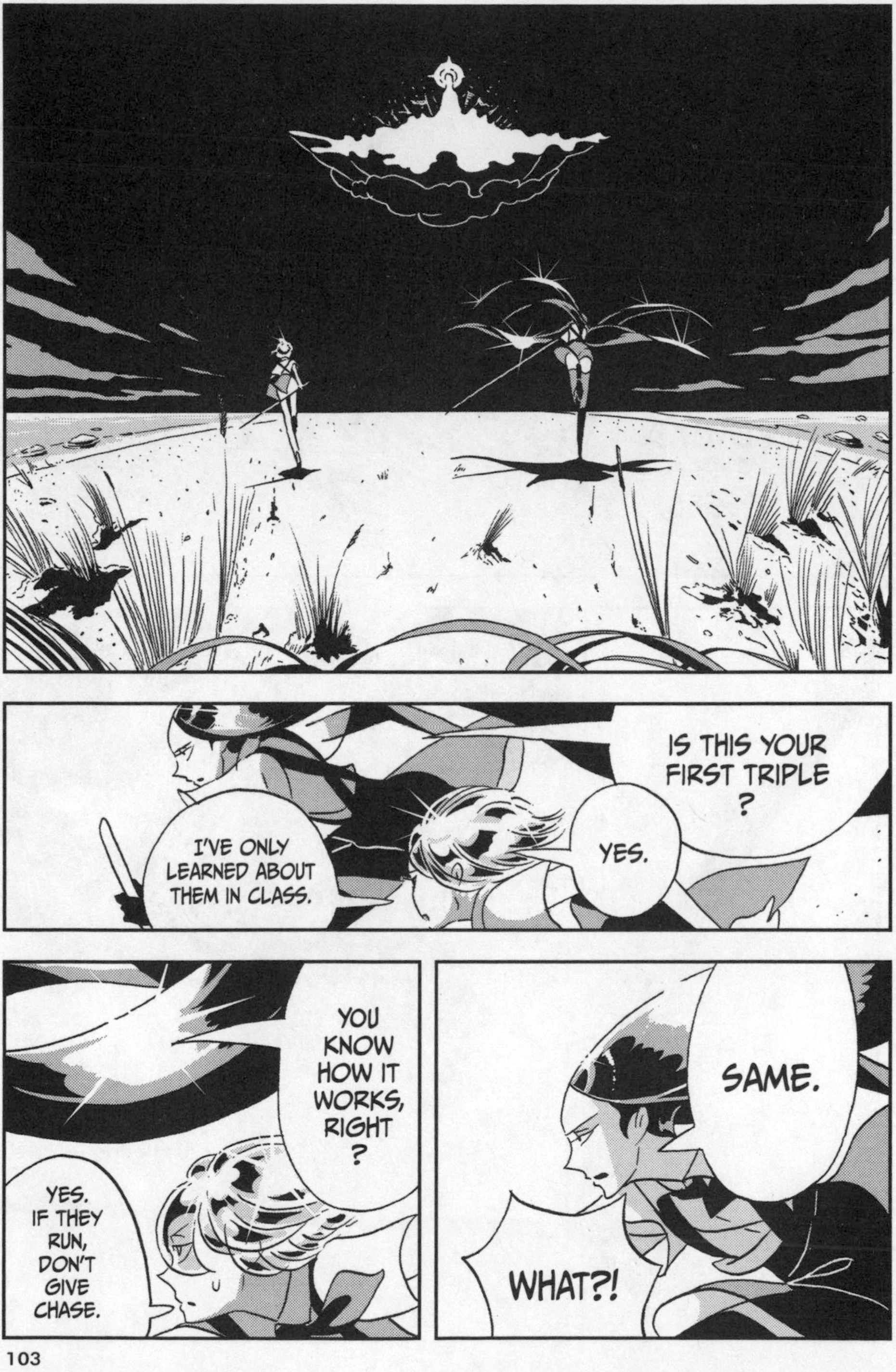
IS THIS YOUR FIRST TRIPLE?
YES.
I'VE ONLY LEARNED ABOUT THEM IN CLASS.
SAME.
WHAT?!
YOU KNOW HOW IT WORKS, RIGHT?
YES. IF THEY RUN, DON'T GIVE CHASE.

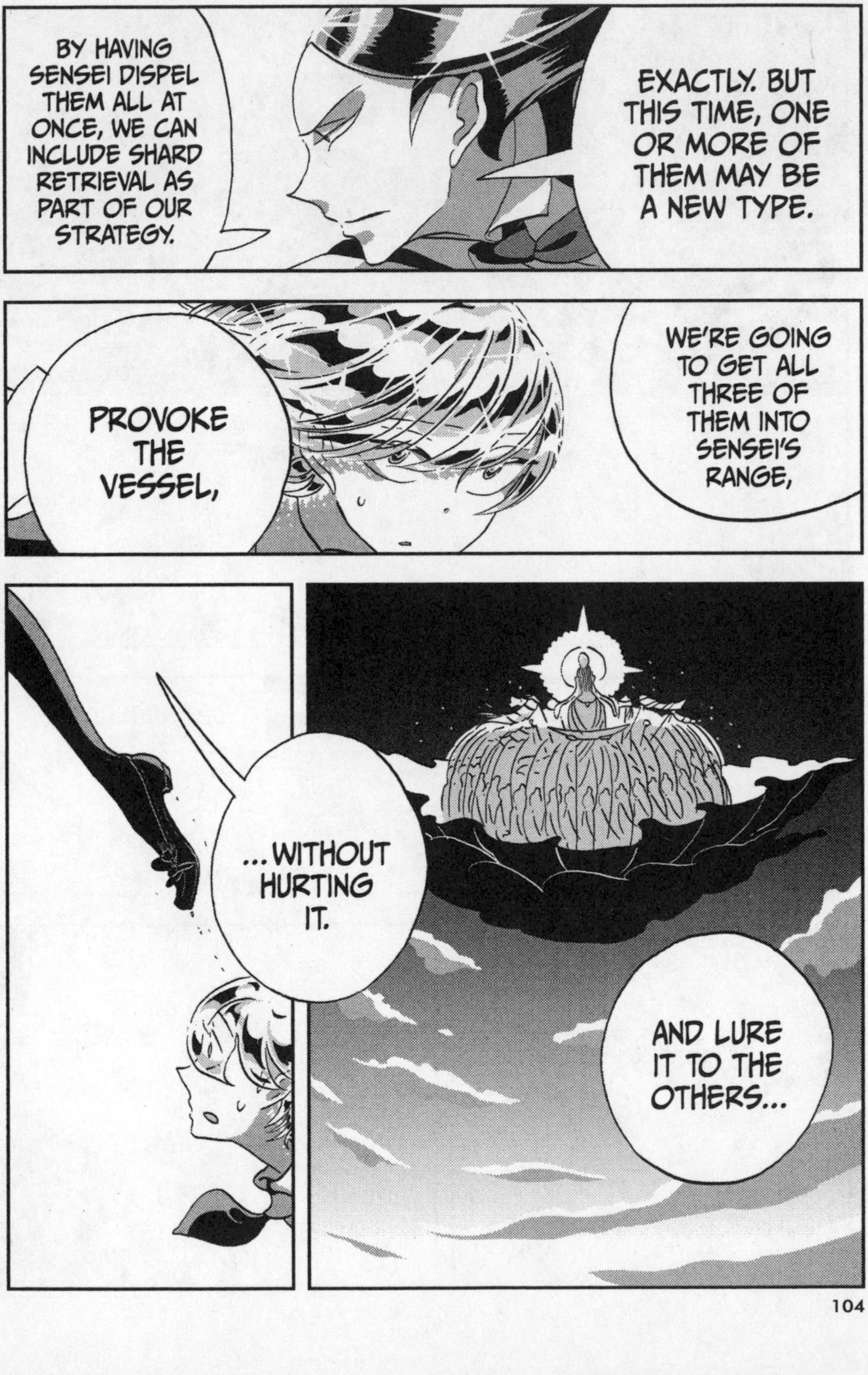
BY HAVING SENSEI DISPEL THEM ALL AT ONCE, WE CAN INCLUDE SHARD RETRIEVAL AS PART OF OUR STRATEGY.
EXACTLY. BUT THIS TIME, ONE OR MORE OF THEM MAY BE A NEW TYPE.
WE'RE GOING TO GET ALL THREE OF THEM INTO SENSEI'S RANGE,
PROVOKE THE VESSEL,
AND LURE IT TO THE OTHERS...
...WITHOUT HURTING IT.

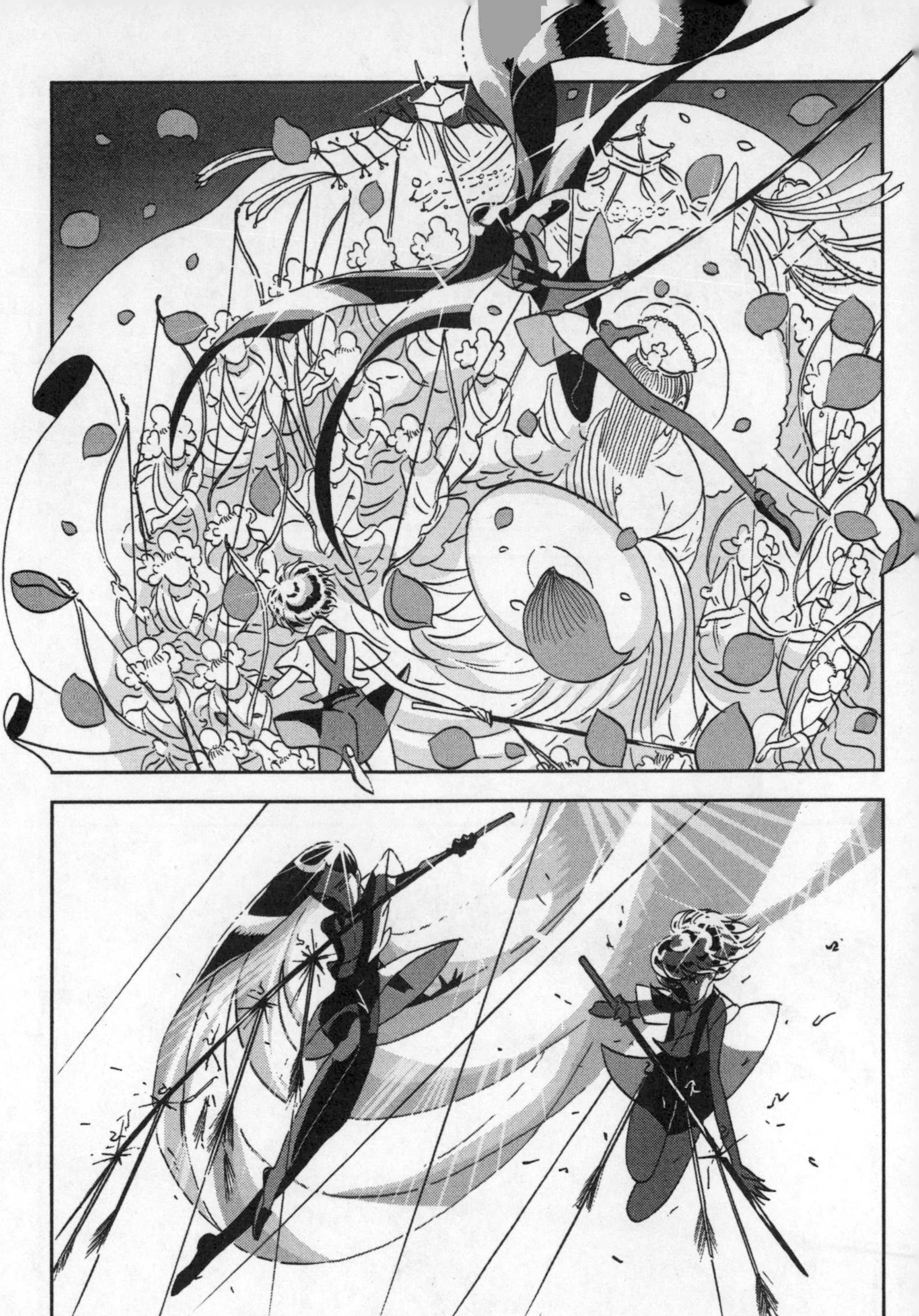

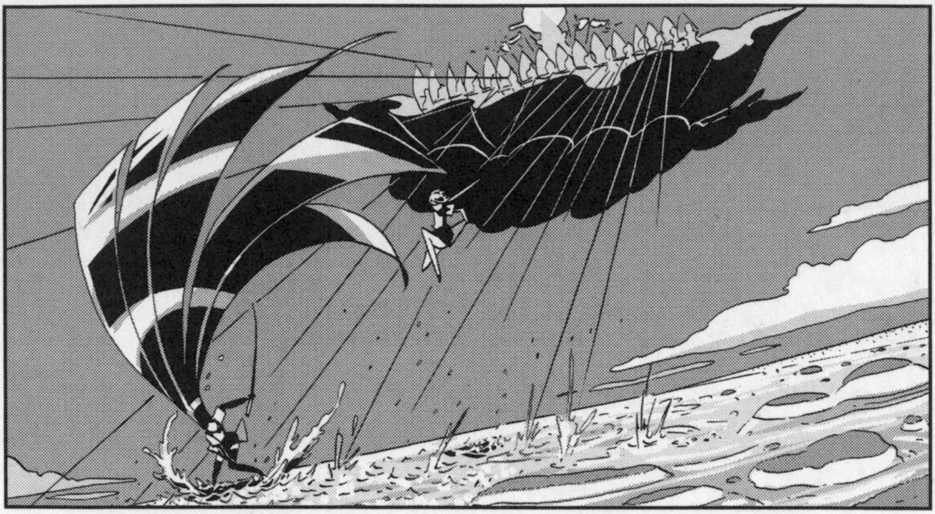
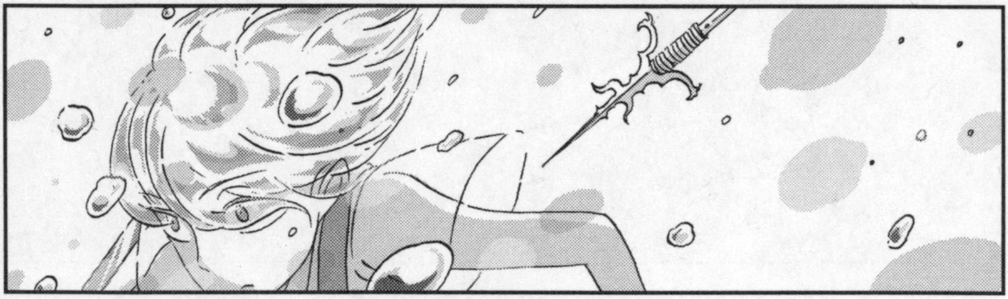
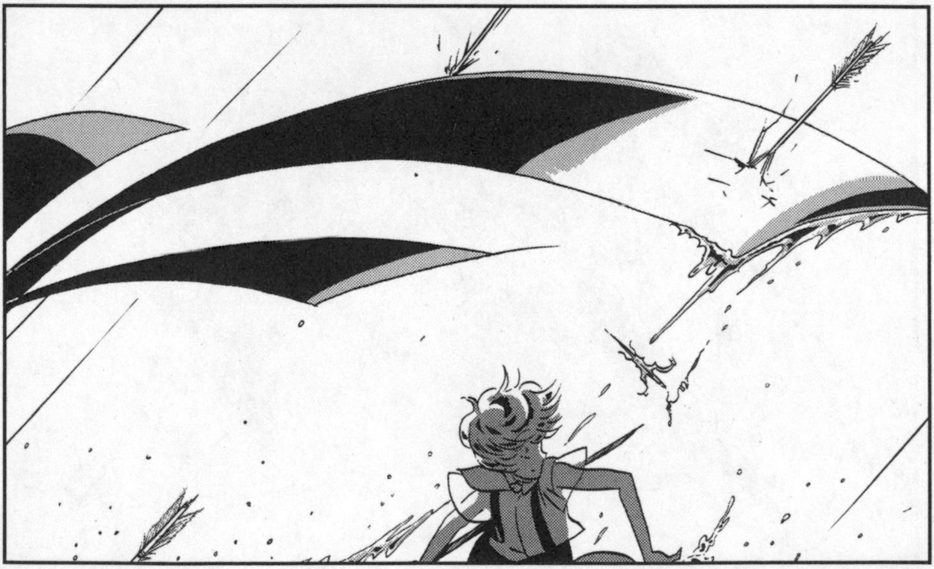

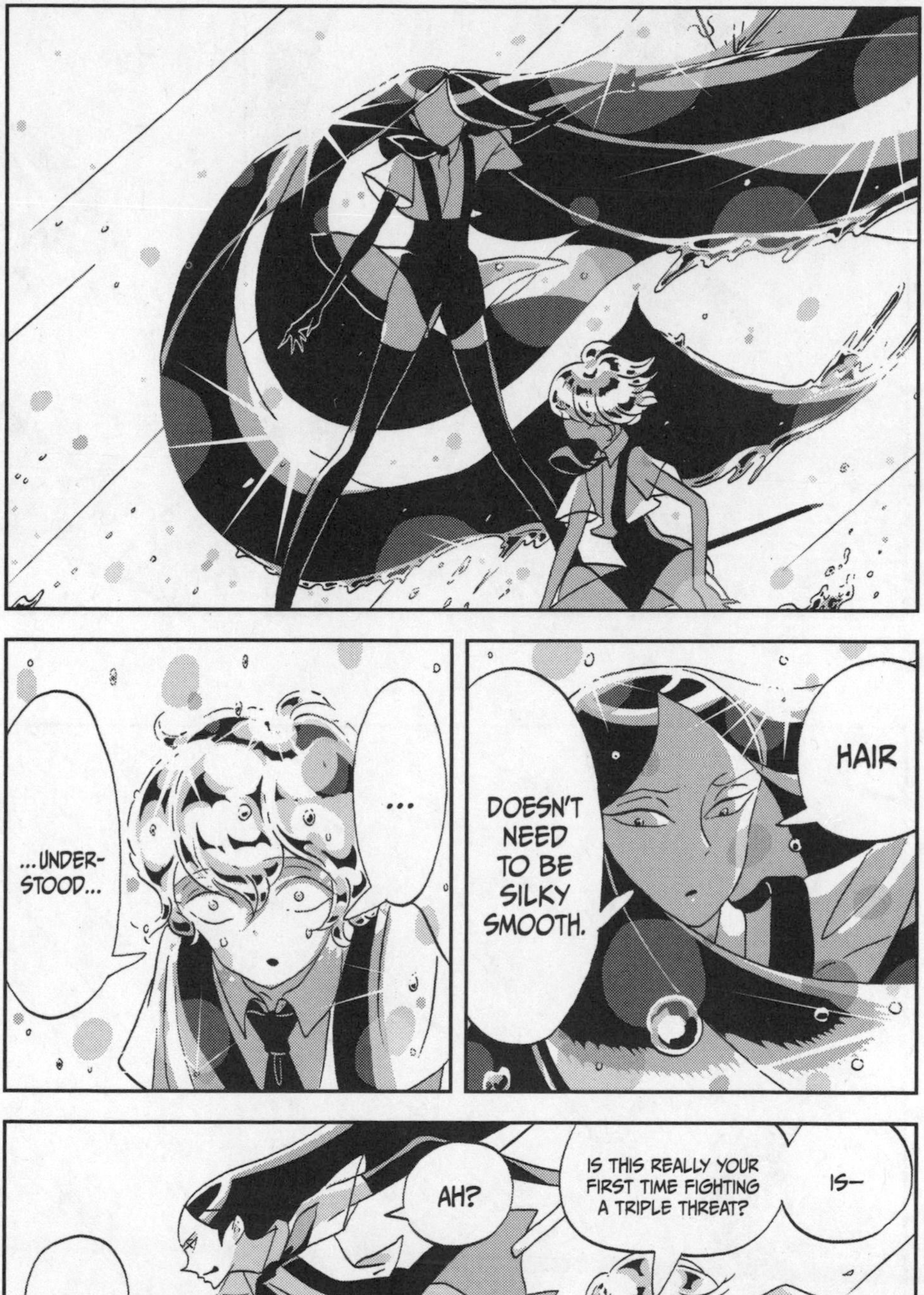
HAIR
DOESN'T NEED TO BE SILKY SMOOTH.
...
...UNDER-STOOD...
IS—
IS THIS REALLY YOUR FIRST TIME FIGHTING A TRIPLE THREAT?
AH?
YES.

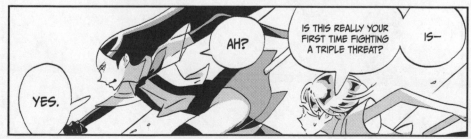

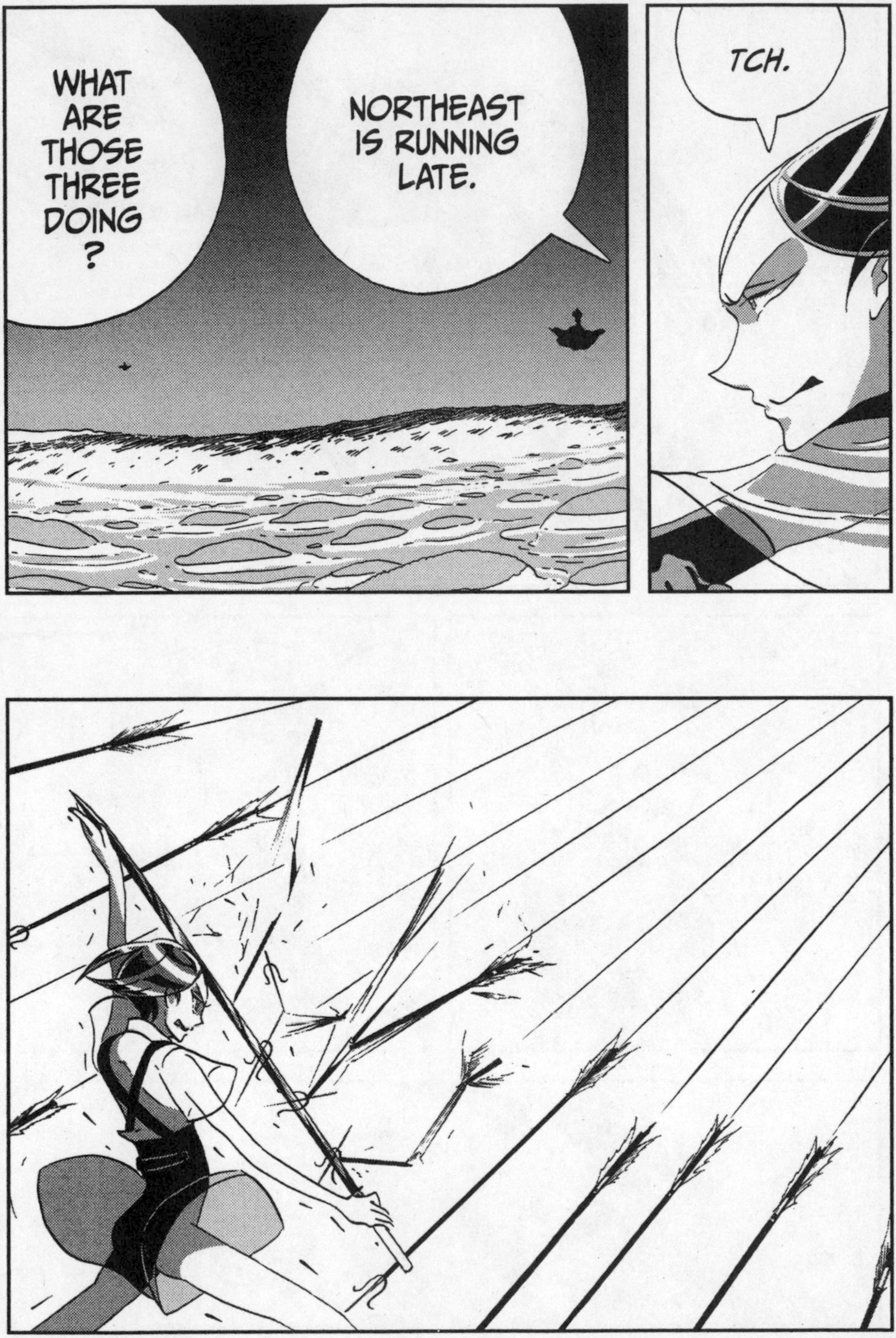
TCH.
NORTHEAST IS RUNNING LATE.
WHAT ARE THOSE THREE DOING?

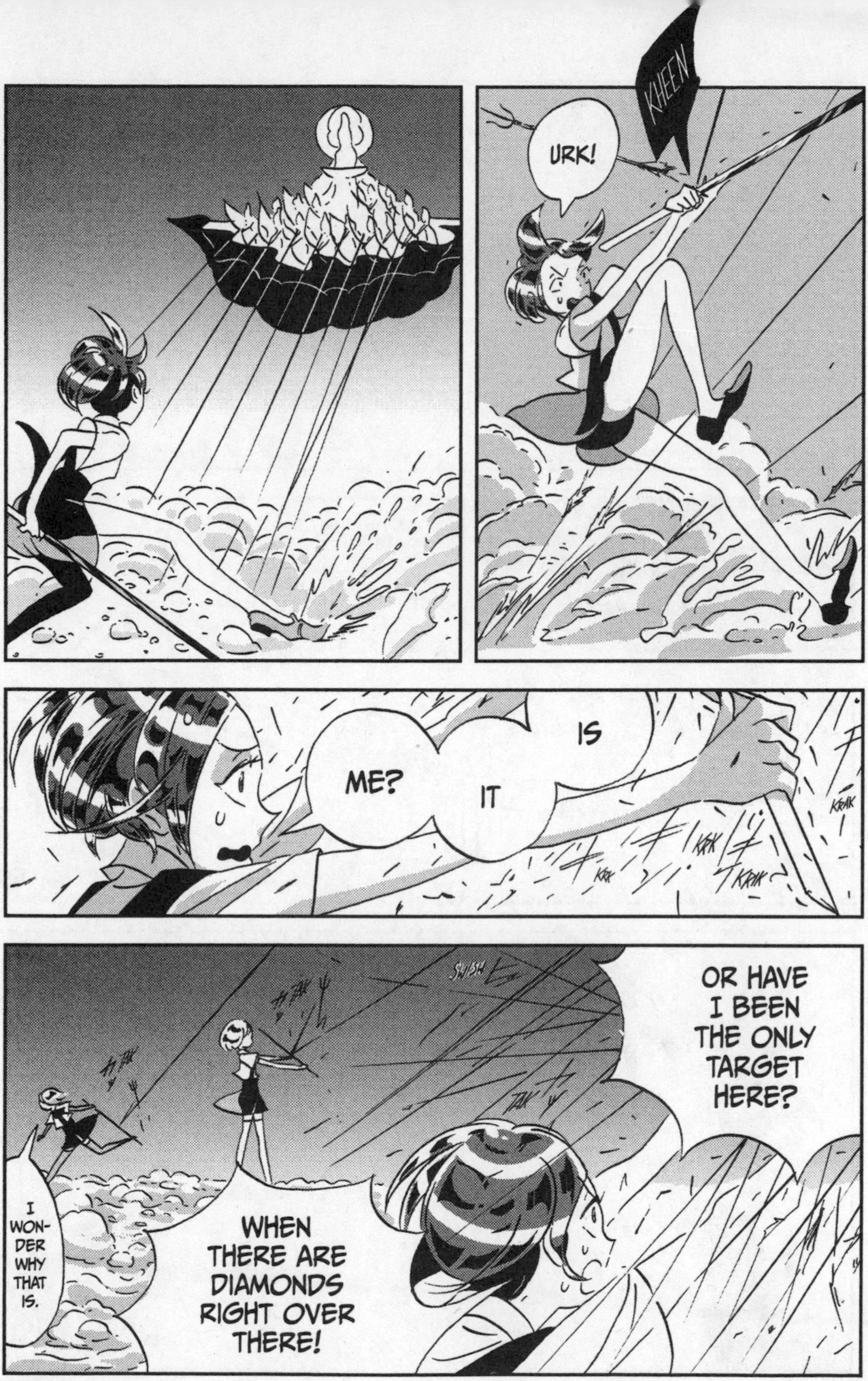
KHEEN
URK!
IS IT ME?
KRAK
KRK
KRK
KRIK
SWISH
OR HAVE I BEEN THE ONLY TARGET HERE?
TAK
TAK
TAK
WHEN THERE ARE DIAMONDS RIGHT OVER THERE!
I WONDER WHY THAT IS.

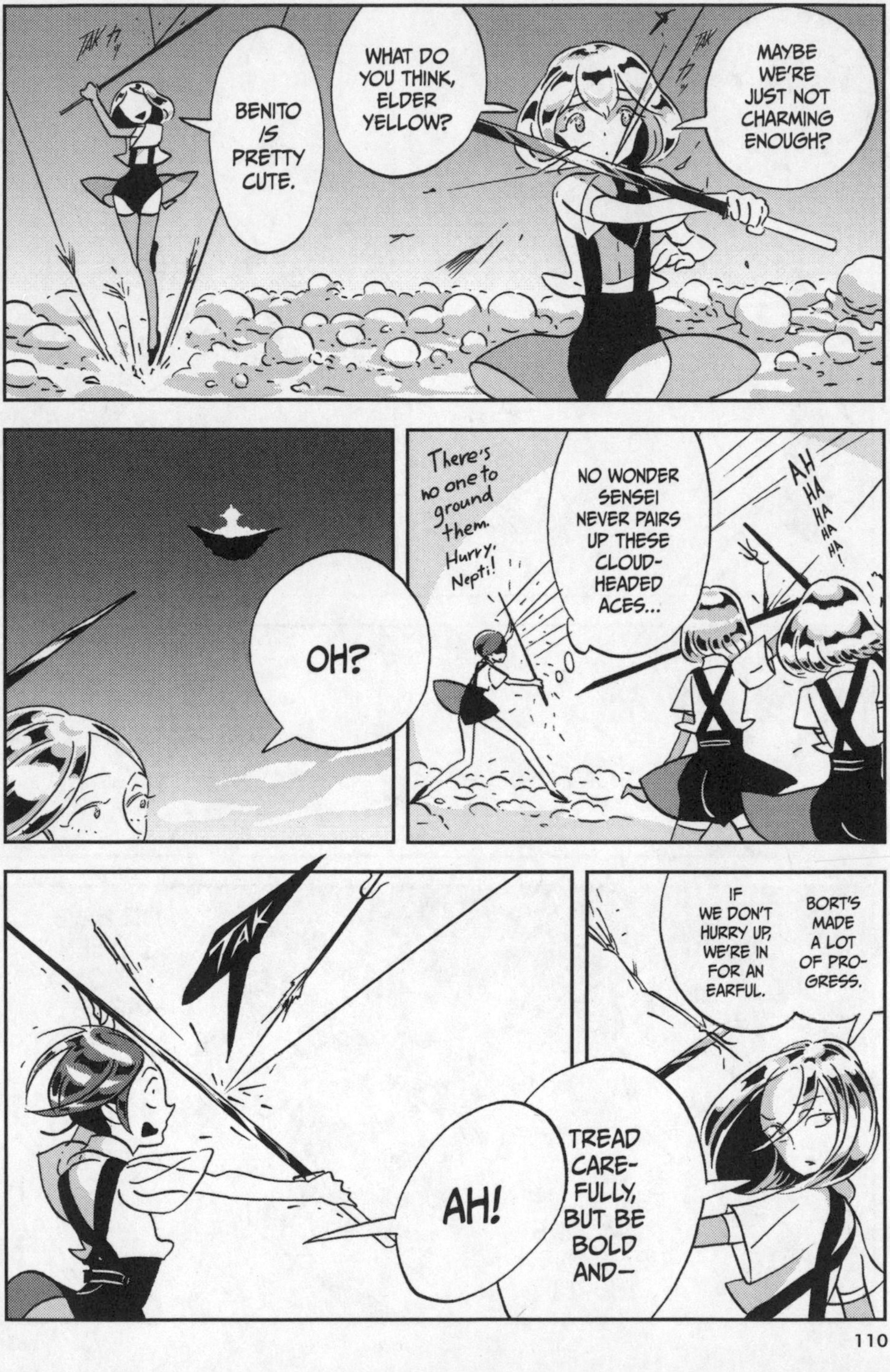
TAK
TAK
MAYBE WE'RE JUST NOT CHARMING ENOUGH?
WHAT DO YOU THINK, ELDER YELLOW?
BENITO IS PRETTY CUTE.
AH HA HA HA HA!
NO WONDER SENSEI NEVER PAIRS UP THESE CLOUD-HEADED ACES...
There's no one to ground them. Hurry, Nepti!
OH?
BORT'S MADE A LOT OF PROGRESS.
IF WE DON'T HURRY UP, WE'RE IN FOR AN EARFUL.
TREAD CAREFULLY, BUT BE BOLD AND—
TAK
AH!

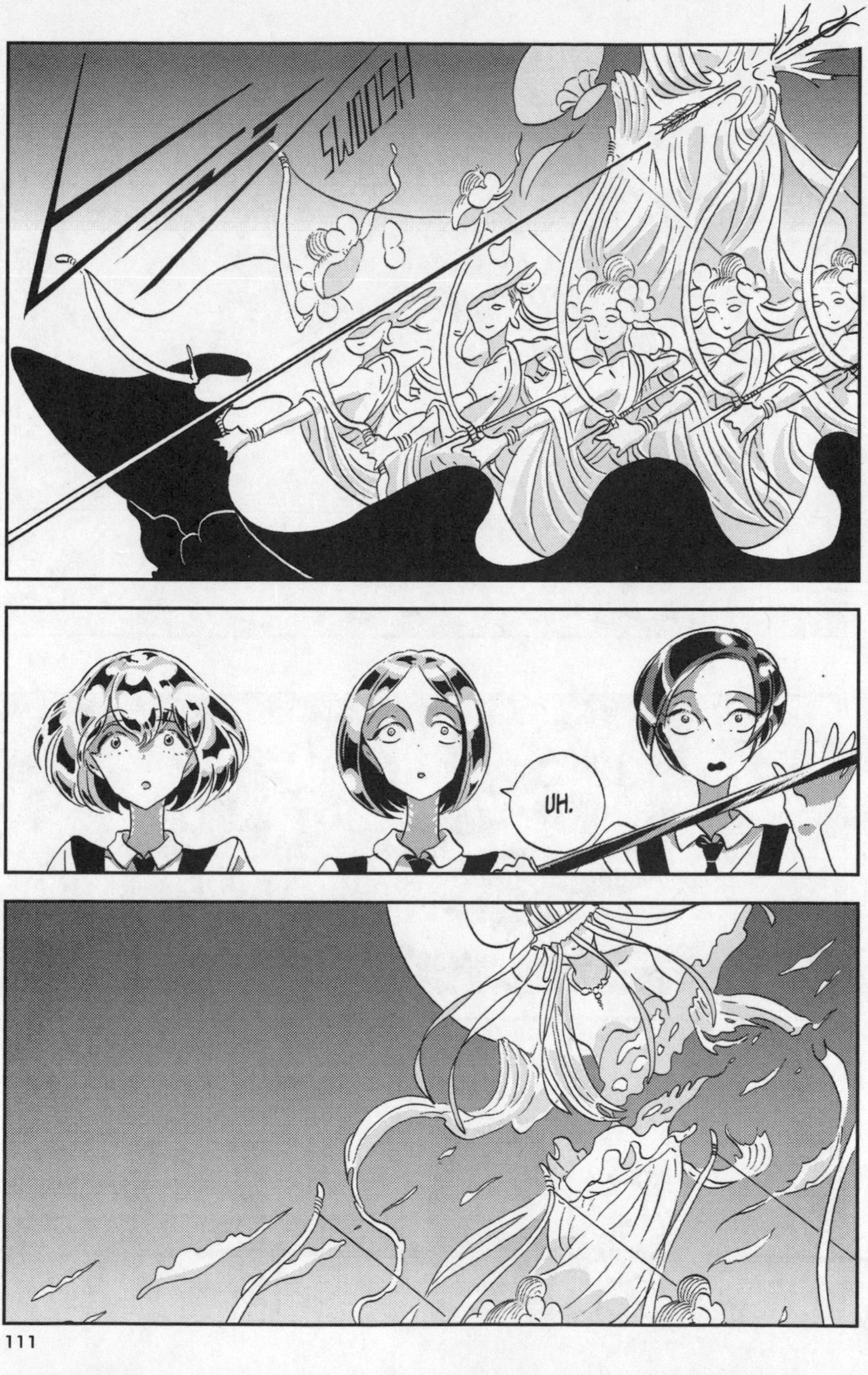
SWOOSH
UH.

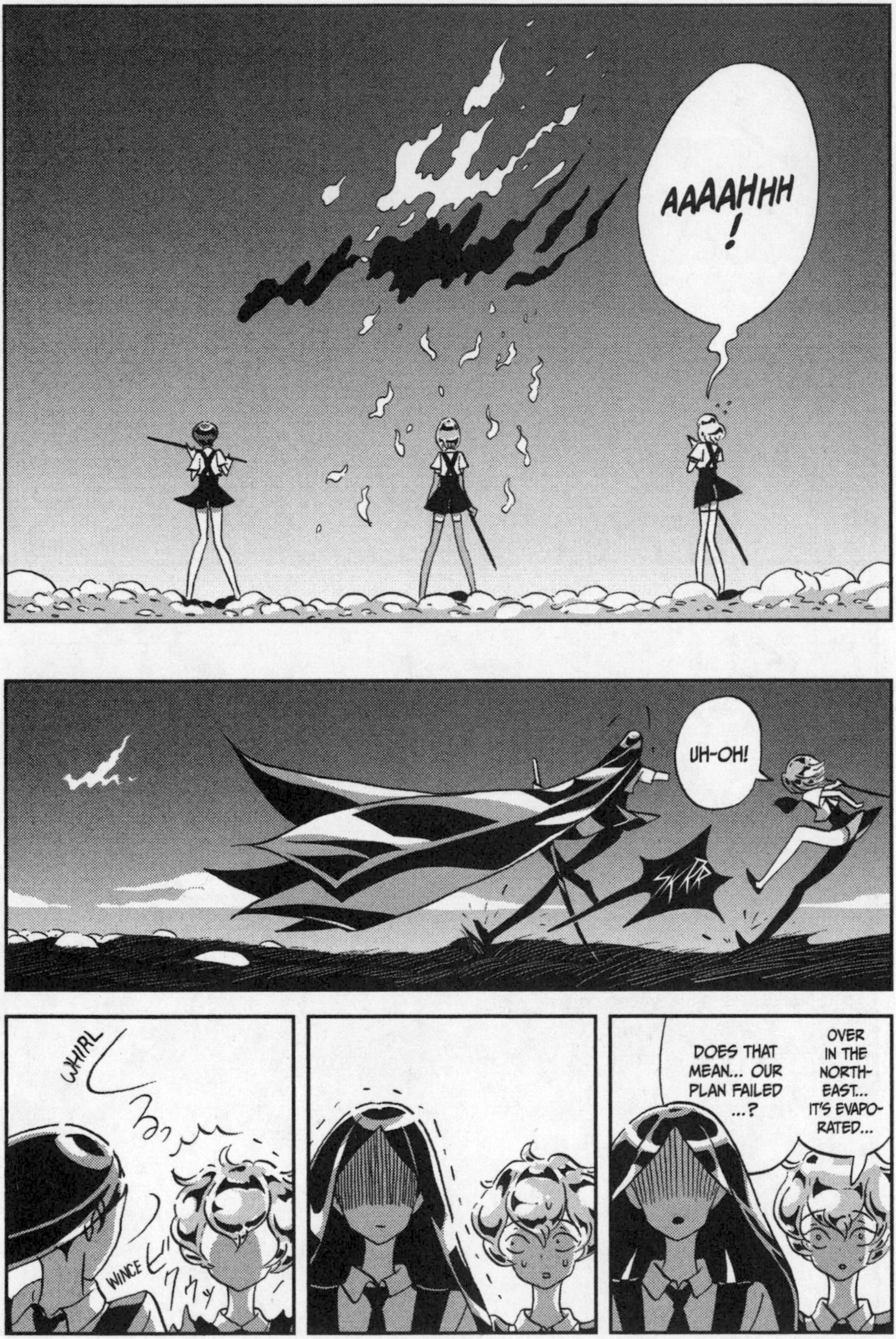
AAAAHHH!
UH-OH!
SKRR
OVER IN THE NORTH-EAST... IT'S EVAPORATED...
DOES THAT MEAN... OUR PLAN FAILED ...?
WHIRL
WINCE

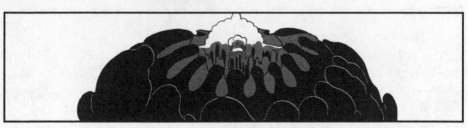

UH...

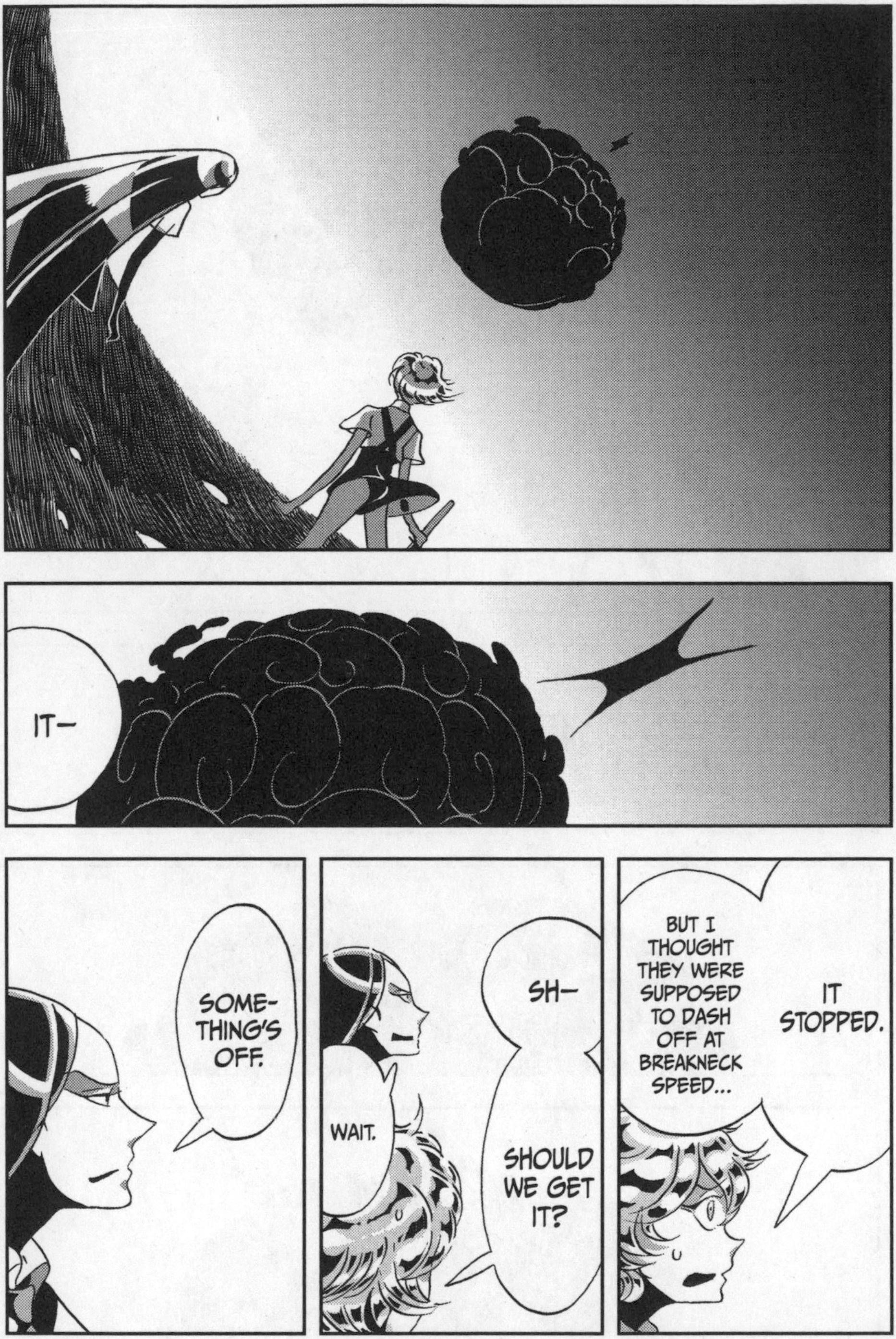
IT—
IT STOPPED.
BUT I THOUGHT THEY WERE SUPPOSED TO DASH OFF AT BREAKNECK SPEED...
SH—
SHOULD WE GET IT?
WAIT.
SOME-THING'S OFF.

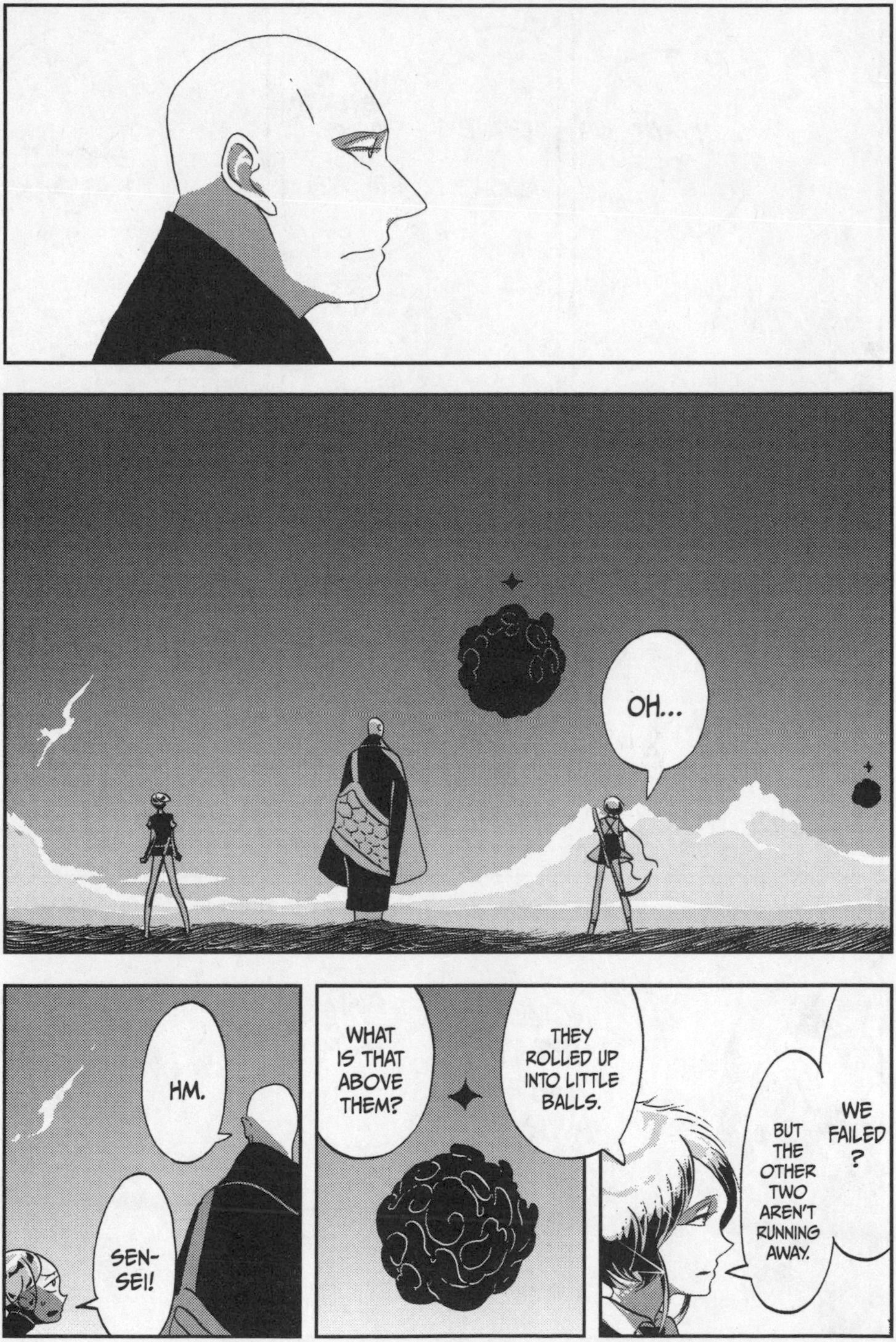
OH...
WE FAILED?
BUT THE OTHER TWO AREN'T RUNNING AWAY.
THEY ROLLED UP INTO LITTLE BALLS.
WHAT IS THAT ABOVE THEM?
HM.
SEN-SEI!

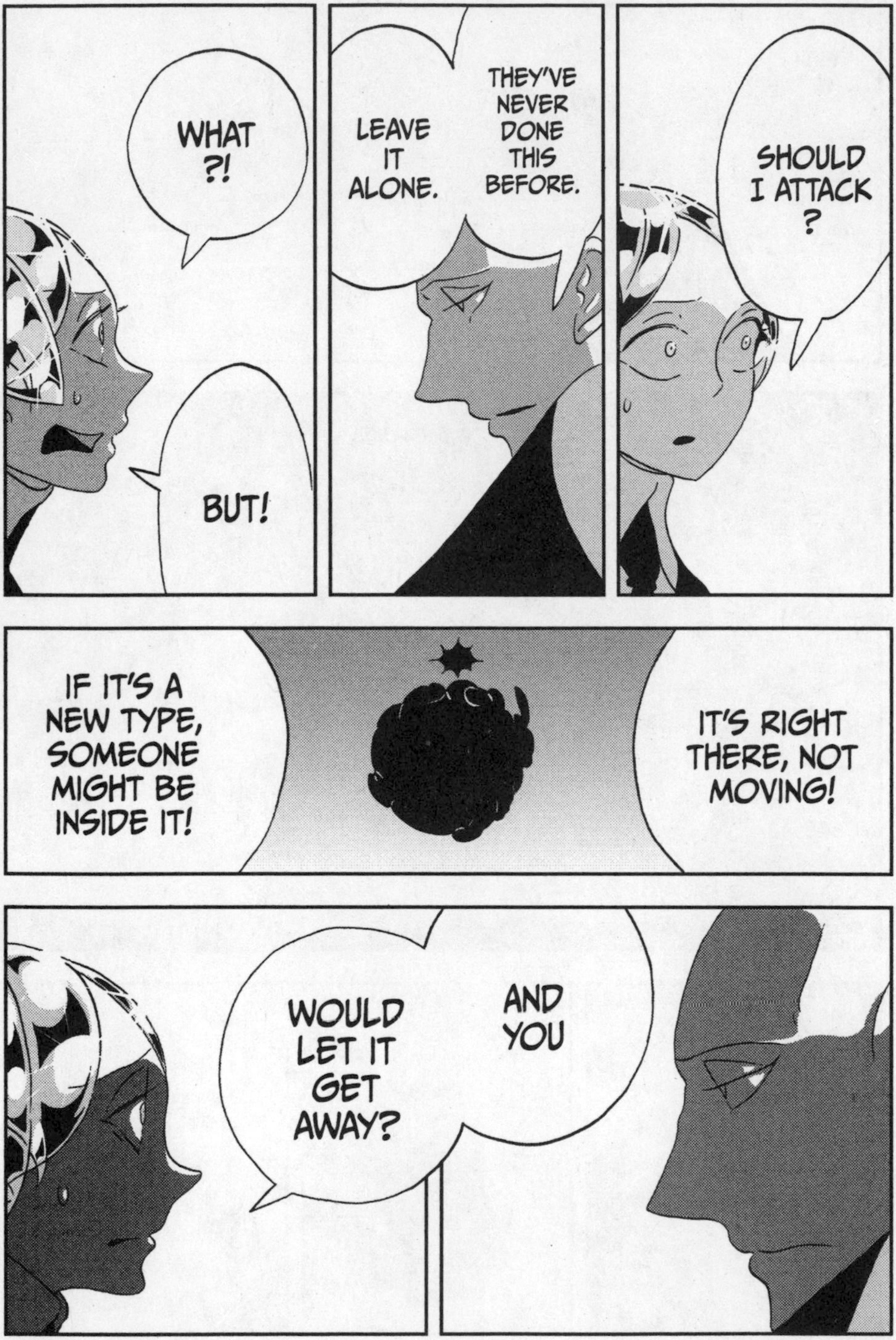

SHOULD I ATTACK ?
THEY'VE NEVER DONE THIS BEFORE.
LEAVE IT ALONE.
WHAT ?!
BUT!
IT'S RIGHT THERE, NOT MOVING!
IF IT'S A NEW TYPE, SOMEONE MIGHT BE INSIDE IT!
AND YOU
WOULD LET IT GET AWAY?

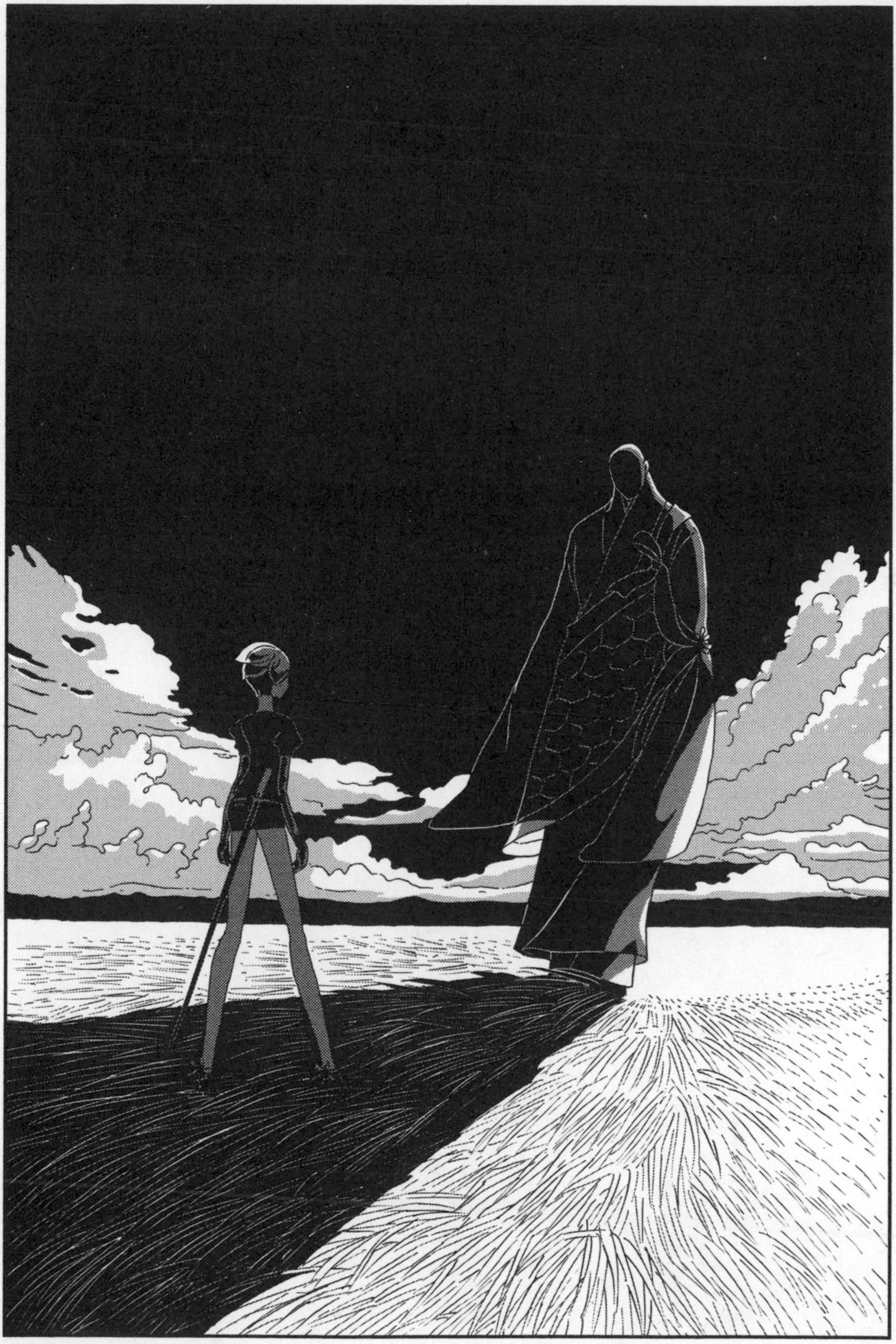

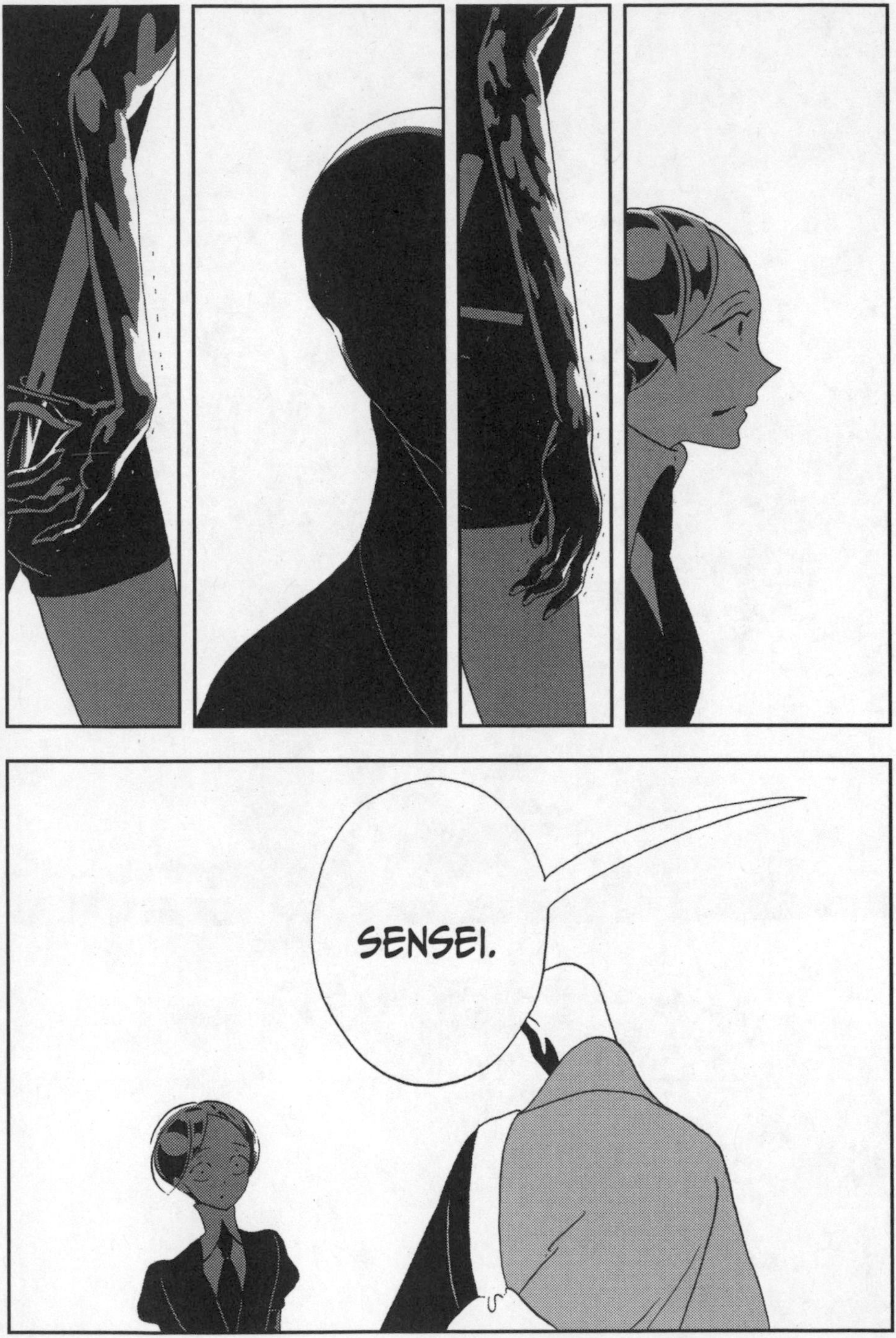
SENSEI.

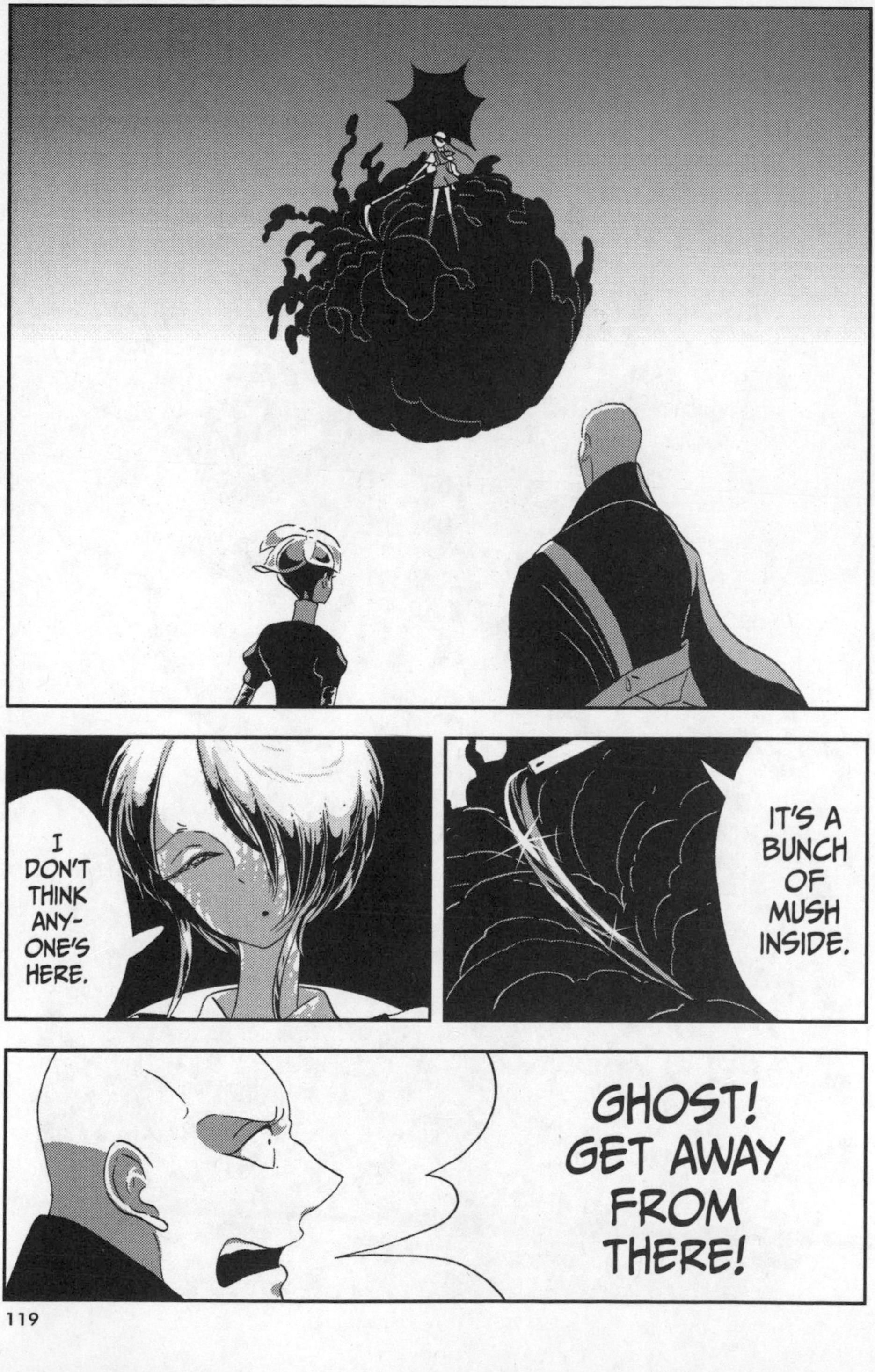
IT'S A BUNCH OF MUSH INSIDE.
I DON'T THINK ANY-ONE'S HERE.
GHOST! GET AWAY FROM THERE!

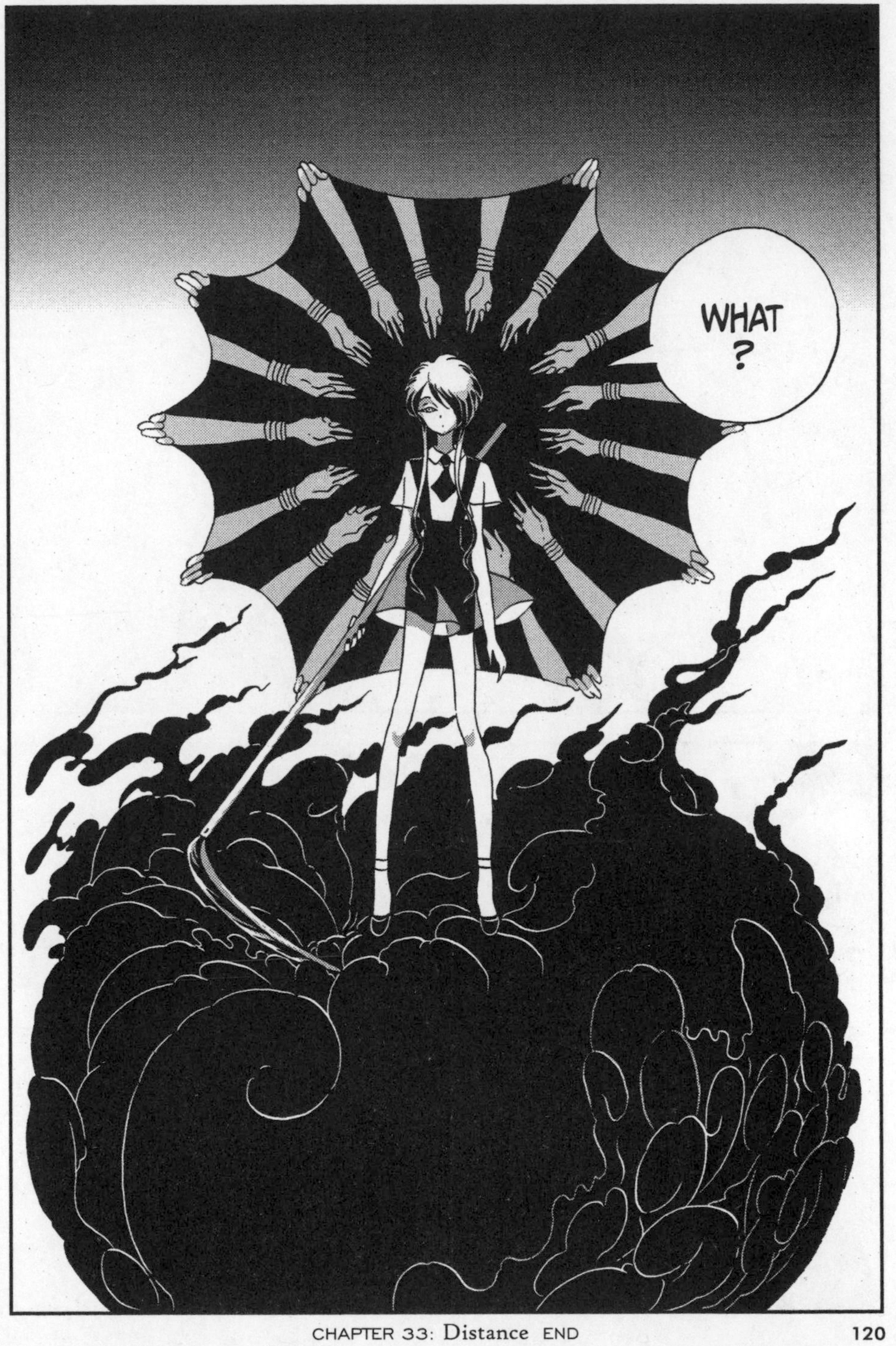
WHAT
?

CHAPTER 33: Distance END

CHAPTER 34:

Reversal

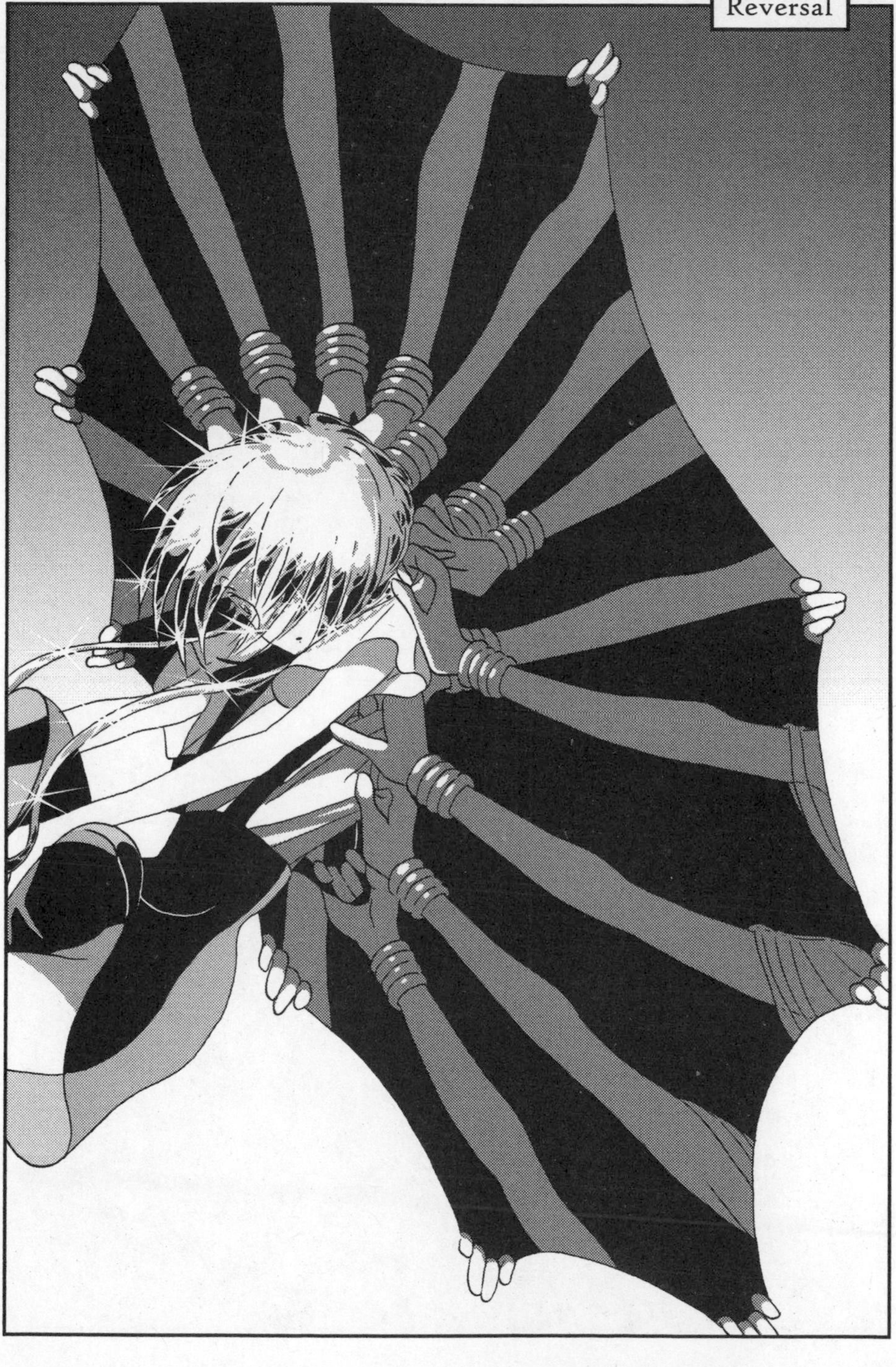

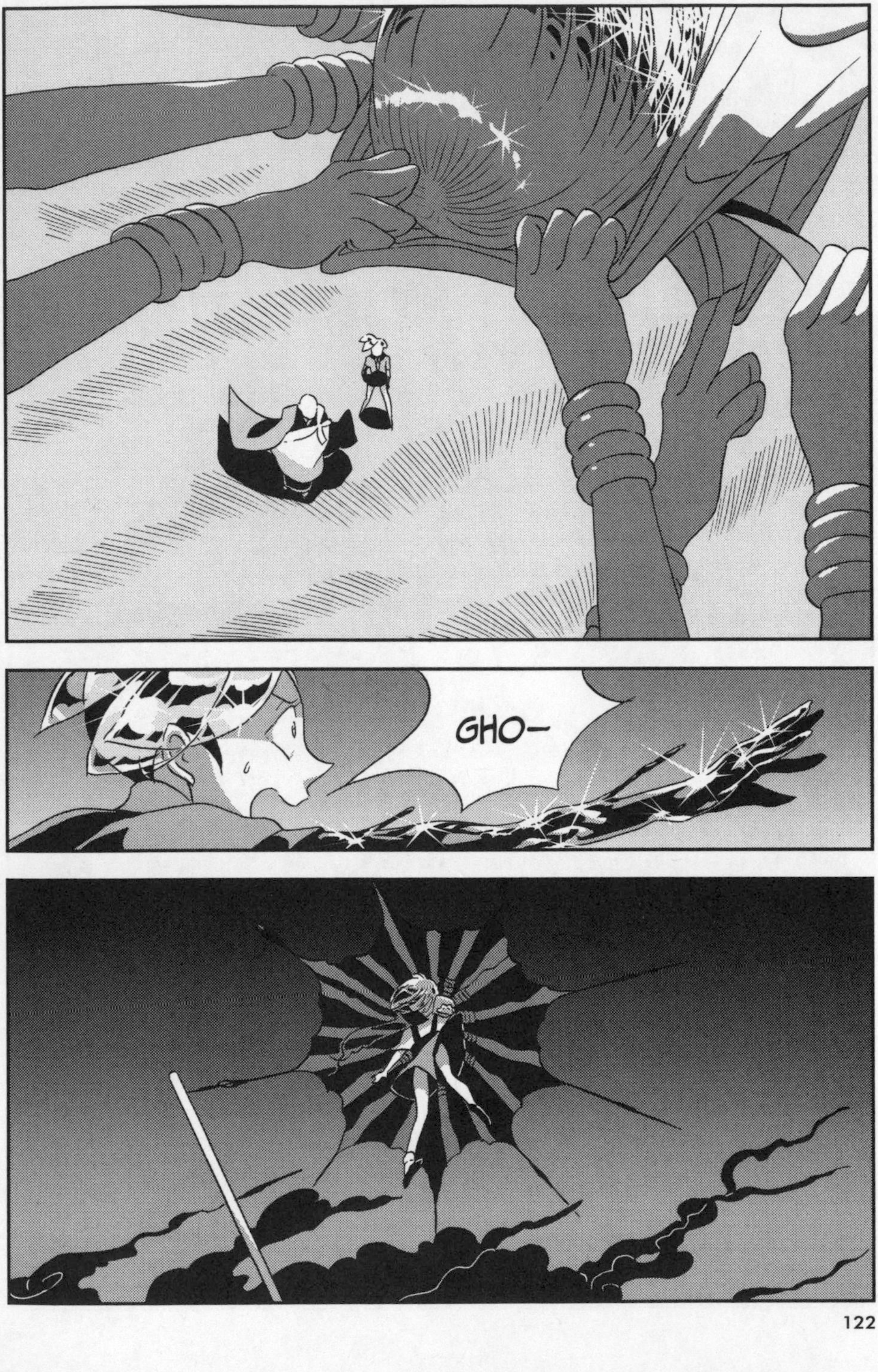
GHO-

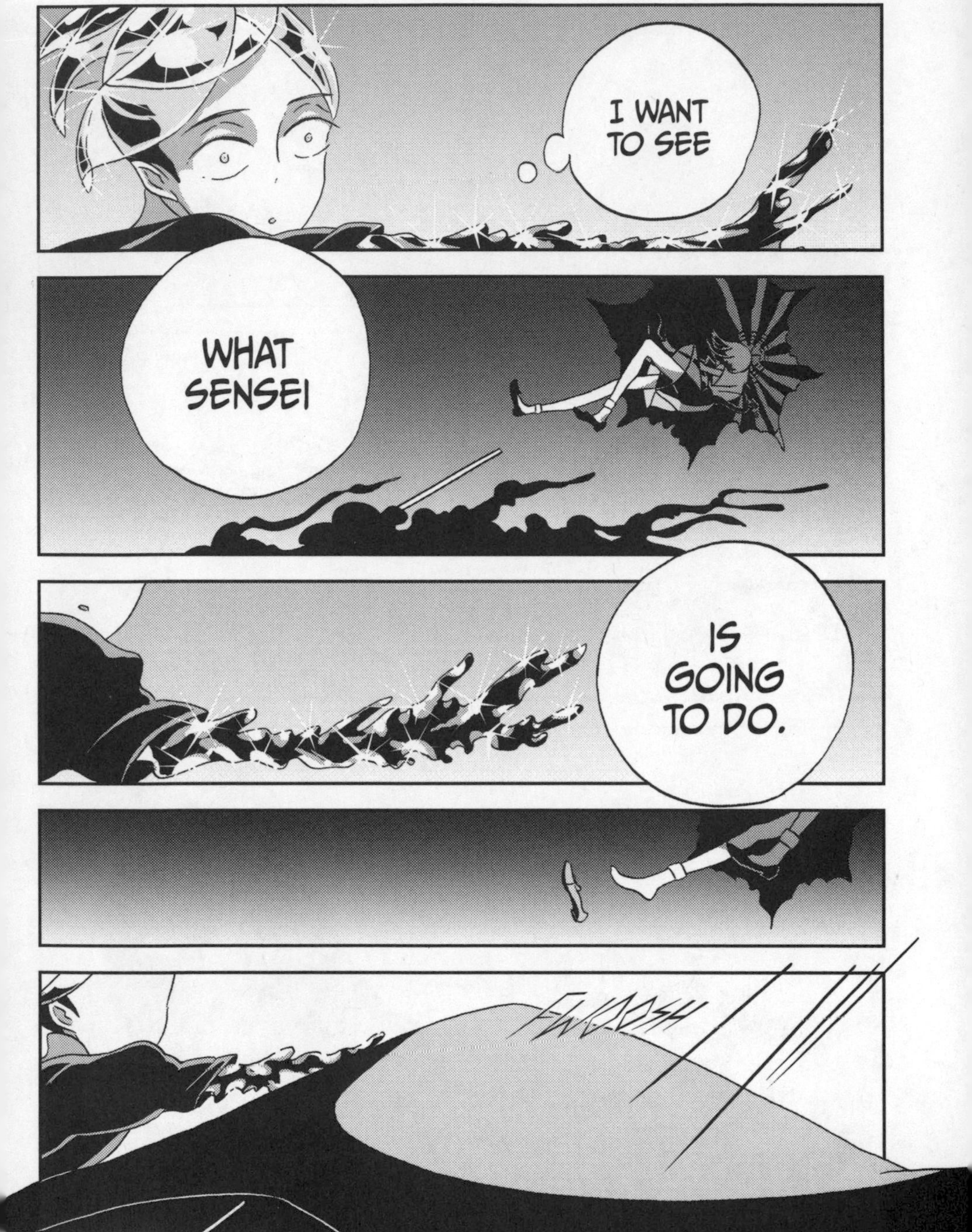
I WANT TO SEE
WHAT SENSEI
IS GOING TO DO.
FWOOSH

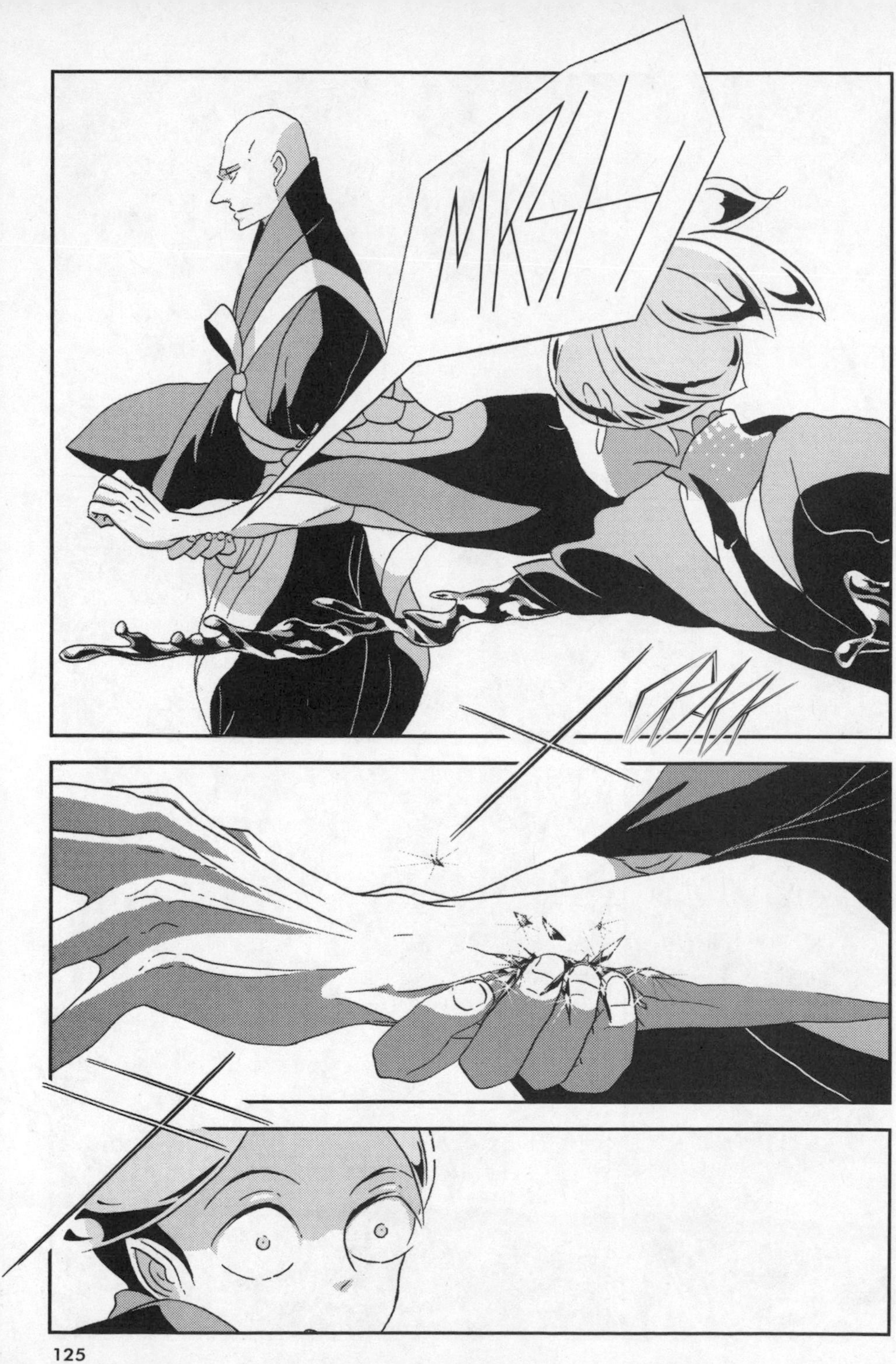
MRSH
CRACK

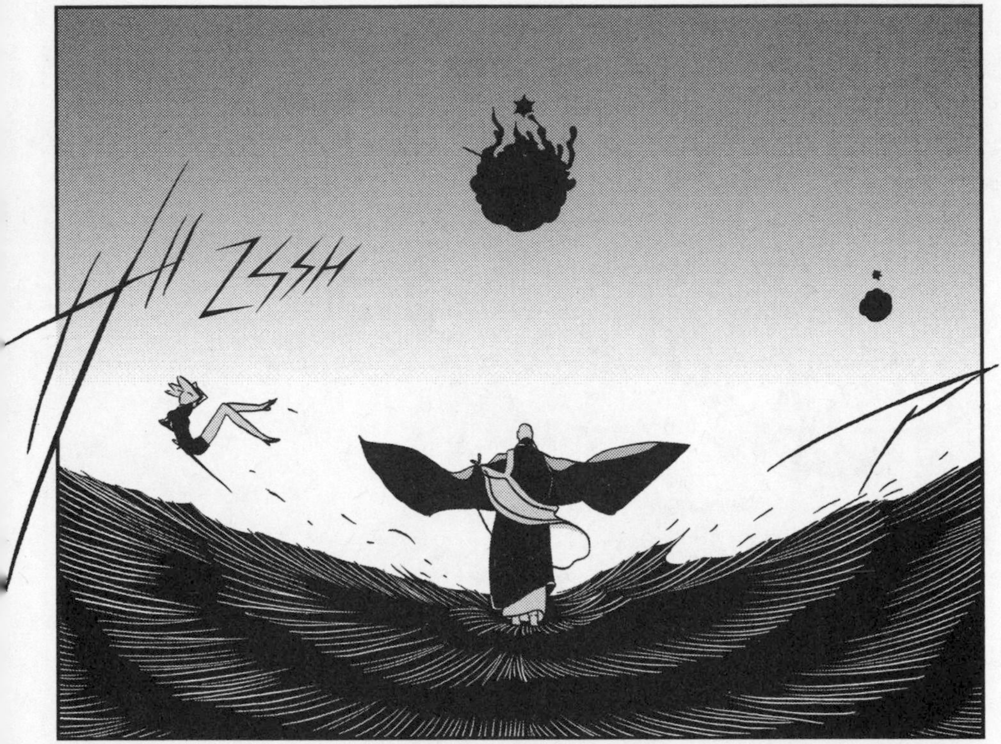
ZSSH

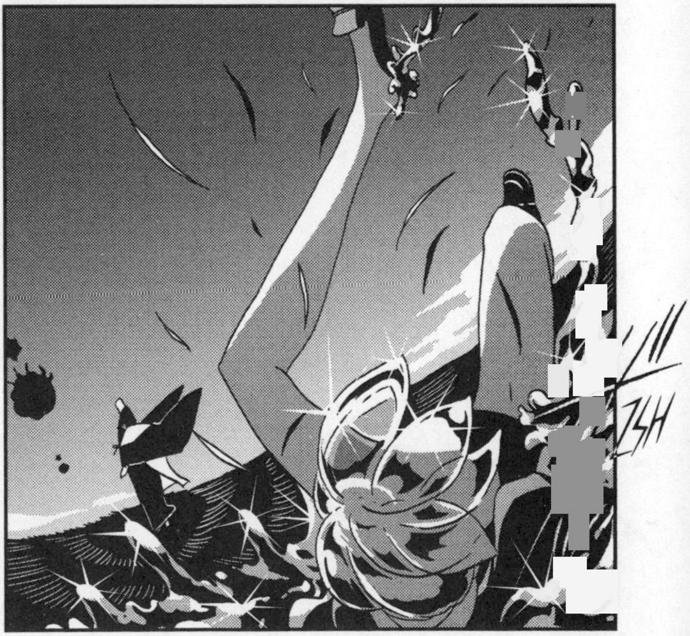
ZSH

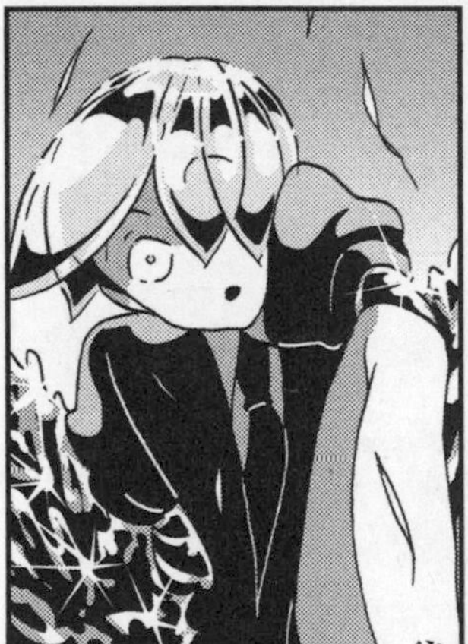

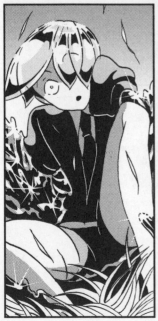

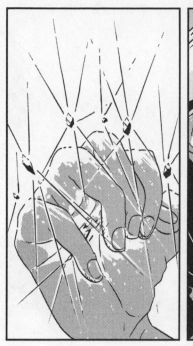

SWISH!

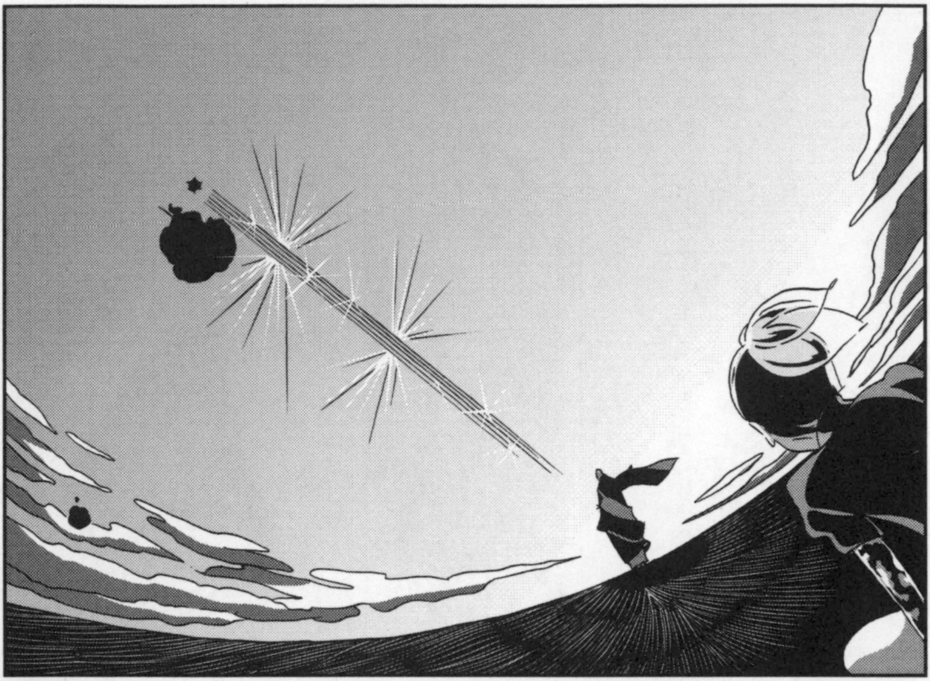

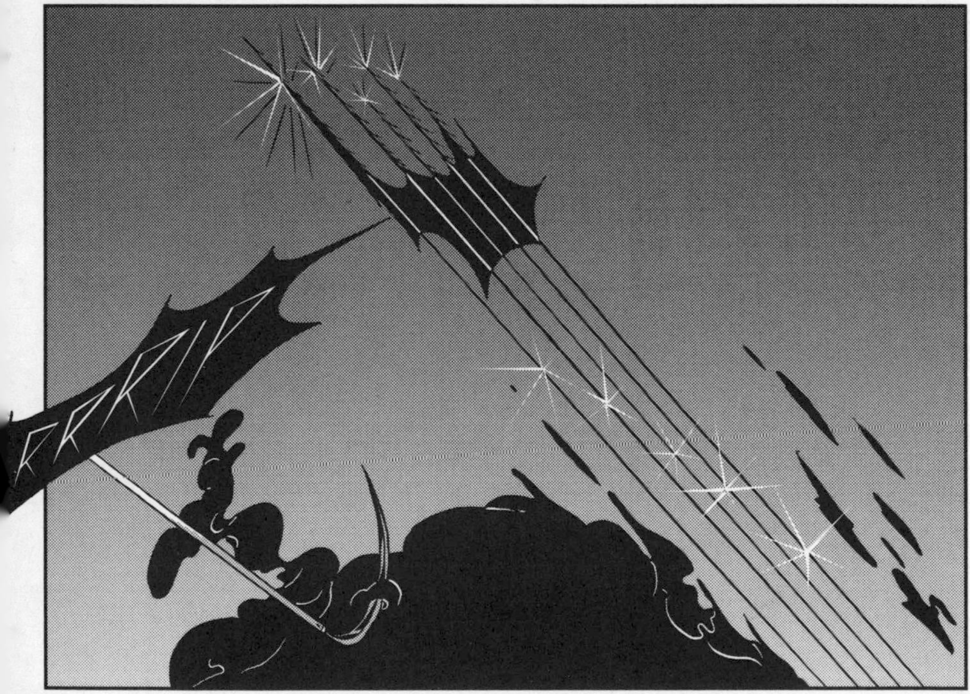
RRRIP

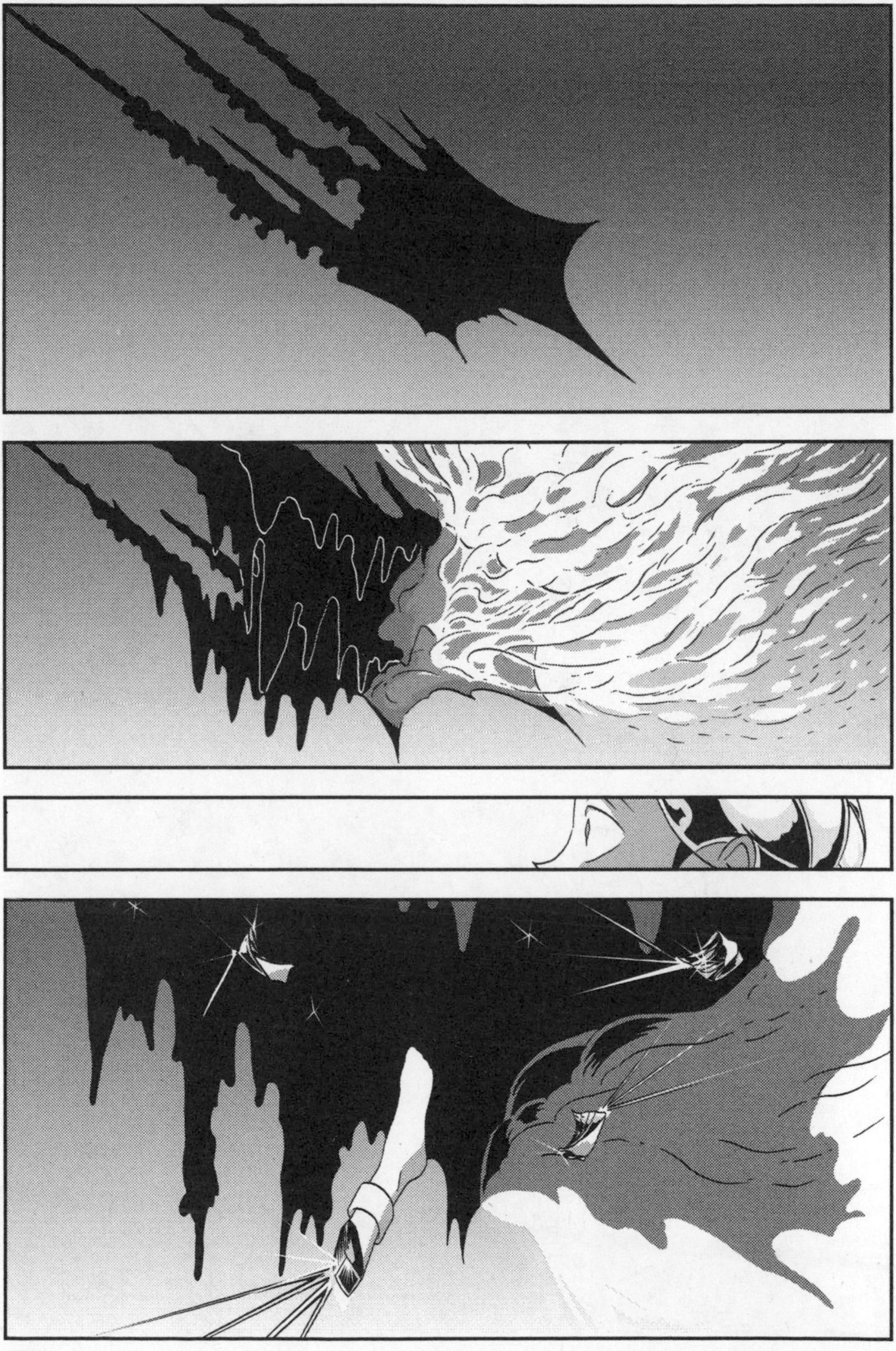

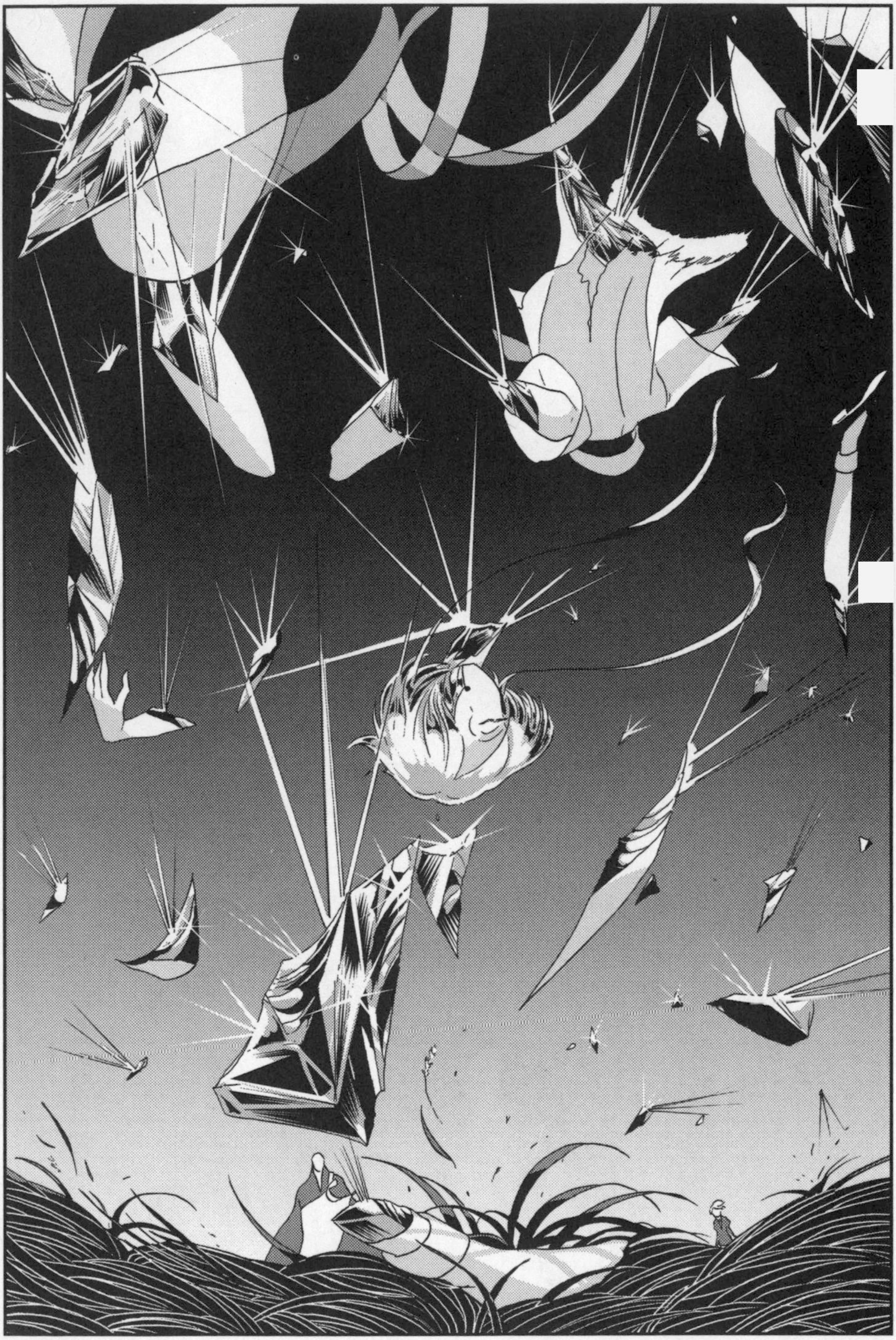

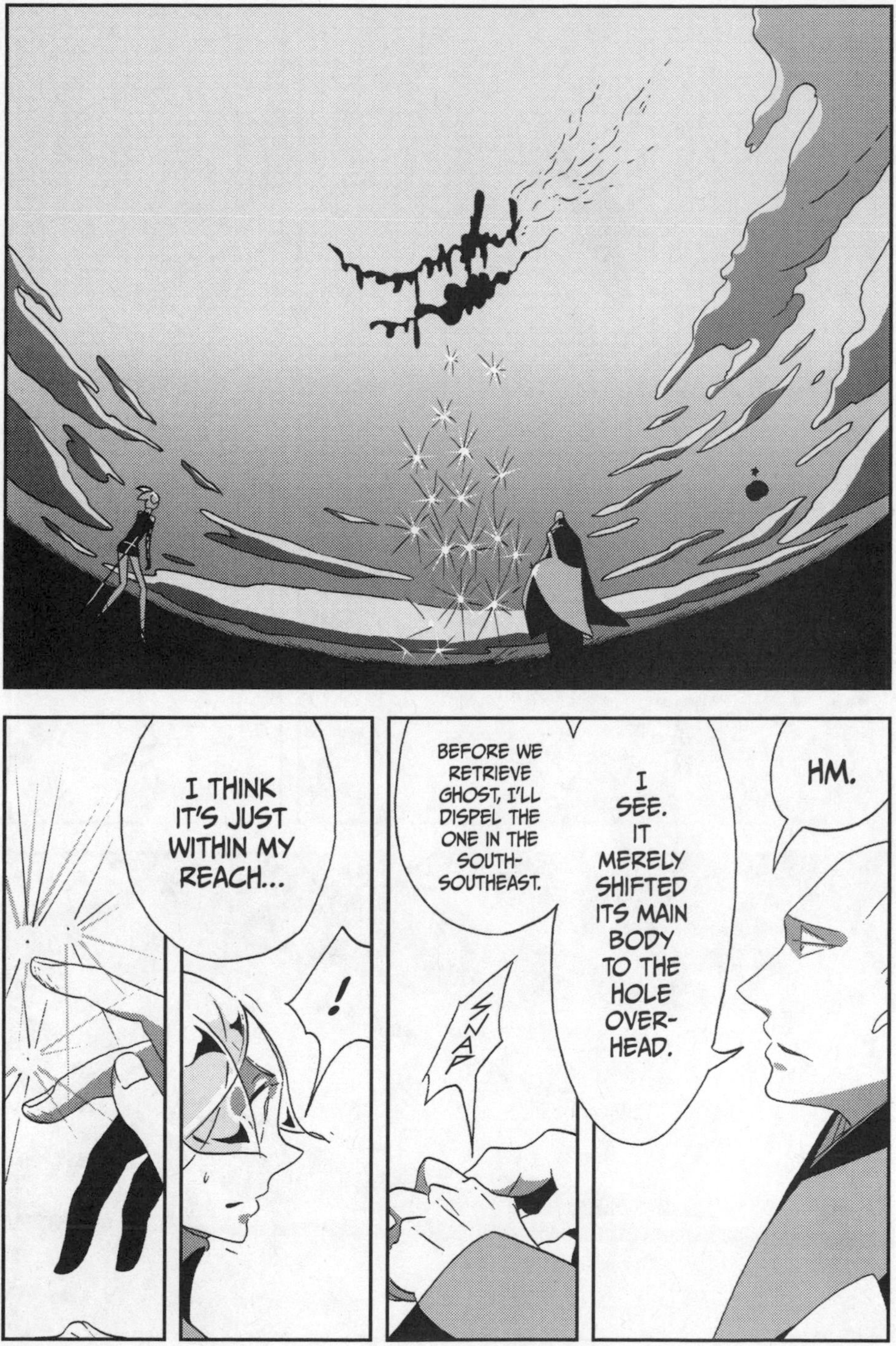

HM.
I SEE. IT MERELY SHIFTED ITS MAIN BODY TO THE HOLE OVERHEAD.
BEFORE WE RETRIEVE GHOST, I'LL DISPEL THE ONE IN THE SOUTH-SOUTHEAST.
SNAP
!
I THINK IT'S JUST WITHIN MY REACH...

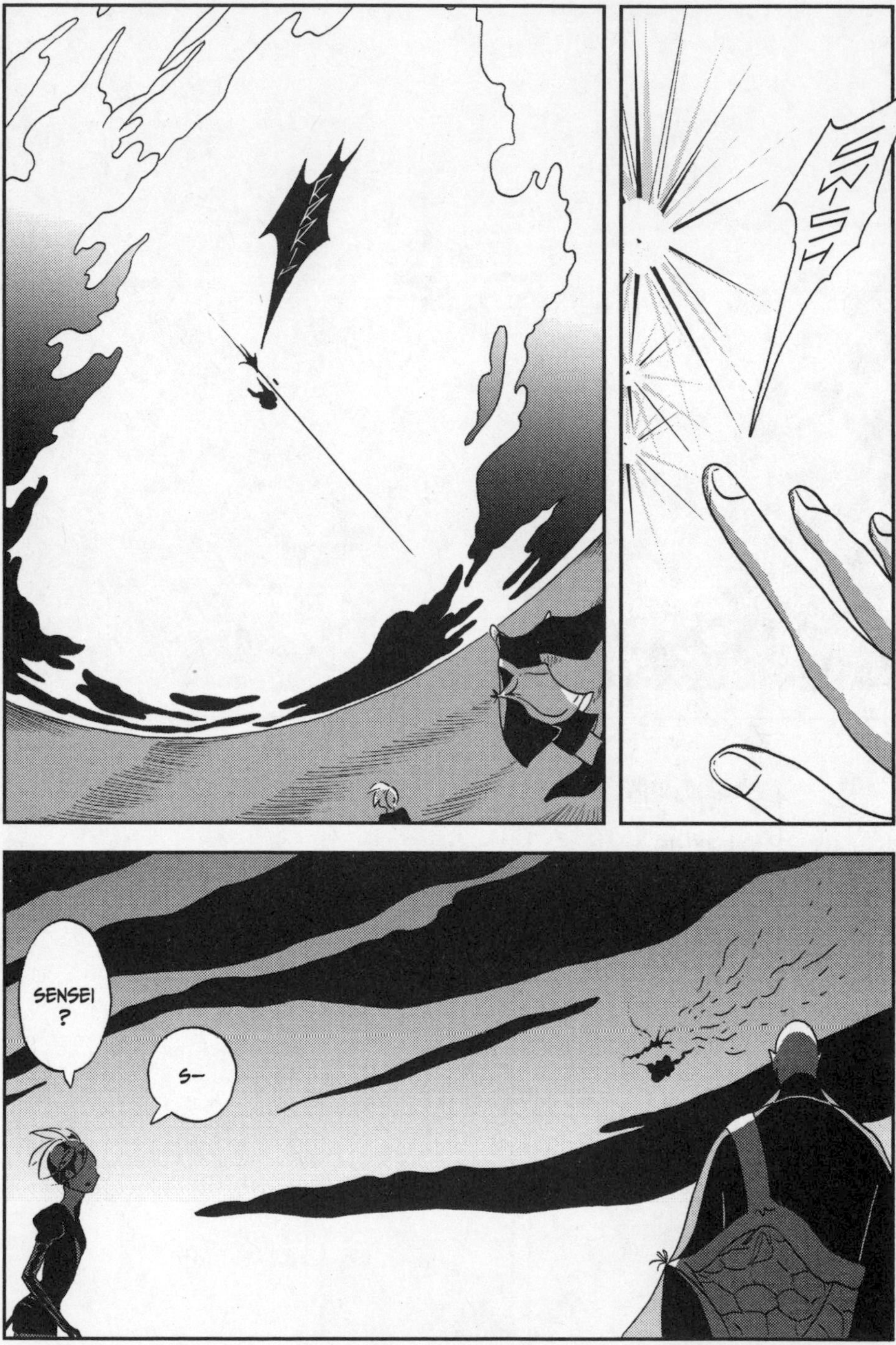
SWISH
SENSEI?
S-

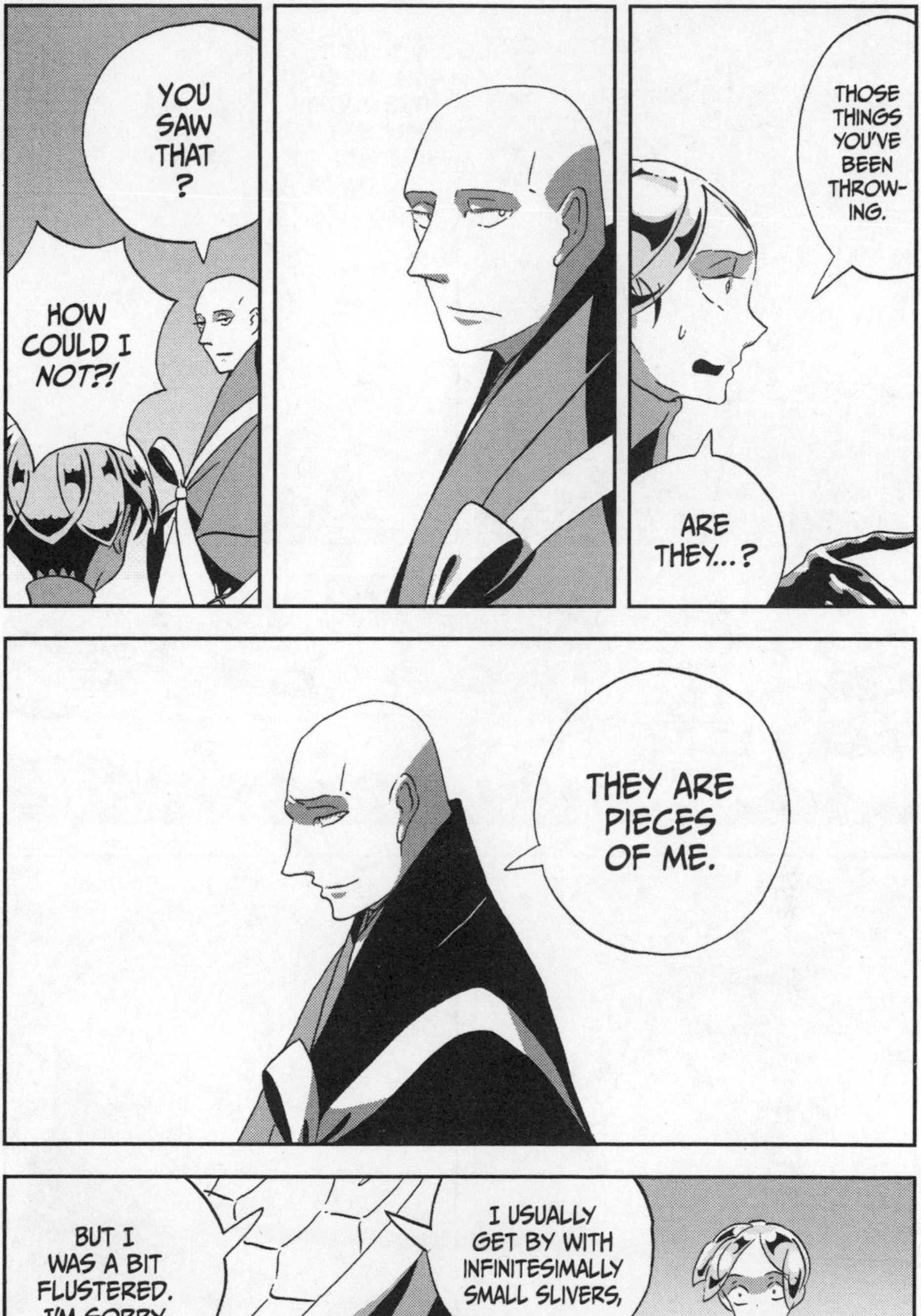
THOSE THINGS YOU'VE BEEN THROW-ING.
ARE THEY...?
YOU SAW THAT?
HOW COULD I NOT?!
THEY ARE PIECES OF ME.
I USUALLY GET BY WITH INFINITESIMALLY SMALL SLIVERS,
BUT I WAS A BIT FLUSTERED. I'M SORRY.

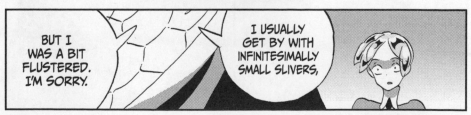

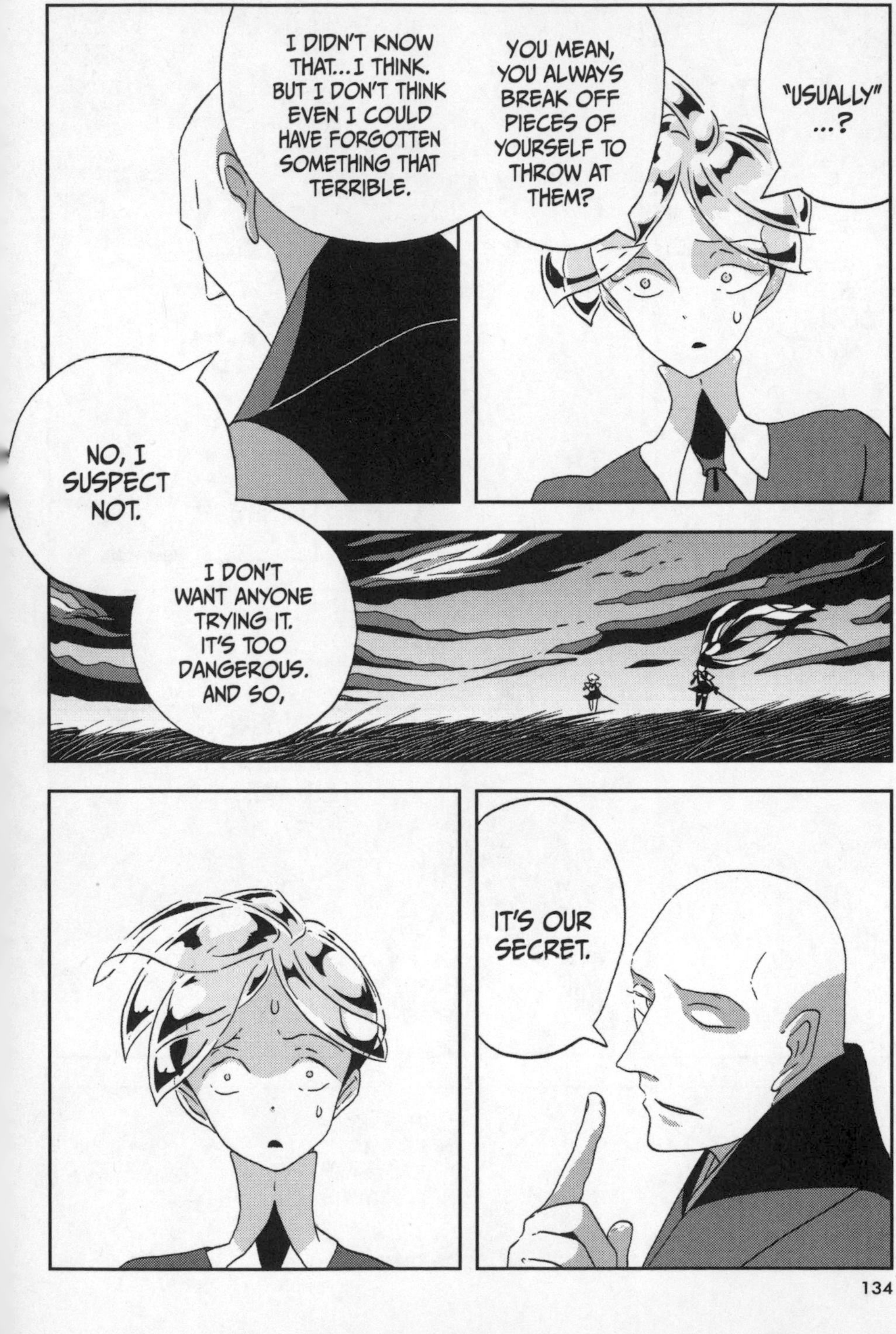
"USUALLY" ...?
YOU MEAN, YOU ALWAYS BREAK OFF PIECES OF YOURSELF TO THROW AT THEM?
I DIDN'T KNOW THAT... I THINK. BUT I DON'T THINK EVEN I COULD HAVE FORGOTTEN SOMETHING THAT TERRIBLE.
NO, I SUSPECT NOT.
I DON'T WANT ANYONE TRYING IT. IT'S TOO DANGEROUS. AND SO,
IT'S OUR SECRET.

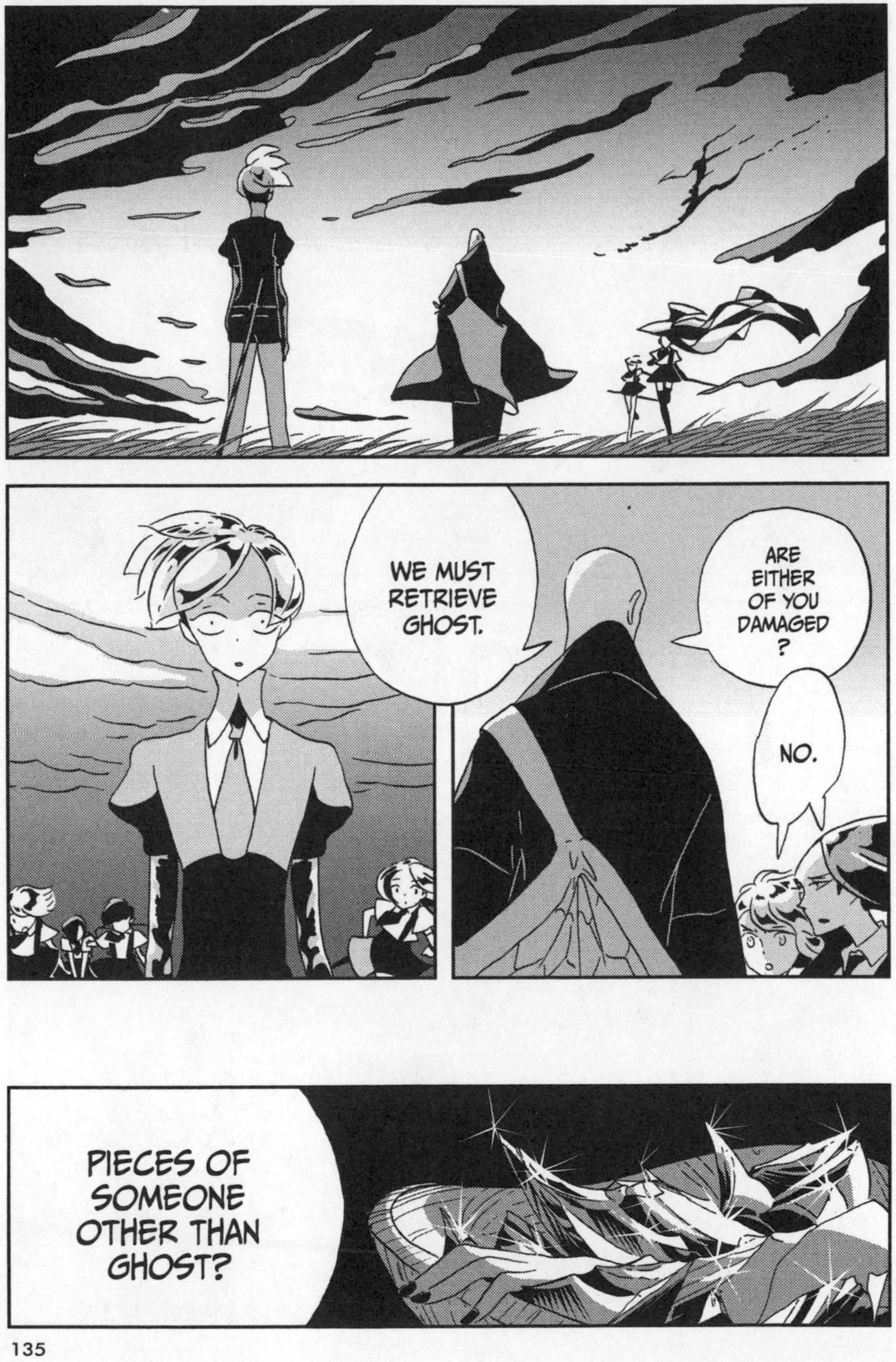
ARE EITHER OF YOU DAMAGED?
NO.
WE MUST RETRIEVE GHOST.
PIECES OF SOMEONE OTHER THAN GHOST?

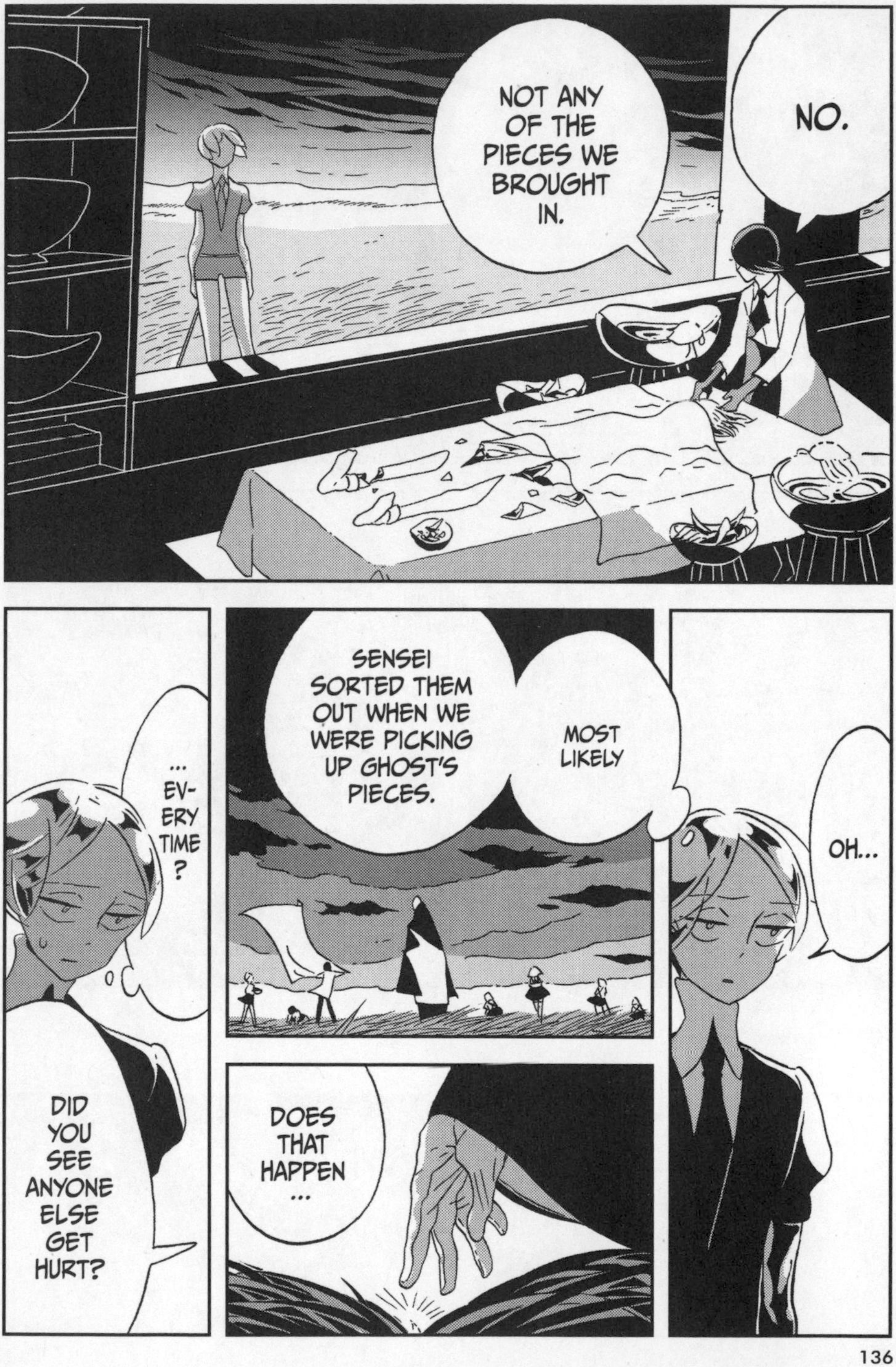
NO.
NOT ANY OF THE PIECES WE BROUGHT IN.
OH...
MOST LIKELY
SENSEI SORTED THEM OUT WHEN WE WERE PICKING UP GHOST'S PIECES.
DOES THAT HAPPEN ...
... EV-ERY TIME ?
DID YOU SEE ANYONE ELSE GET HURT?

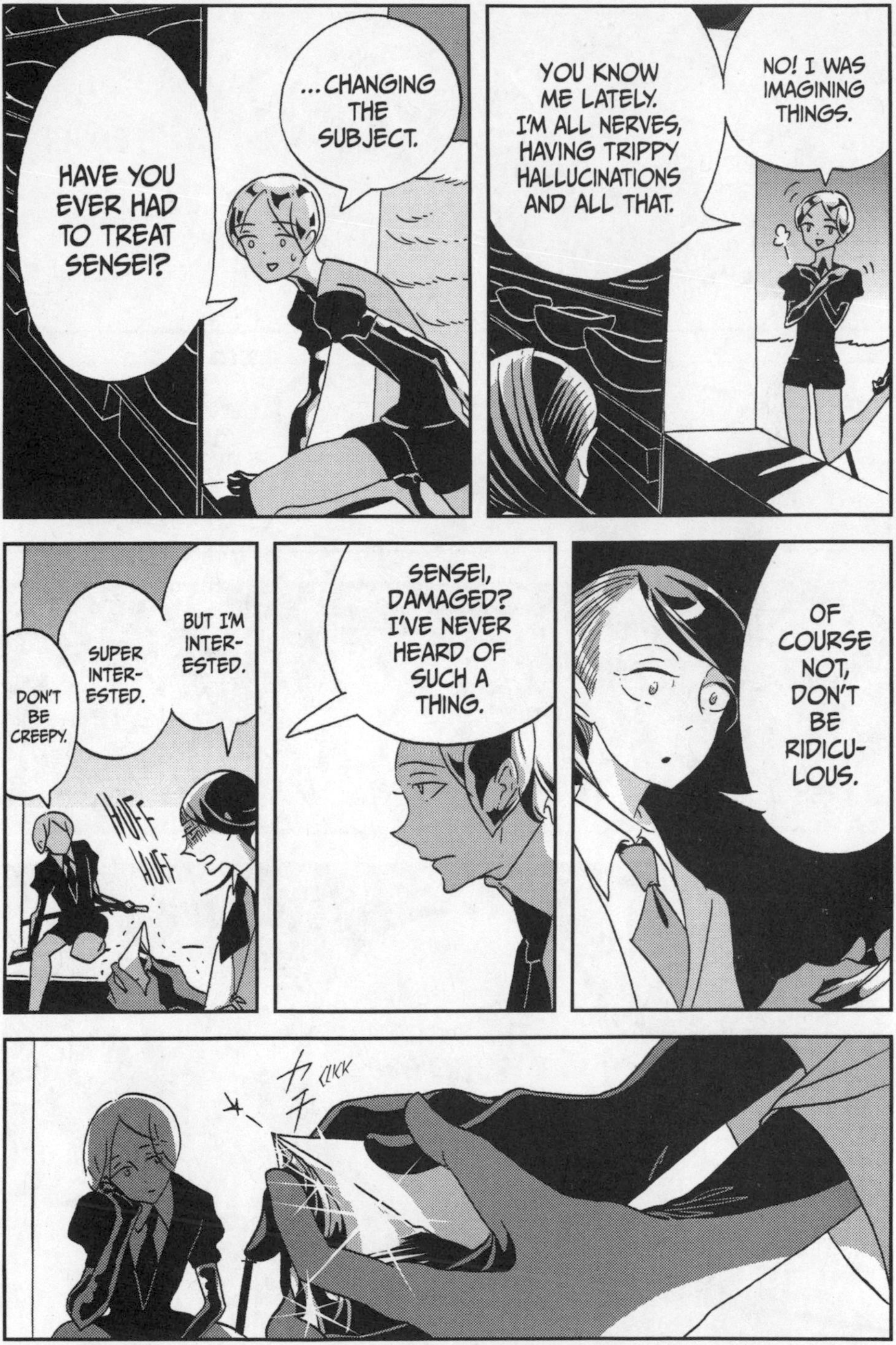
NO! I WAS IMAGINING THINGS.
YOU KNOW ME LATELY. I'M ALL NERVES, HAVING TRIPPY HALLUCINATIONS AND ALL THAT.
...CHANGING THE SUBJECT.
HAVE YOU EVER HAD TO TREAT SENSEI?
OF COURSE NOT, DON'T BE RIDICU-LOUS.
SENSEI, DAMAGED? I'VE NEVER HEARD OF SUCH A THING.
BUT I'M INTER-ESTED.
SUPER INTER-ESTED.
DON'T BE CREEPY.
HUFF HUFF
カチ CLICK

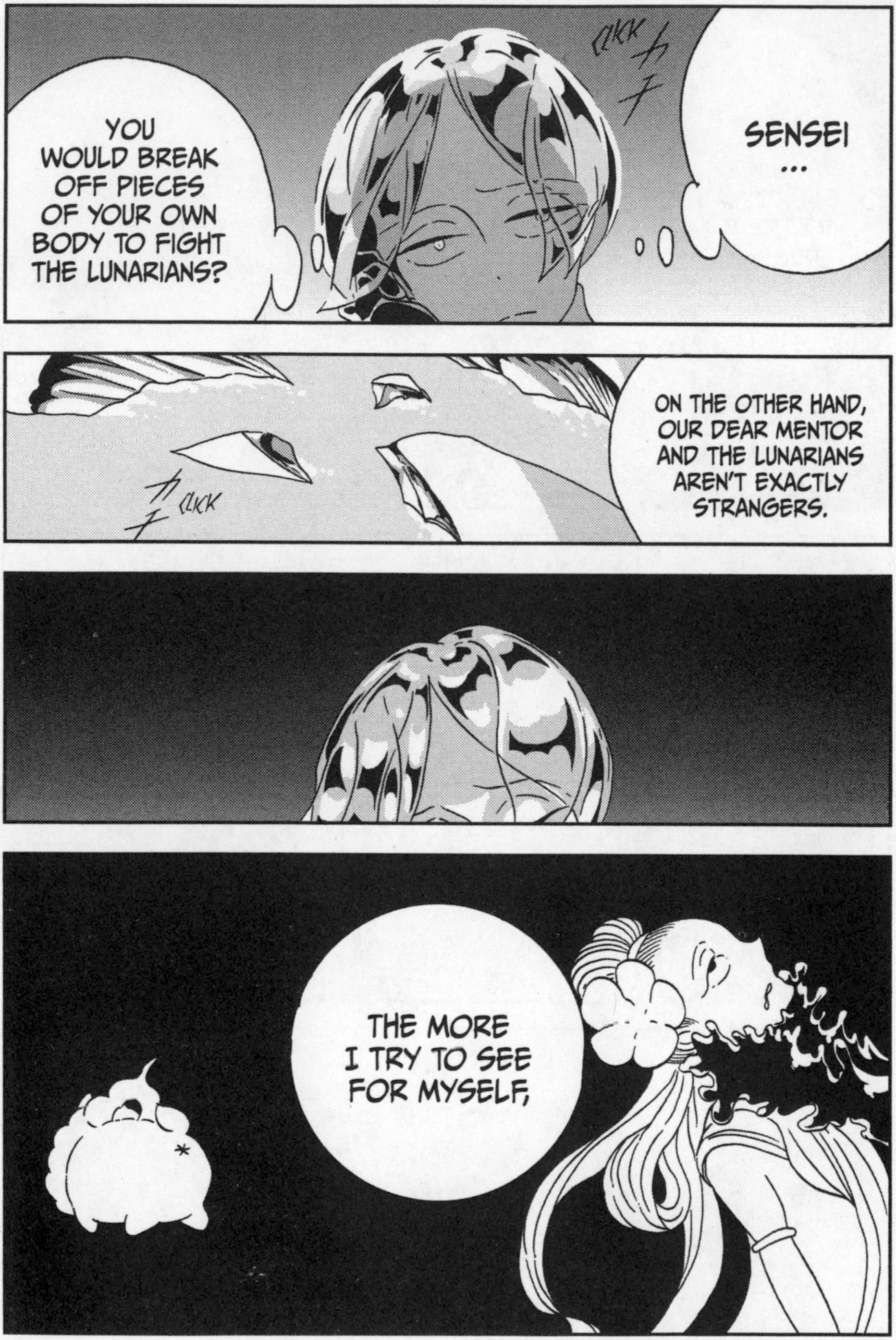
SENSEI ...
CLKK
カチ
YOU WOULD BREAK OFF PIECES OF YOUR OWN BODY TO FIGHT THE LUNARIANS?
ON THE OTHER HAND, OUR DEAR MENTOR AND THE LUNARIANS AREN'T EXACTLY STRANGERS.
カチ
CLKK
THE MORE I TRY TO SEE FOR MYSELF,

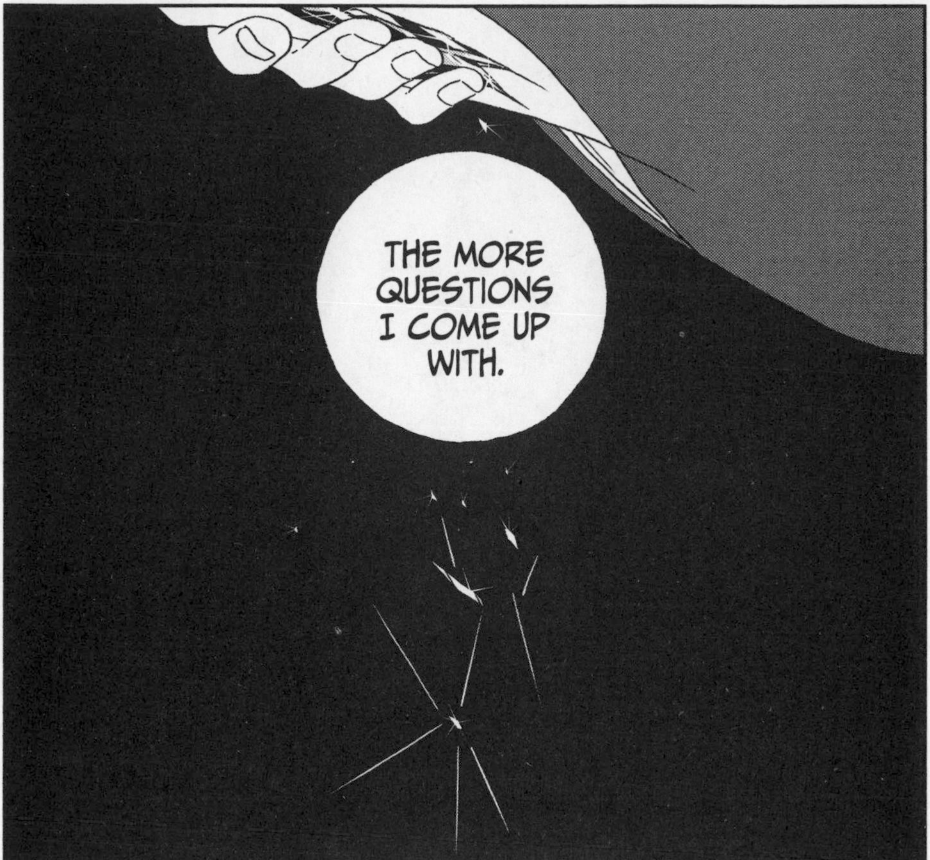
THE MORE QUESTIONS I COME UP WITH.

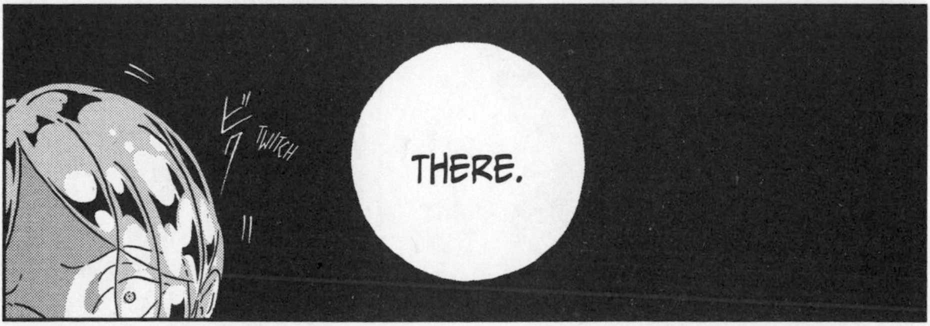
ビク
TWITCH
THERE.

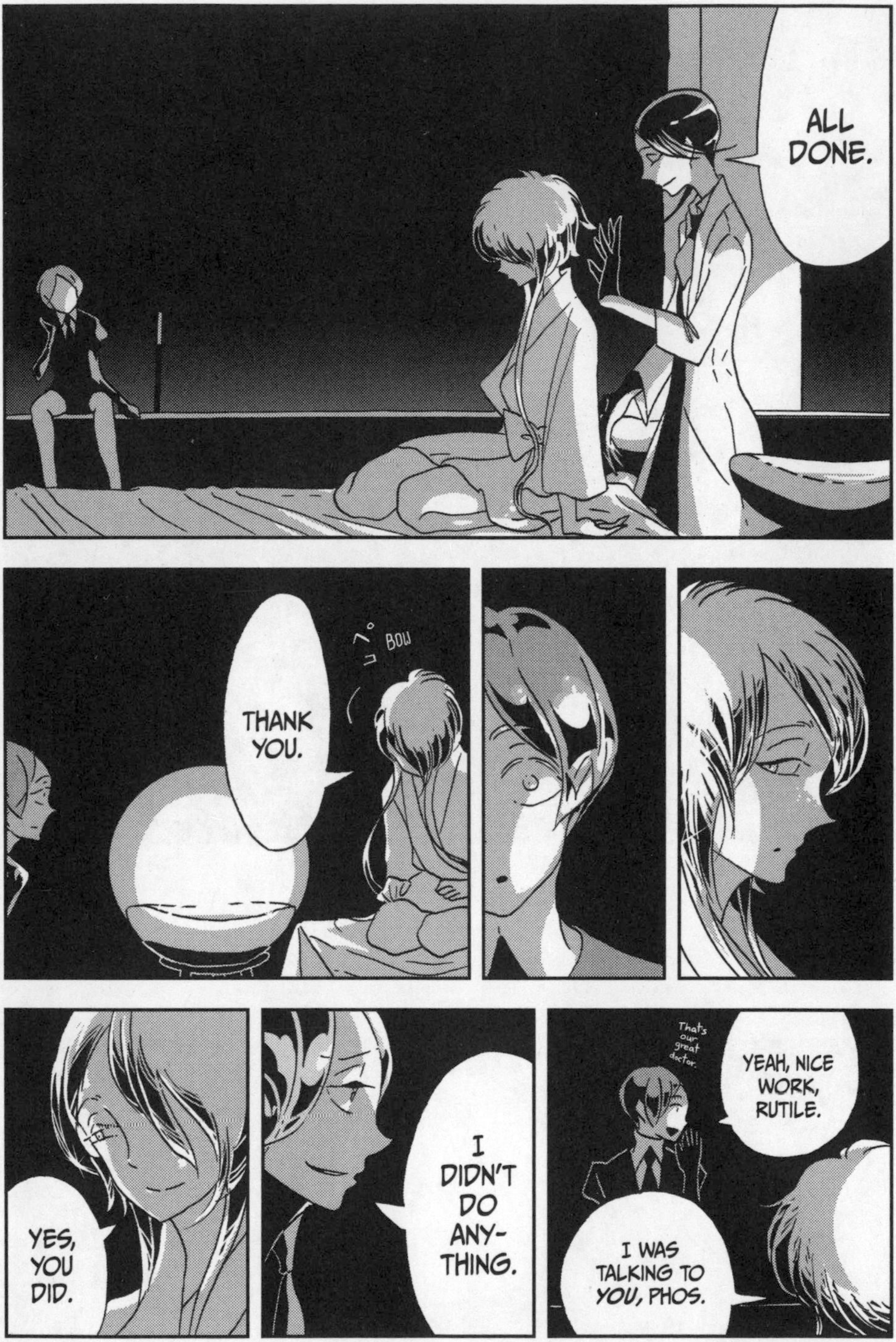
ALL DONE.
BOW
THANK YOU.
YEAH, NICE WORK, RUTILE.
That's our great doctor.
I WAS TALKING TO *YOU*, PHOS.
I DIDN'T DO ANY-THING.
YES, YOU DID.

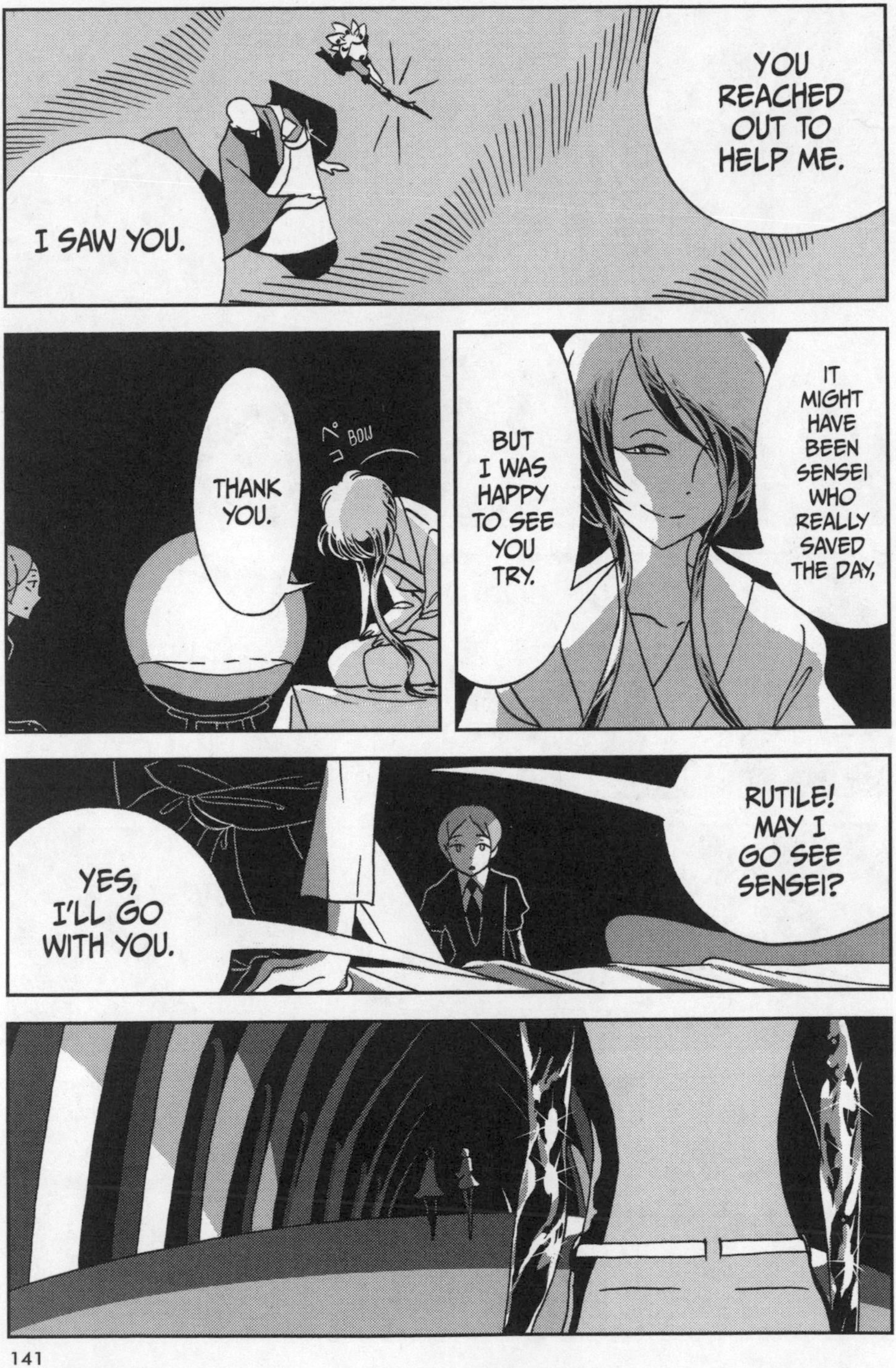

YOU REACHED OUT TO HELP ME.
I SAW YOU.
IT MIGHT HAVE BEEN SENSEI WHO REALLY SAVED THE DAY,
BUT I WAS HAPPY TO SEE YOU TRY.
BOW
THANK YOU.
RUTILE! MAY I GO SEE SENSEI?
YES, I'LL GO WITH YOU.

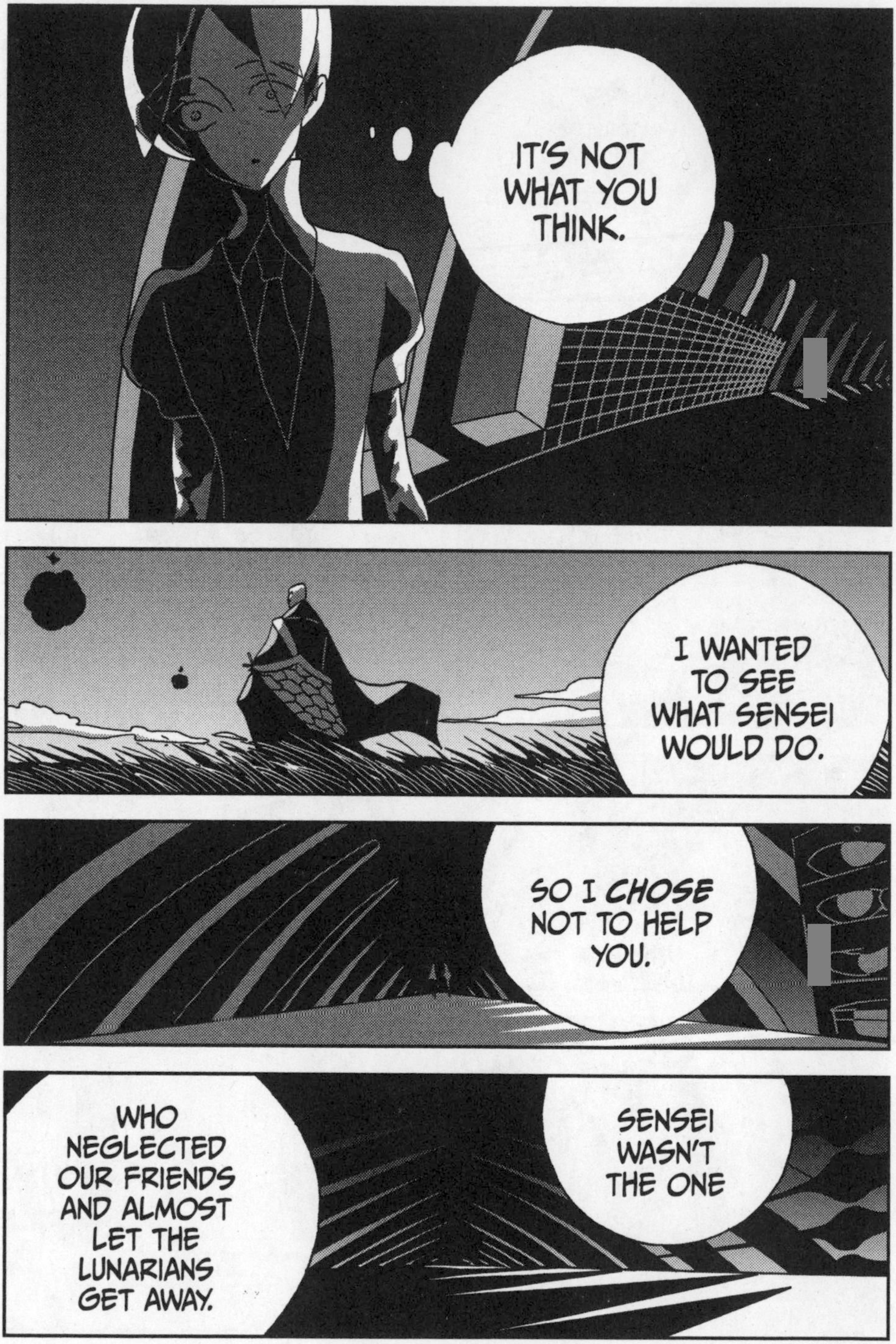
IT'S NOT WHAT YOU THINK.
I WANTED TO SEE WHAT SENSEI WOULD DO.
SO I *CHOSE* NOT TO HELP YOU.
SENSEI WASN'T THE ONE
WHO NEGLECTED OUR FRIENDS AND ALMOST LET THE LUNARIANS GET AWAY.

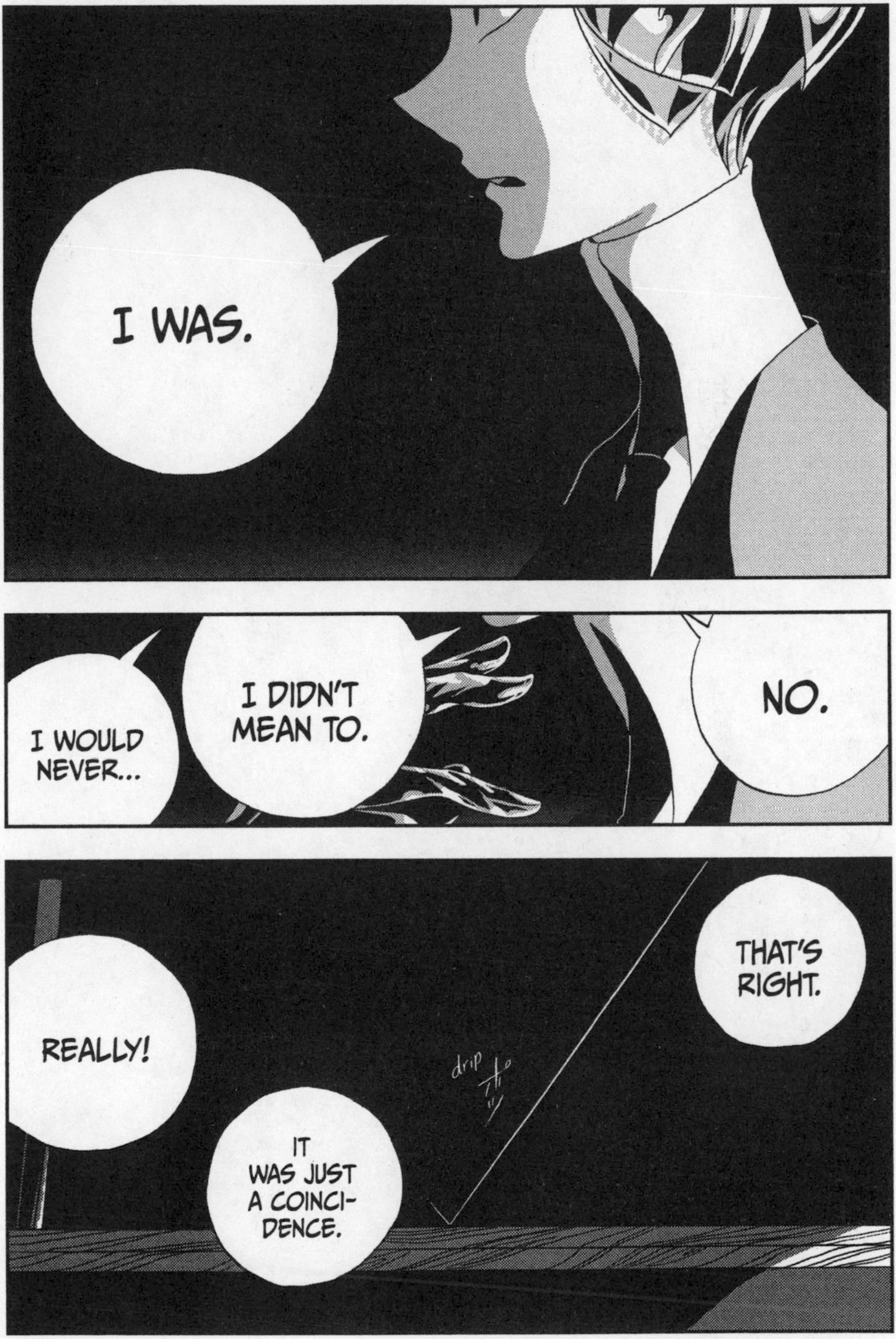
I WAS.
NO.
I DIDN'T MEAN TO.
I WOULD NEVER...
THAT'S RIGHT.
drip
IT WAS JUST A COINCI-DENCE.
REALLY!

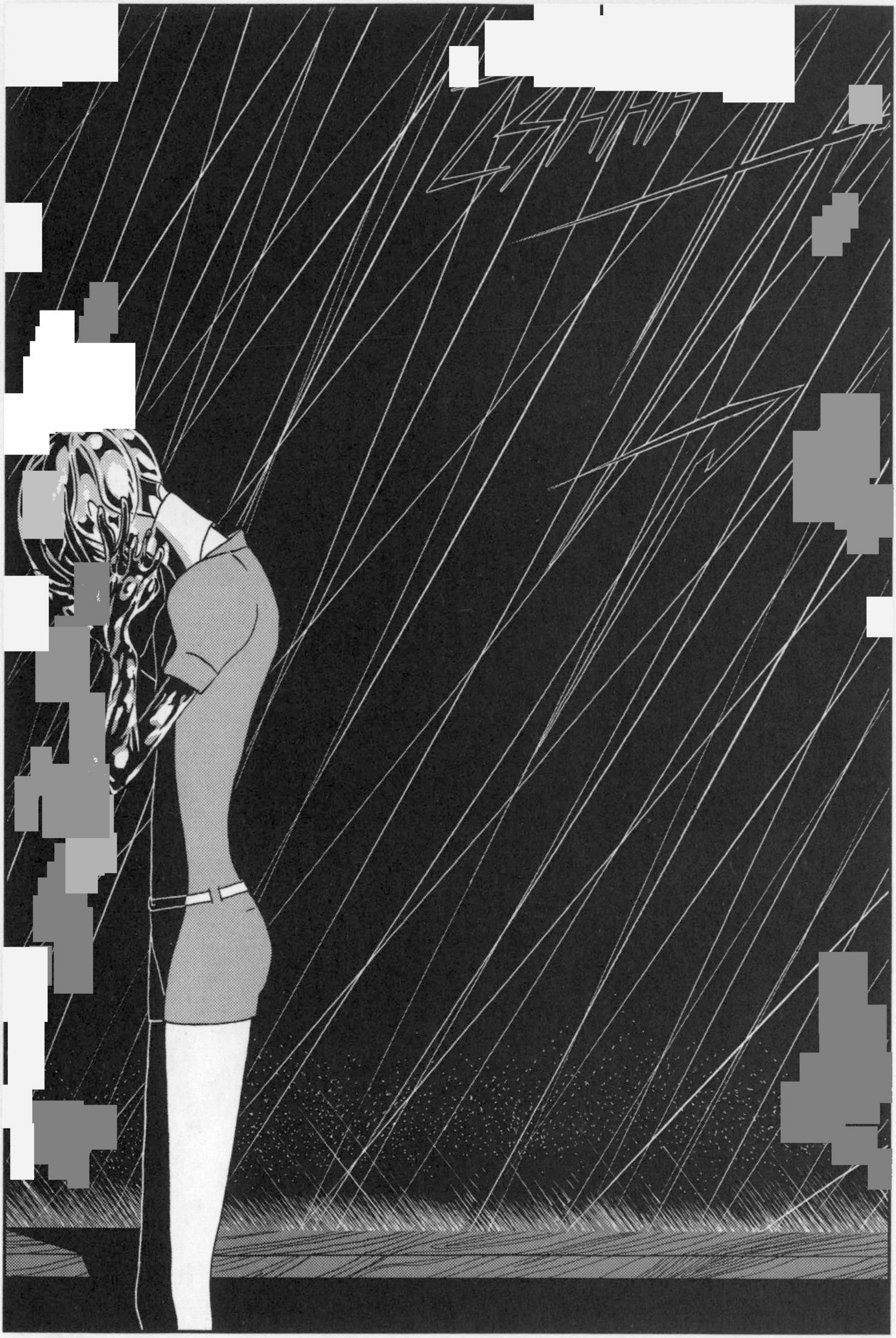

CHAPTER 34: Reversal END

CHAPTER 35:

A Pair

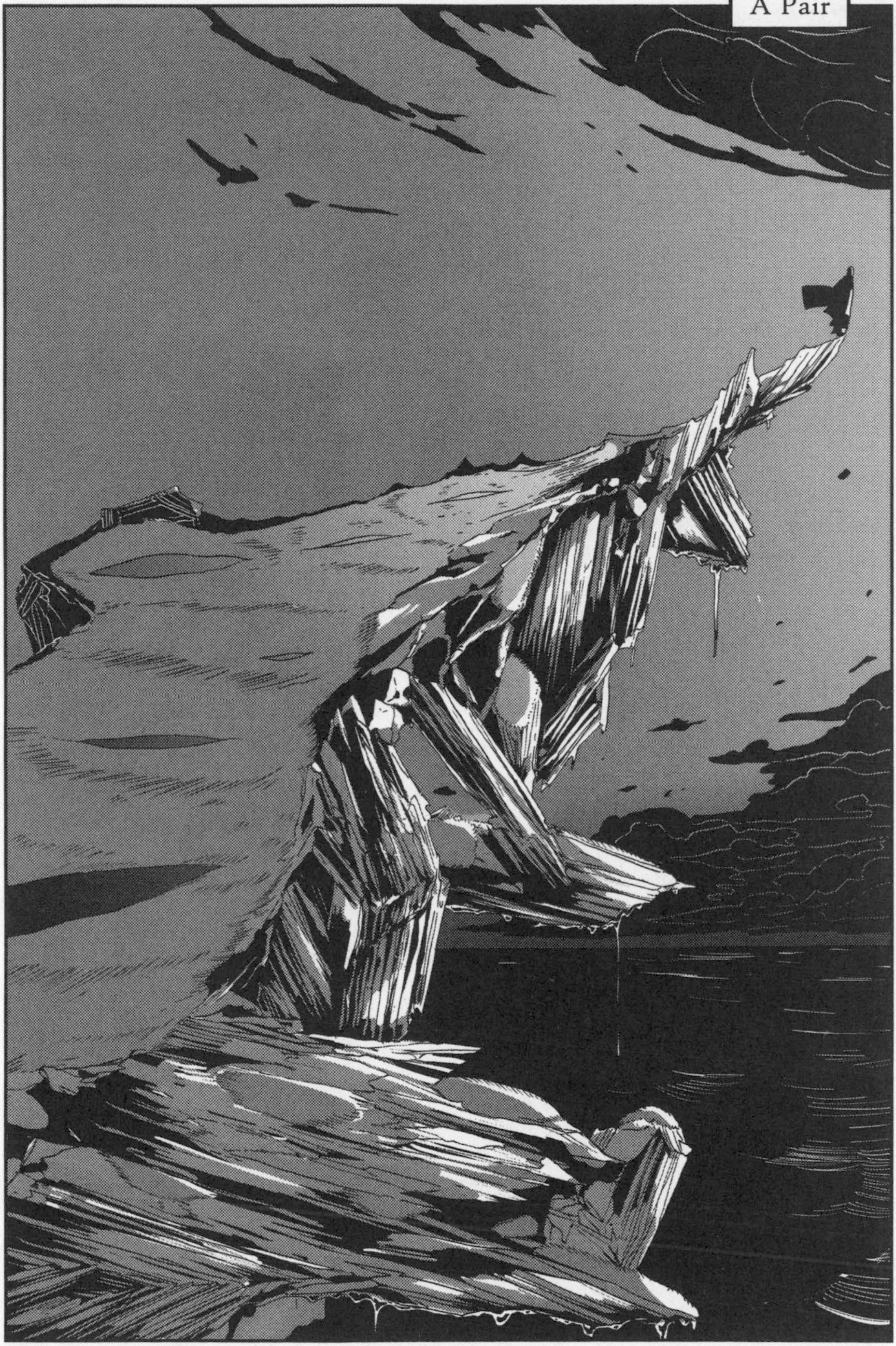

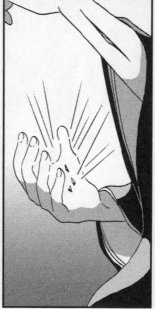

RUSTLE

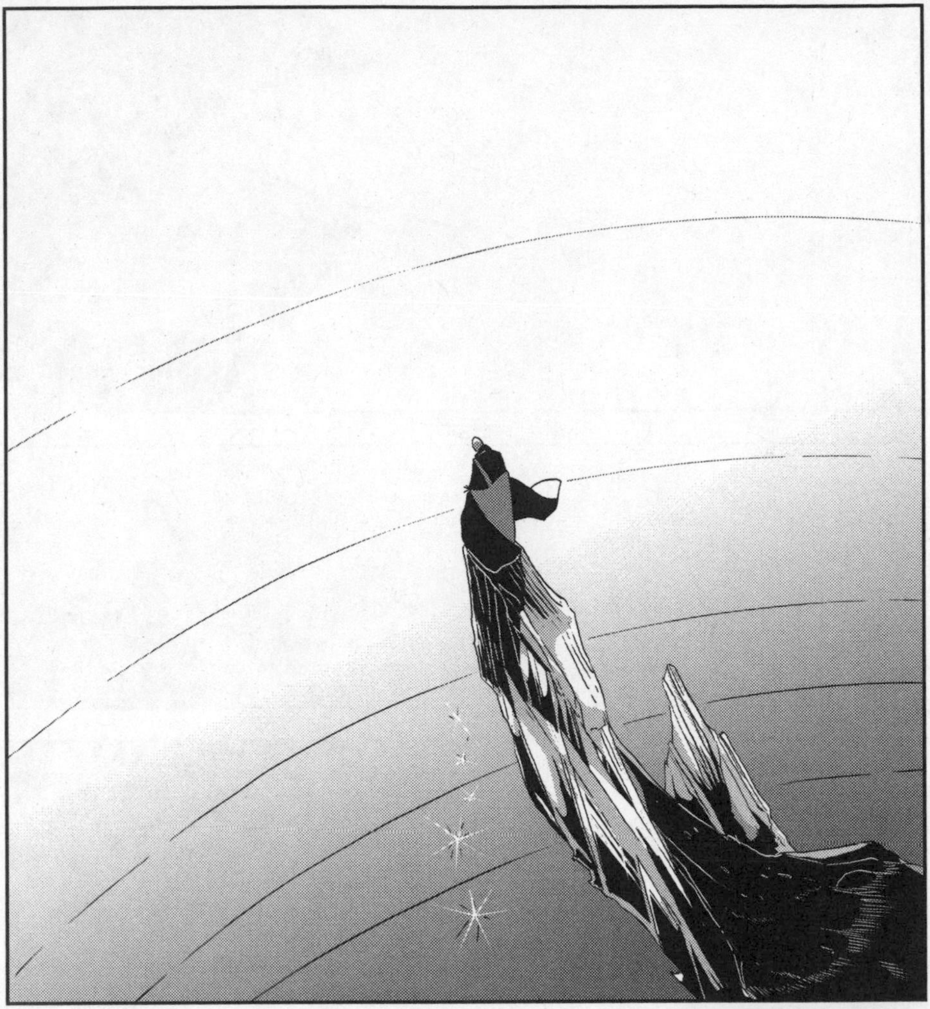

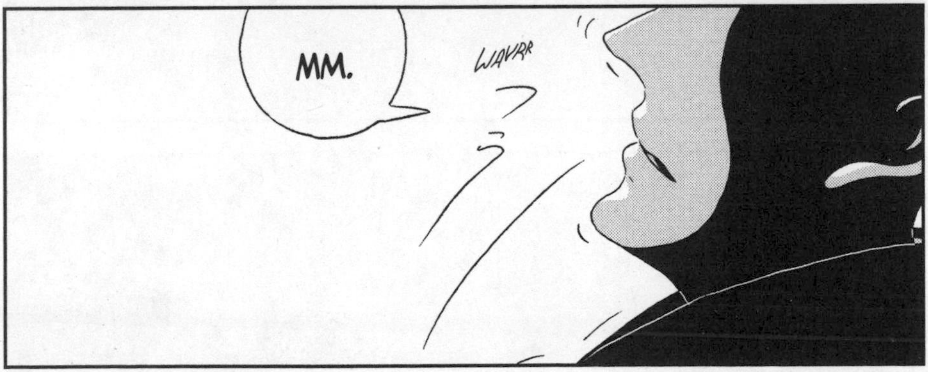
WAVRR
MM.

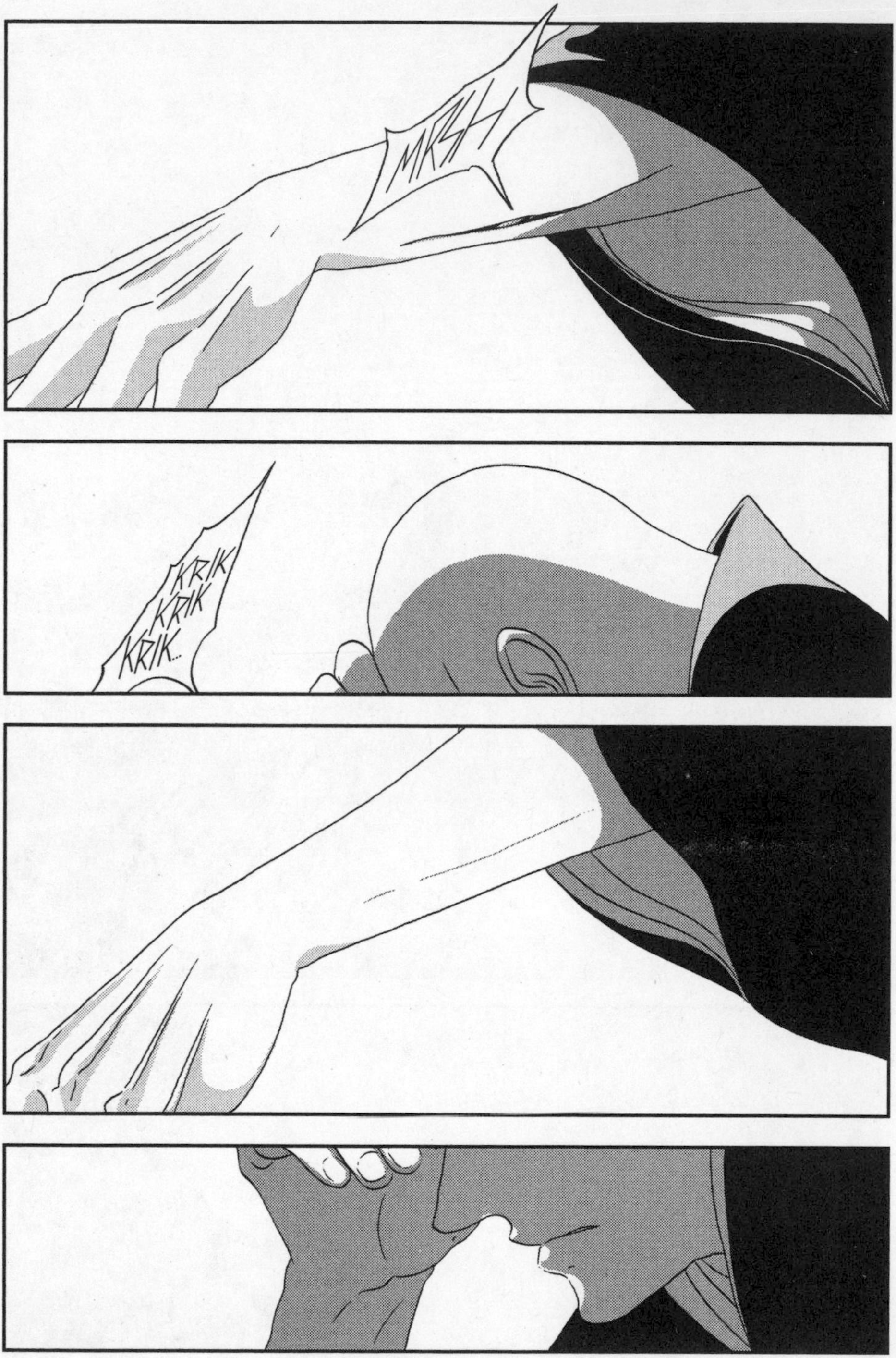
MRSH
KRIK KRIK KRIK...

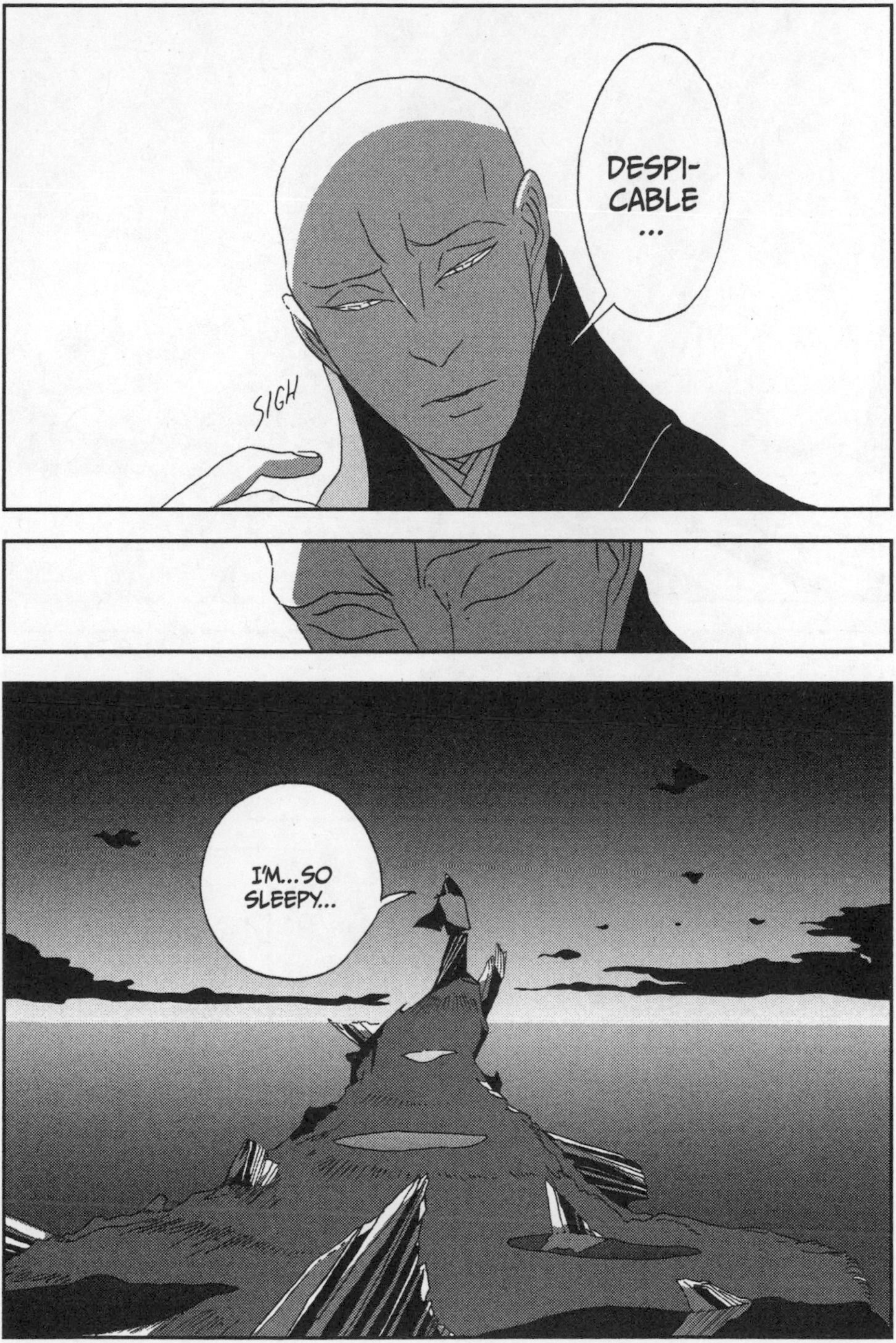
DESPI-
CABLE
...
SIGH
I'M...SO SLEEPY...

I DON'T MEAN TO BETRAY EVERYONE.

AM I...

BUT EVERY TIME I TRY TO FIND OUT ABOUT SENSEI'S SECRETS,

I END UP WITH MORE OF MY OWN.

...GOING TO KEEP REPEATING THIS?
FOREVER ?
ALL ALONE?

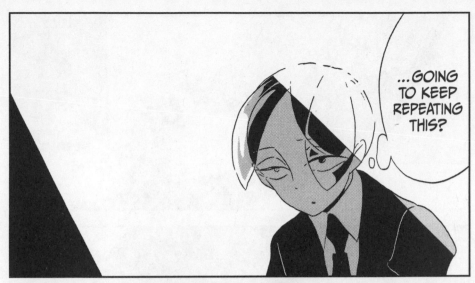

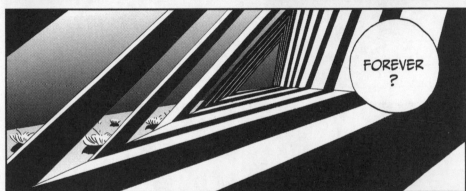

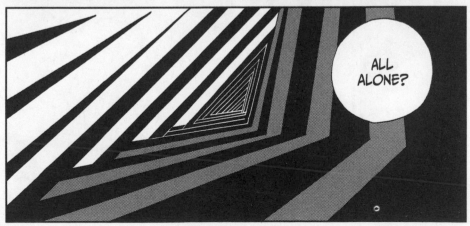

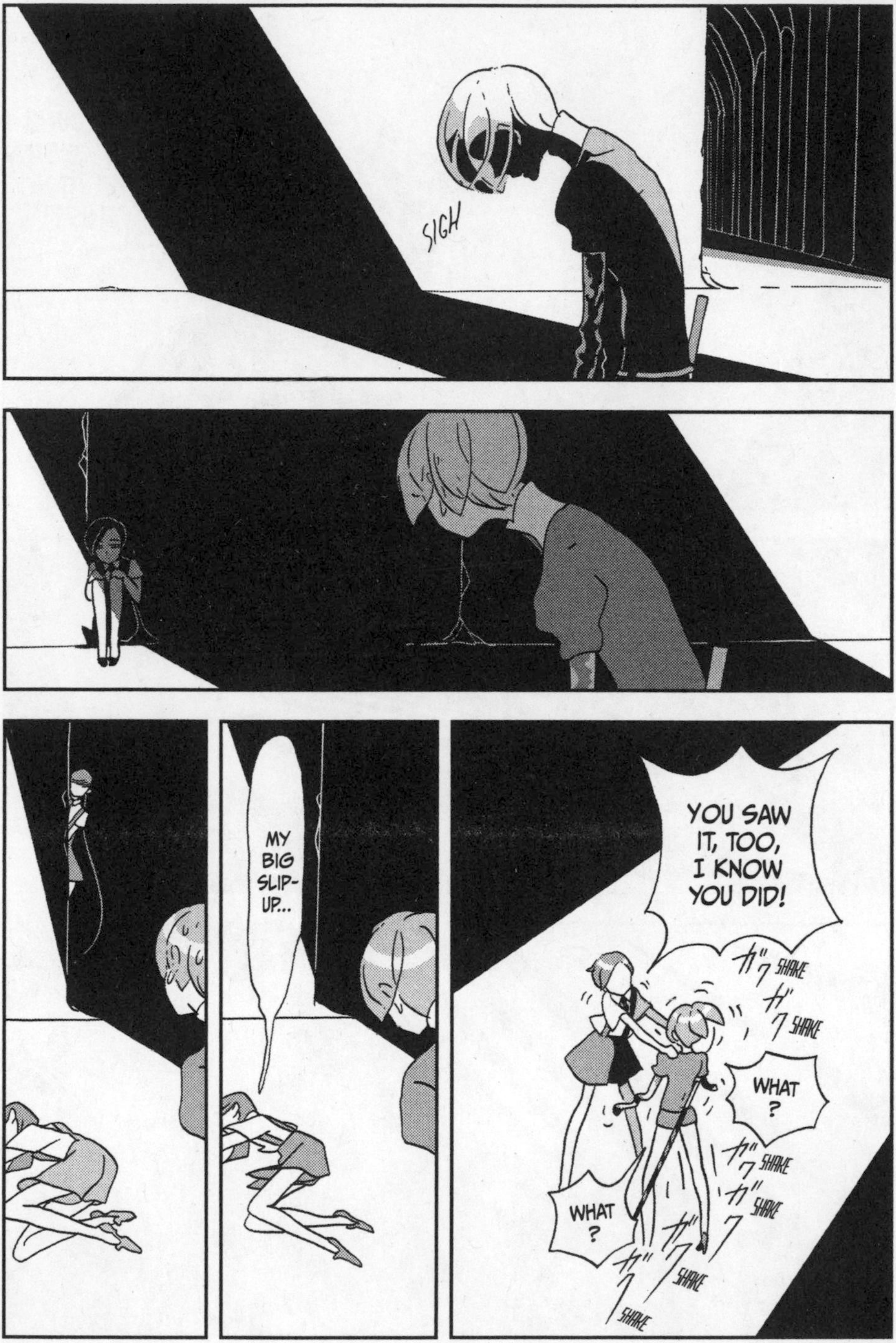
SIGH
YOU SAW IT, TOO, I KNOW YOU DID!
ガク SHAKE
ガク SHAKE
WHAT?
ガク SHAKE
ガク SHAKE
WHAT?
ガク SHAKE
ガク SHAKE
MY BIG SLIP-UP...

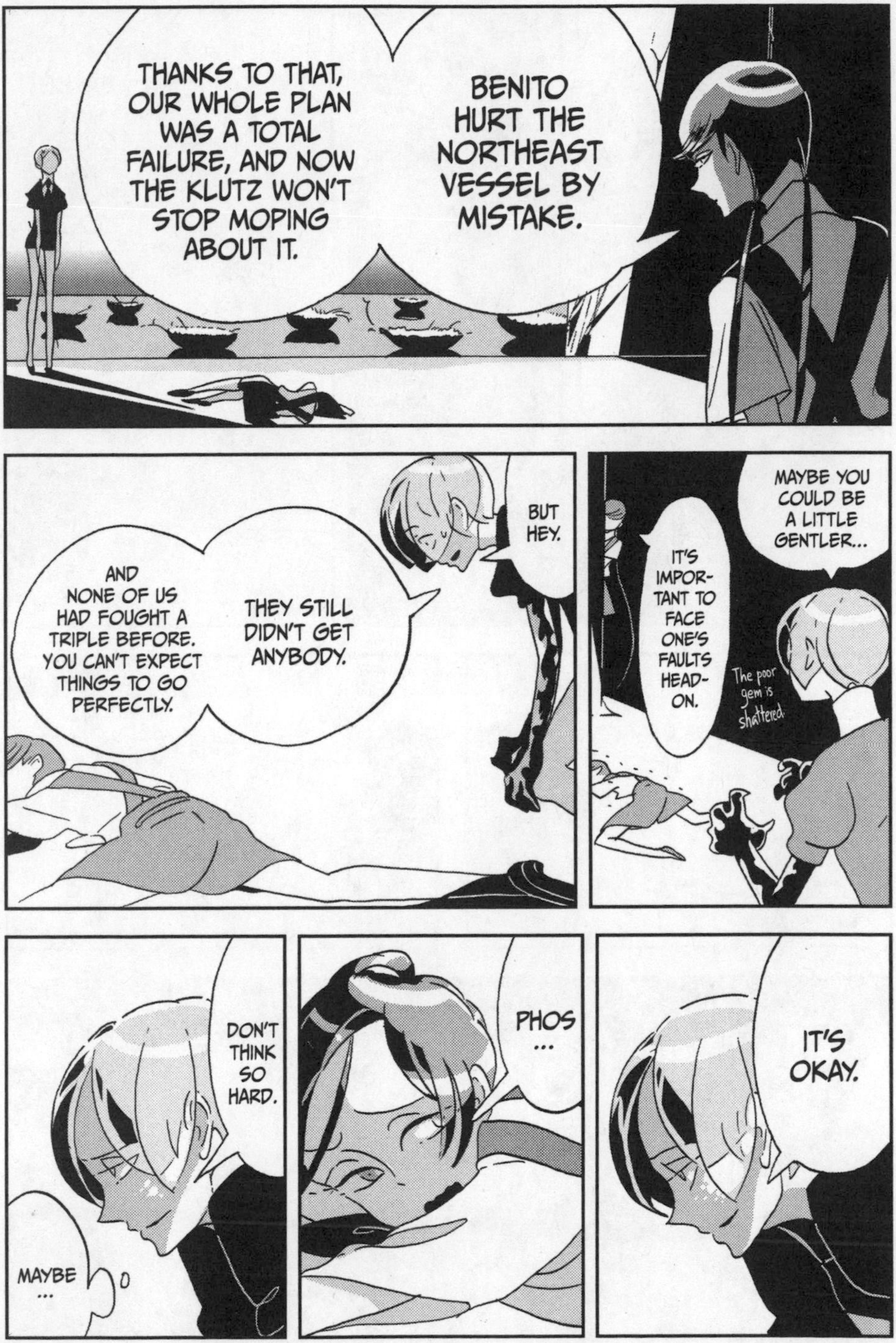
BENITO HURT THE NORTHEAST VESSEL BY MISTAKE.
THANKS TO THAT, OUR WHOLE PLAN WAS A TOTAL FAILURE, AND NOW THE KLUTZ WON'T STOP MOPING ABOUT IT.
MAYBE YOU COULD BE A LITTLE GENTLER...
IT'S IMPORTANT TO FACE ONE'S FAULTS HEAD-ON.
The poor gem is shattered.
BUT HEY.
THEY STILL DIDN'T GET ANYBODY.
AND NONE OF US HAD FOUGHT A TRIPLE BEFORE. YOU CAN'T EXPECT THINGS TO GO PERFECTLY.
IT'S OKAY.
PHOS ...
DON'T THINK SO HARD.
MAYBE ...

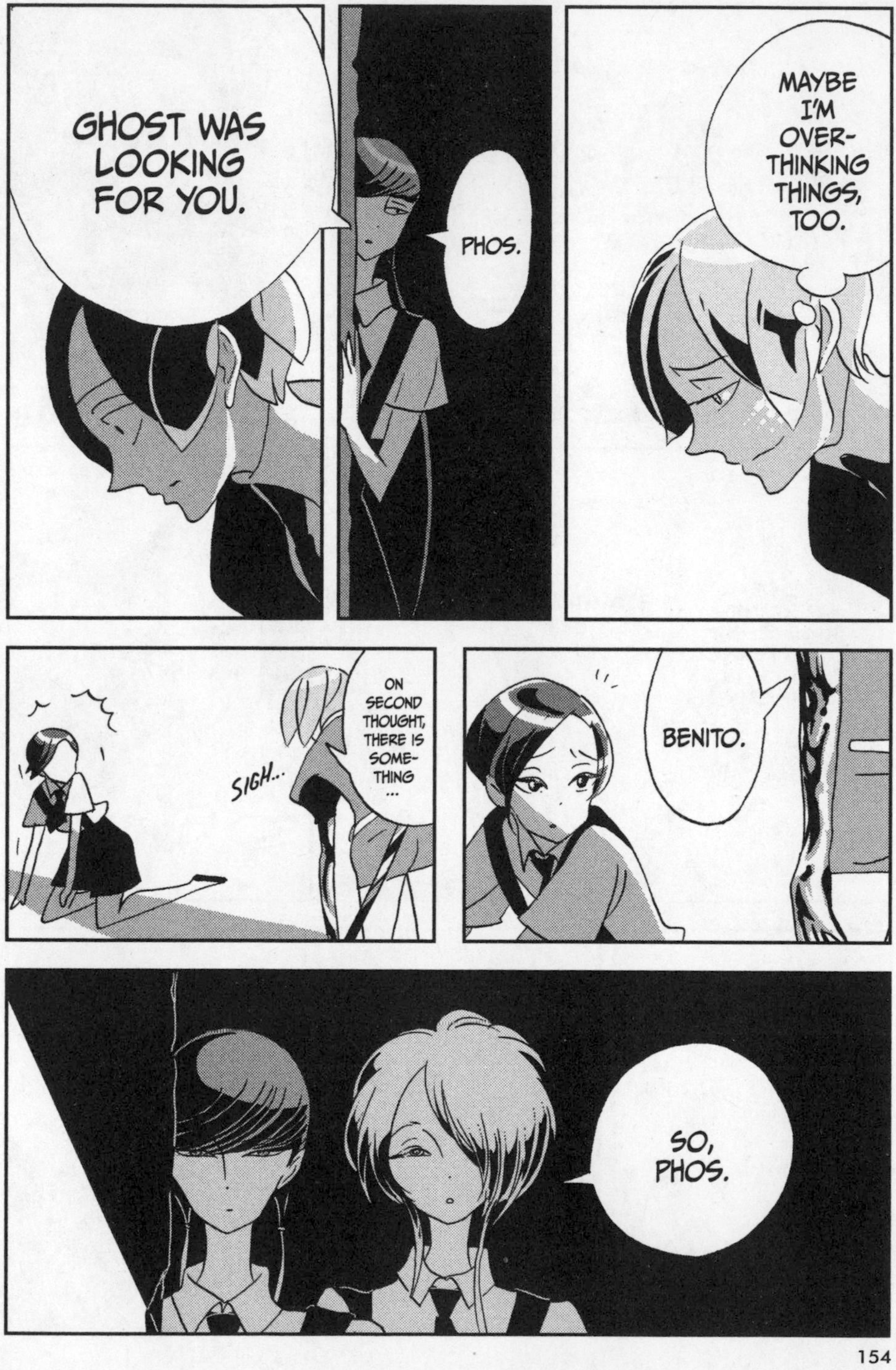
MAYBE I'M OVER-THINKING THINGS, TOO.
PHOS.
GHOST WAS LOOKING FOR YOU.
BENITO.
ON SECOND THOUGHT, THERE IS SOME-THING ...
SIGH...
SO, PHOS.

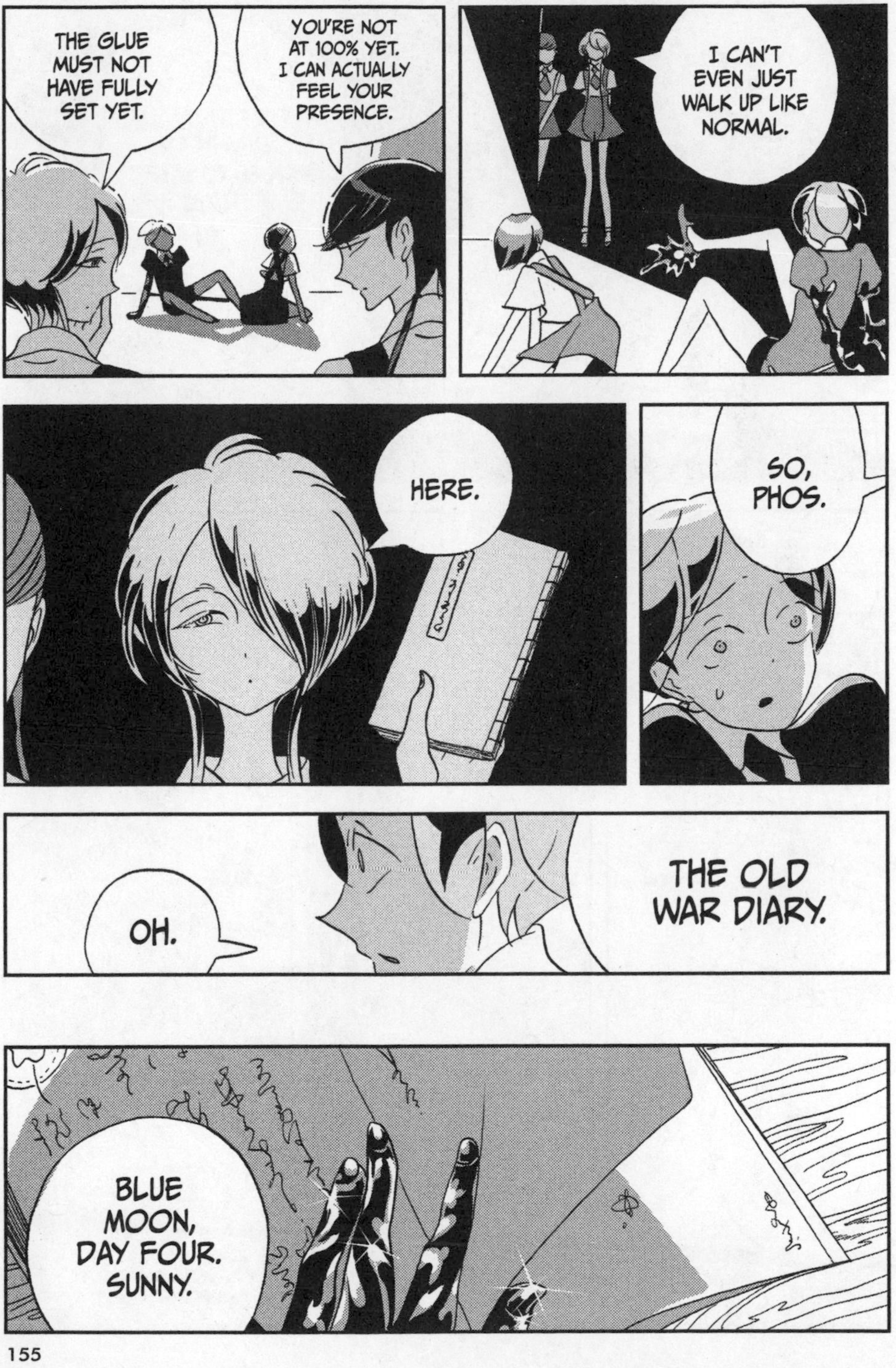
I CAN'T EVEN JUST WALK UP LIKE NORMAL.
YOU'RE NOT AT 100% YET. I CAN ACTUALLY FEEL YOUR PRESENCE.
THE GLUE MUST NOT HAVE FULLY SET YET.
SO, PHOS.
HERE.
THE OLD WAR DIARY.
OH.
BLUE MOON, DAY FOUR. SUNNY.

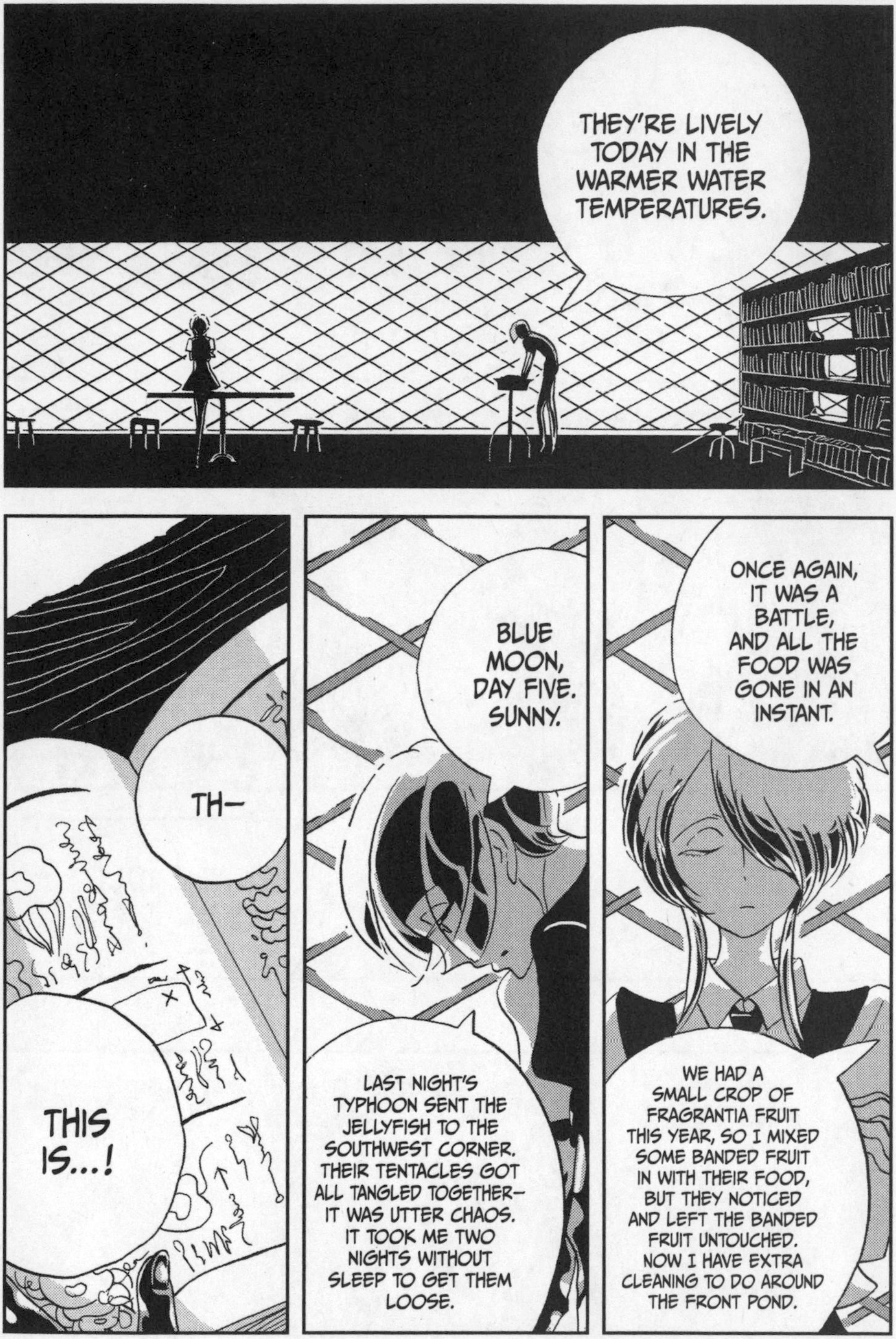
THEY'RE LIVELY TODAY IN THE WARMER WATER TEMPERATURES.
ONCE AGAIN, IT WAS A BATTLE, AND ALL THE FOOD WAS GONE IN AN INSTANT.
WE HAD A SMALL CROP OF FRAGRANTIA FRUIT THIS YEAR, SO I MIXED SOME BANDED FRUIT IN WITH THEIR FOOD, BUT THEY NOTICED AND LEFT THE BANDED FRUIT UNTOUCHED. NOW I HAVE EXTRA CLEANING TO DO AROUND THE FRONT POND.
BLUE MOON, DAY FIVE. SUNNY.
LAST NIGHT'S TYPHOON SENT THE JELLYFISH TO THE SOUTHWEST CORNER. THEIR TENTACLES GOT ALL TANGLED TOGETHER— IT WAS UTTER CHAOS. IT TOOK ME TWO NIGHTS WITHOUT SLEEP TO GET THEM LOOSE.
TH—
THIS IS...!

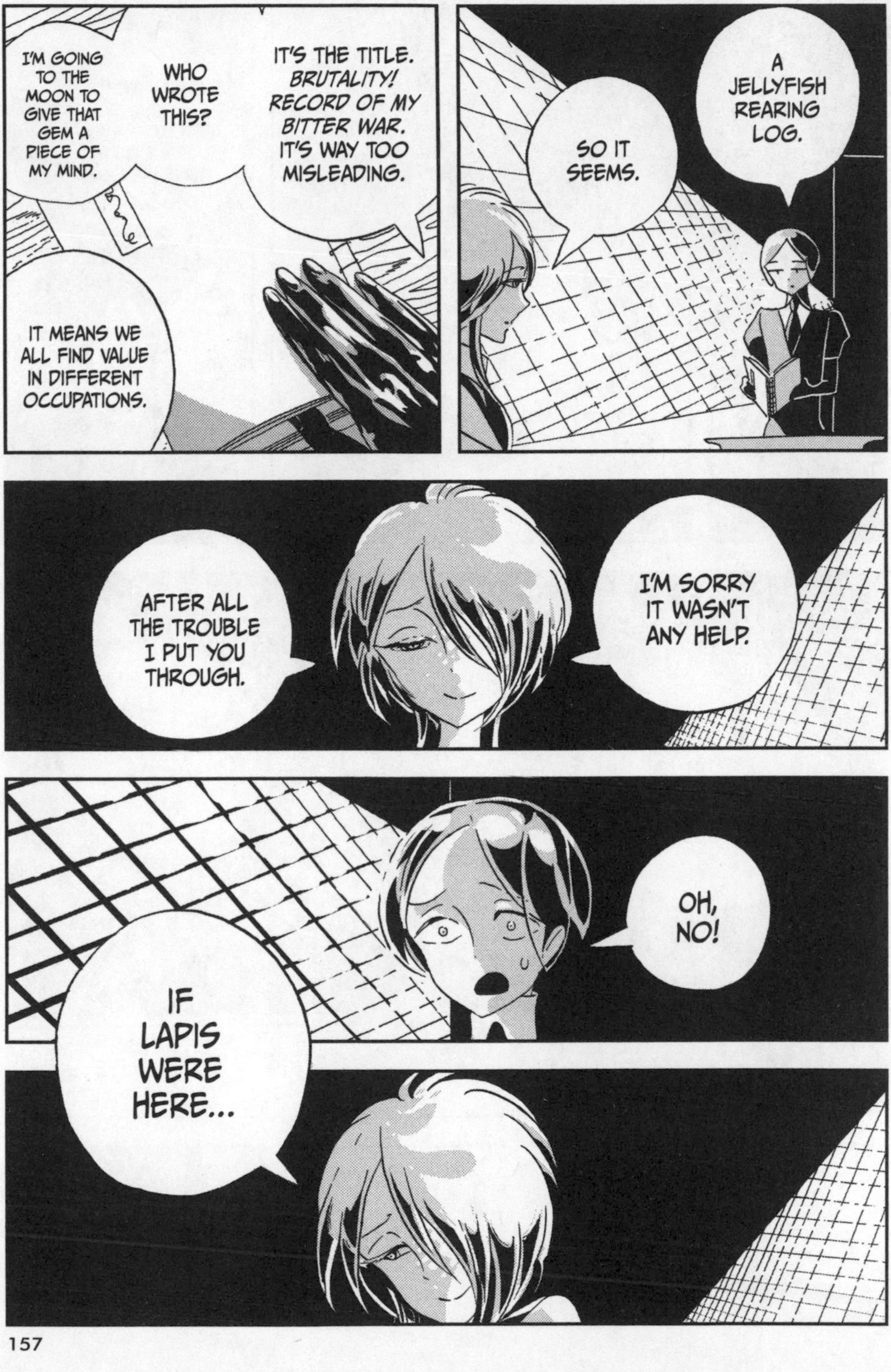
A JELLYFISH REARING LOG.
SO IT SEEMS.
IT'S THE TITLE. *BRUTALITY! RECORD OF MY BITTER WAR.* IT'S WAY TOO MISLEADING.
WHO WROTE THIS?
I'M GOING TO THE MOON TO GIVE THAT GEM A PIECE OF MY MIND.
IT MEANS WE ALL FIND VALUE IN DIFFERENT OCCUPATIONS.
I'M SORRY IT WASN'T ANY HELP.
AFTER ALL THE TROUBLE I PUT YOU THROUGH.
OH, NO!
IF LAPIS WERE HERE...

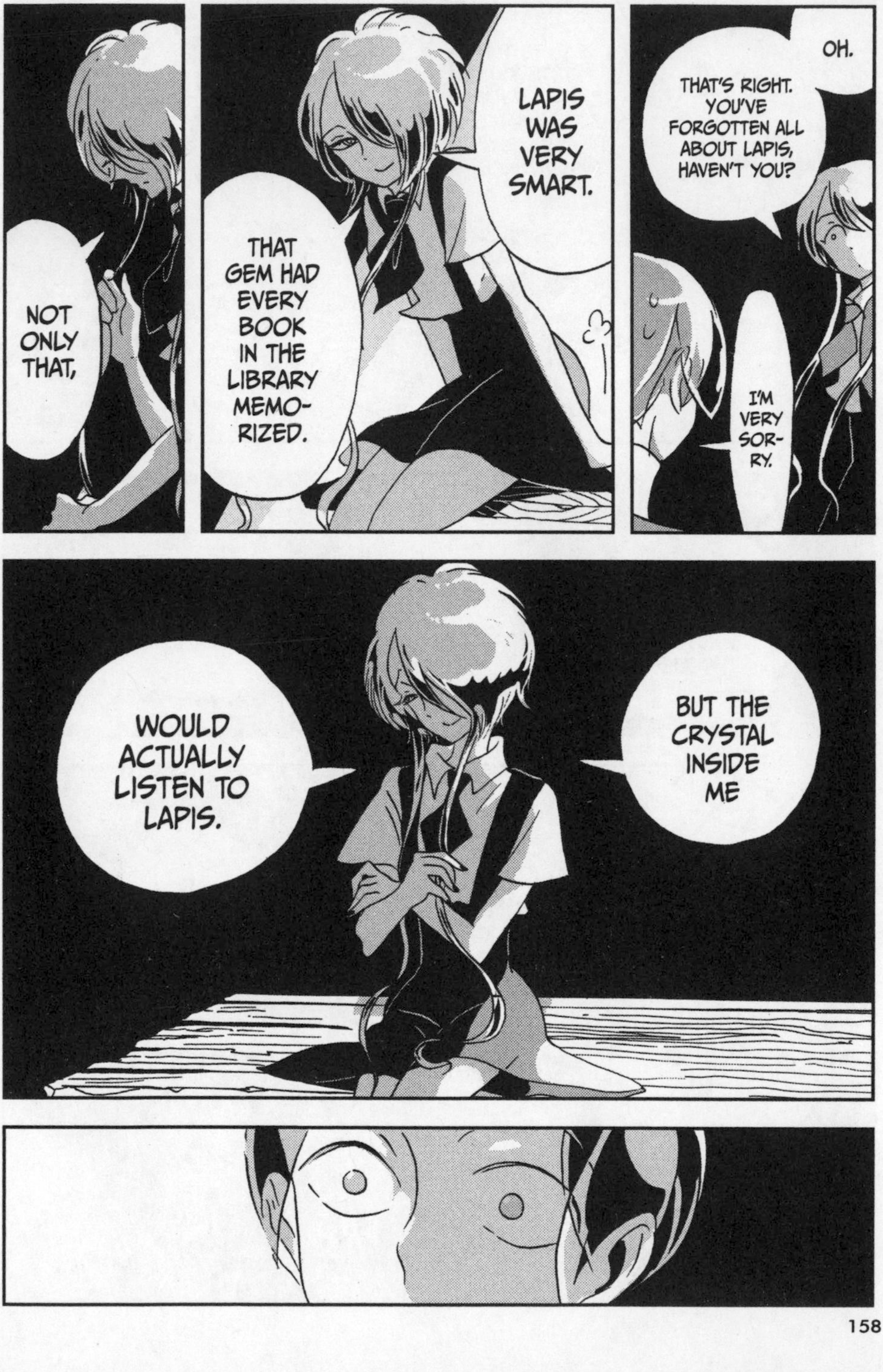
OH.
THAT'S RIGHT. YOU'VE FORGOTTEN ALL ABOUT LAPIS, HAVEN'T YOU?
I'M VERY SORRY.
LAPIS WAS VERY SMART.
THAT GEM HAD EVERY BOOK IN THE LIBRARY MEMORIZED.
NOT ONLY THAT,
BUT THE CRYSTAL INSIDE ME
WOULD ACTUALLY LISTEN TO LAPIS.

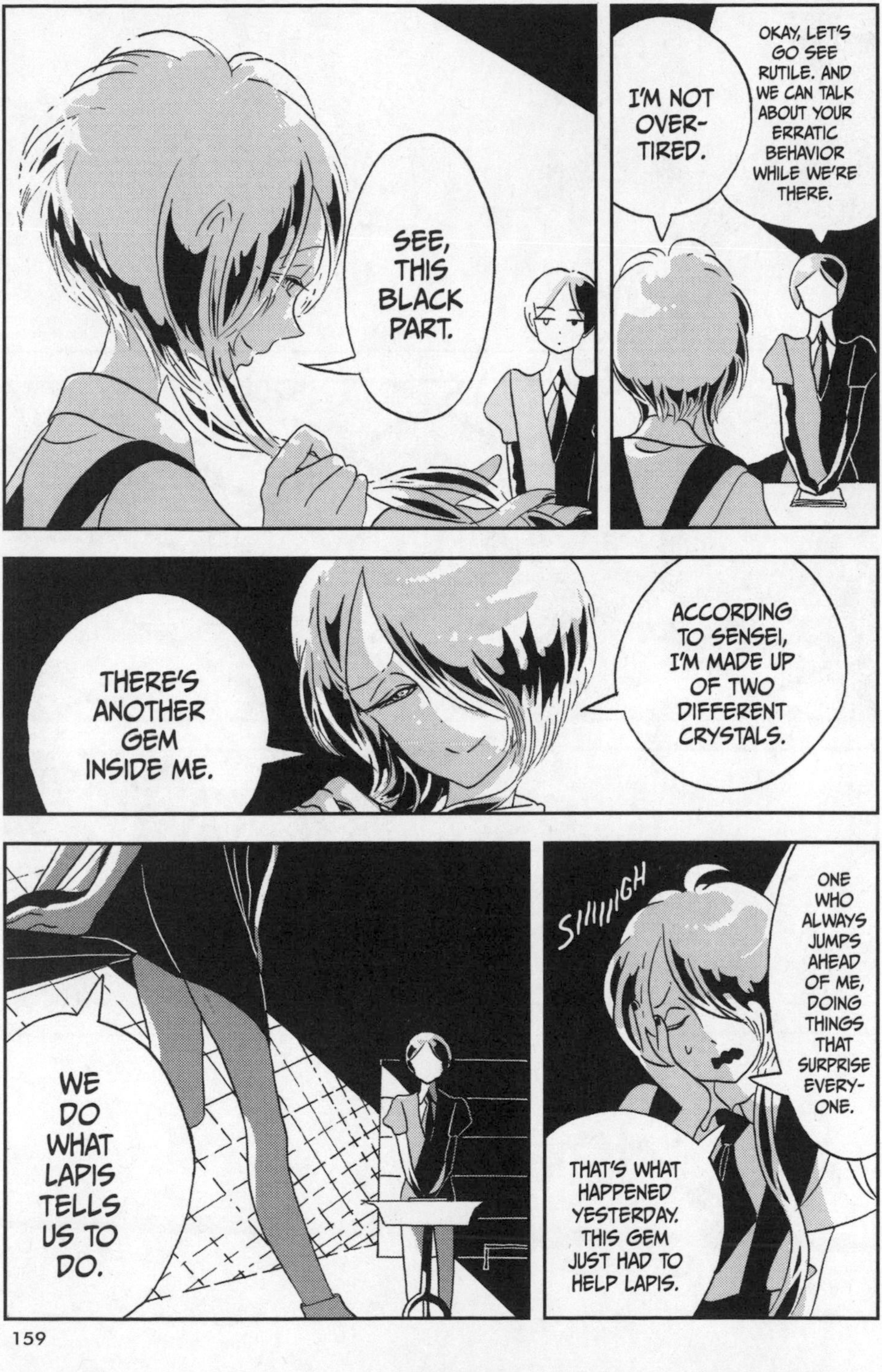
OKAY, LET'S GO SEE RUTILE. AND WE CAN TALK ABOUT YOUR ERRATIC BEHAVIOR WHILE WE'RE THERE.
I'M NOT OVER-TIRED.
SEE, THIS BLACK PART.
ACCORDING TO SENSEI, I'M MADE UP OF TWO DIFFERENT CRYSTALS.
THERE'S ANOTHER GEM INSIDE ME.
ONE WHO ALWAYS JUMPS AHEAD OF ME, DOING THINGS THAT SURPRISE EVERY-ONE.
SIIIIIIGH
THAT'S WHAT HAPPENED YESTERDAY. THIS GEM JUST HAD TO HELP LAPIS.
WE DO WHAT LAPIS TELLS US TO DO.

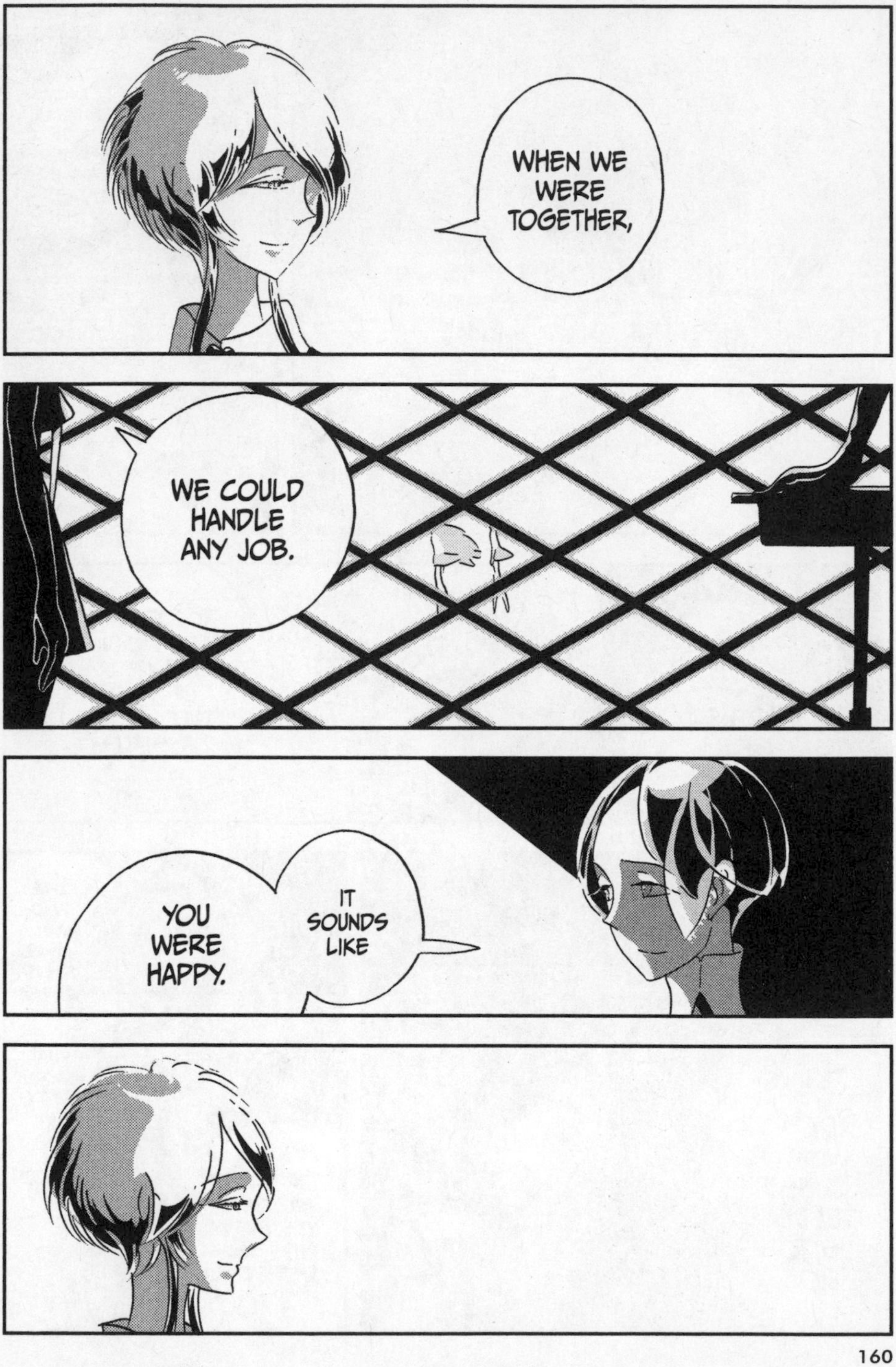
WHEN WE WERE TOGETHER,
WE COULD HANDLE ANY JOB.
IT SOUNDS LIKE
YOU WERE HAPPY.

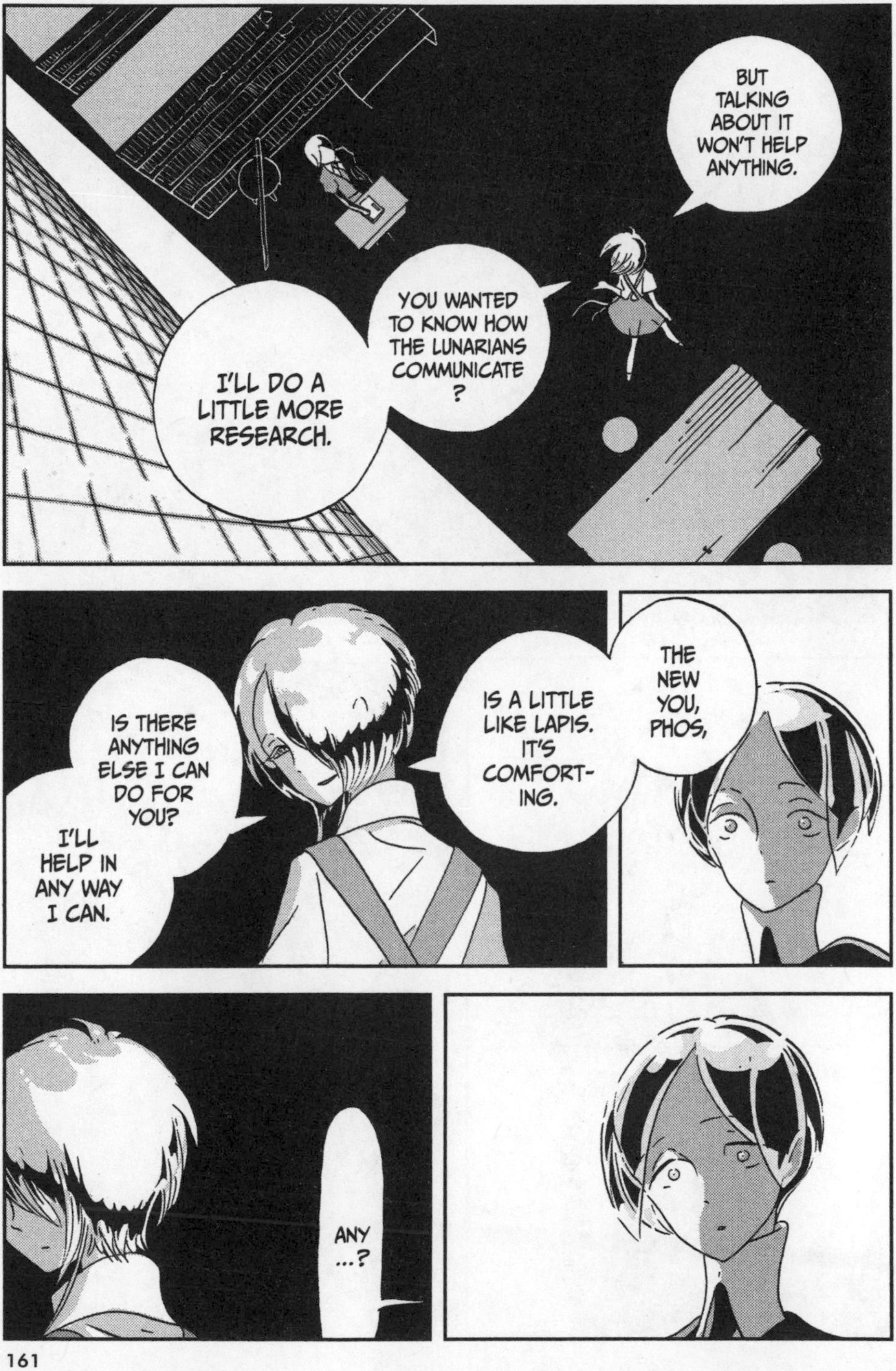
BUT TALKING ABOUT IT WON'T HELP ANYTHING.
YOU WANTED TO KNOW HOW THE LUNARIANS COMMUNICATE ?
I'LL DO A LITTLE MORE RESEARCH.
THE NEW YOU, PHOS,
IS A LITTLE LIKE LAPIS. IT'S COMFORT-ING.
IS THERE ANYTHING ELSE I CAN DO FOR YOU?
I'LL HELP IN ANY WAY I CAN.
ANY ...?

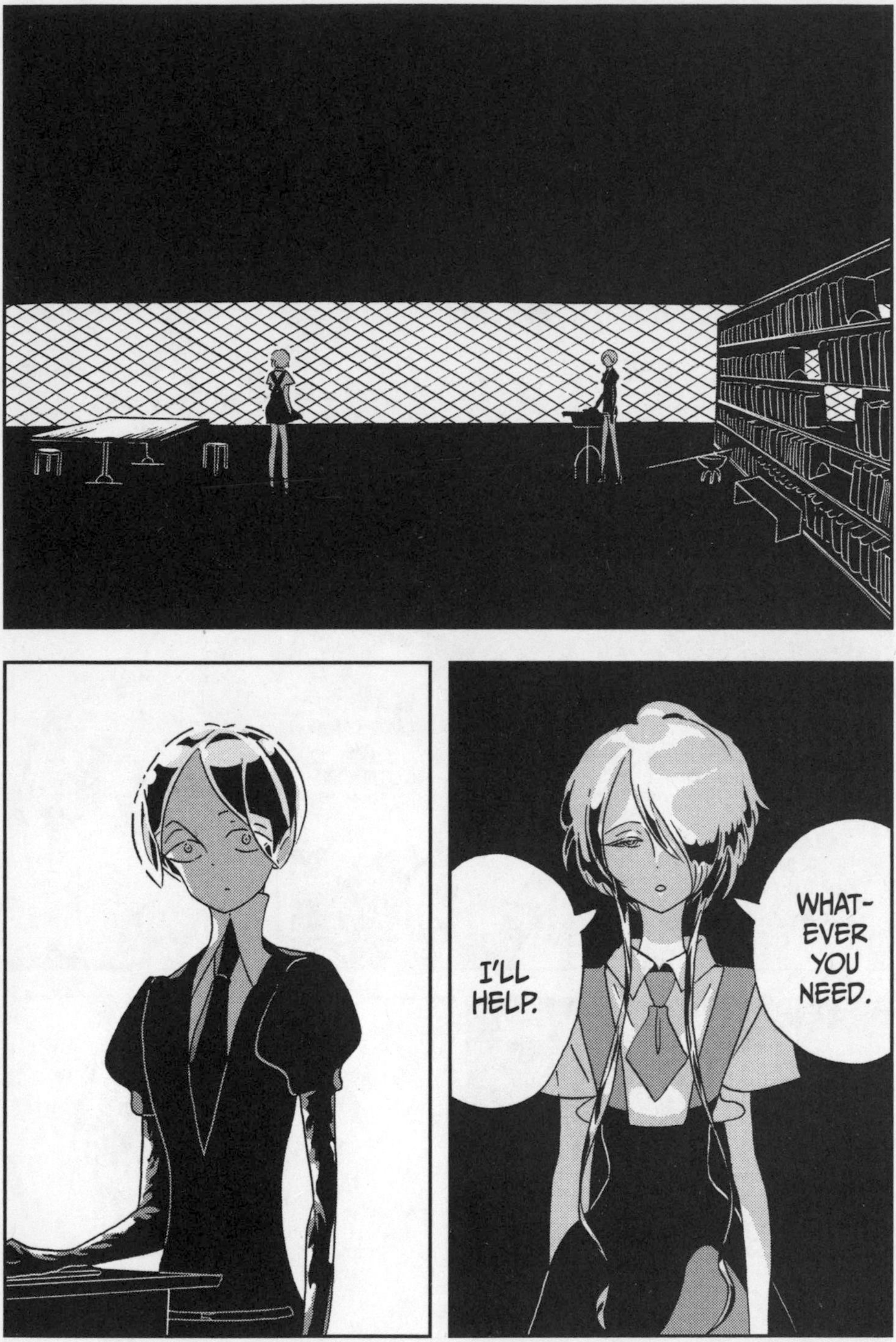
WHAT-EVER YOU NEED.
I'LL HELP.

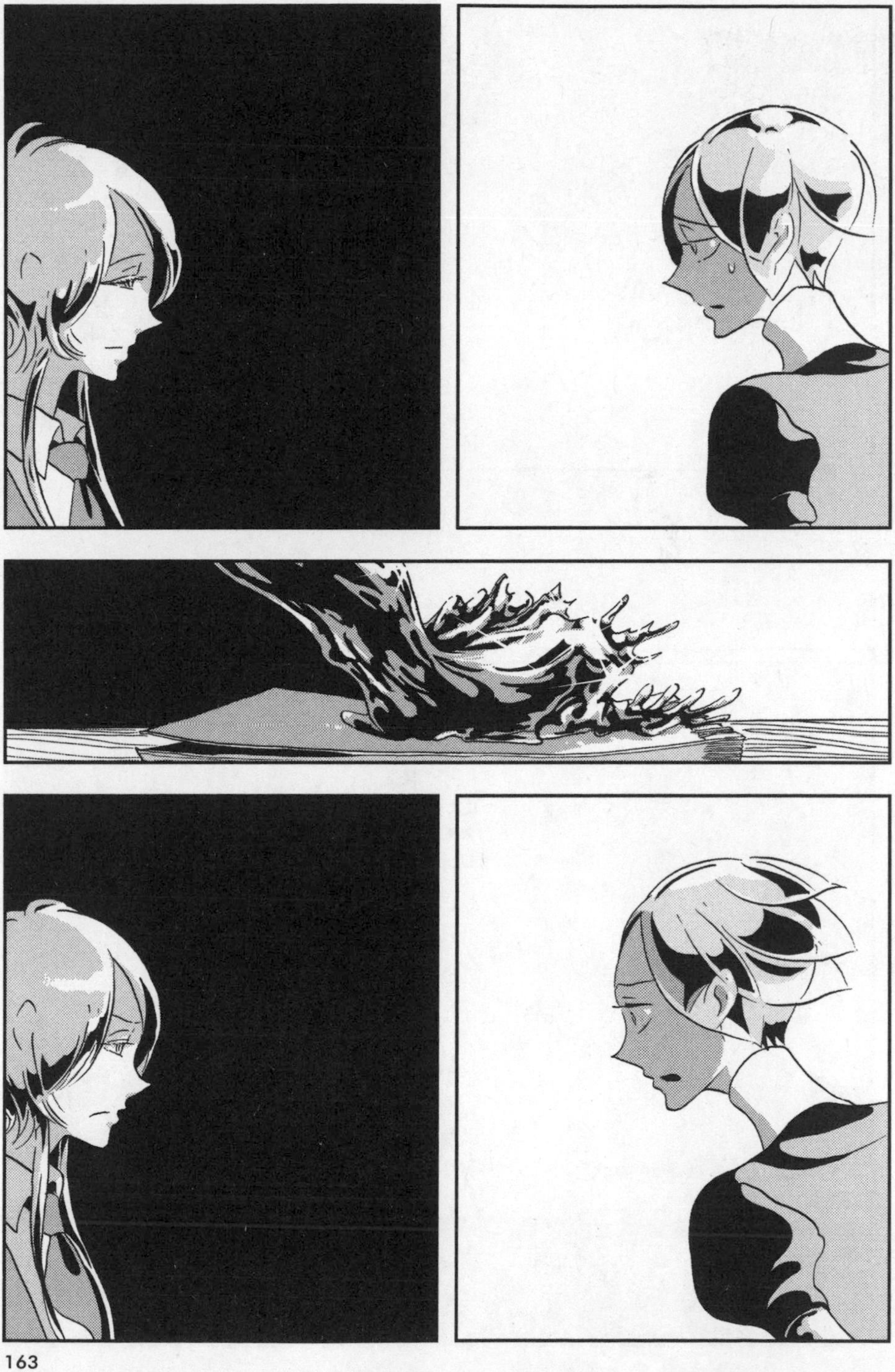

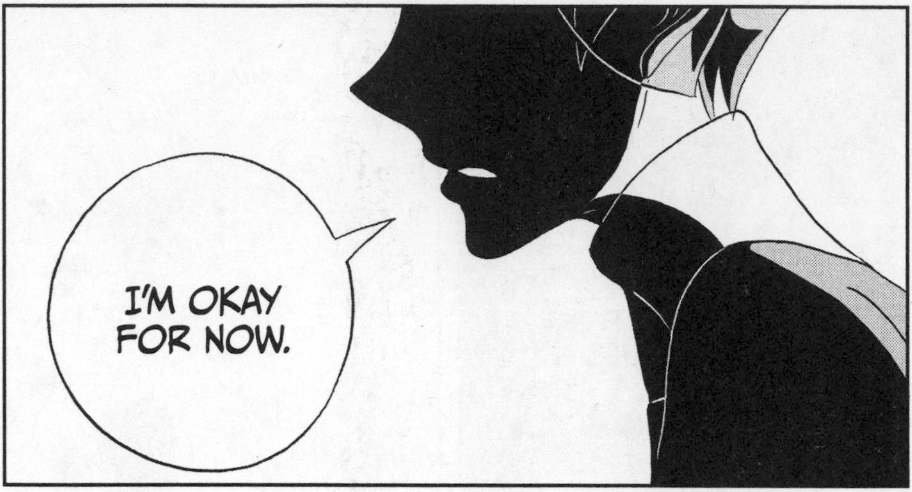
I'M OKAY FOR NOW.
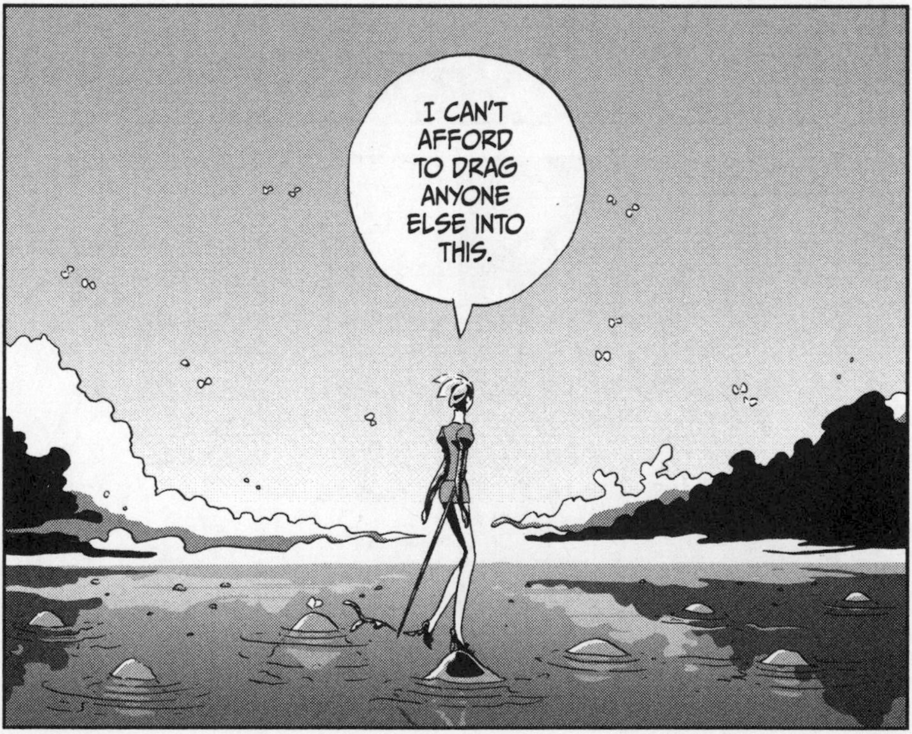
I CAN'T AFFORD TO DRAG ANYONE ELSE INTO THIS.

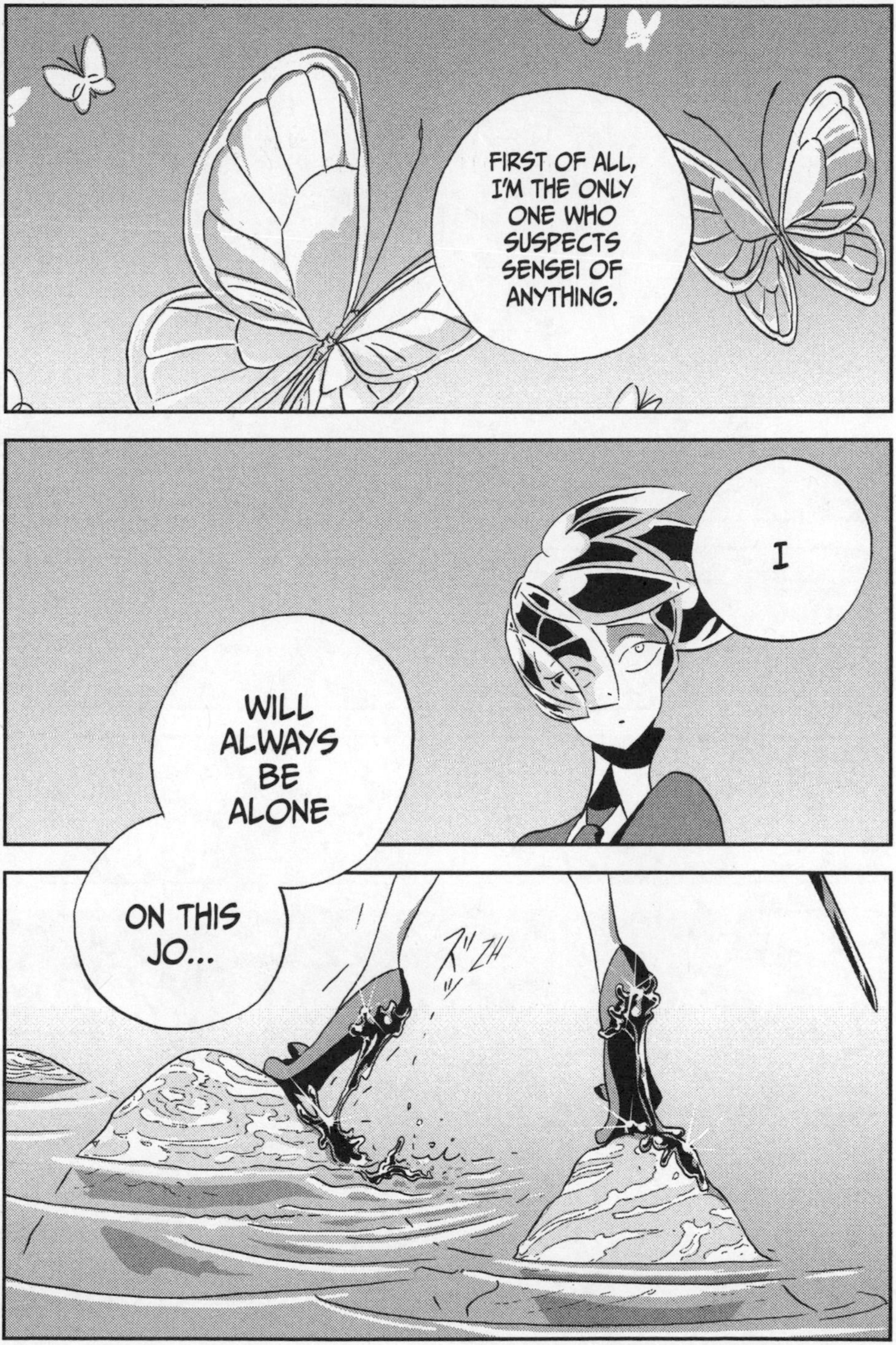
FIRST OF ALL, I'M THE ONLY ONE WHO SUSPECTS SENSEI OF ANYTHING.
I
WILL ALWAYS BE ALONE
ON THIS JO...
ZH

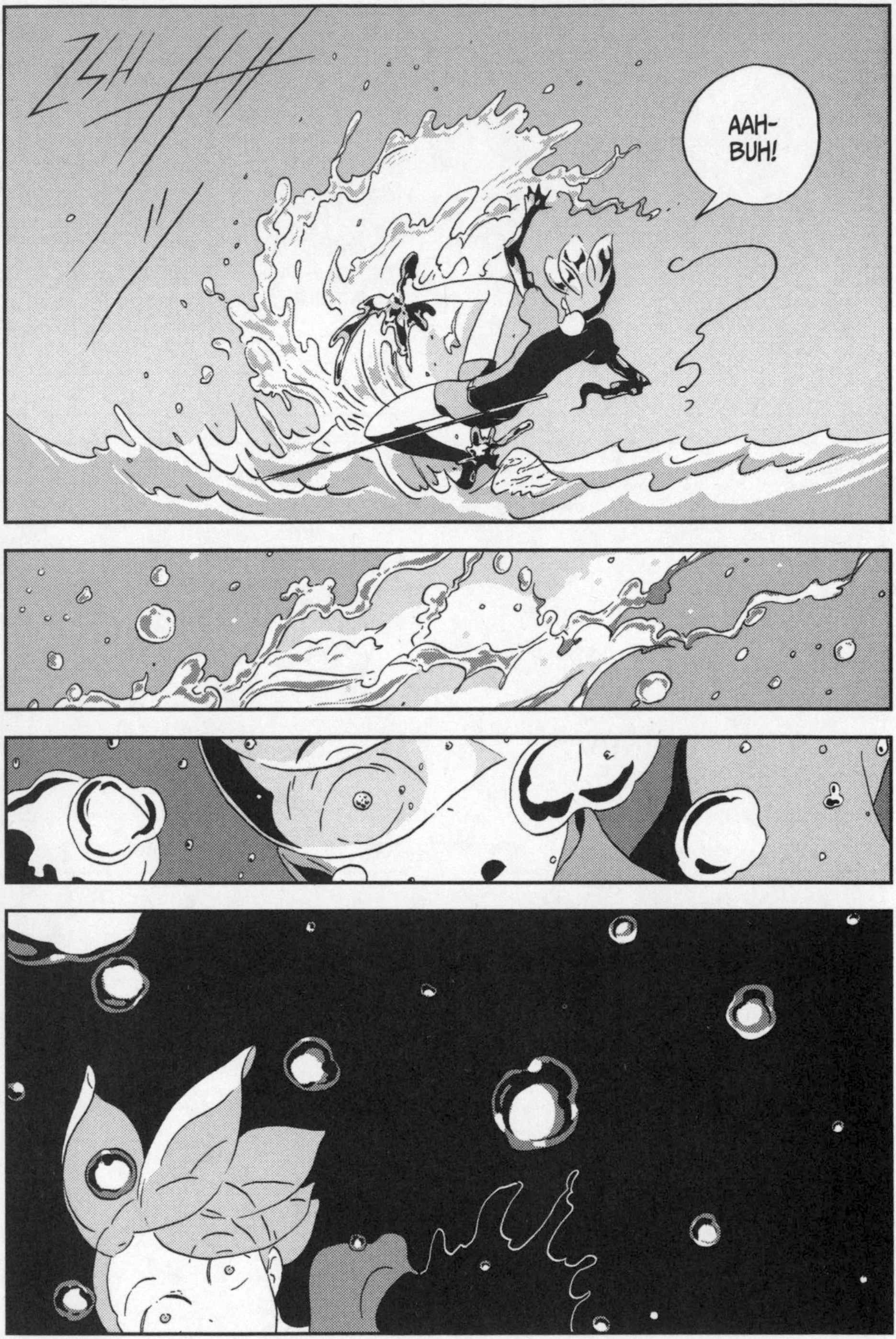
AAH-
BUH!
ZSH

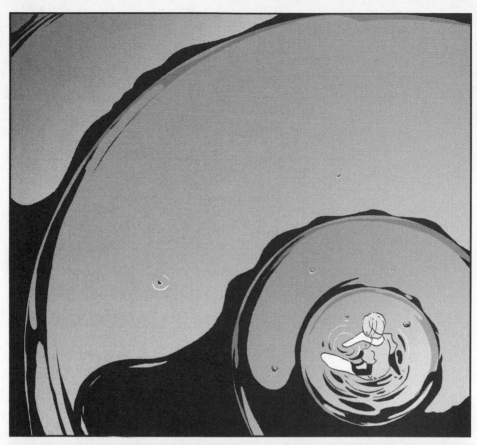

A NEW...

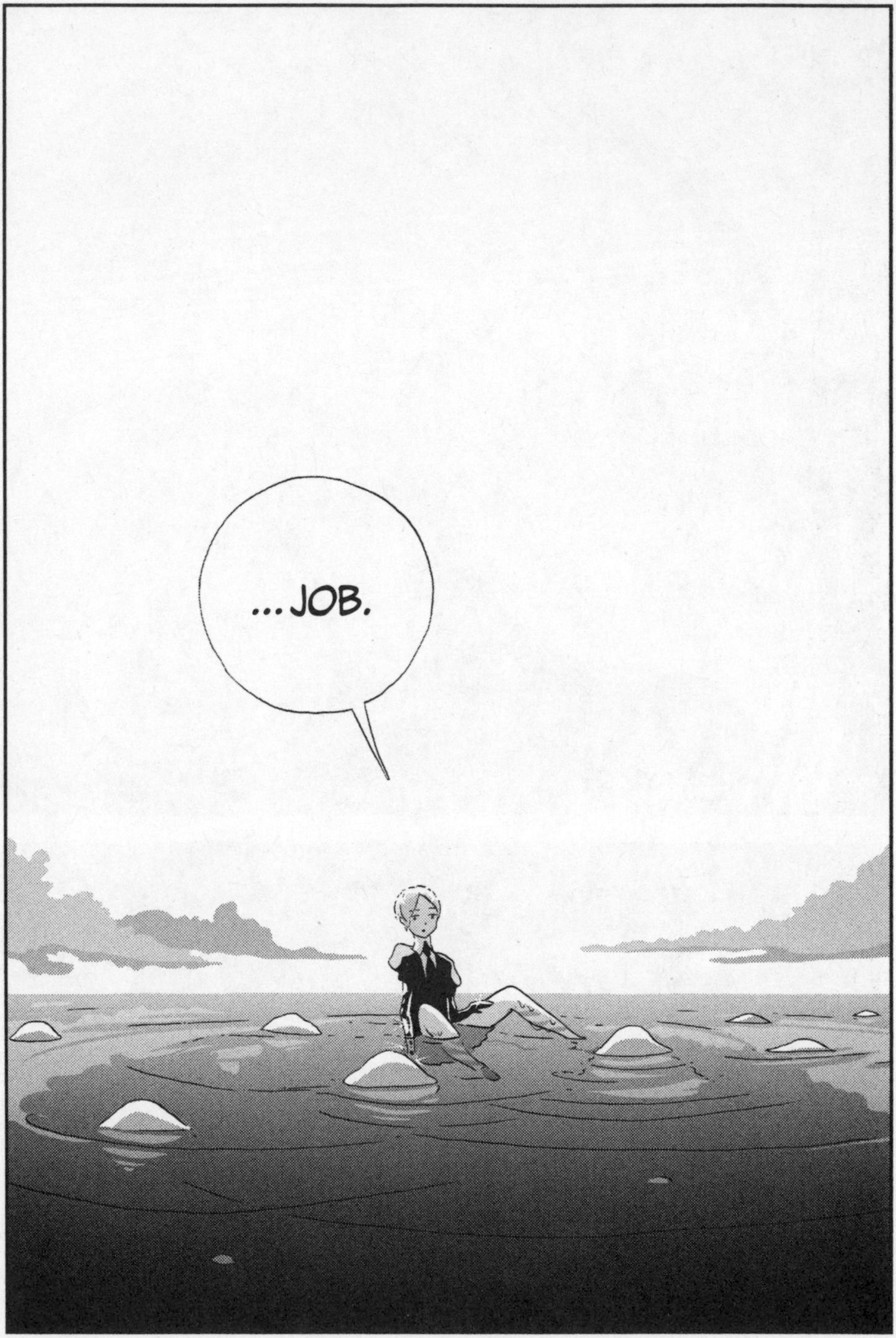
...JOB.

CHAPTER 35: A Pair END

CHAPTER 36:

A New Job

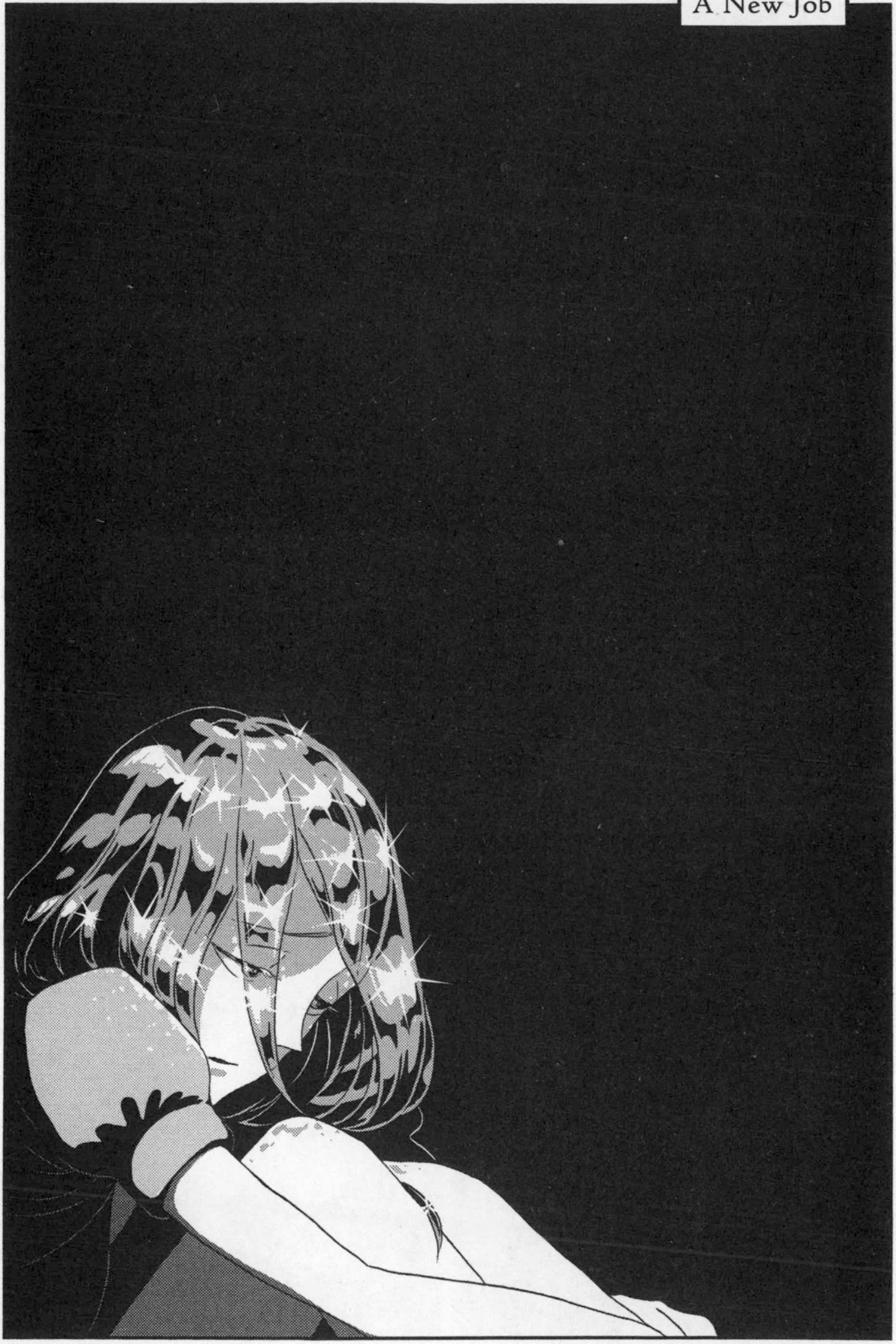

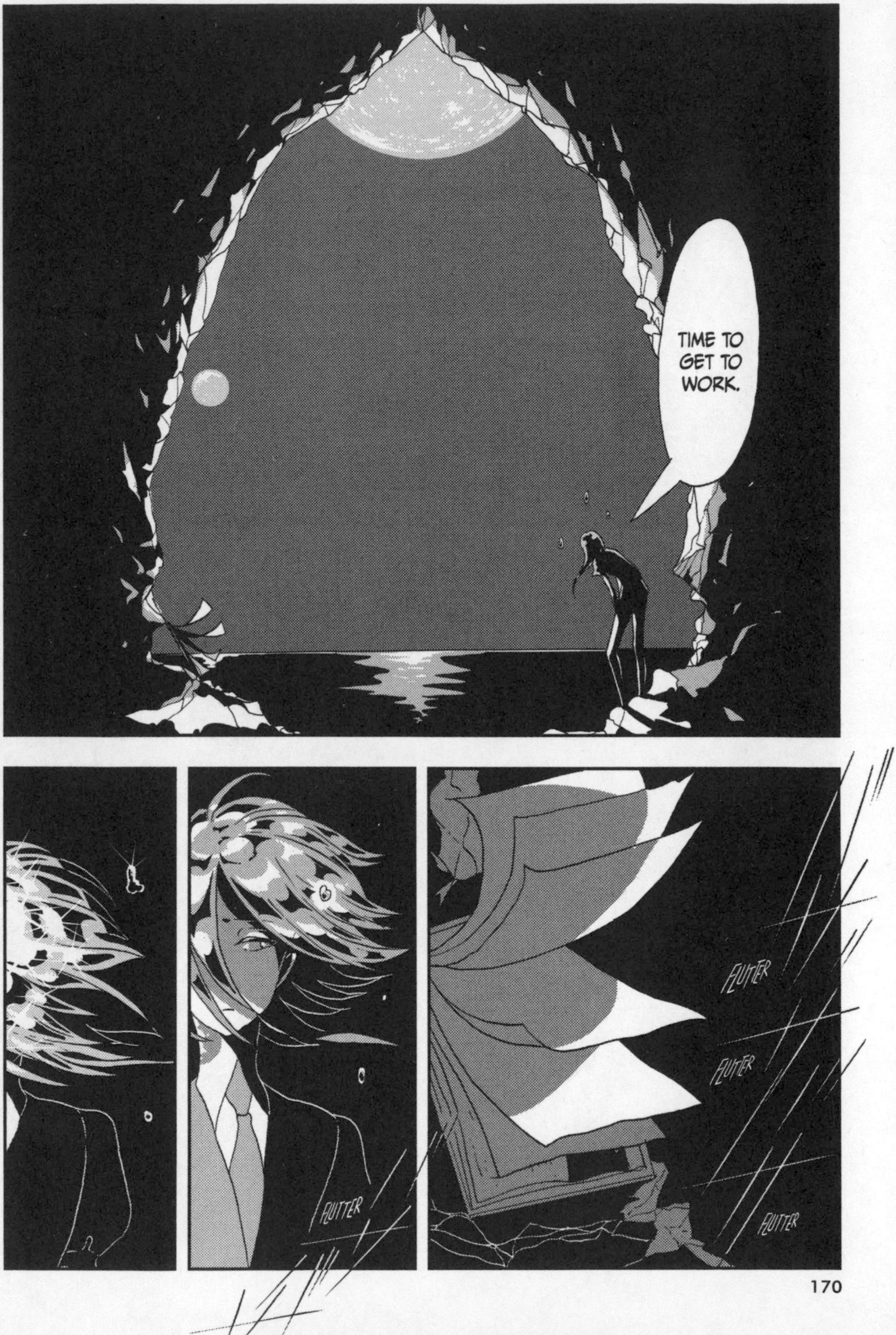
TIME TO GET TO WORK.
FLUTTER
FLUTTER
FLUTTER
FLUTTER

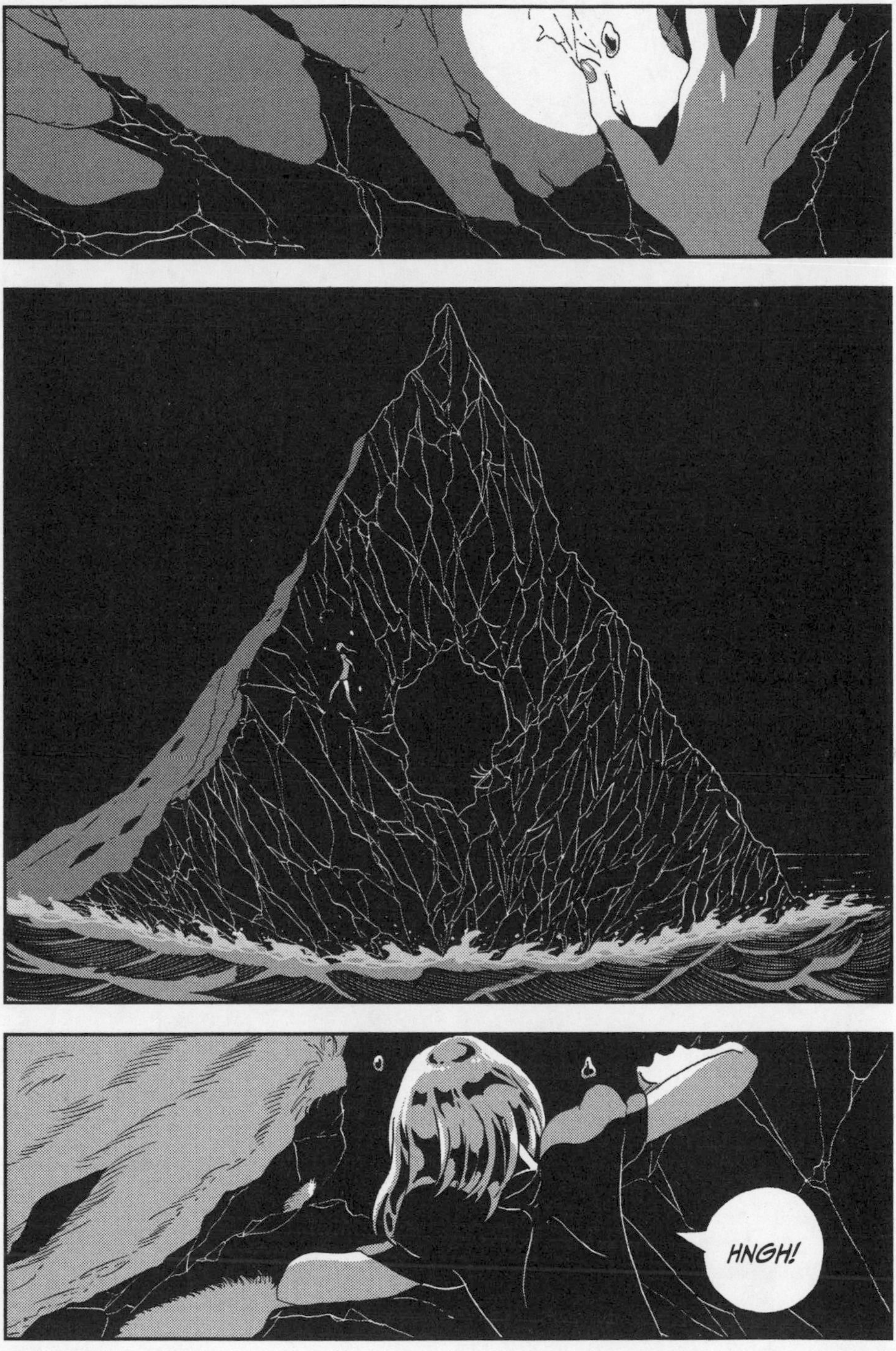
HNGH!

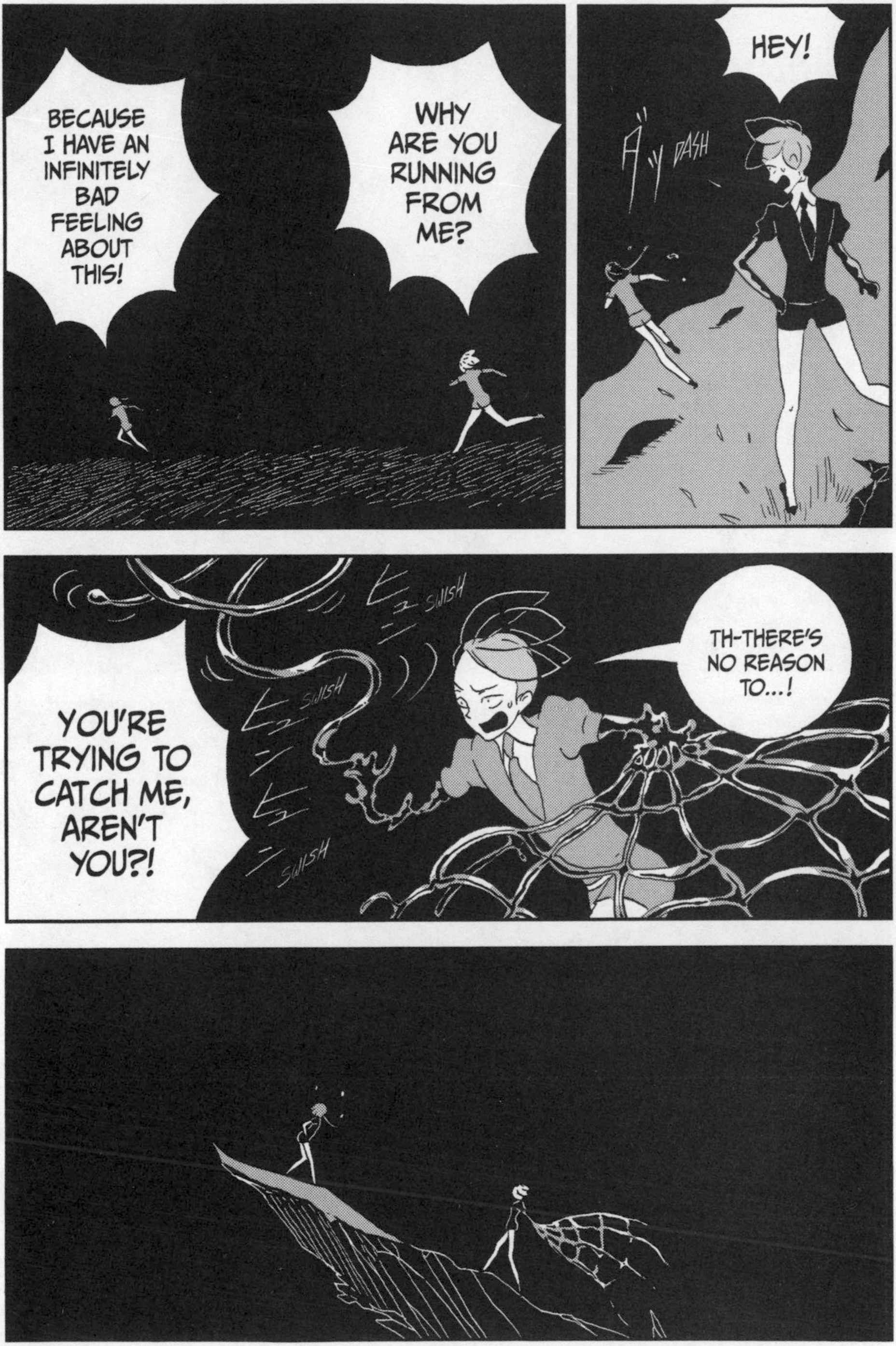
HEY!
DASH
WHY ARE YOU RUNNING FROM ME?
BECAUSE I HAVE AN INFINITELY BAD FEELING ABOUT THIS!
SWISH
TH-THERE'S NO REASON TO...!
SWISH
YOU'RE TRYING TO CATCH ME, AREN'T YOU?!
SWISH

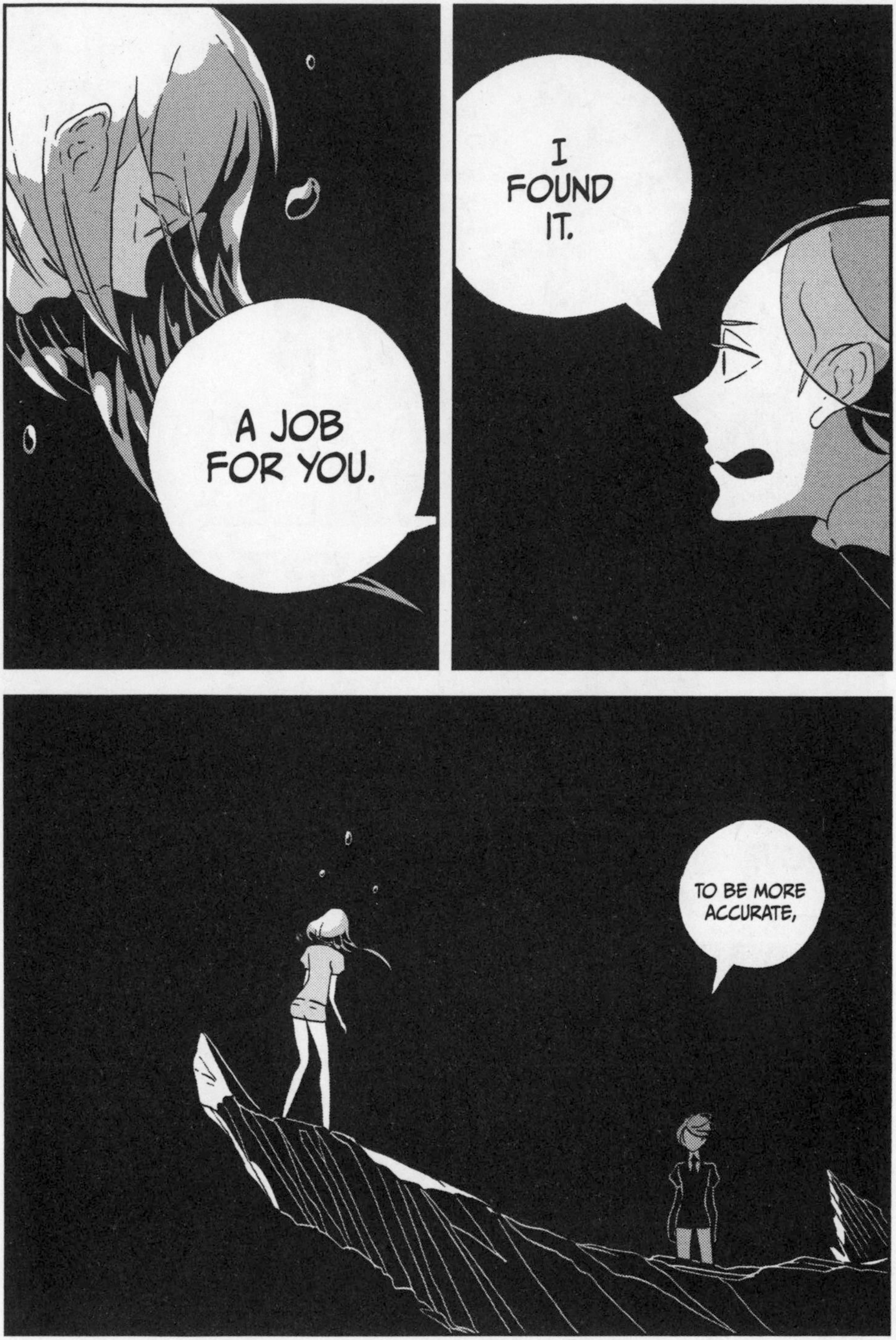
I FOUND IT.
A JOB FOR YOU.
TO BE MORE ACCURATE,

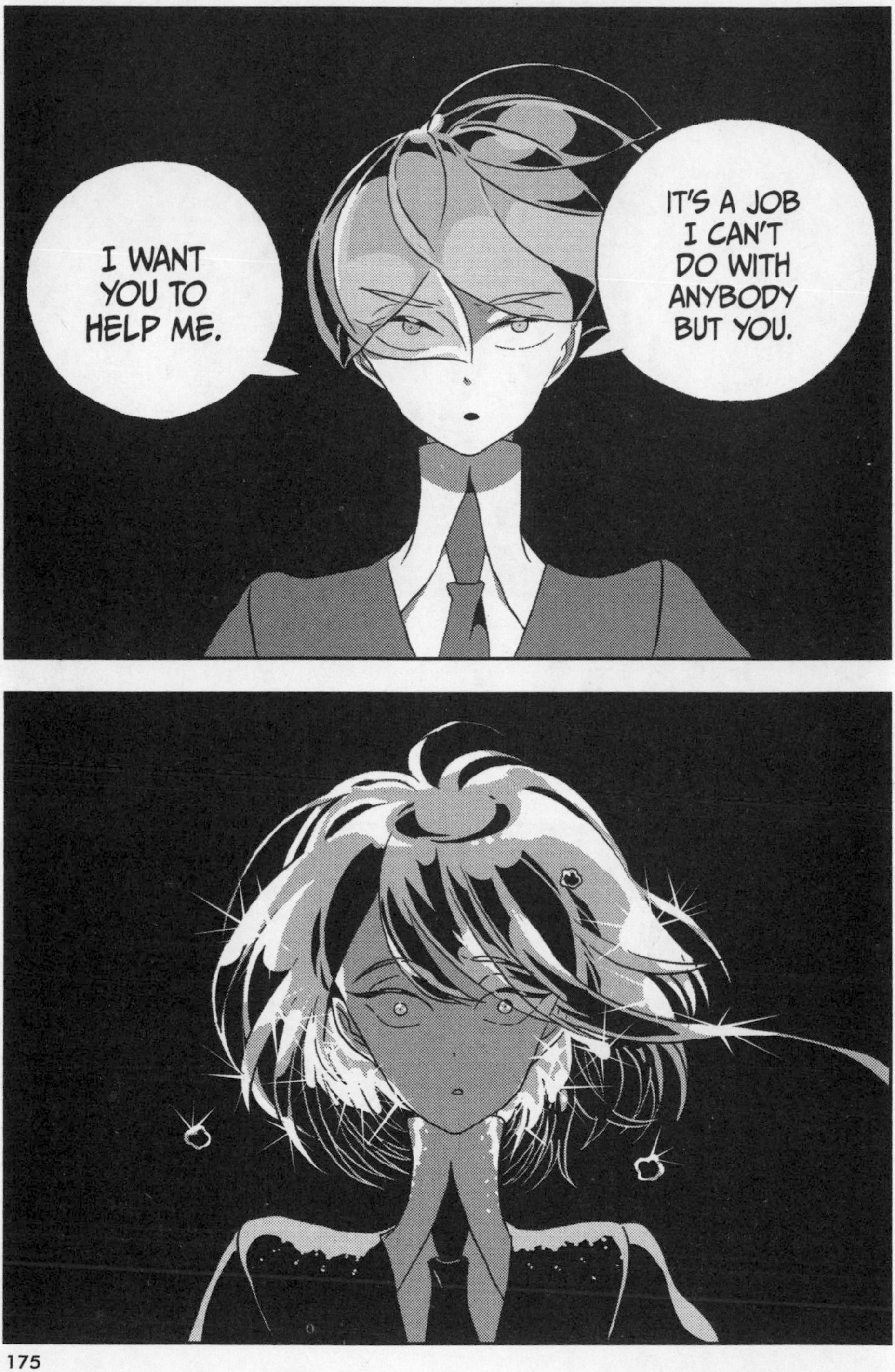
IT'S A JOB I CAN'T DO WITH ANYBODY BUT YOU.
I WANT YOU TO HELP ME.

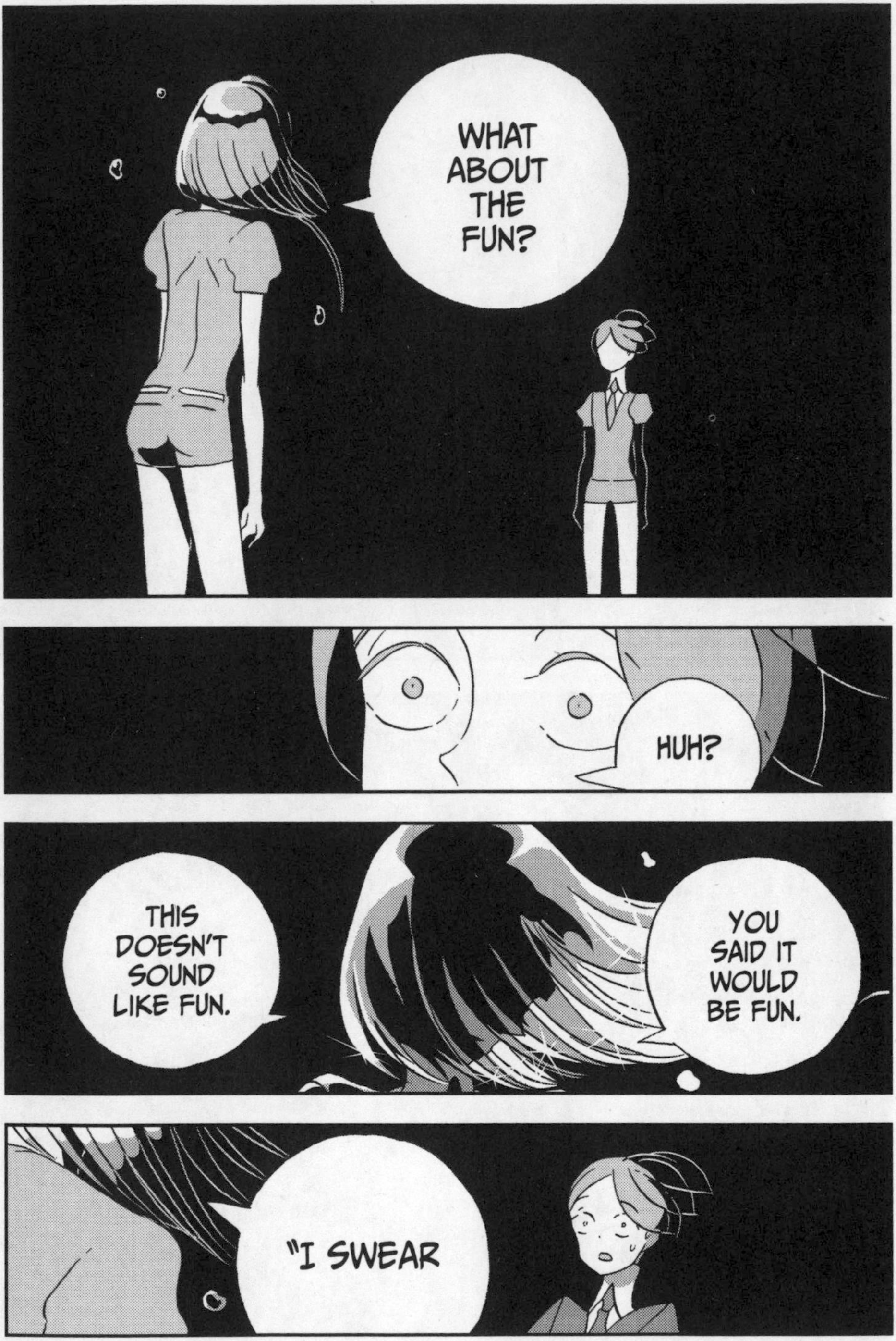
WHAT ABOUT THE FUN?
HUH?
YOU SAID IT WOULD BE FUN.
THIS DOESN'T SOUND LIKE FUN.
"I SWEAR

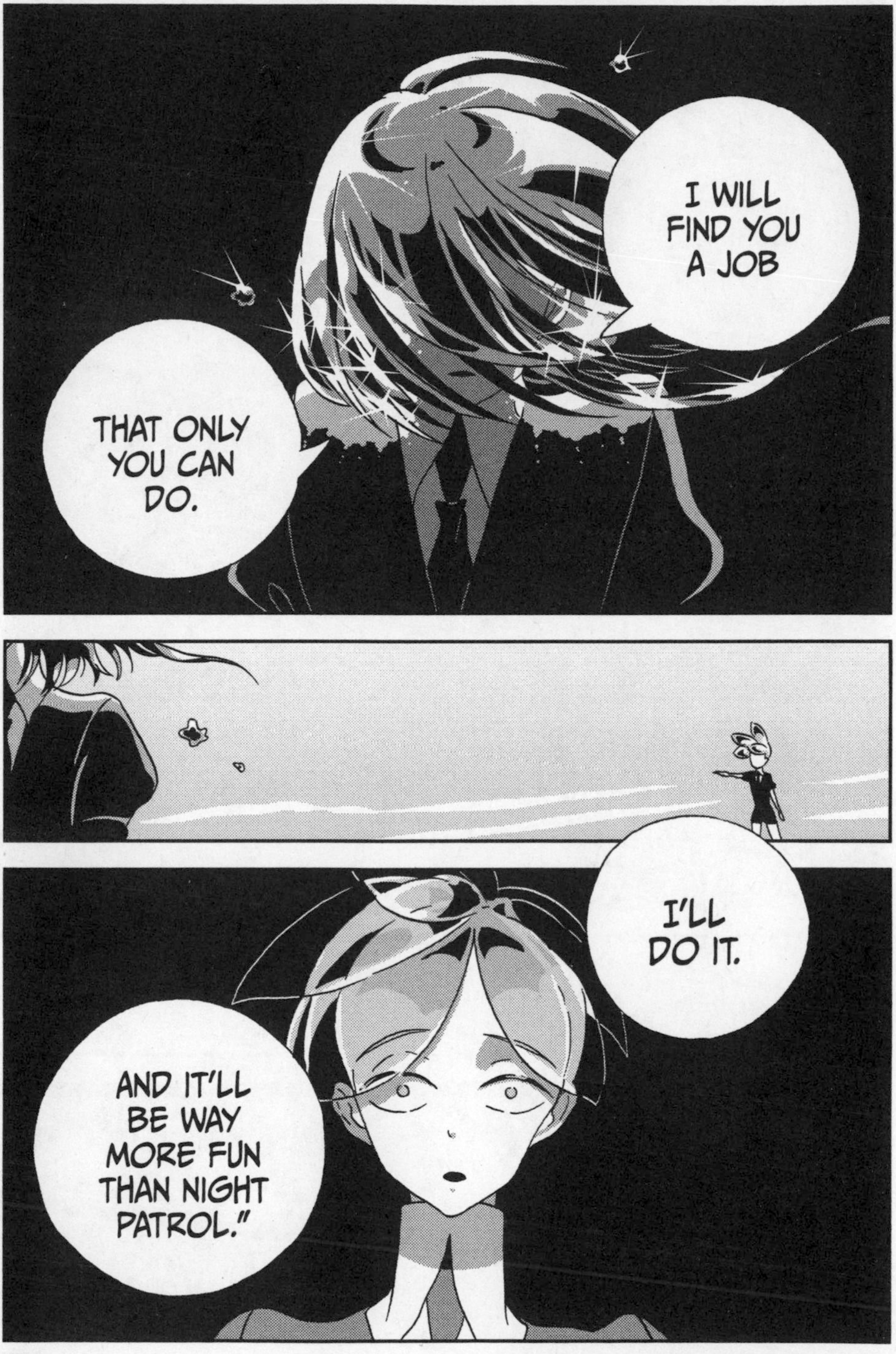
I WILL FIND YOU A JOB
THAT ONLY YOU CAN DO.
I'LL DO IT.
AND IT'LL BE WAY MORE FUN THAN NIGHT PATROL."

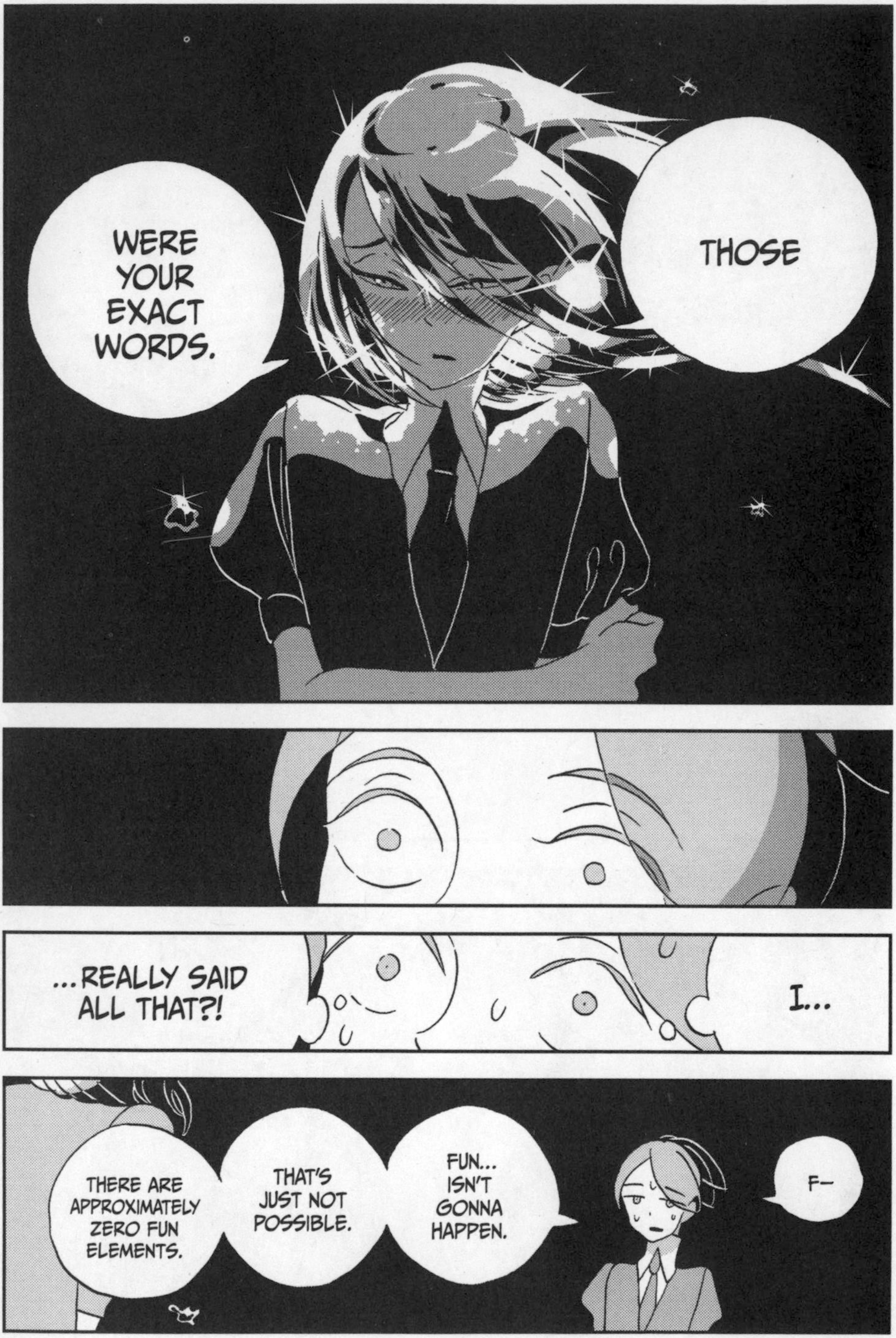
THOSE
WERE YOUR EXACT WORDS.
I...
...REALLY SAID ALL THAT?!
F–
FUN... ISN'T GONNA HAPPEN.
THAT'S JUST NOT POSSIBLE.
THERE ARE APPROXIMATELY ZERO FUN ELEMENTS.

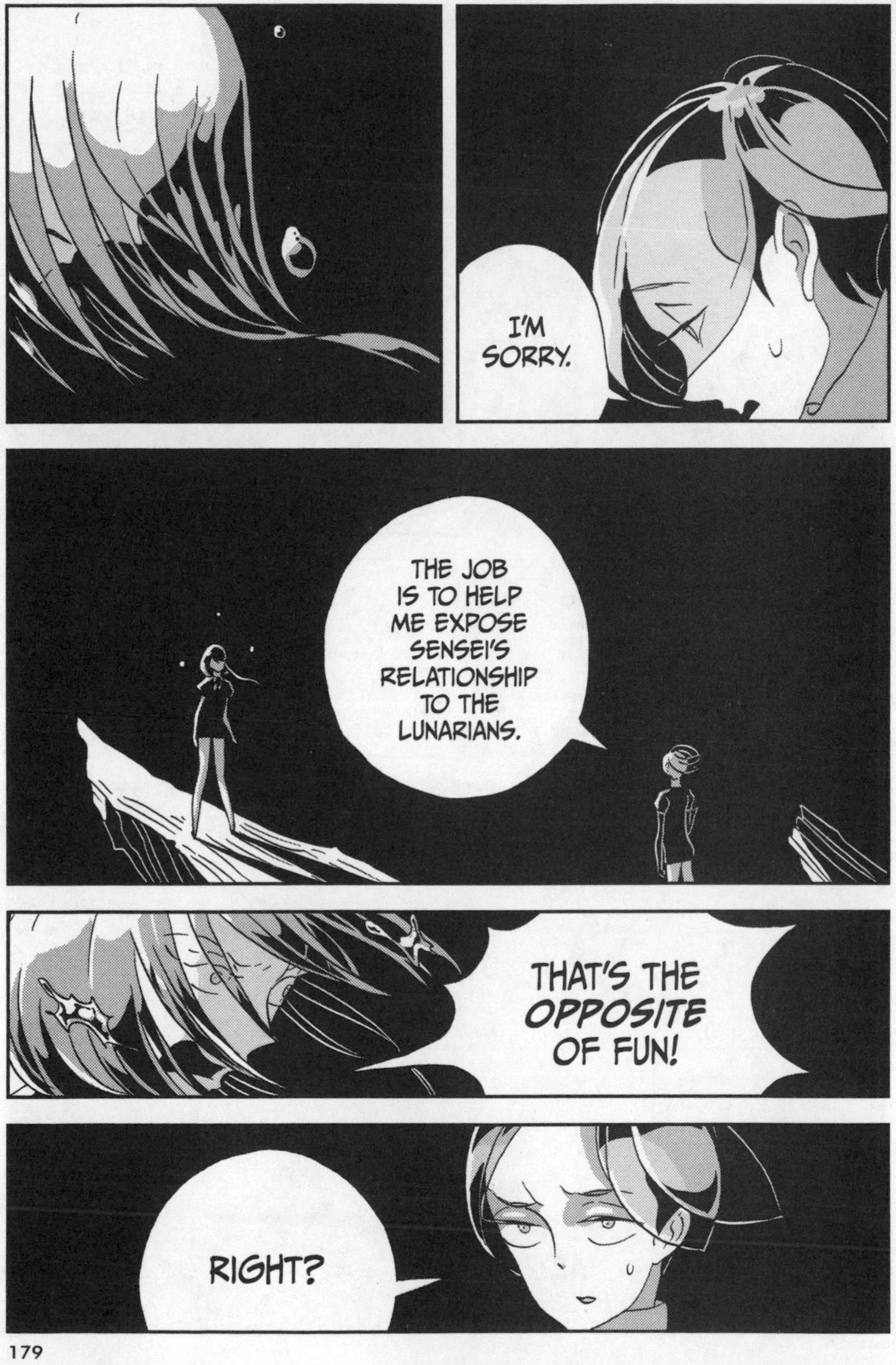
I'M SORRY.
THE JOB IS TO HELP ME EXPOSE SENSEI'S RELATIONSHIP TO THE LUNARIANS.
THAT'S THE OPPOSITE OF FUN!
RIGHT?

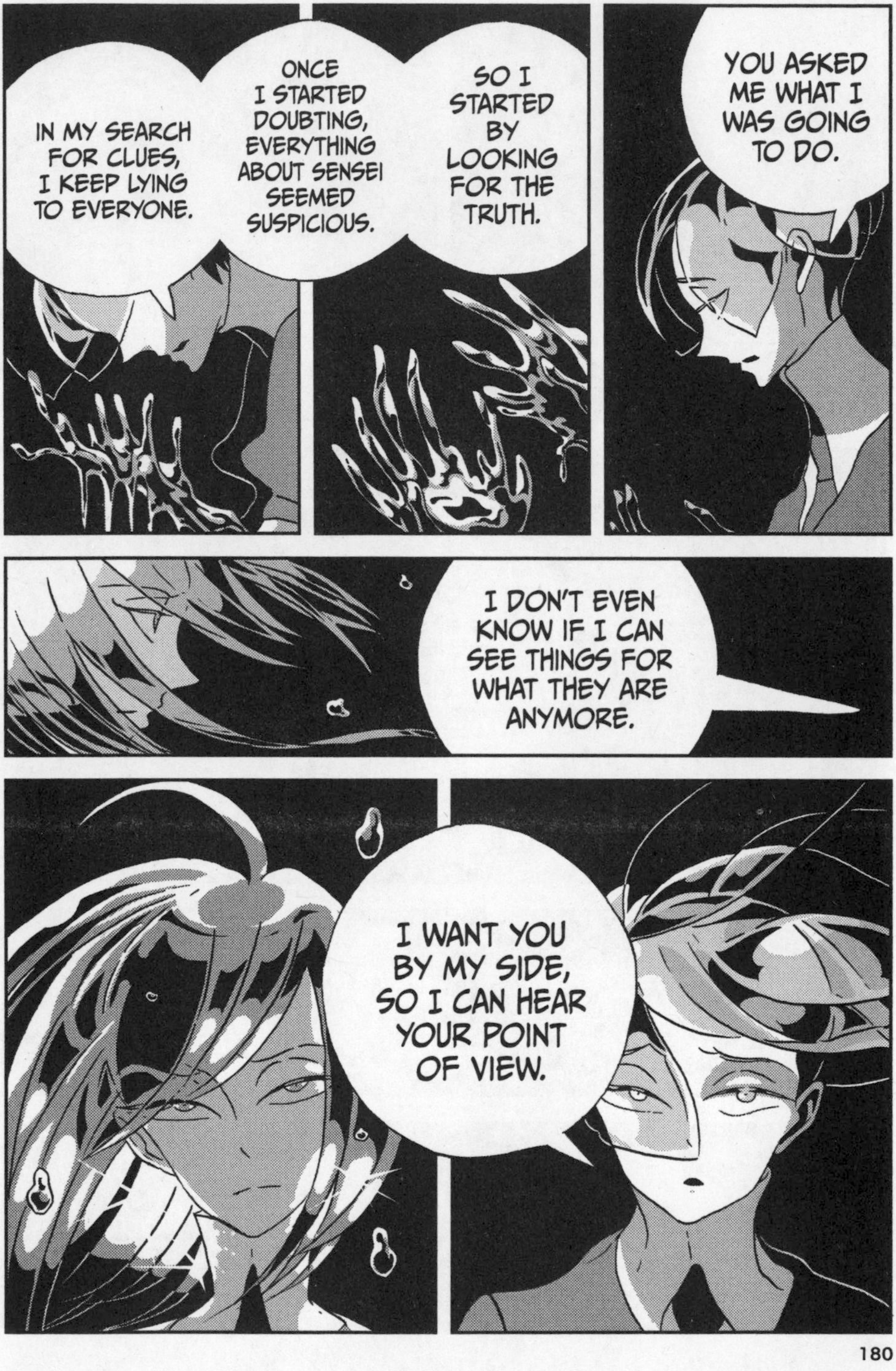
YOU ASKED ME WHAT I WAS GOING TO DO.
SO I STARTED BY LOOKING FOR THE TRUTH.
ONCE I STARTED DOUBTING, EVERYTHING ABOUT SENSEI SEEMED SUSPICIOUS.
IN MY SEARCH FOR CLUES, I KEEP LYING TO EVERYONE.
I DON'T EVEN KNOW IF I CAN SEE THINGS FOR WHAT THEY ARE ANYMORE.
I WANT YOU BY MY SIDE, SO I CAN HEAR YOUR POINT OF VIEW.

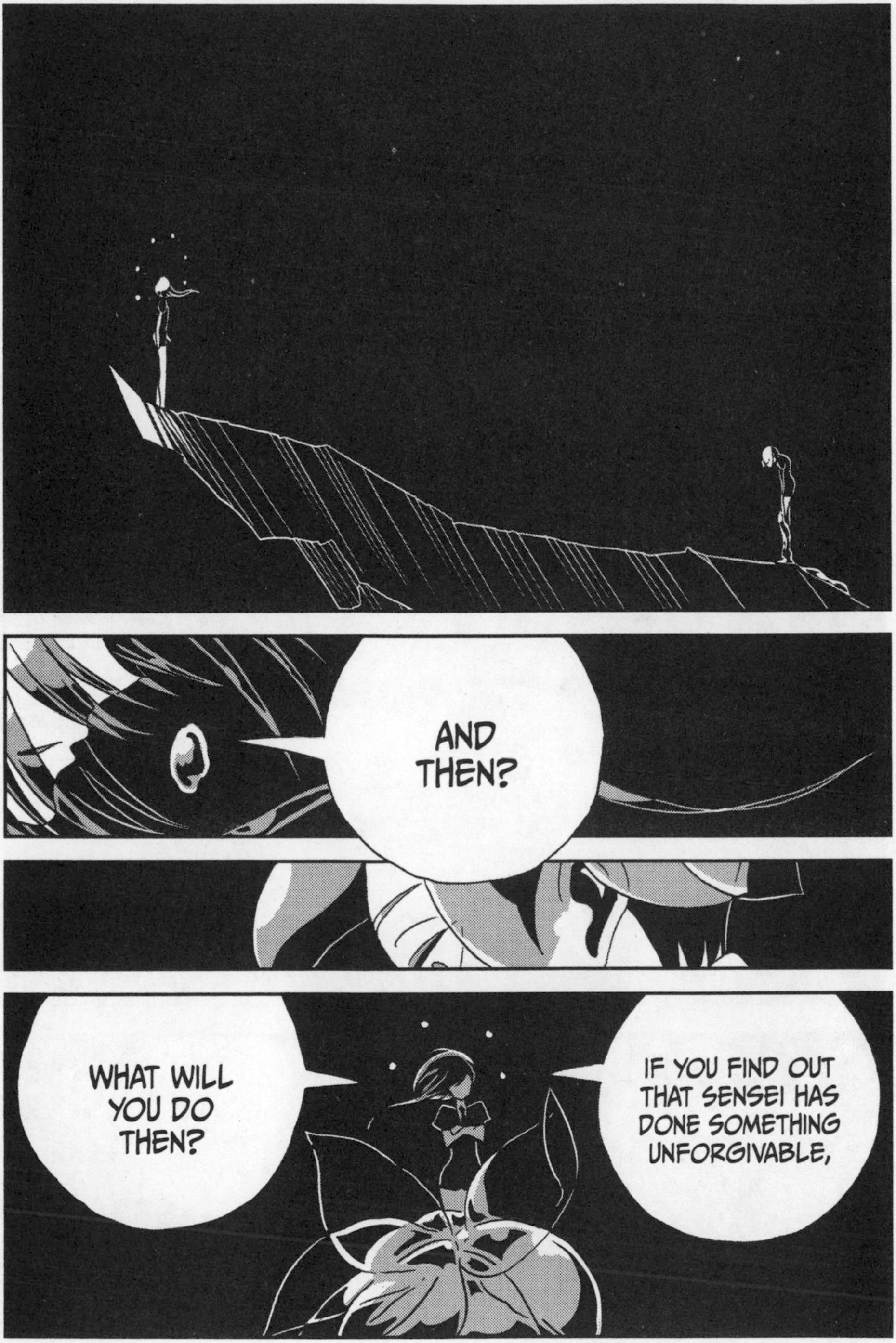
AND THEN?
IF YOU FIND OUT THAT SENSEI HAS DONE SOMETHING UNFORGIVABLE,
WHAT WILL YOU DO THEN?

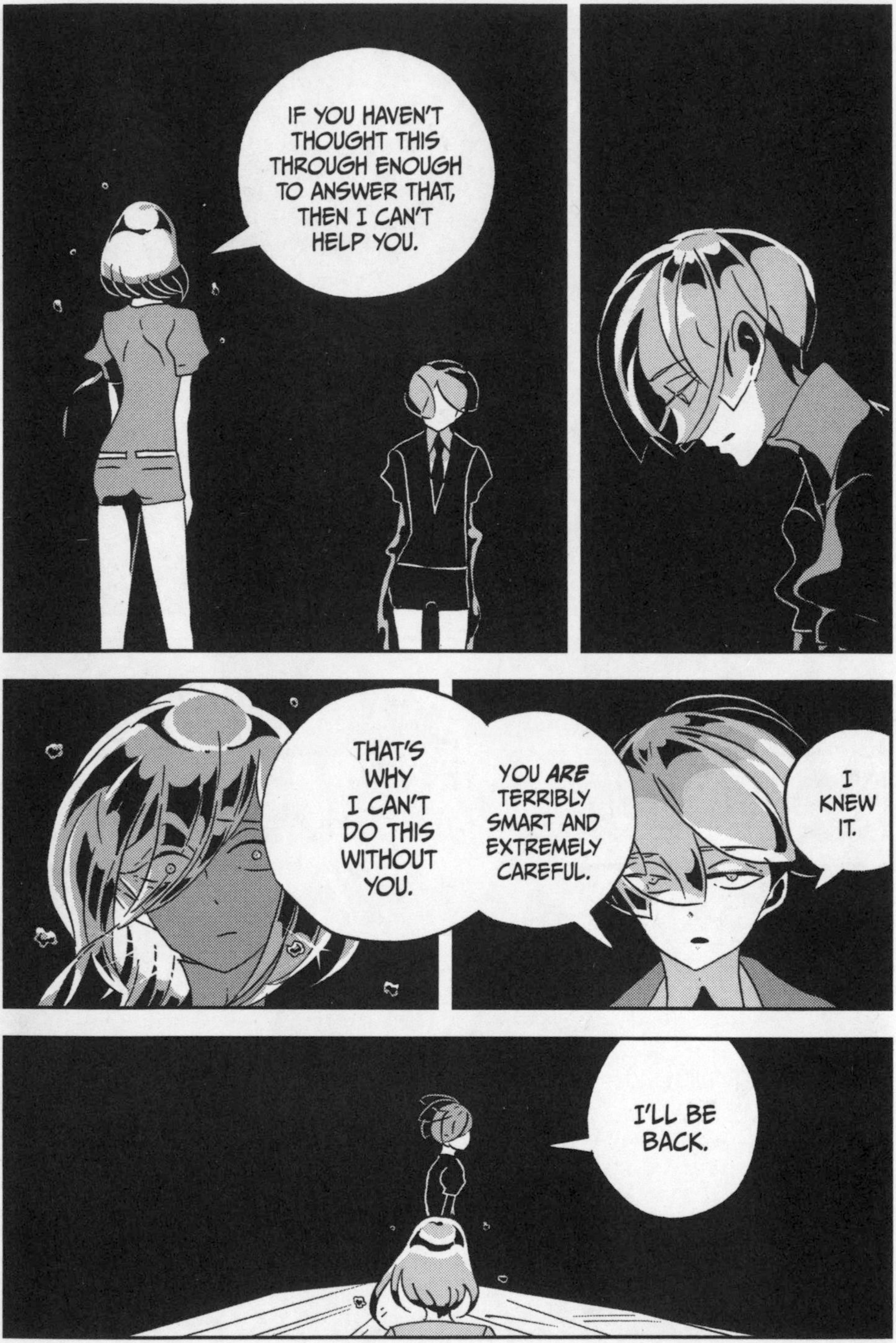
IF YOU HAVEN'T THOUGHT THIS THROUGH ENOUGH TO ANSWER THAT, THEN I CAN'T HELP YOU.
I KNEW IT.
YOU *ARE* TERRIBLY SMART AND EXTREMELY CAREFUL.
THAT'S WHY I CAN'T DO THIS WITHOUT YOU.
I'LL BE BACK.

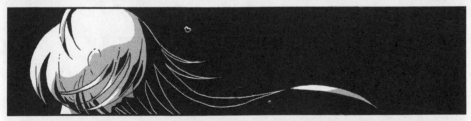

BUT...

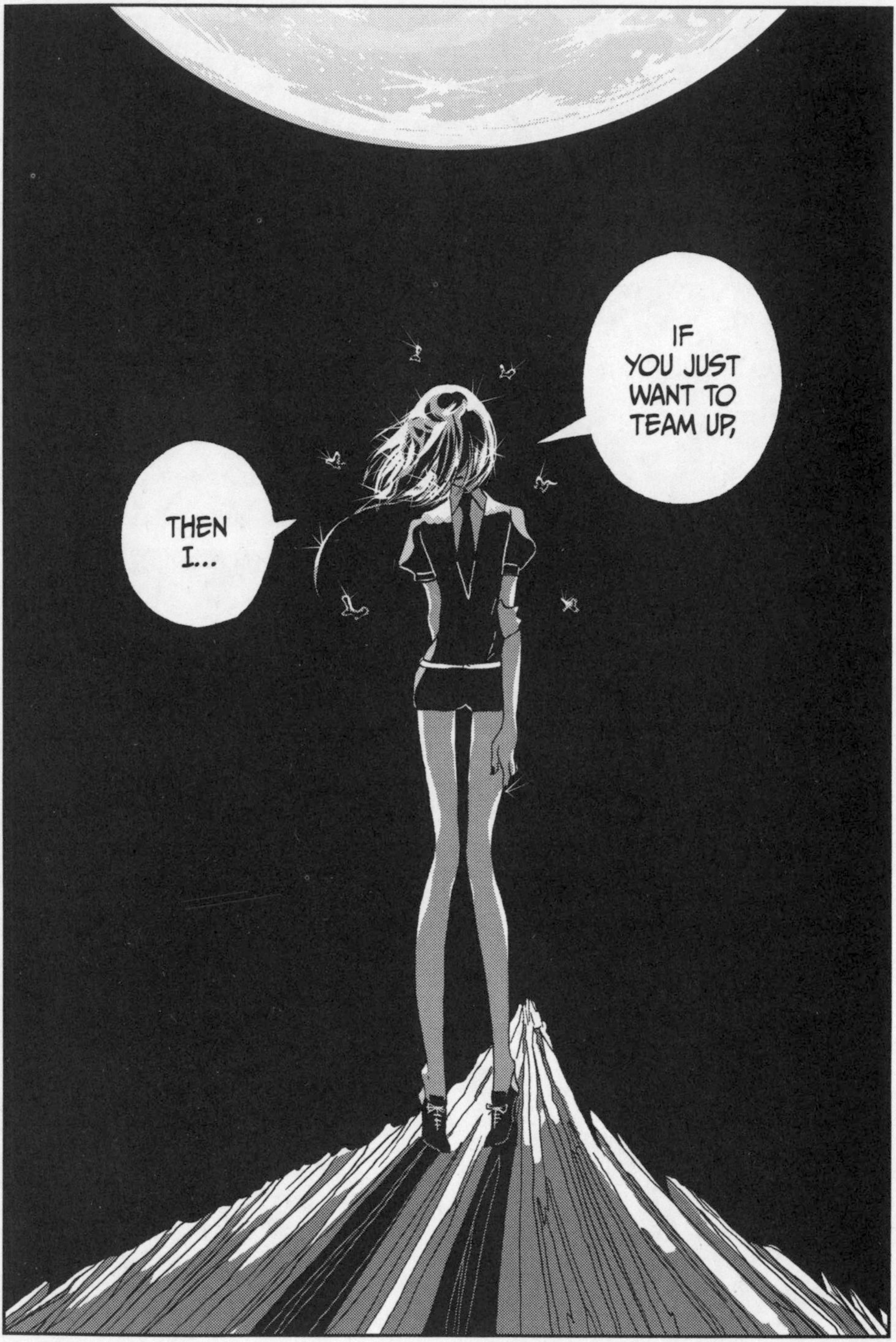
IF YOU JUST WANT TO TEAM UP,
THEN I...

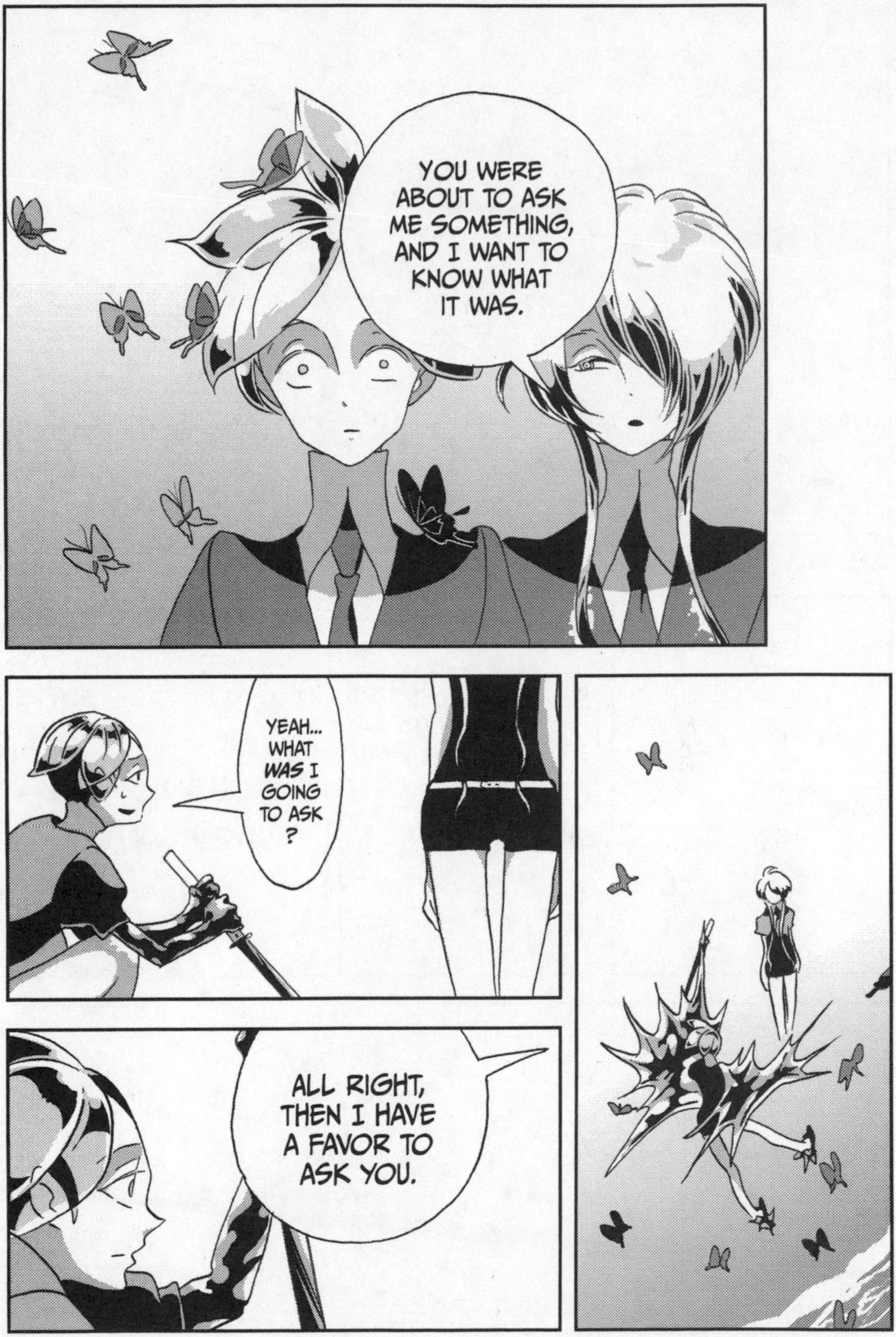
YOU WERE ABOUT TO ASK ME SOMETHING, AND I WANT TO KNOW WHAT IT WAS.
YEAH... WHAT *WAS* I GOING TO ASK ?
ALL RIGHT, THEN I HAVE A FAVOR TO ASK YOU.

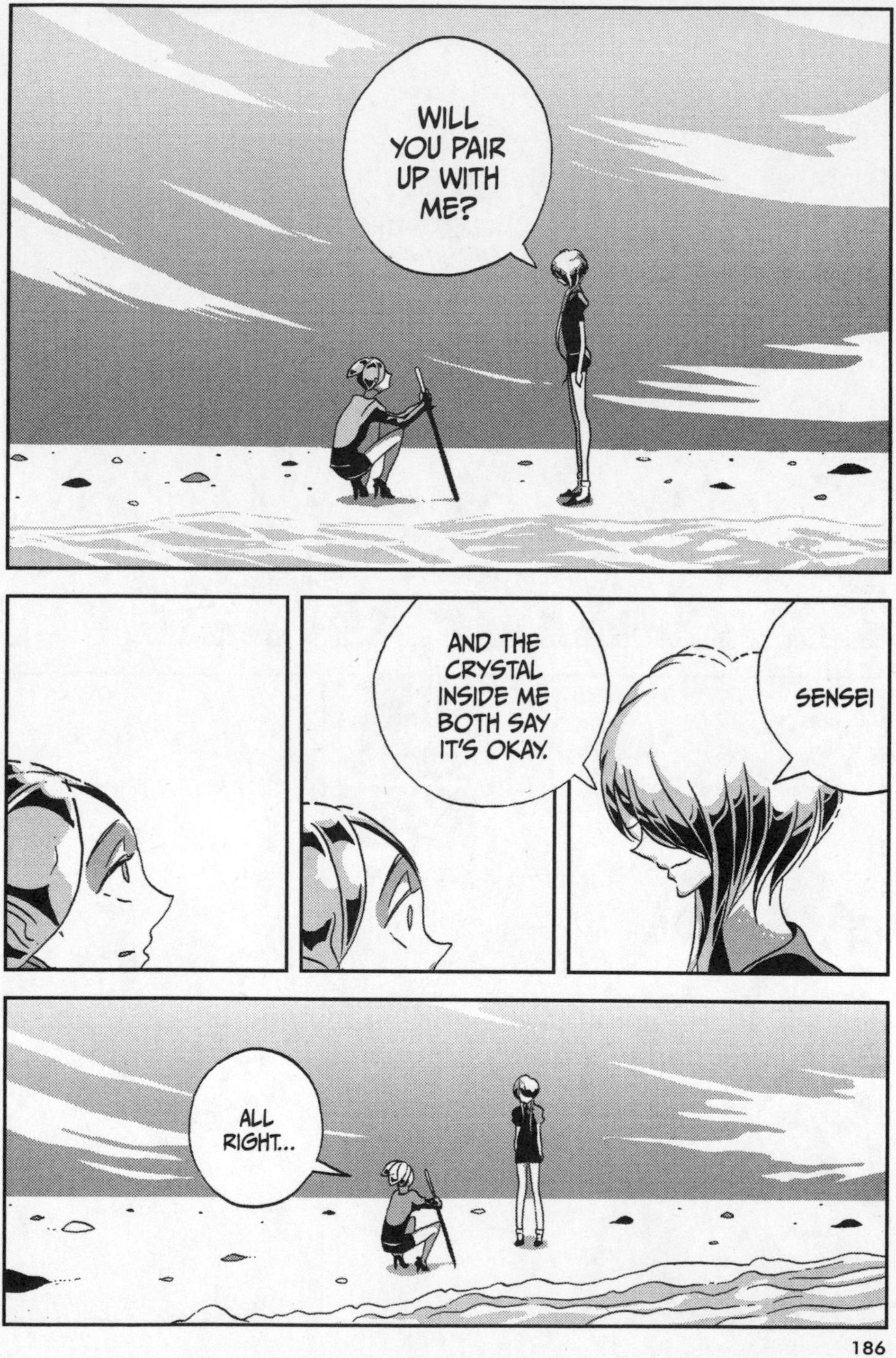
WILL YOU PAIR UP WITH ME?
SENSEI
AND THE CRYSTAL INSIDE ME BOTH SAY IT'S OKAY.
ALL RIGHT...

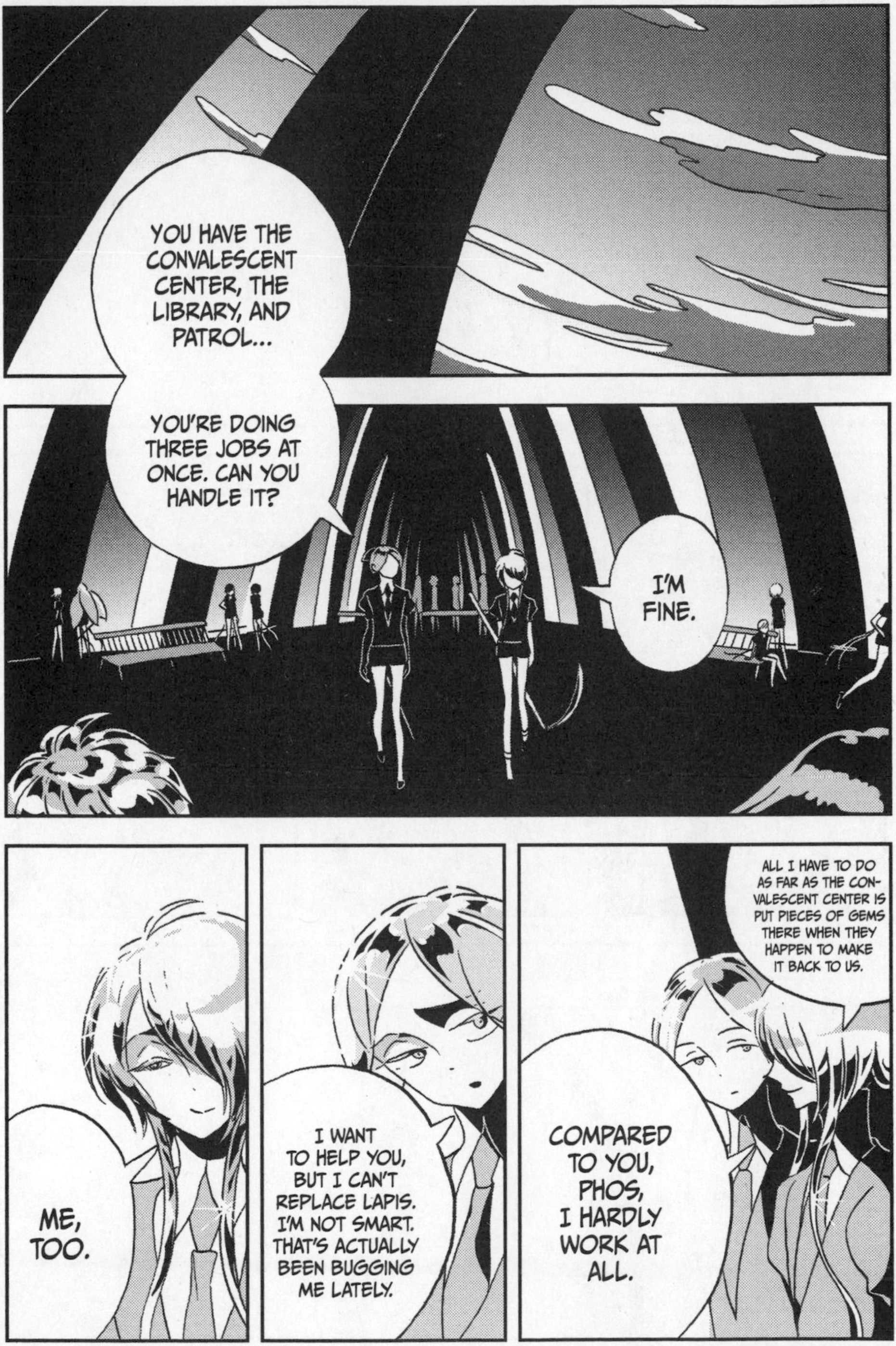
YOU HAVE THE CONVALESCENT CENTER, THE LIBRARY, AND PATROL...
YOU'RE DOING THREE JOBS AT ONCE. CAN YOU HANDLE IT?
I'M FINE.
ALL I HAVE TO DO AS FAR AS THE CONVALESCENT CENTER IS PUT PIECES OF GEMS THERE WHEN THEY HAPPEN TO MAKE IT BACK TO US.
COMPARED TO YOU, PHOS, I HARDLY WORK AT ALL.
I WANT TO HELP YOU, BUT I CAN'T REPLACE LAPIS. I'M NOT SMART. THAT'S ACTUALLY BEEN BUGGING ME LATELY.
ME, TOO.

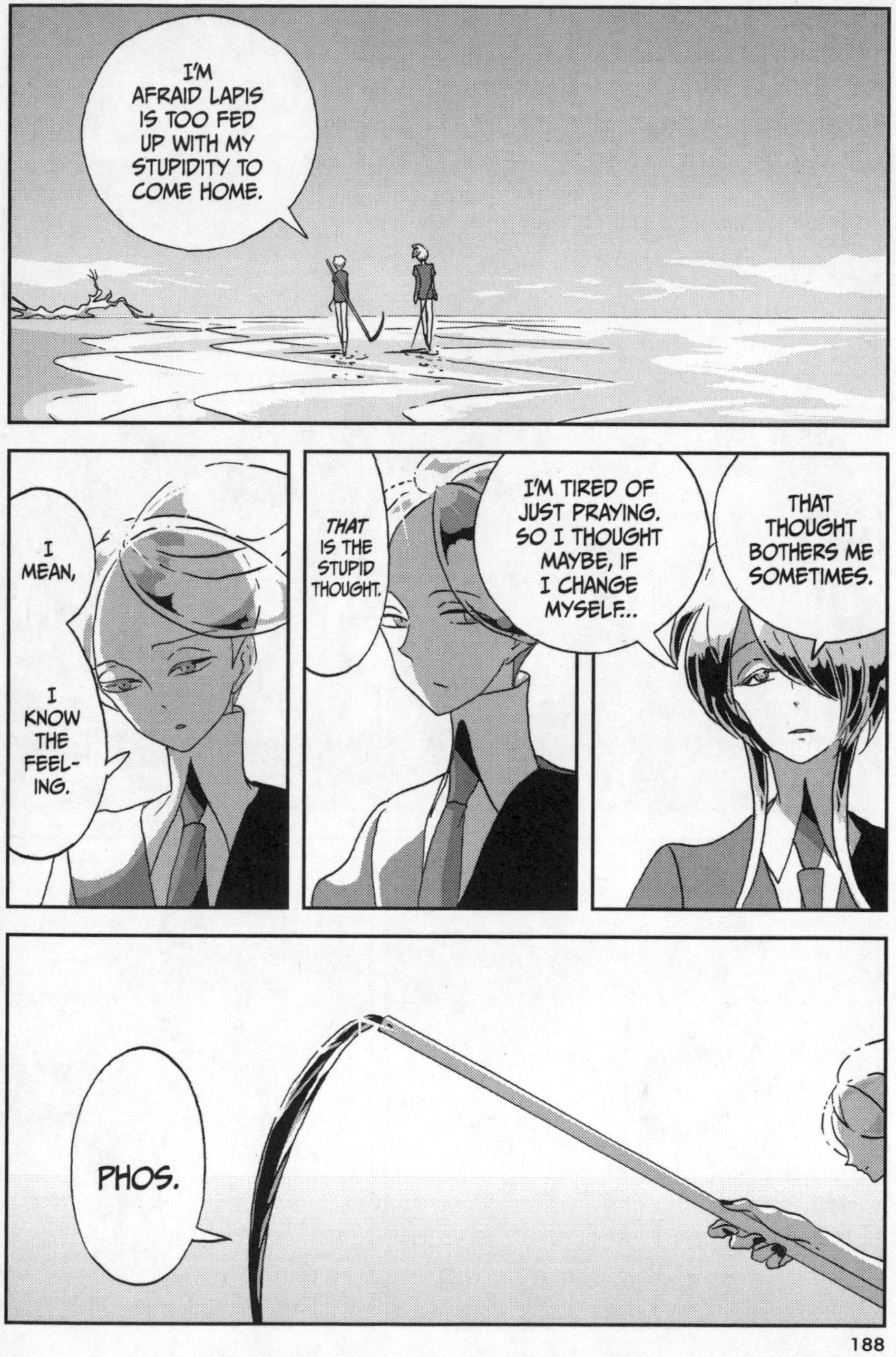
I'M AFRAID LAPIS IS TOO FED UP WITH MY STUPIDITY TO COME HOME.
THAT THOUGHT BOTHERS ME SOMETIMES.
I'M TIRED OF JUST PRAYING. SO I THOUGHT MAYBE, IF I CHANGE MYSELF...
THAT IS THE STUPID THOUGHT.
I MEAN,
I KNOW THE FEEL- ING.
PHOS.

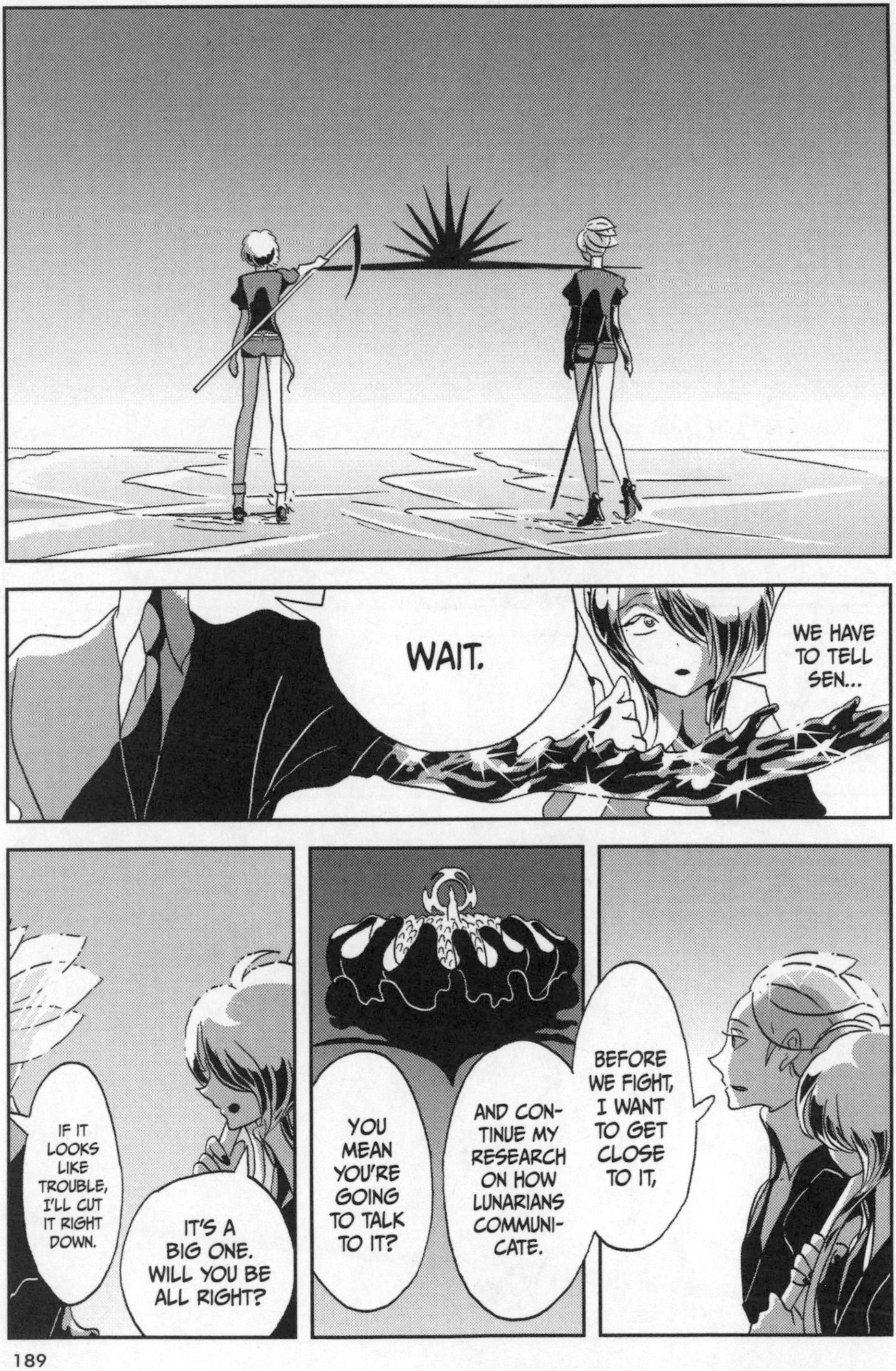
WE HAVE TO TELL SEN...
WAIT.
BEFORE WE FIGHT, I WANT TO GET CLOSE TO IT,
AND CON-TINUE MY RESEARCH ON HOW LUNARIANS COMMUNI-CATE.
YOU MEAN YOU'RE GOING TO TALK TO IT?
IT'S A BIG ONE. WILL YOU BE ALL RIGHT?
IF IT LOOKS LIKE TROUBLE, I'LL CUT IT RIGHT DOWN.

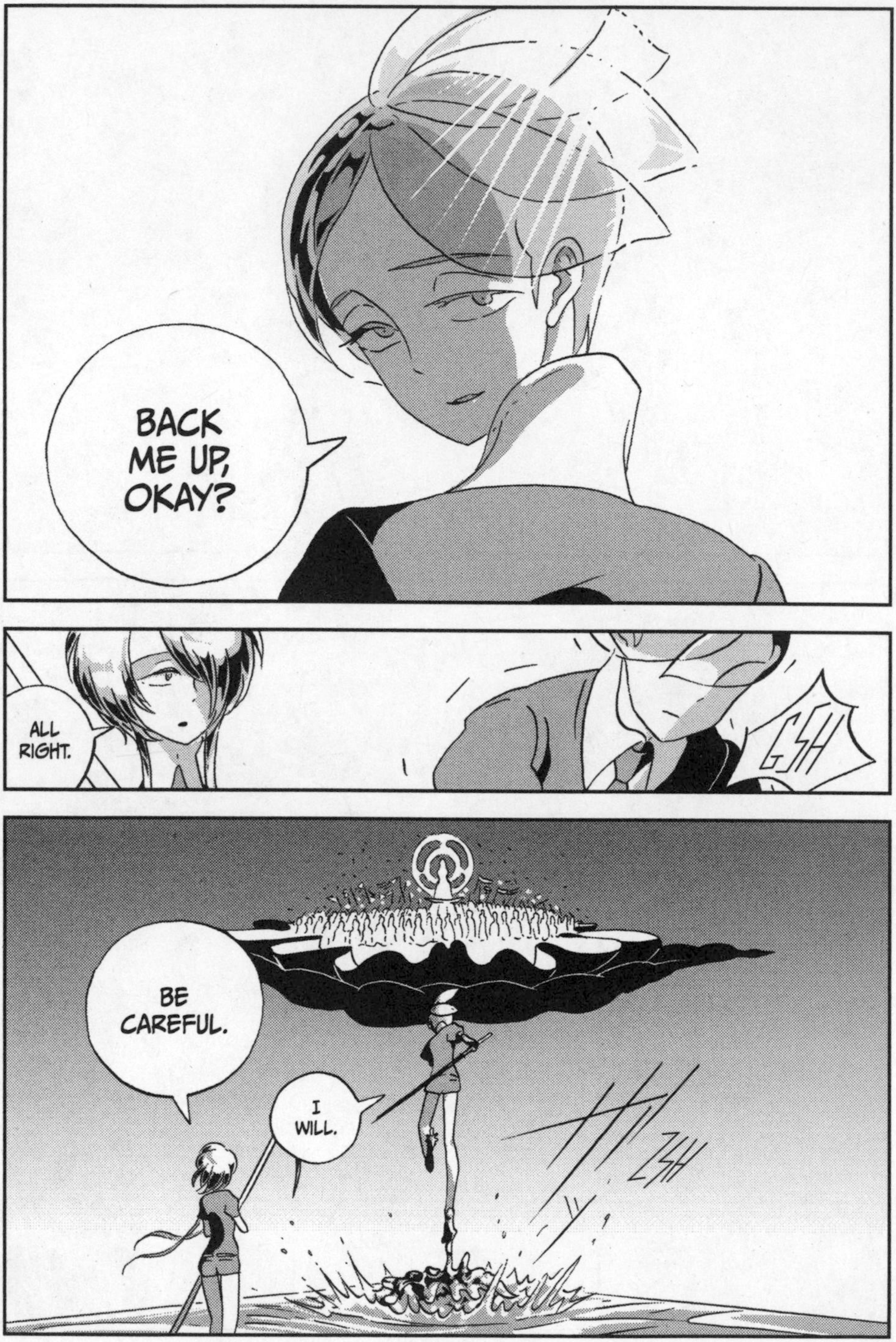
BACK ME UP, OKAY?
GSH
ALL RIGHT.
BE CAREFUL.
I WILL.
ZSH

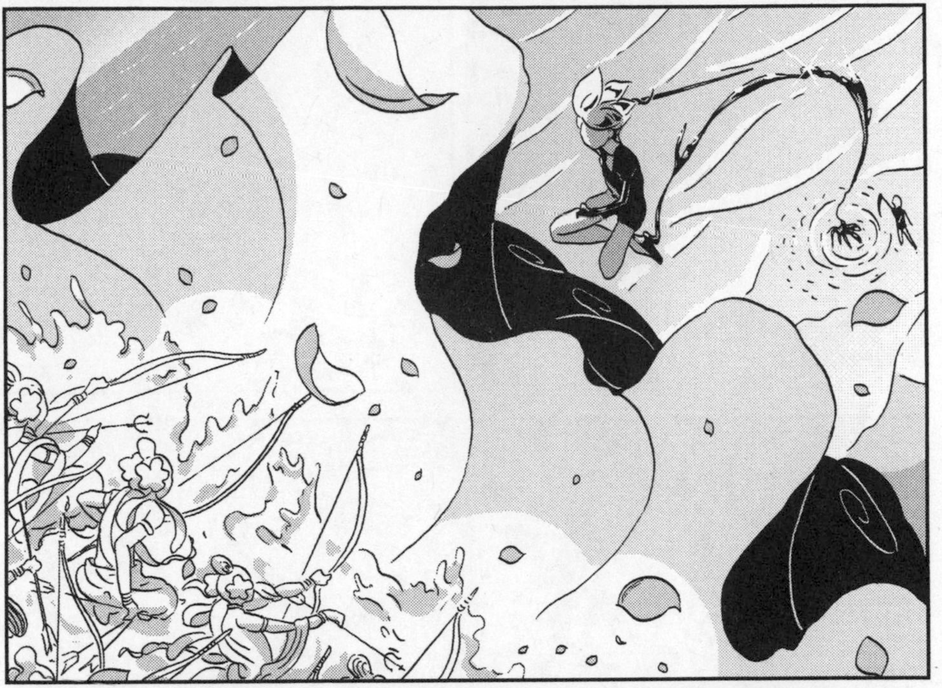

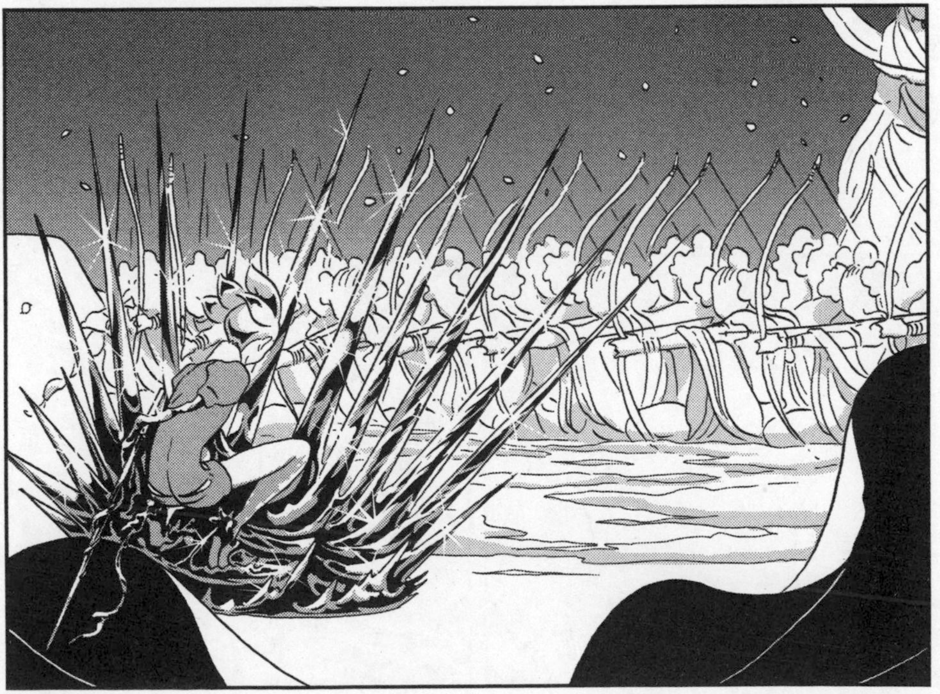

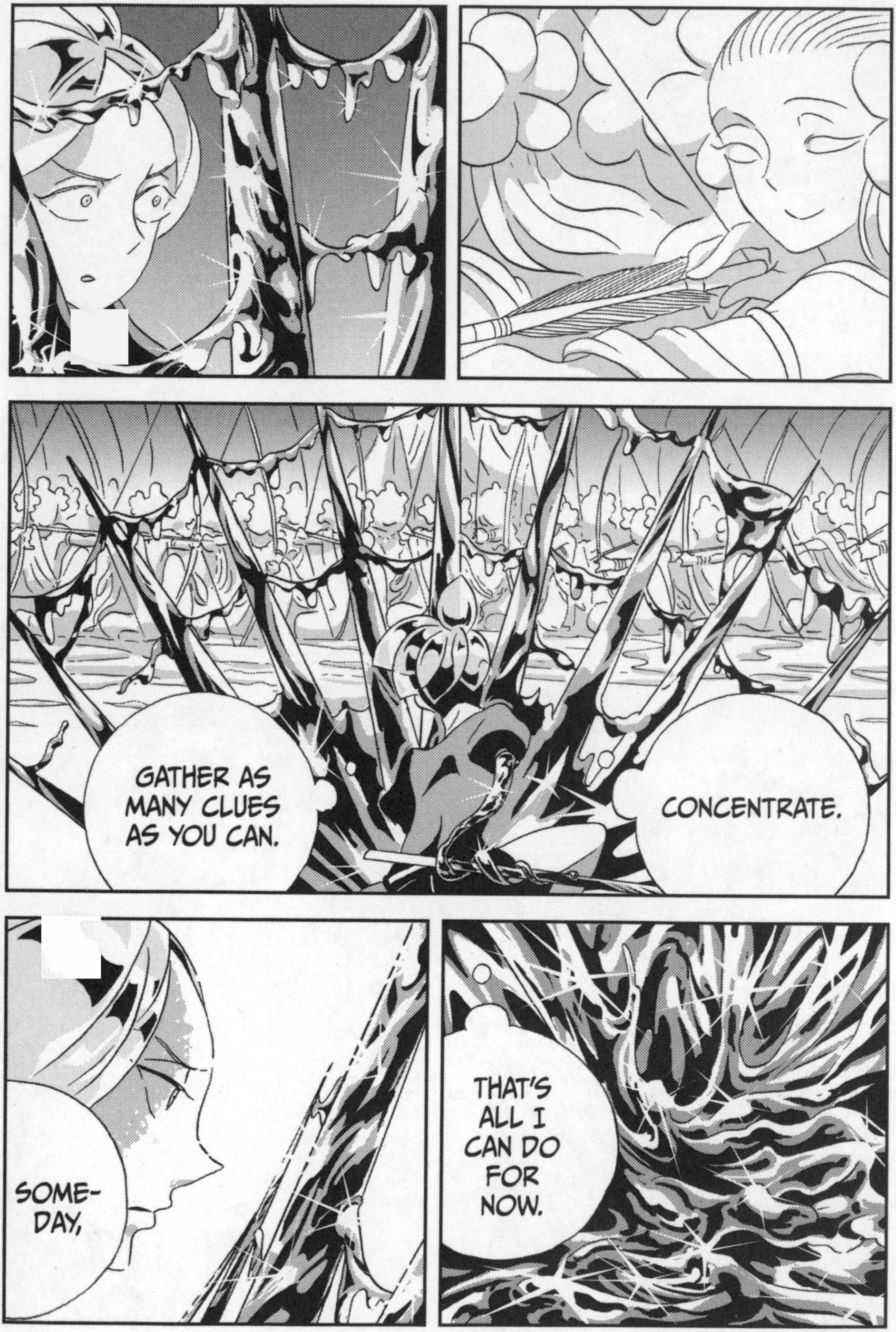
CONCENTRATE.
GATHER AS MANY CLUES AS YOU CAN.
THAT'S ALL I CAN DO FOR NOW.
SOME-DAY,

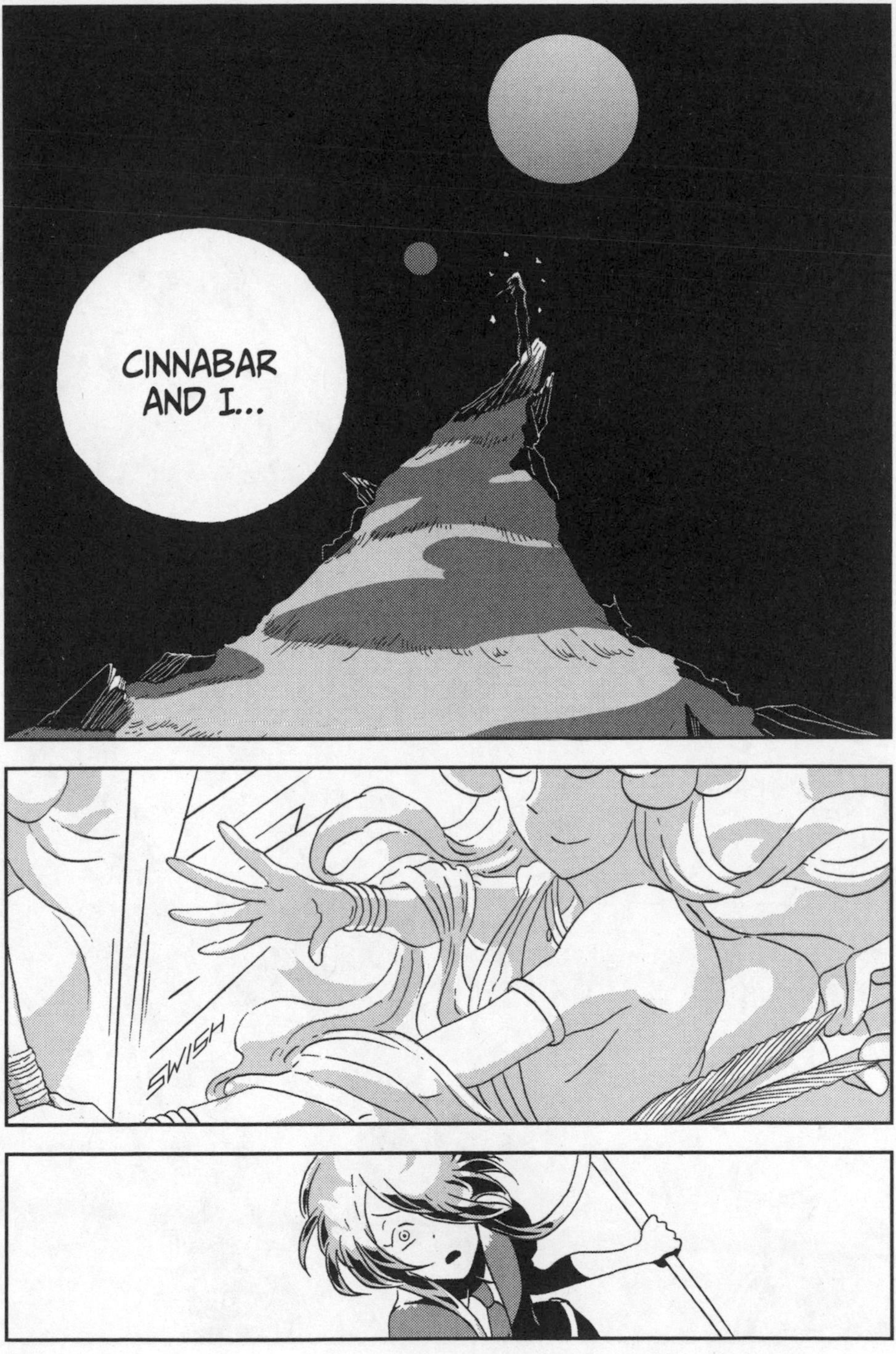
CINNABAR AND I...
SWISH

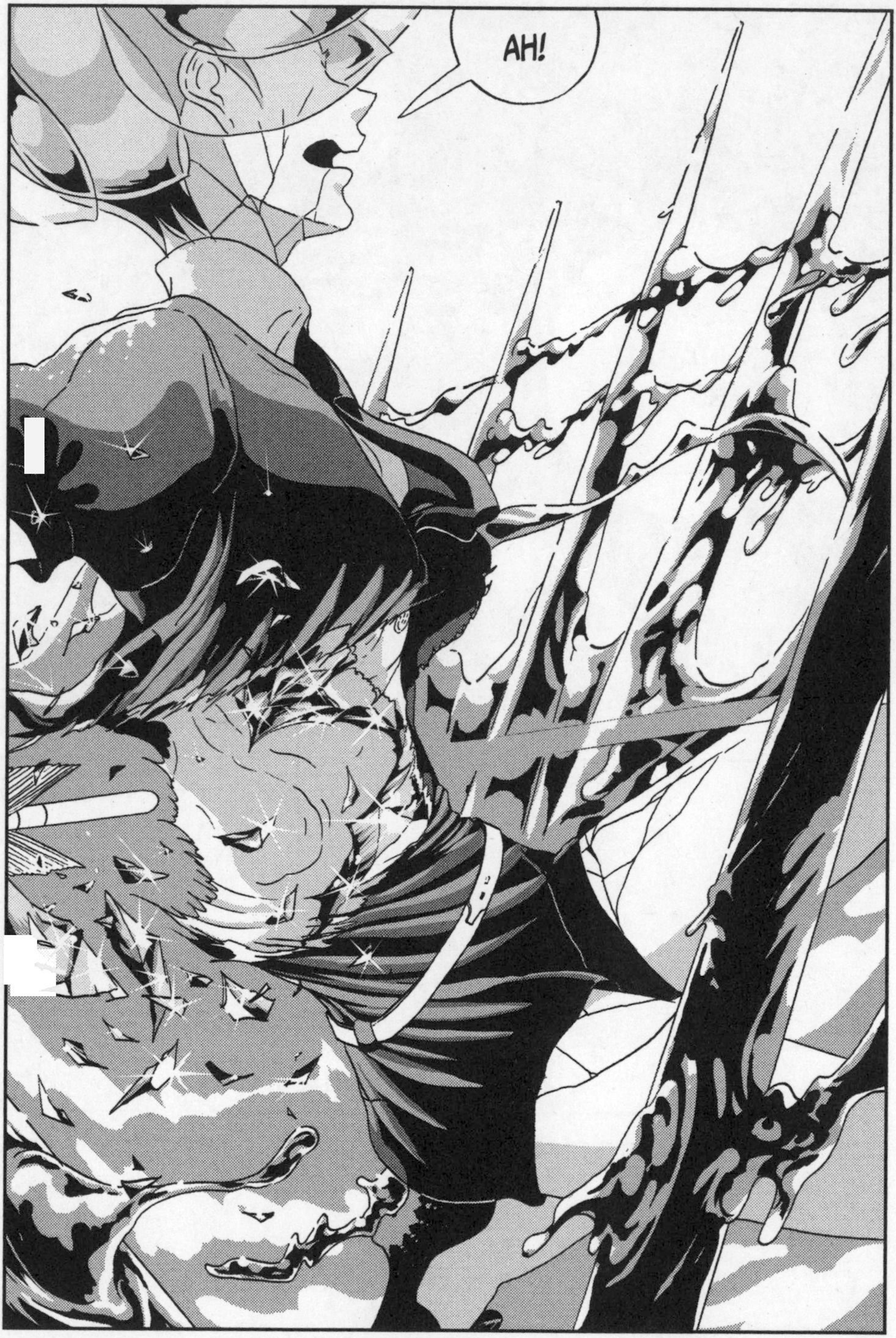
AH!

CHAPTER 36: A New Job END

LAND OF THE LONGSTANDING PUZZLE

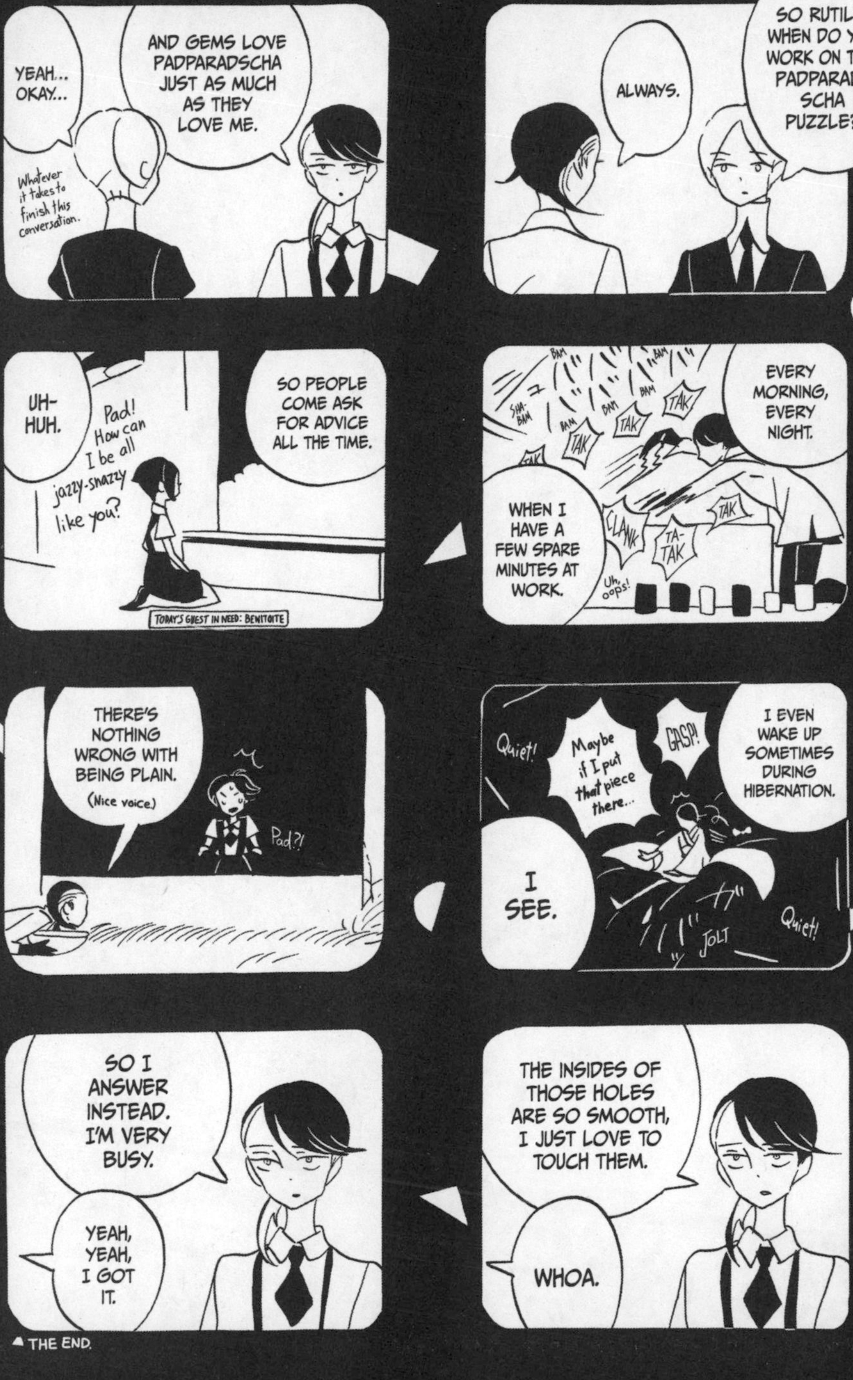
SO RUTILE, WHEN DO YOU WORK ON THIS PADPARAD-SCHA PUZZLE?
ALWAYS.
EVERY MORNING, EVERY NIGHT.
BAM
BAM
SHA-BAM
BAM
BAM
BAM
TAK
TAK
TAK
TAK
CLANK
TA-TAK
TAK
Uh, oops!
WHEN I HAVE A FEW SPARE MINUTES AT WORK.
I EVEN WAKE UP SOMETIMES DURING HIBERNATION.
GASP!
Maybe if I put that piece there...
Quiet!
Quiet!
JOLT
I SEE.
THE INSIDES OF THOSE HOLES ARE SO SMOOTH, I JUST LOVE TO TOUCH THEM.
WHOA.
AND GEMS LOVE PADPARADSCHA JUST AS MUCH AS THEY LOVE ME.
YEAH... OKAY...
Whatever it takes to finish this conversation.
SO PEOPLE COME ASK FOR ADVICE ALL THE TIME.
Pad! How can I be all jazzy-snazzy like you?
UH-HUH.
TODAY'S GUEST IN NEED: BENITOITE
THERE'S NOTHING WRONG WITH BEING PLAIN.
(Nice voice.)
Pad?!
SO I ANSWER INSTEAD. I'M VERY BUSY.
YEAH, YEAH, I GOT IT.

▲ THE END.

TRANSLATION NOTES

BODY FULL OF HOLES *page 13*

While the translators were unable to find any information indicating that padparadscha sapphires have a tendency to be full of holes, they are able to offer a linguistic explanation. The name padparadscha is derived from the Sanskrit *padma ranga*, meaning "lotus color," because of their pink-orange hue. Lotus pods and roots are full of holes similar to the ones seen in Padparadscha. It may be interesting to note that, because the lotus flowers rise above the muddy waters that they grow in, they have come to be a Buddhist symbol of spiritual purity.

BLUE MOON *page 155*

In the world of the Lustrous, the months don't have the same names as they do in our time. So here, this isn't referring to an extra full moon during a single calendar month, but a month (or moon) that is designated by the color blue. Likely, this entry took place sometime in spring.

THE CRYSTAL INSIDE ME *page 158*

Ghost quartz, also known as phantom quartz, is so named because it is a crystal with another fully formed crystal (or several) inside of it. Because quartz is clear, the inner crystal is visible from the outside, creating an image that looks like a phantom, or ghost.

LAND OF THE LUSTROUS

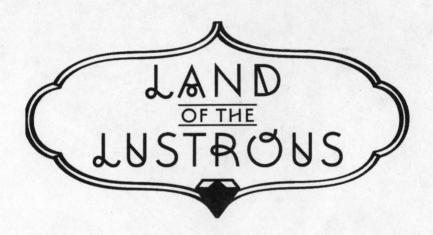

Japanese Edition Inside Cover Gallery

Volume 1

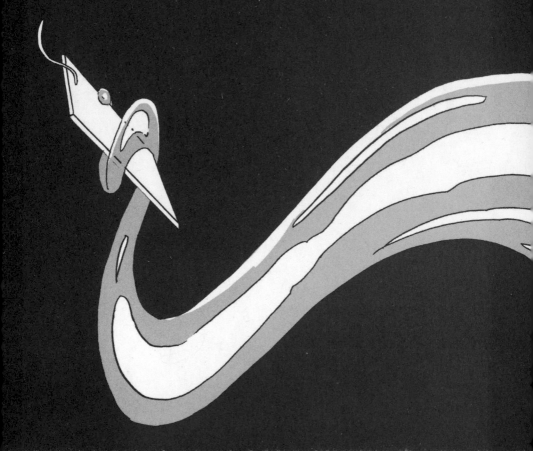

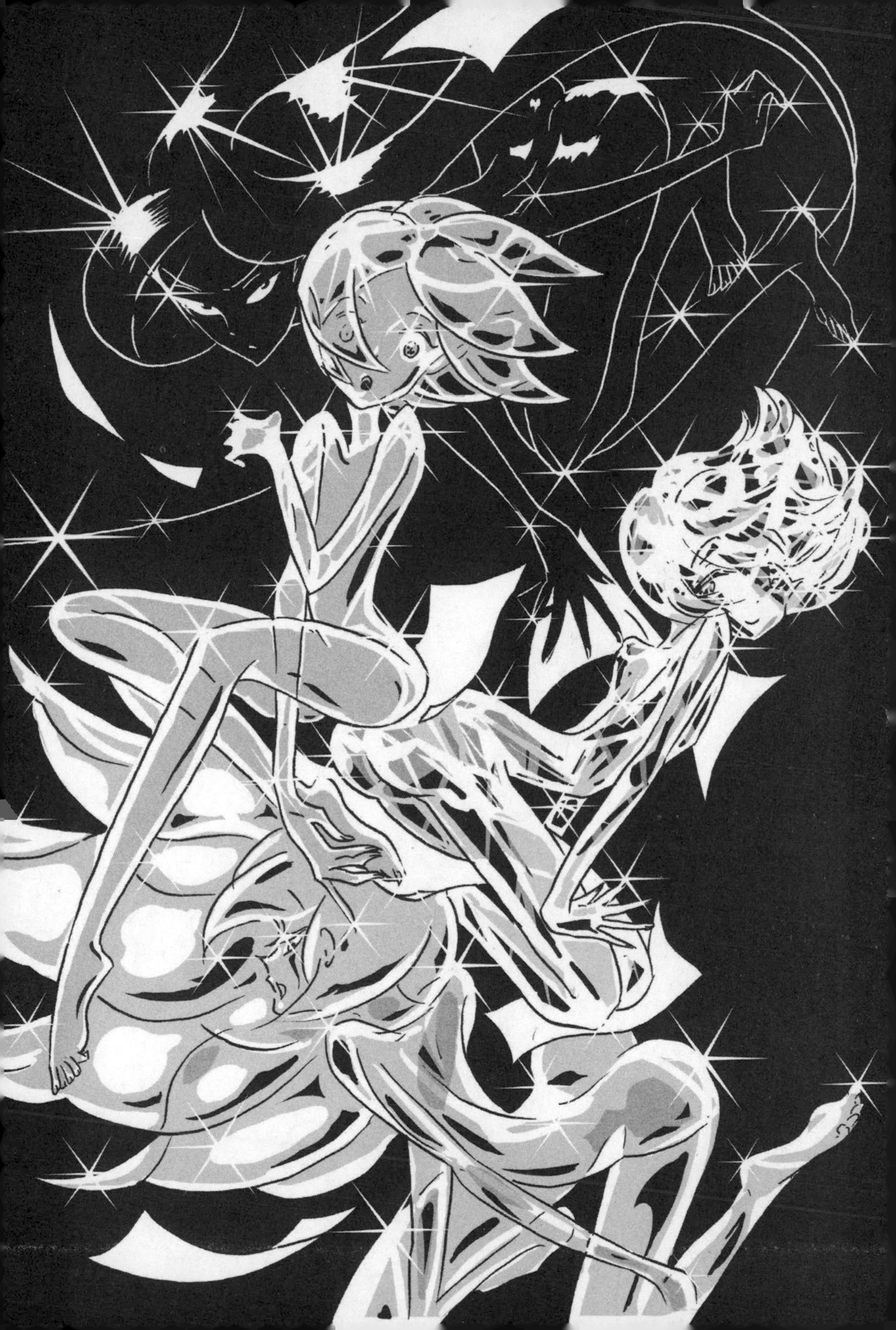

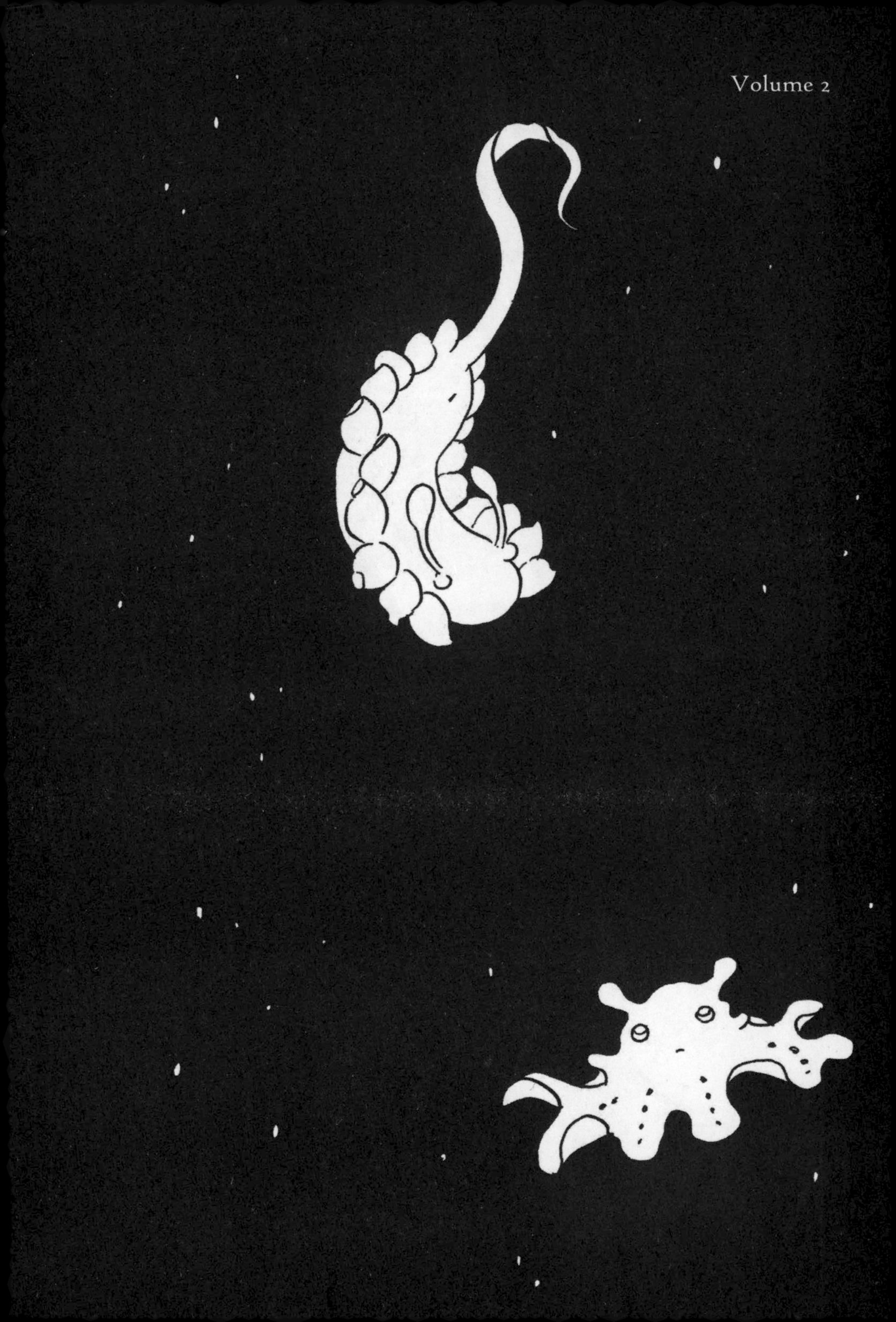
Volume 2

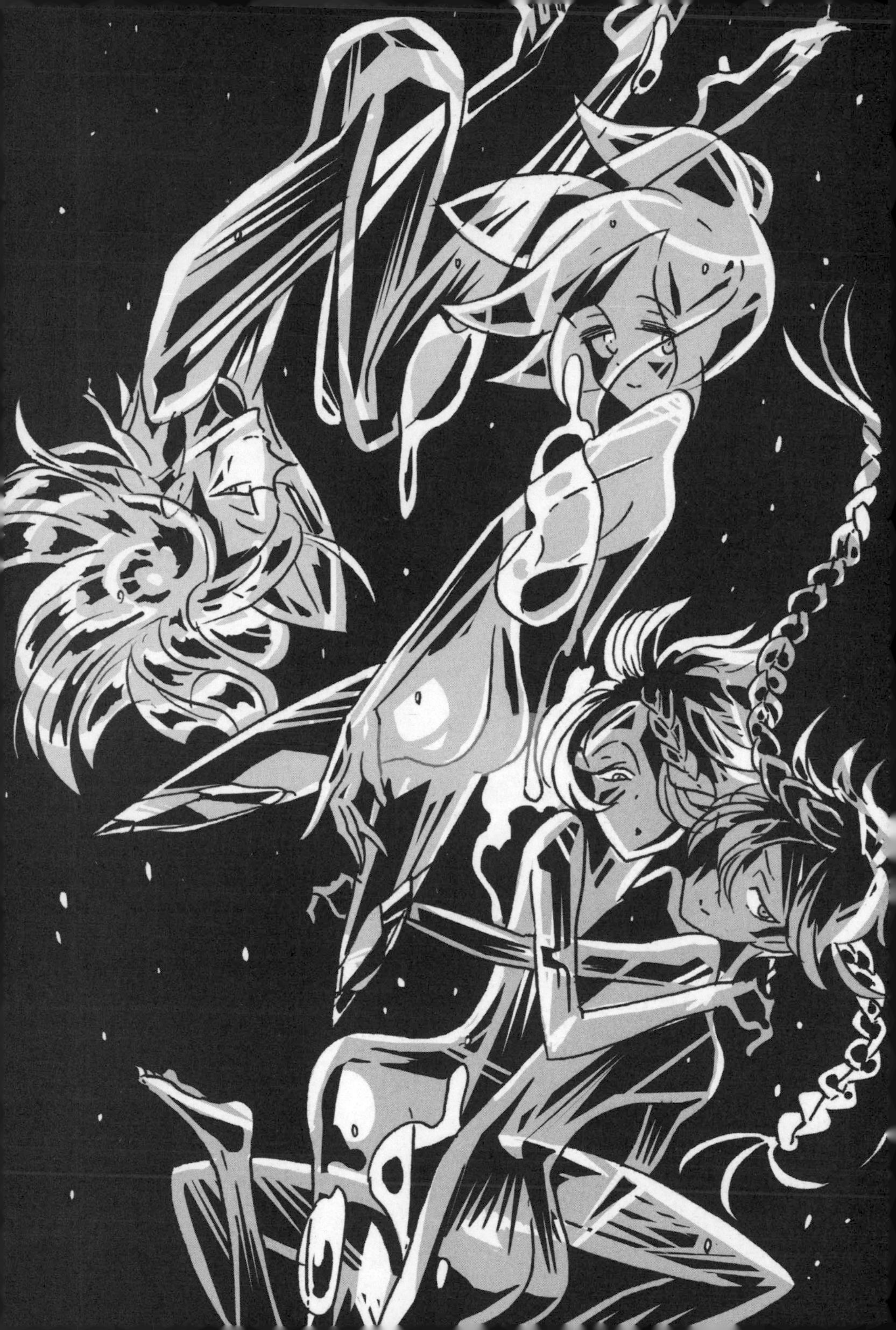

KC KODANSHA COMICS

FIRE SOLDIER
8
TOKYO

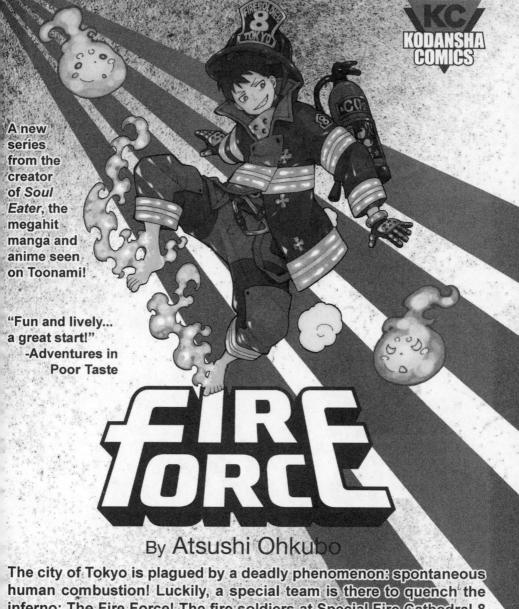

A new series from the creator of *Soul Eater*, the megahit manga and anime seen on Toonami!

"Fun and lively... a great start!"
-Adventures in Poor Taste

FIRE FORCE

By Atsushi Ohkubo

The city of Tokyo is plagued by a deadly phenomenon: spontaneous human combustion! Luckily, a special team is there to quench the inferno: The Fire Force! The fire soldiers at Special Fire Cathedral 8 are about to get a unique addition. Enter Shinra, a boy who possesses the power to run at the speed of a rocket, leaving behind the famous "devil's footprints" (and destroying his shoes in the process). Can Shinra and his colleagues discover the source of this strange epidemic before the city burns to ashes?

HAPPINESS

—ハピネス—

By Shuzo Oshimi

From the creator of *The Flowers of Evil*

Nothing interesting is happening in Makoto Ozaki's first year of high school. His life is a series of quiet humiliations: low-grade bullies, unreliable friends, and the constant frustration of his adolescent lust. But one night, a pale, thin girl knocks him to the ground in an alley and offers him a choice. Now everything is different. Daylight is searingly bright. Food tastes awful. And worse than anything is the terrible, consuming thirst...

Praise for Shuzo Oshimi's *The Flowers of Evil*

"A shockingly readable story that vividly—one might even say queasily—evokes the fear and confusion of discovering one's own sexuality. Recommended." —The Manga Critic

"A page-turning tale of sordid middle school blackmail." —Otaku USA Magazine

"A stunning new horror manga." —Third Eye Comics

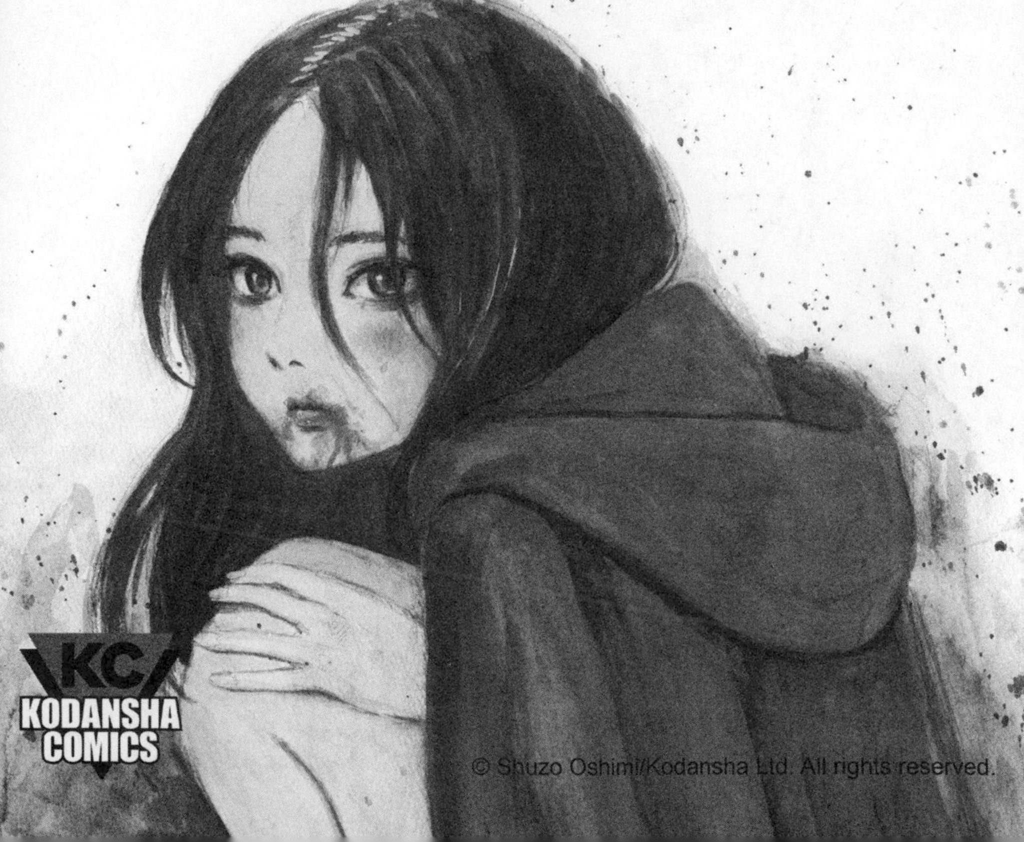

KC KODANSHA COMICS

"I'm pleasantly surprised to find modern shojo using cross-dressing as a dramatic device to deliver social commentary... Recommended."

-Otaku USA Magazine

The prince in his dark days

By Hico Yamanaka

A drunkard for a father, a household of poverty... For 17-year-old Atsuko, misfortune is all she knows and believes in. Until one day, a chance encounter with Itaru–the wealthy heir of a huge corporation–changes everything. The two look identical, uncannily so. When Itaru curiously goes missing, Atsuko is roped into being his stand-in. There, in his shoes, Atsuko must parade like a prince in a palace. She encounters many new experiences, but at what cost...?

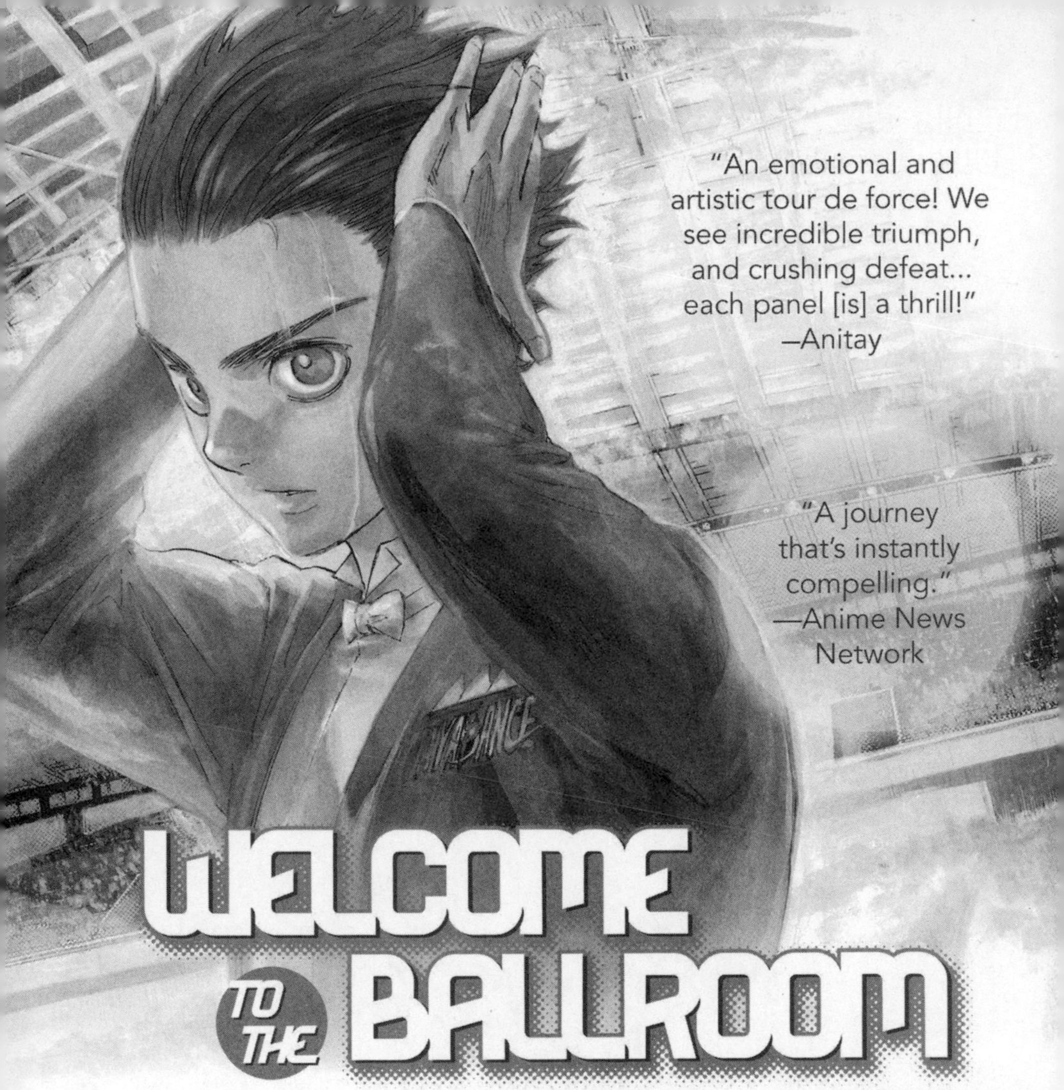
"An emotional and artistic tour de force! We see incredible triumph, and crushing defeat... each panel [is] a thrill!"
–Anitay
"A journey that's instantly compelling."
—Anime News Network
WELCOME TO THE BALLROOM

By Tomo Takeuchi

Feckless high school student Tatara Fujita wants to be good at something—anything. Unfortunately, he's about as average as a slouchy teen can be. The local bullies know this, and make it a habit to hit him up for cash, but all that changes when the debonair Kaname Sengoku sends them packing. Sengoku's not the neighborhood watch, though. He's a professional ballroom dancer. And once Tatara Fujita gets pulled into the world of ballroom, his life will never be the same.

KC KODANSHA COMICS

KC
KODANSHA
COMICS

Japan's most powerful spirit medium delves into the ghost world's greatest mysteries!

Story by Kyo Shirodaira, famed author of mystery fiction and creator of *Spiral*, *Blast of Tempest*, and *The Record of a Fallen Vampire*.

Both touched by spirits called yôkai, Kotoko and Kurô have gained unique superhuman powers. But to gain her powers Kotoko has given up an eye and a leg, and Kurô's personal life is in shambles. So when Kotoko suggests they team up to deal with renegades from the spirit world, Kurô doesn't have many other choices, but Kotoko might just have a few ulterior motives...

IN/SPECTRE

STORY BY KYO SHIRODAIRA
ART BY CHASHIBA KATASE

Based on the critically acclaimed classic horror manga

The first new *Parasyte* manga in over 20 years!

NEO Parasyte f

BY ASUMIKO NAKAMURA, EMA TOYAMA, MIKI RINNO, LALAKO KOJIMA, KAORI YUKI, BANKO KUZE, YUUKI OBATA, KASHIO, YUI KUROE, ASIA WATANABE, MIKIMAKI, HIKARU SURUGA, HAJIME SHINJO, RENJURO KINDAICHI, AND YURI NARUSHIMA

A collection of chilling new *Parasyte* stories from Japan's top shojo artists!

Parasites: shape-shifting aliens whose only purpose is to assimilate with and consume the human race... but do these monsters have a different side? A parasite becomes a prince to save his romance-obsessed female host from a dangerous stalker. Another hosts a cooking show, in which the real monsters are revealed. These and 13 more stories, from some of the greatest shojo manga artists alive today, together make up a chilling, funny, and entertaining tribute to one of manga's horror classics!

KODANSHA COMICS

New action series from Hiroyuki Takei, creator of the classic shonen franchise Shaman King!

In medieval Japan, a bell hanging on the collar is a sign that a cat has a master. Norachiyo's bell hangs from his katana sheath, but he is nonetheless a stray — a ronin. This one-eyed cat samurai travels across a dishonest world, cutting through pretense and deception with his blade.

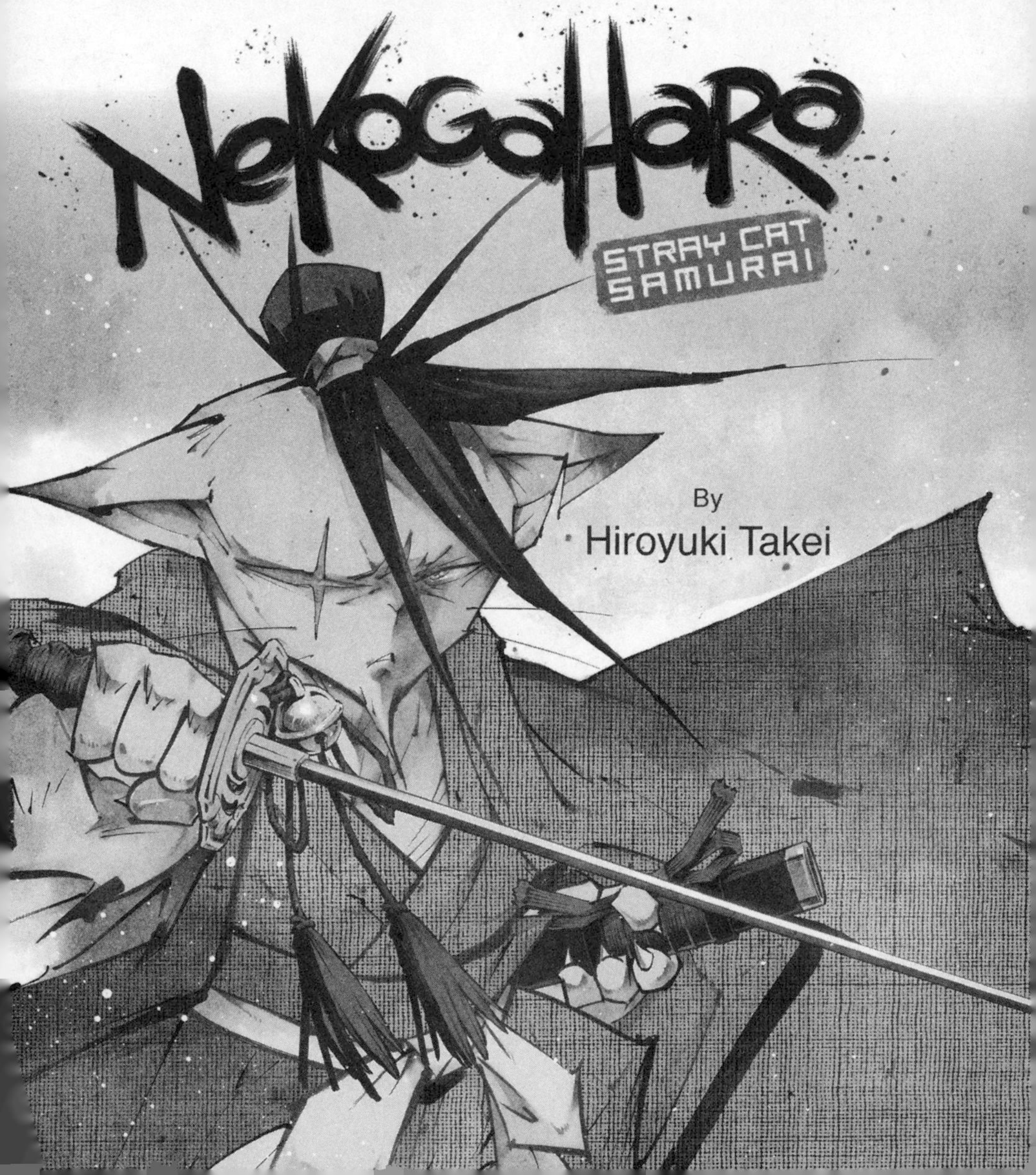
NekoGaHara
STRAY CAT
SAMURAI
By
Hiroyuki Takei

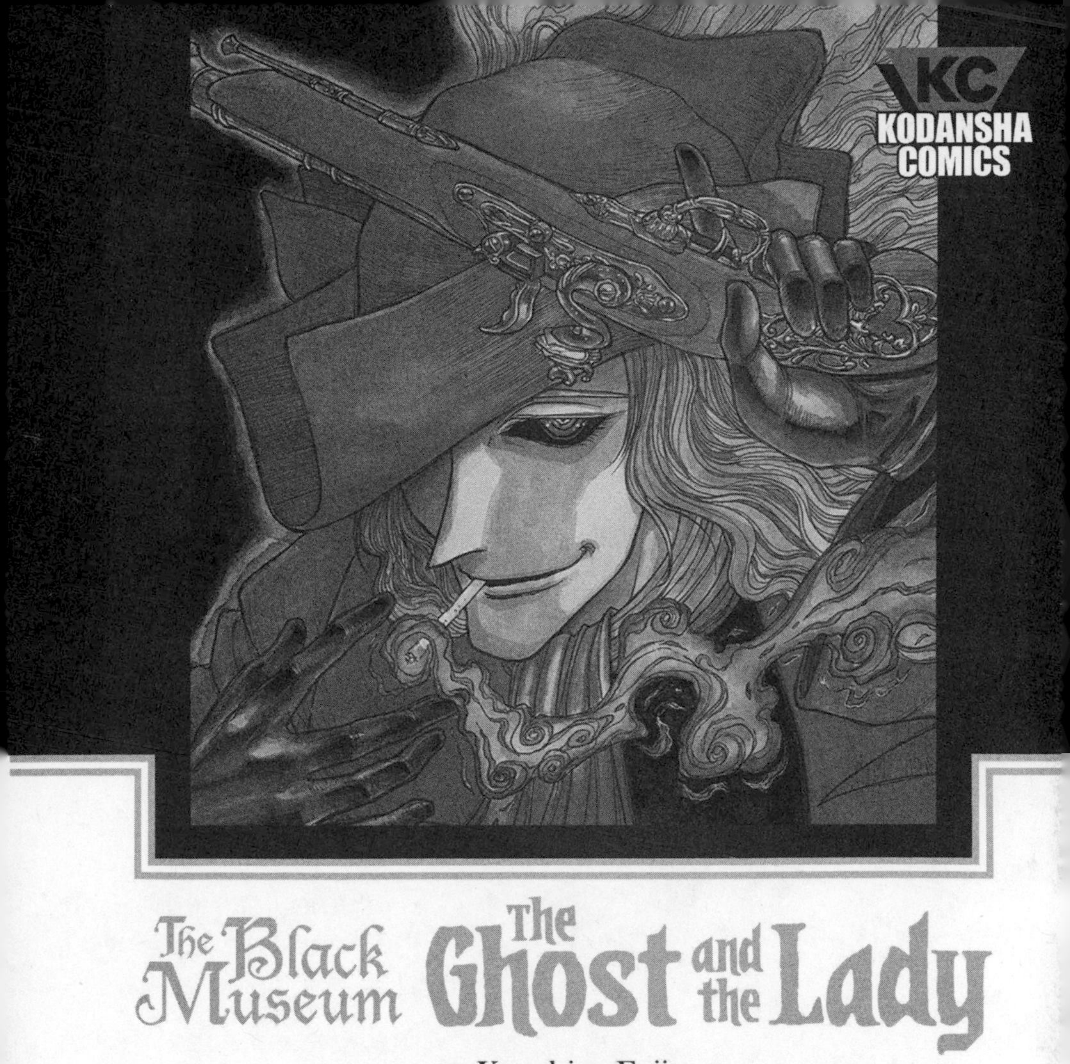
KC
KODANSHA COMICS

The Black Museum The Ghost and the Lady

By Kazuhiro Fujita

Deep in Scotland Yard in London sits an evidence room dedicated to the greatest mysteries of British history. In this "Black Museum" sits a misshapen hunk of lead–two bullets fused together–the key to a wartime encounter between Florence Nightingale, the mother of modern nursing, and a supernatural Man in Grey. This story is unknown to most scholars of history, but a special guest of the museum will tell the tale of The Ghost and the Lady...

Praise for Kazuhiro Fujita's *Ushio and Tora*

"A charming revival that combines a classic look with modern depth and pacing... **Essential viewing both for curmudgeons and new fans alike.**" — Anime News Network

"**GREAT!** The first episode of Ushio and Tora captures the essence of '90s anime." — IGN

The award-winning manga about what happens inside you!

"Far more entertaining than it ought to be... what kid doesn't want to think that every time they sneeze a torpedo shoots out their nose?"
—Anime News Network

Strep throat! Hay fever! Influenza! The world is a dangerous place for a red blood cell just trying to get her deliveries finished. Fortunately, she's not alone…she's got a whole human body's worth of cells ready to help out! The mysterious white blood cells, the buff and brash killer T cells, even the cute little platelets— everyone's got to come together if they want to keep you healthy!

Cells at Work!

はたらく細胞

By Akane Shimizu

a Silent Voice

The New York Times bestselling manga and Eisner Award nominee—now available in a complete box set!

Now a feature-length animation from Kyoto Animation!

- Exclusive 2-sided poster
- Replica of Shoko's notebook
- Preview of Yoshitoki Oima's new series, To Your Eternity

Shoya is a bully. When Shoko, a girl who can't hear, enters his elementary school class, she becomes their favorite target, and Shoya and his friends goad each other into devising new tortures for her. But the children's cruelty goes too far. Shoko is forced to leave the school, and Shoya ends up shouldering all the blame. Six years later, the two meet again. Can Shoya make up for his past mistakes, or is it too late?

Land of the Lustrous volume 5 is a work of fiction. Names, characters, places, and incidents are the products of the author's imagination or are used fictitiously. Any resemblance to actual events, locales, or persons, living or dead, is entirely coincidental.

A Kodansha Comics Trade Paperback Original.

Land of the Lustrous volume 5 copyright © 2015 Haruko Ichikawa
English translation copyright © 2018 Haruko Ichikawa

All rights reserved.

Published in the United States by Kodansha Comics, an imprint of Kodansha USA Publishing, LLC, New York.

Publication rights for this English edition arranged through Kodansha Ltd., Tokyo.

First published in Japan in 2015 by Kodansha Ltd., Tokyo.

ISBN 978-1-63236-635-1

Printed in the United States of America.

www.kodansha.us

9 8 7 6 5

Translator: Alethea Nibley & Athena Nibley
Lettering: Evan Hayden
Editing: Lauren Scanlan